# BIBLIOPHILES, MURDEROUS BOOKMEN, AND MAD LIBRARIANS

## The Story of Books in Modern Spain

# Bibliophiles, Murderous Bookmen, and Mad Librarians

## *The Story of Books in Modern Spain*

ROBERT RICHMOND ELLIS

UNIVERSITY OF TORONTO PRESS
Toronto Buffalo London

Toronto Buffalo London
utorontopress.com
Printed in the U.S.A.

ISBN 978-1-4875-4236-8 (cloth)
ISBN 978-1-4875-4237-5 (PDF)
ISBN 978-1-4875-4238-2 (EPUB)

Toronto Iberic

---

**Library and Archives Canada Cataloguing in Publication**

Title: Bibliophiles, murderous bookmen, and mad librarians : the story of books in modern Spain / Robert Richmond Ellis.
Names: Ellis, Robert Richmond, author.
Series: Toronto Iberic ; 67.
Description: Series statement: Toronto Iberic series ; 67 | Includes bibliographical references and index.
Identifiers: Canadiana (print) 20210346620 | Canadiana (ebook) 20210346752 | ISBN 9781487542368 (hardcover) | ISBN 9781487542382 (EPUB) | ISBN 9781487542375 (PDF)
Subjects: LCSH: Books in literature. | LCSH: Books and reading in literature. | LCSH: Book collecting in literature. | LCSH: Bibliomania. | LCSH: Book collecting – Spain. | LCSH: Spanish literature – 19th century – History and criticism. | LCSH: Spanish literature – 20th century – History and criticism. | LCSH: Spain – Intellectual life.
Classification: LCC PQ6072 .E45 2022 | DDC 860.9/39–dc23

---

We wish to acknowledge the land on which the University of Toronto Press operates. This land is the traditional territory of the Wendat, the Anishnaabeg, the Haudenosaunee, the Métis, and the Mississaugas of the Credit First Nation.

This book has been published with the assistance of Occidental College and the Brown Humanities Book Publication Fund.

University of Toronto Press acknowledges the financial support of the Government of Canada, the Canada Council for the Arts, and the Ontario Arts Council, an agency of the Government of Ontario, for its publishing activities.

Canada Council for the Arts

Conseil des Arts du Canada

Funded by the Government of Canada

Financé par le gouvernement du Canada

Canada

*In memory of my mother, grandmother, and grandfather,*
*and to José Horacio, as always*

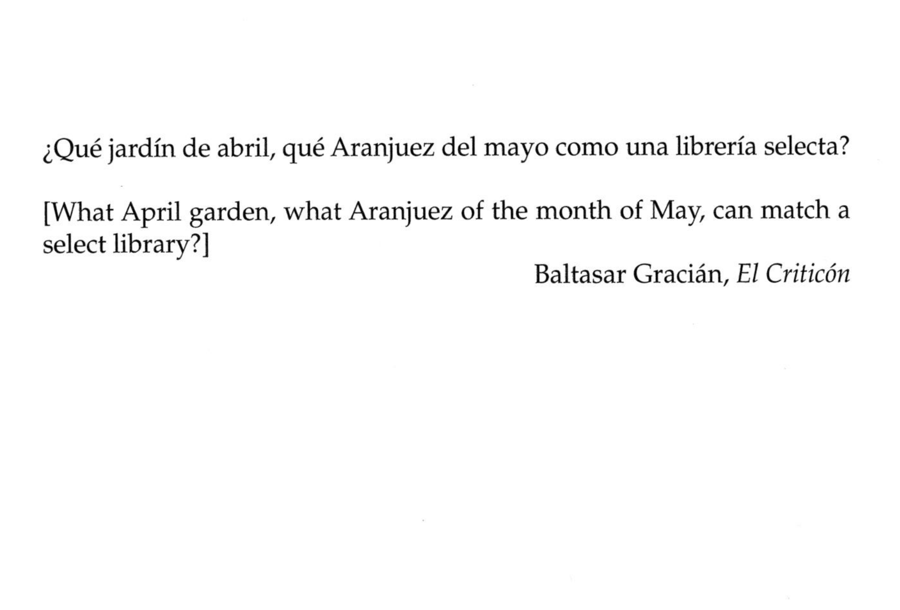

¿Qué jardín de abril, qué Aranjuez del mayo como una librería selecta?

[What April garden, what Aranjuez of the month of May, can match a select library?]

Baltasar Gracián, *El Criticón*

# Contents

# Illustrations

# Acknowledgments

There are many people and institutions whose support over the years has helped make this book possible.

I am particularly grateful to Occidental College for helping fund my research in the Biblioteca Nacional de España and the Biblioteca de Catalunya through a MacArthur International Grant, and for generously providing financial assistance for the publication of the book. I am also grateful to my colleagues in the Department of Spanish and French Studies for their steadfast support and good cheer over the years.

I want to thank my primary editor at the University of Toronto Press, Mark Thompson, for his judicious guidance throughout the editorial process, and all the people at the Press for helping bring the project to fruition. I am also deeply appreciative of the wisdom and good advice of the readers of the manuscript.

# BIBLIOPHILES, MURDEROUS BOOKMEN, AND MAD LIBRARIANS

## The Story of Books in Modern Spain

# Introduction

The most famous depiction of books in all of Spanish literature is a scene in Miguel de Cervantes's *Don Quixote* in which the title character's library is destroyed. Don Quixote is a voracious reader whose passion for the tales of knight-errantry has supposedly led him to madness, and for this reason his niece, housekeeper, barber, and local curate decide that his library must be burned. Just prior to the book burning, the curate examines the library and expresses a keen interest in the importance and quality of many of the volumes. In so doing, he reveals the temperament of a bibliophile, even if he is the person most responsible for the obliteration of what in his day would have been a large and valuable collection. Don Quixote, although beside himself with anger when he discovers that his treasured books have vanished, ultimately blames the incident on the machinations of an evil enchanter – a figure that originally entered his imagination through reading. He thus regards his books (and, by extension, the entire world) through the lens of the discourses that he has encountered in them. The episode is nevertheless paradigmatic in the history of the Spanish book. Not only does it affirm both a love of reading and an appreciation of the aesthetic appeal of physical books, but it also, in the context of the seventeenth-century Inquisition, exposes the threat posed to books by forces of oppression, and even suggests that their destruction is tantamount to the destruction of human life itself. What is more, it captures the almost wild despair felt by those who lose books, when in the wake of the crime Don Quixote lashes out in a blind and hopeless rage. Yet through his imagination, Don Quixote does retain much of what he has lost, just as Cervantes, through his narrative, gives renewed life to the voices and stories of the past.[1]

The great themes expressed in *Don Quixote* regarding books and bibliophilia are present throughout the history of Spanish book culture, and feature prominently in Spanish book-centred narratives of subsequent centuries. My aim in the work that follows is precisely to examine how books are represented in modern Spanish writing, both literally and metaphorically, and how modern Spanish commentators of books reflect on the role of books in their lives and in the cultural life of modern Spain. The overarching subject of my study is bibliophilia, a love of books both as texts to be read and objects to be cherished for their physical qualities. Like their counterparts in other countries, Spanish bibliophiles have painstakingly described the characteristics of books, the book arts, libraries, and bookshops, and have attempted to explain the psychological experiences of reading and collecting books, as well as the social and economic conditions of book production. They have also used images of books to tell a multitude of stories. Whereas some of these stories highlight the diverse histories, politics, and nationalisms of the modern Spanish state, others engage in a more philosophical meditation on such topics as personal identity, the nostalgia for the past, the nature of good and evil, and mortality and immortality.

Spanish bibliophilia precedes the advent of printing in the West in the fifteenth century, but it flourishes in the ensuing centuries of print culture, culminating in the mid-nineteenth century when the central state confiscated large monastic libraries and either transferred them to public institutions or sold them. The entry of vast numbers of old books into the marketplace, coupled with the beginning of the mass production of new books made possible by the Industrial Revolution, led to what might be called a "Golden Age" of Spanish bibliophilia, a period spanning the second half of the nineteenth century and the first half of the twentieth century. This high point of print culture lasted until other forms of media, including radio, film, and television, gained ascendency and began to augment, if not in some instances replace, print media. In the late twentieth century, with the advent of digital technology, non-print media has become the dominant form of communication, to the point that some commentators of book culture believe that physical books will one day disappear. Yet even though writers such as Enrique Vila-Matas suggest that we are reaching what he calls "el fin de la era Gutenberg" (*Dublinesca* 119) ["the end of the Gutenberg era" (*Dublinesque* 109)], physical books will surely continue to be produced. As book historian Leah Price wryly puts it, this is perhaps because "the idea of the book remains more powerful than any ideas that it contains" (168).

Given the changes in text production that have occurred as a result of digital technology, scholars have become increasingly interested in the nature of books as material objects. As Alan Liu notes, the field of book history "has lately advanced a cutting-edge research agenda focused on a dimension of the book that hardly used to matter but that recently seems to be all that matters: the materiality of the book ... [including] material forms of writing and reading that, however physically long-lived, do not have the metaphysical permanence of language or meaning" (513).[2] Despite this new emphasis in the historiography of books, a heightened consciousness of physical books and their perceived impermanence has been the hallmark of the literature of bibliophilia for centuries, and is central to current Spanish narratives about books.

Some contemporary Spanish authors express a preoccupation with physical books because they are concerned that digital technology might eventually lead to their extinction. But others are also painfully aware that at certain moments within recent historical memory (including the Spanish Civil War and the Franco dictatorship) large numbers of books were in fact intentionally destroyed or made to disappear. By making books the focal point of their narratives, these writers hope to recover a past that they fear might be lost or forgotten. In a society traumatized by violence, the physicality of books is also a powerful metaphor for the fragility and vulnerability of the human body. If, as throughout the western tradition, books are thought to embody the human spirit, then their destruction at the hands of repressive regimes can easily be compared to the murder of individual human beings, or even the annihilation of an entire people. Books about books are thus often sites of re-embodiment and restitution, both of books themselves and of the intentions of others now gone.

Although the nostalgia for books expressed in contemporary fiction might seem indicative of a desire to escape from the real world, more often than not it represents an attempt to engage more deeply with it, as evidenced by historically focused Spanish narratives about books. Jessica Pressman in fact detects in certain contemporary narratives an "aesthetic of bookishness," which in her view "is not merely a nostalgia for print" (480) or a "fetishized focus on textuality and the book-bound reading object" (466) but rather a way of addressing current cultural concerns. She further maintains that traditional books will never be rendered obsolete by new technologies precisely because they fulfill human needs and desires related specifically to their "book-bound physicality and potentiality" (467). Unlike digital media, traditional books, and in particular those that foreground their plasticity, such as artists' books, have a distinct corporality, and, as N. Katherine Hayles argues, they entwine their materialities with those of our own bodies: "Texts that employ their bodies to create narrative complexity must be read not for their words alone but also for the physical involvements readers undertake to access their materialities – including smells, tactile sensations, muscular manipulations, kinesthetic perceptions, and proprioceptive feedback" (231). Both Pressman and Hayles focus on contemporary authors who manipulate the physical format of books, often through the use of digital technology itself. But their comments are relevant to authors who highlight through their narratives the physical format of traditional books, as well as those whose book-centred narratives actually preceded the digital revolution.

Even though physical books are unlikely to be entirely superseded by new textual formats, their production, as Hayles notes, is already so fully tied to digital technology that "they may more appropriately be considered an output form of digital texts than a separate medium" (226). Yet for bibliophiles throughout modern history what matters most is not the mode of book production but the final, three-dimensional, bound volume that they can hold in their hands. According to Jim Collins, the most significant change wrought by the development of digital books is not a change of medium (for instance, the "long-form narrative" ["Reading" 211]), but rather the delivery system, which has moved from "wood pulp to e-reader" (210). In his view, those who regard the proliferation of new reading platforms as a threat to traditional reading practices engage in "an exercise in nostalgia, grounded in a discourse of inevitable loss that ignores what reading already is" (212).[3] Nevertheless, a delivery system can profoundly alter a discursive medium, especially for readers most keenly attuned to the spatial dimensions of texts, or what Pressman calls "the power of the print page" (465). As she sees it, books about books can "harness the power and potential, as well as the fears and frustrations of new media *into* print and *onto* paper" (480).

Traditional commentators of the nature of books and the practice of bibliophilia have often attempted to distinguish between the book as a physical object and the book as a text.[4] In so doing, they implicitly replicate a dichotomy between matter and spirit that in Christian practice has been applied to the Bible. From the perspective of Christian belief, the Bible houses the spirit in a way that is analogous to how the mortal body houses the soul. From a secular perspective, however, the physical book is not ontologically different from the discourses that it conveys precisely because both are material realities. As Judith Still and Michael Worton succinctly remark in their study of textuality, "the apparent opposition between texts and *material* reality is a false one, as suggested even by the restricted meaning of the term *text* where a Shakespeare text, say, may appear to be essentially immaterial and yet can exist and be known to us only via artifacts (books) and practices (theatre)" (8). If all texts are material, the materiality of books is also always textual, and their physical features are necessarily interpreted and thereby rendered meaningful. The physical book is not brute matter but, like all texts, mediated matter, which can be read not only through printed words but also through colour, texture, scent, and even sound. Just as the text/matter dichotomy is specious, so too then is the even more commonly held notion that the aesthetic apprehension of physical books and the reading of texts are diametrically opposed activities.

Because physical books might seem more tangible than other forms of textuality, such as oral or digital productions, they can often evoke emotions more closely related to the physical senses, especially touch. But their greater tangibility can also make them seem more out of reach, for unless they are actually ingested through an act of bibliophagy, they can never be fully internalized. As the literature of bibliophilia reveals, physical books thus often exacerbate a desire for possession in a way that a musical piece or a literary text might not. This apparent inaccessibility of books can in certain cases make books a site of nostalgia or melancholy longing, as if through them bibliophiles are attempting to recover something essential but irrevocable from their pasts. In book-centred narratives, books are in fact frequently depicted as absent, whether as a result of loss, theft, or destruction. In portraying them as such, however, authors not only express their own psychological dispositions but also, on occasion, an even existential intuition of the emptiness of the human condition and the impossibility of ever achieving a lasting ontological fulfilment.

During the modern period in Spain two strains of bibliophilia coalesce: one that envisions books as a means of achieving personal fulfilment, and another that envisions books as a means of cultivating linguistic, cultural, and regional or national identities. In the nineteenth and early twentieth centuries, bibliophiles like Bartolomé José Gallardo (1776–1852), Vicente Salvá (1786–1849), Pedro Salvá (1811–70), Dionisio Hidalgo (1809–66), and Azorín (born José Martínez Ruiz, 1873–1967) reflected on the subjective experience of bibliophilia, while simultaneously engaging in the consolidation of a national book heritage that they believed would foster both the advancement of the Spanish state and the affirmation of a distinctively Hispanic ethos. In their writings on books they thus often focused on the formation of bibliographies, archives, and libraries that would further promote the project of national identity, especially in the great moments of national regeneration following the Napoleonic Wars in the early nineteenth century and the Spanish–American War in the late nineteenth century. Their efforts paralleled those of bibliophiles from the non-Castilian parts of Spain, including Catalonia, Galicia, and the Basque Country, who cultivated books in the languages of these regions in order to foment what they regarded as either regional or national identities distinct from the Castilian-language identity asserted by the Spanish state. A prime example from the late nineteenth and early twentieth centuries is the Catalan bibliophile, publisher, novelist, and essayist Ramon Miquel i Planas (1874–1950), whose love of books was intimately intertwined with his love of the Catalan language and Catalan history and culture.[5]

Throughout the twentieth and early twenty-first centuries the practice of bibliophilia in regions like Catalonia, Galicia, and the Basque Country remains distinct from the bibliophilia of the primarily Castilian-speaking parts of Spain. Catalan-born Nuria Amat (1950–), for instance, highlights the effect of her dual linguistic and cultural heritage on her bibliophilia while engaging in an introspective reflection on the role of books in her life. Juan Goytisolo (1931–2017), also a Catalan native, directs his attention beyond the Iberian Peninsula in his depiction of bibliophiles struggling to maintain the integrity of historically minoritized cultural and national groups threatened by more powerful state actors. In their short stories and novels, the Catalan authors Montserrat Roig (1946–91) and Carlos Ruiz Zafón (1964–), and the Galician author Manuel Rivas (1957–) often situate bibliophilia within the context of the Spanish Civil War and the Franco dictatorship in an effort to recover and revitalize social and political traditions – as well as the cultural heritages of Catalonia and Galicia – attacked and repressed during those periods. Yet regardless of the particular linguistic, cultural, political, and national affiliations of modern Spanish bibliophiles, their writings remain grounded in a personal love of books and are therefore deeply individualistic.

In my study I focus on all of the aforementioned Spanish bibliophiles. These figures clearly have a passion for physical books. Yet some are bibliographers and librarians, who catalogue, organize, and archive books, whereas others are publishers, artists, and writers, who actually create them. What they produce, moreover, are often books about books in which they meditate on the role of books in their lives and in society at large, especially at pivotal moments in the history of modern Spain and the regions of the modern Spanish state. For this reason, I feature not only Castilian-language bibliophiles but also those working in other languages of the Peninsula, including Catalan and Galician.

In Part 1, I highlight a fictional tale of bibliomania about the so-called murderous bookman of Barcelona, which had its origins in nineteenth-century France in an anonymous newspaper report (possibly penned by Charles Nodier) and in a short story of Gustave Flaubert, and which formed the basis for Jean-Paul Sartre's decisive existentialist interpretation of the phenomenon of bibliomania. Throughout the nineteenth and twentieth centuries the tale was recounted and republished by numerous European and Spanish commentators and writers, chief of whom were Miquel i Planas in the early twentieth century and Roig in the late twentieth century. Whereas Miquel i Planas transformed the French tale into a Catalan linguistic and cultural text, Roig recontextualized it in the period of Spain's transition from dictatorship to democracy. By virtue of the number of iterations of the tale in literature, folklore, and music (including a song by the Catalan folk singer, Jaume Arnella [1943–]), the murderous bookman of Barcelona stands as the quintessential (and most notorious) incarnation of the Iberian bookman of the modern period. More significant, the genealogy of the story reveals how the image of the book in modern Spanish culture emerges through an intersection of the languages, histories, and traditions of the various regions of the Spanish state, as well as those of Spain, France, and western Europe in general.

In Part 2, I focus on nineteenth- and early twentieth-century Spanish bibliophilia through a discussion of Gallardo, the Salvás, Hidalgo, and Azorín in order to delineate the contours of modern Spanish bibliophilia as a project of both personal fulfilment and national self-affirmation. In so doing, I examine portions of their essays, autobiographies, and correspondences in which they comment on their careers as readers and writers as well as book collectors, bibliographers, and librarians. Whereas Gallardo, the Salvás, and Hidalgo often represent their experiences as bibliophiles through the Romantic tropes prevalent in the literary discourse of their period, Azorín publishes the majority of his writings on bibliophilia in newspapers and magazines, melding a journalistic discourse with his own subjective and often impressionistic perceptions of the bibliophile life.

In Part 3, I focus on more recent expressions of bibliophilia through an analysis of the book-centred narratives of Ruiz Zafón, Rivas, and Goytisolo. Whereas the figures discussed in Part 2 are Castilian-identified, these writers, albeit to differing degrees, all recognize how their worldviews have been informed by non-Castilian linguistic, historical, and cultural traditions. They also depict the theme of bibliophilia in explicitly political frameworks, and in their books about books they at times create new archives representing the lives and experiences of individuals and groups excluded from dominant national libraries and compendia.

In Part 4, I examine the essays and fictional narratives of Amat, who situates bibliophilia in the context of both Catalan- and Castilian-language cultures as well as print and digital technologies. She also highlights how the dynamics of gender and family inform the bibliophile life. Amat is perhaps the most introspective yet wide-ranging contemporary Spanish commentator of bibliophilia, and in her nuanced and reflective writings she draws together many of the diverse themes of bibliophilia expressed in Spain during the last two centuries.

In Part 5, I conclude with a discussion of the artists' books of Miquel Plana (1943–2012). Although unrelated to Miquel i Planas (despite their similar names), Plana is his greatest artistic successor, and his work marks the culmination of the modern, Catalan book-arts movement begun in the nineteenth century. It also, in my view, can be regarded as the culmination of the history of modern Spanish bibliophilia and the Spanish book as an object of aesthetic appreciation.

## Bibliophilia

The word "bibliophilia" (or "bibliophily") indicates a love of books, and a bibliophile, according to dictionary definition, is one who loves "beautiful or rare qualities of format" (*Webster's* 212), or one who expresses an interest in collecting books, especially rare and unusual ones (*Diccionario de la lengua española*). The word "bibliomania," in contrast, indicates an "extreme preoccupation with books, especially with their acquisition and possession" (*Webster's* 212).[6] The two dispositions or practices thus differ primarily in intensity (Albero 144), although as most commentators remark, bibliophilia is generally regarded as positive and bibliomania as negative (Mendoza Díaz-Maroto, *La pasión* 42). The commonly held view is that bibliophiles value both the form and content of books, whereas bibliomaniacs are fixated on their external aspects and are obsessed with collecting and possessing them. Nevertheless, when commenting on their proclivities, most bibliophiles reveal a keen appreciation of physical books as well as pleasure in acquiring and owning them. They thus distinguish themselves from those interested solely in reading, even if their lives as bibliophiles and readers are inseparable. As the definitions indicate, bibliophiles are drawn to beautiful and rare books. Yet some specifically seek out old volumes, while others prize contemporary editions published in limited numbers and deluxe formats. At times, bibliophiles conflate their perceptions of the beauty and rarity of books, but the two are in fact distinct qualities that function differently in the literature of bibliophilia and in narratives about books.

Within the Spanish tradition the list of bibliophiles who have commented on the nature of bibliophilia is extensive, and their observations tend to reflect their own personal experiences.[7] Yet most striking is the number of bibliophiles who feel compelled not simply to describe their love of books but to distinguish between bibliophilia and bibliomania, or what the French theorist, Maurice Robert, calls the two species of bibliophiles: the true and the false (17). In this vein, Francisco Mendoza Díaz-Maroto writes:

> Sin embargo, e incomprensiblemente para los que somos bibliófilos, abundan en la república de las letras las personas que dicen amar los libros sólo por su contenido, y consideran excéntricos – cuando no ridiculizan abiertamente – a quienes adoramos los libros *también* – y en ocasiones, *sobre todo* – por su continente. Estas personas deben de pensar que no hay gran diferencia entre *bibliofilia* y *bibliomanía*. (*Introducción* 17)
>
> [Nevertheless, and incomprehensibly for those of us who are bibliophiles, there abound in the Republic of Letters people who say that they love books only for their content, and who consider eccentric – when they do not openly mock them – those of us who love books *also* – and occasionally *above all* – for their container. These people must think that there is no great difference between *bibliophilia* and *bibliomania*.]

Mendoza Díaz-Maroto's words are significant in that they reveal a defensive attitude present in many bibliophiles, who seemingly fear that they might be regarded by serious readers and scholars as dilettantes. As examples, José Ignacio Montobbio Jover declares that society almost always assumes that bibliophiles do not read (5), and José María Serret challenges the supposed myth that the bibliophile is "un mero coleccionista de libros, como el de sellos o el de vitolas de cigarros puros" (253) [a mere collector of books, like a collector of stamps or cigar bands]. Miquel i Planas likewise complains, albeit humorously, that the love of books could ever be labeled a mania: "[N]o sé ... que se haya hecho costumbre el incluir en el grupo de monomanías la afición a los toros, al boxeo, y aun el bugui-bugui" (*De tonterías* 4) [I do not know if anyone has ever made a habit of including in the group of manias an attraction to bullfighting, boxing, or even boogey boogey]. Miquel i Planas recommends that bibliophiles ignore criticism and continue enjoying what he regards as an edifying and ennobling pastime (110).

Commentators of bibliophilia have often attempted to describe the elements that bibliophiles share as a group. Enis Batur, a contemporary Turkish author, essayist, and self-identified bibliophile, compares the bonds between bibliophiles to those of members of a family or a tribal or ethnic community. In observing the way that a fellow library patron takes hold of a book, he imagines that he has discovered "un frère utérin, un être de mon espèce" (37) [a brother of the same womb, a being of my species]. Books, he maintains, function like arteries, linking readers, writers, and book lovers across generations (36). Batur's reflections on books are clearly metaphorical, and his essay is a personal meditation on his life with books. Yet some scholars of bibliophilia press the notion of a common identity even further, including Renaud Muller, who likens his effort to describe bibliophiles to the work of an ethnographer studying a discrete group of human beings. As Muller sees it, bibliophilia is a practice through which bibliophiles attempt to flee society and affirm a personal identity that sets them apart from the masses. Although they all engage in a similar enterprise, they differ from each other according to the books that they gather in their libraries, which reflect back to them their distinctive characteristics as bibliophiles. What they have in common is hence a strong sense of individualism and at times a belief that they are actually superior to those who do not cultivate books.

Throughout European history many bibliophiles have expressed this view of bibliophilia, as if they constituted a sort of aristocracy of cultural and artistic connoisseurs. In a preface to a book by Miquel i Planas, Fernando Bruner Prieto identifies him as a member of a rarefied group of individuals, "diseminados en las múltiples clases de la sociedad y que forman una casta escogida de muy limitado número" (Miquel i Planas, *La formación* xv) [scattered throughout all classes of society and who form an exclusive caste of limited number]. This caste is determined not by social class (although undoubtedly some economic means are required if one is to practise bibliophilia) but by a temperament akin to a religious calling. Bruner Prieto describes the bibliophile as an "idealista que persigue con el sentimiento de una predestinación un objetivo magnífico, cabe un apostolado" (xv) [idealist who pursues with a feeling of predestination a magnificent objective, or even a mission]. For Bruner Prieto, this "magnificent objective" ultimately relates to taste ("[el] buen gusto de los libros" (xv) [the good taste of books]), a notion more closely associated with the standards of social decorum and, by extension, the established social order, than any philosophical or religious conception of beauty or truth.

Bruner Prieto's comments are representative of an elitist strain of bibliophilia dominant in the nineteenth and early twentieth centuries, and in defending bibliophiles against the charge that they do not read, he even remarks that they are not what "el vano vulgo" (xvi) [the ignorant masses] might imagine. More recently, bibliophiles such as Jaume Pla have rejected the notion that bibliophilia is a luxury or a business that caters to the snobbism of the moneyed classes (166). Yet Pla employs much of the same vocabulary as Bruner Prieto to characterize the practice of bibliophilia, maintaining that bibliophiles know how to appreciate "los detalles de perfección, de buen gusto y de sensibilidad" [the details of perfection, good taste, and sensitivity], and even a "tono espiritual" [spiritual tone] that bibliophile books express (166). Critics of these attitudes, which from a political perspective are clearly conservative, have at times gone well beyond recognizing the social pretentions of some bibliophiles and have depicted them as members of an almost perverse or degenerate species. As Julián Martín Abad notes, Elena Pita once described bibliophilia as an "oscuro laberinto" [dark labyrinth], and bibliophiles as "personajes hoscos" [antisocial people] who have been infected by "un virus extraño, difícil de erradicar" [a strange virus, which is difficult to eradicate] (57–8).[8] These comments differ markedly from the satirical but humorous self-portraits penned by bibliophiles throughout much of the modern period, and are decidedly hostile. That something as seemingly innocuous as an interest in books and book collecting might be so thoroughly disparaged is more telling of society's general attitudes towards books than the attitudes of bibliophiles themselves.

The history and practice of bibliophilia has been inflected not only by ideologies of class but also gender. The majority of bibliophiles in the modern period have been men, and most bibliophile societies have been largely, if not exclusively, male enclaves. Some male bibliophiles express overtly misogynistic attitudes, as when Miquel i Planas depicts women as enemies of books in his novel *El purgatori del bibliòfil* [The purgatory of the bibliophile]. In her rich and exhaustive analysis of French book culture at the turn of the twentieth century and the consummate French bibliophile, Octave Uzanne, Willa Z. Silverman observes that during this period women were imagined as "a particularly dangerous breed of biblioclasts, or book destroyers" (169). She regards the relationships of male bibliophiles as examples of "homosociality" insofar as their shared interest in books made possible affective bonds that were "safeguarded" from homosexuality to the extent that books were fetishized as the objects of their sexual desire (167).[9] Whether or not all male bibliophiles of the period should be regarded as fetishists or latent homosexuals (Silverman cites Richard von Krafft-Ebing and Havelock Ellis, who drew a connection between male fetishism and homosexuality [192]), male bibliophiles do sometimes represent their passion for books in amorous, if not erotic terms. The nineteenth-century Spanish bibliophile and bibliographer, Hidalgo, describes the intense physical excitement and satisfaction he experienced when purchasing a book and taking it home and reading it (*Diccionario* 13), and Azorín, one of the most iconic writers of early twentieth-century Spain, speaks of impregnating the pages of a book (*Libros* 84). Luis Antonio de Villena, the contemporary Spanish poet and bibliophile, nuances the erotic dynamic of the relationship between bibliophiles and books when he suggests that the books we most ardently desire seduce us (145). For Villena, what makes books seductive are their unique qualities (145), whereas for Juan Van-Halen, their power of attraction derives from our awareness of their previous readers and owners (149). Perhaps the most extreme example of the sexualization of books is expressed by a character in a novel by the Argentine author, Carlos María Domínguez: "[Y]o cojo con cada libro y si no hay marca, no hay orgasmo" (*La casa* 42) ["I fuck with every book, and if I don't leave a mark, there's no orgasm" (*The House* 43)].

Among male bibliophiles of the late nineteenth and early twentieth centuries, the material book, as Willa Z. Silverman notes, was typically portrayed "not as inimical to women but in fact as women themselves" (4). The homosocial dynamic of bibliophilia was thus often characterized as competitive, as if male bibliophiles were engaged in a struggle for a mate or an animal of prey. Indeed, one of the most frequent images of the male bibliophile is the hunter.[10] In many male-authored commentaries on bibliophilia, including some by contemporary Spanish-speaking bibliophiles, the act of possessing a book is depicted in heteroerotic and at times sexist terms. For Fernando Lázaro Carreter, "[e]l ejemplar intonso de un libro antiguo o viejo posee el indudable encanto de romper una virginidad" (108) [the uncut copy of an antiquarian or old book affords the undeniable charm of breaking a virginity]. According to Fernando Iwasaki, "[n]o hay ceremonia más turbadora y placentera que desvirgar un viejo libro" (125) [there is no ceremony more unsettling yet delightful than deflowering an old book]. Antonio Mingote even declares that "[l]eer un libro que ya ha sido leído es como amar a una mujer que ya ha tenido otros hombres" (101) [reading a book that has already been read is like loving a woman who has already had other men].

The contemporary Spanish author Juan Manuel de Prada pens what is perhaps the lengthiest erotic depiction of bibliophilia in Spanish literature, in a scene in which a character entrusted with a trove of antiquarian books spends a night in his bed pouring over them before delivering them to a bookstore for sale the following morning. He speaks of the thrill of tearing open uncut pages and caressing their rough and brittle surfaces, like those of pressed flowers, as well as "un placer envilecido de necrofilia" (33) [a pleasure degraded by necrophilia] when he discerns the bas-relief of letters engraved on the pages like epitaphs. He even goes so far as to revel in feeling the books' "humedad contagiosa infiltrándose en [su] carne" [damp contagion infiltrating his flesh] and sharing his bed with "los ácaros que anidaban entre el encolado de las encuadernaciones" (33) [the mites that nested in the glue of the bindings]. Yet his description differs from typical male erotizations of bibliophilia precisely because of the emphasis that he places on the chasteness of book love – "la lujuria casta de los libros, que no se agota nunca, a diferencia de otras lujurias" (34) [the chaste lust of books, that is never exhausted, unlike other kinds of lust]. For Prada's character, the desire for books is thus not a substitute for other forms of desire, and although it might be compared to the sexual desire for the human other, it is ultimately sui generis.

Prada's view of book love as inexhaustible appears in the testimony of numerous bibliophiles, including certain male writers who describe not only an erotic pleasure in acquiring books but also a loss of interest in them once they have been obtained. For these bibliophiles, like the Don Juan and Casanova figures, satisfaction is to be had solely in the act of conquest. As the late nineteenth-century bookman, Édouard Rouveyre, declares, bibliomaniacal desire often expresses itself with frenzied zeal, and like an insatiable Eros, the bibliomaniac "devient amoureux [des livres], et les poursuit avec acharnement jusqu'à ce qu'il les ait entre les mains; alors il les dédaigne, les oublie, et finalement il cherche une autre victime" (26) [falls in love (with books), and pursues them with furious energy until he has them in his hands; then he spurns them, forgets them, and finally seeks out another victim]. In commenting on this dynamic from the perspective of psychology, Nicholas A. Basdenes cites the work of the Freudian psychoanalyst Norman D. Weiner:[11]

> The quality of the boasting, the constant search for new conquests, and the delight in recounting the tales of acquisition and success brings to mind the activities of the hypersexual male hysteric who must constantly reassure himself that he has not been castrated. It seems germane to this point that Casanova, after his many amatory adventures, settled down as a librarian. (Weiner 220 qtd. in Basdenes, *A Gentle* 28)

Weiner concludes that the connection between bibliophilia and castration anxiety applies exclusively to males, and for this reason he argues that most compulsive book collectors throughout history have been men. Basdenes, nevertheless, challenges this view and identifies many noted female bibliophiles from the past including Gabrielle d'Estrées, Madame de Pompadour, Catherine de' Medici, and Queen Christina of Sweden (28–9).

In representations of male bibliophilia not only do books sometimes function as objects of male sexual desire, but the bonds between male bibliophiles are occasionally depicted in what might be interpreted as veiled references to same-sex eroticism or a shared homosexual identity. In the introduction to an English version of the tale of the murderous bookman of Barcelona, Holbrook Jackson almost uncannily evokes the homosexual closet when he describes how male bibliophiles come to know one another: "Those within the pale will understand. They will understand because they also recognize their kind in a word or a phrase, as well as by the tenderness with which books are fondled and the gusto with which the fragrance of libraries is inhaled: and there are other and more esoteric means of recognition which it would be profane for me to unveil" (2). In the literature of bibliophilia, male bibliophiles are wont to stalk their fellow bibliophiles, spy on them in their private quarters, and at times even attack and kill them. But they also long to share their company, and often they regard the community of bibliophiles as a kind of extended family or brotherhood.

In keeping with the Freudian theory of collecting, books can function as objects of the bibliophile's surplus libido, but they are also what Marxists would regard as fetishized commodities (Willa Z. Silverman 17–18). Not only are they produced within a particular economic system, but so too is the bibliophile's desire to acquire and possess them, even if this desire makes possible the expression of an inner psychological disposition. The bibliophilia of Uzanne was significant insofar as it marked a moment in high capitalism when some bibliophiles began to turn from the pursuit of old and rare books to the creation of new, deluxe editions directed to an elite circle of consumers. These books were considered first and foremost works of art rather than vehicles of discursive communication. In *La nouvelle bibliopolis: Voyage d'un novateur au pays des néo-icono-bibliomanes* [The new bibliopolis: the journey of an innovator to the land of the neo-iconic-bibliomaniacs], Uzanne even imagined a time in the future when new technologies would transform book production and paper would be replaced with some other medium – perhaps, as he speculated, a kind of phonographic material. Uzanne's goal was to create books of an unmatched aesthetic quality. But, as Willa Z. Silverman asks, "[w]as the new luxury book, then – echoing an aesthetic debate at the heart of Symbolism – an expression of materialism or of idealism?" (11). Her conclusion, albeit tentative, is that it was "[p]erhaps both" (11).

Although clearly present in the writings of Uzanne and his contemporaries, the perception of books as both matter and ideal characterizes the entire history of western bibliophilia and reveals the extent to which it has been informed by a religious tradition founded in a faith in the sacredness of certain writings and in the divinity itself as an incarnate word. In fact, Christians, Jews, and Muslims have collectively been described as the "people of the book" because of their conviction that specific texts, including some that they share, convey God's ultimate revelation to humanity. Other religions, such as Brahmanism, Buddhism, and Confucianism, are also grounded in fundamental sacred writings (Carrière and Eco, *This* 291). Christianity is nevertheless distinct insofar as it conceives of God as a word ("In the beginning was the Word, and the Word was with God, and the Word was God" [John 1:1, *The New Oxford Annotated Bible*]). What is more, the Christian scriptures are thought not only to communicate the divine will but also in a sense to embody it, even if they and the languages in which they are written have not actually undergone a transubstantiation and become divine.

According to Muller, the material and the spiritual are conjoined during the Catholic Mass when the Bible is held up to the congregation as an object of veneration: "Le livre devient ainsi un moyen d'édification non par le contenu, mais par le contenant; le rapport au livre qu'entretient la communauté n'est pas la lecture, mais l'assistance à un spectacle du Sacré" (40) [The book thus becomes a means of edification not through the content but through the container; the community is bound to the book not by reading but by witnessing a spectacle of the Sacred]. Something similar occurs on the Jewish holiday, Simchat Torah, when the Torah scrolls are removed from the ark in the synagogue and venerated. In Jewish tradition not only are physical scrolls revered but, as Mario Satz explains in his study of Cabbalism, so too are actual words and letters: "Cada letra tiene, pues, su vida individual, su carácter y su valor numérico. Son, en cierto modo, criaturas vivas a las que hay que prestar atención" (28) [Each letter thus has its individual life, its character, and its numeric value. They are, in a way, living creatures to which one must pay attention]. If, for the believer, letters, words, texts, and ultimately books are living creatures with a spirit that derives from the divine, then they are comparable to human bodies insofar as humans are endowed with a divinely created life force, or soul. The body-book metaphor is particularly potent in Spain given the history of the Spanish Inquisition, which condemned to the bonfires both books and persons deemed inimical to Catholicism, including Jews and crypto-Judaizers as well as Muslims, Protestants, and others accused of heresy.[12] It informs the scene of book burning in *Don Quixote*, and it appears in the writings of numerous Spanish bibliophiles from the early modern period to the present day.

In the western bibliophile tradition, the belief that God is present in sacred texts can extend to books as a whole, as when Richard de Bury (putatively the first European bibliophile) declares that in books "the mighty and incomprehensible God is apprehensibly contained and worshiped" (9). According to Yvonne Johannot, western readers continue to regard books as sites of truth long after they have been dissociated from Christian ideology and desacralized (184). Given this deeply entrenched attitude towards books, commentators of bibliophilia often regard an excessive reverence for physical books not merely as a psychological disorder but also as sinful. Nodier, one of the most noted French bibliophiles of the nineteenth century, employed a quasi-medical terminology in his depictions of bibliomania (Steinmetz 13); however, he continued to rely on Christian conceptions of good and evil when portraying his fictional characters, including the archetypal bibliomaniac, Théodore, in the short story "Le Bibliomane" [The Bibliomaniac], first published in 1831. Through Théodore, Nodier satirizes the figure of the bibliomaniac, but he also chastises him because he focuses his attention exclusively on the physical qualities of books while ignoring the truths conveyed through language. As the narrator remarks, Théodore mistakenly spent his life engaged in "la vaine étude de la lettre" (42–3) [the vain study of the letter] and failed to adhere to the spirit behind words. Yet in the process he discovered something akin to the divine in the materiality of books, which he perceives as extraordinarily beautiful. Théodore's belief, as it exists, is therefore tantamount to idolatry, or bibliolatry.[13]

Despite the warnings of commentators like Nodier, what most bibliophiles share in common is a love of physical books. A book, of course, can take many forms, from a papyrus scroll to an e-reader. But in the early modern and modern periods, between the introduction of the printing press and moveable type in mid-fifteenth-century Europe and the advent of digital technology in the late twentieth century, the primary focus of bibliophilia has been an object comprised of printed sheets of paper, fastened together on one side and bound within a cover. Most important for bibliophiles is the three-dimensionality of books, a quality that sets them apart from ostensibly less tangible texts (such as those expressed orally or digitally) and makes them appear more real. As Jorge Carrión observes in his study of bookstores, books provide a "textura" (31) [texture] to the human experience, and as a result "la textualidad se vuelve más física" (68) [textuality becomes more physical]. What is of significance here is not physicality itself but the degree of physicality perceived and experienced by the bibliophile. This greater degree of physicality makes books seem not only more real but also more permanent. As James Salter remarks in his introduction to Jacques Bonnet's reflection on libraries, a digital book can be accessed as easily as a physical book, but when one "closes" it, it gives the impression of disappearing into cyberspace, as if it never existed: "Comme le djinn, on pourra le faire apparaître mais il restera irréel" (9) [Like the genie, one can make it reappear, but it will remain unreal]. Salter's observation is metaphorical – the digital book is not unreal but is rather expressed through a form of materiality different from that of traditional books. Yet it might seem less real to those accustomed to experiencing books through multiple senses, including touch and smell. Physical books thus appear to have a corporality that digital texts do not, even considering the physical aspects of devices like e-readers, which for bibliophiles would likely convey far less emotive and aesthetic potential than paper-based volumes. As Johannot notes, the physical features of books are in fact typically described in anthropomorphic terms, including their "spine," the component that holds them together and allows them to stand upright (8).

Like human bodies, no two physical books are identical, and even if the volumes in a given print run seem indistinguishable from one another (despite the inevitable differences in their material components), they eventually reveal the markings of their particular circulation histories. Like human bodies, they are also prone to decay, and although they might evoke an illusion of fixedness, they often remind bibliophiles of their own mortality. In reflecting on their love of books, many bibliophiles express a sense of wistfulness, if not anguish, when faced with the passage of time made visible by books. In this context Italo Calvino contemplates with regret the short life of new books, whose pages quickly yellow and fray "nel rapido autunno delle biblioteche" (*Se* 7) ["in the rapid autumn of libraries" (*If* 6)]. For some bibliophiles, however, the materiality of old books retains the life of the past. As Villena remarks, old books convey "el olor del papel de su tiempo" (145) [the scent of the paper of their time]. And for Francisco Nieva they are in fact like mummies that talk (132). As this unusual metaphor suggests, when reading old books, we not only reactivate the voices of the past (and, by extension, what Antonio Bonet Correa calls "el insondable arcano del tiempo" (138) [the inscrutable mystery of time]) but also the medium through which these voices were originally embedded. If physical books portend our mortality, they thus also provide a site for imagining that the body is immortal.

Bibliophiles are attracted to all the physical features of books including the typeface, the layout, the texture and weight of the paper, the binding, the cover, the illustrations and designs, and the signs of previous ownership, such as bookplates and other revealing markings. Many of these qualities can be perceived not only visually but also through the tactile and olfactory senses, and even through sound (as when one cuts or turns the pages) and taste (in the case of bibliophages). For those whose sole interest is reading, a book's physical aspects might seem secondary to the written text, but for many bibliophiles they often enhance reading, and for some they are really all that matters. Manuel Carrión Gútiez argues that "[l]os textos no son el libro; la literatura no es el libro; la comunicación escrita y aun impresa no son el libro" ("Encuadernación" 63) [texts are not the book; literature is not the book; written and even printed communication is not the book].[14] Carrión Gútiez's radical distinction between books and texts is not typical of bibliophiles, whose interest in books is more often than not intricately tied to reading. In fact, those who seem to value only the visual or plastic qualities of books usually do engage in a kind of reading, even when they attempt to ignore the meaning of the printed words. In *La casa de papel*, for instance, Domínguez remarks that with some books "una página es, también, un formidable dibujo[,] ... [u]n juego de líneas y pequeñas figuras que se reiteran, de vocal en consonante, con sus propias leyes de ritmo y composición" (53) ["a printed page is also a completed drawing(,) ... a play of lines and tiny figures that flows from vowel to consonant, obeying its own laws of rhythm and composition" (*The House* 57)]. These laws of rhythm and composition are meanings that are ultimately read, if not through the syntax of the words, then through their spatial structure and arrangement on the page.[15]

What matters for most bibliophiles is not whether books are or are not texts (they are, but their textuality is more multifaceted than is conventionally assumed), but rather how the cultivation of books provides a logic and significance to their lives. In one of his many essays on books and bibliophilia, Hermann Hesse states: "[O]utre leur lecture, la possession des textes eux-mêmes génère ses propres joies et sa propre *morale*" (23, emphasis added) [in addition to reading, the possession of texts themselves generates its own joys and its own *moral*]. This comment is significant, given that so many critics of bibliophilia privilege reading over the multitude of other experiences that books make possible. As Hesse sees it, bibliophilia is ethical because both reading *and* the aesthetic appreciation of the physical features of books are edifying pursuits. For him, the project of selecting and assembling books in a personal library is also a way of forging an identity. In his view, a personal library gives coherence to one's acts of reading and grounds in tangible form what are inevitably temporal and transitory experiences. If Sartre once believed that "la bibliothèque, c'était le monde pris dans un miroir" (*Les Mots* 44) ["(t)he library was the world caught in a mirror" (*The Words* 49)], for bibliophiles like Hesse it is the objective site of their own self-fashioning.[16]

Bibliophiles throughout the modern period have often imagined that their personal library reflects their true, inner self, and stands, as Jacques-Rémi Dahan remarks in his study of Nodier, as "l'expression infaillible du caractère de l'homme qui l'a formée" (16) [the infallible expression of the character of the man who formed it]. The ultimate aim of such book collectors is to achieve an inimitable identity through a collection of unique and incomparable books. But this project of self-realization is doomed to failure precisely because of the ephemeral nature of rarity, the attribute that bibliophiles like Nodier most treasure in books. Although no two books are absolutely identical, rarity does not inhere in books but instead appears solely through their perceived differences from other books. Rarity is thus a relational quality and, as such, unstable and ever changing. The upshot is that if the bibliophile's ideal library is an illusion, then so too is the self that seeks grounding through books.

Among contemporary bibliophiles, Virgile Stark, an outspoken critic of digital books and libraries, perhaps most subtly depicts how his personal library gives form and structure to his life. In an intriguing metaphor he compares his library to a rebus, a puzzle that represents words through both pictures and letters. The word "rebus" itself derives from the Latin word "res" [thing], and indeed it is the thingness of books that constitutes much of their appeal for bibliophiles. Books are also cherished for their various visual qualities, including the shapes and colours of type fonts and illustrations that characterize rebuses. As Stark puts it, his library spells out all the syllables of his interior life and connects them through "une impalpable texture de sens" (206) [an impalpable texture of meaning]. Although this texture is paradoxically intangible, it is nevertheless visible to Stark's inner eye as he gazes on his volumes: "Je vois les sillons de mon âme et les liens discrets qui relient tous les instants de ma vie spirituelle" (206) [I see the furrows and folds of my soul and the discrete ties that bind together all the moments of my spiritual life]. Stark's library is thus like a window onto a self that is forever elusive, but that can be conjured forth through a kind of bibliomancy that only paper-based books make possible (206).

Physical books are clearly paramount in the lives of most bibliophiles. Yet an attentiveness to the metaphorical possibilities of books is also a significant aspect of bibliophilia, especially for those who are also writers, including Ruiz Zafón, Rivas, Goytisolo, and Amat. Two of the most internationally renowned twentieth-century authors of book-centred narratives, Jorge Luis Borges and Umberto Eco, depict books and libraries as symbols of the structure of knowledge and of human reality and infinity, although Eco, according to Michael F. Winter, is also keenly interested in actual libraries and how they have functioned throughout history (119).[17] Eco in fact believes that despite the ever-increasing advances in digital technology, physical books as discrete entities will survive, even if their material form ultimately changes. As he remarks to Jean-Claude Carrière, the French novelist, screen writer, and collaborator of Luis Buñuel,

> [l]e livre est comme la cuiller, le marteau, la roue ou le ciseau. Une fois que vous les avez inventés, vous ne pouvez pas faire mieux. ... Le livre a fait ses preuves et on ne voit pas comment, pour le même usage, nous pourrions faire mieux que le livre. Peut-être évoluera-t-il dans ses composantes, peut-être ses pages ne seront-elles plus en papier. Mais il demeurera ce qu'il est. (Carrière and Eco, *N'espérez* 19)

> [(t)he book is like the spoon, scissors, the hammer, the wheel. Once invented, it cannot be improved. ... The book has been thoroughly tested, and it's very hard to see how it could be improved on for its current purposes. Perhaps it will evolve in terms of components; perhaps the pages will no longer be made of paper. But it will still be the same thing. (Carrière and Eco, *This* 4–5)]

Although these words clearly express the nostalgia of a lifelong bibliophile, for the short run, at least, they ring true.

## The Spanish Context

The history of Spanish bibliophilia, following the revolution in book production launched by Johannes Gutenberg in 1439, can be divided into several distinct periods (see Checa Cremades, *El libro* 2011, 142–3). Beginning in the late fifteenth century and throughout the Renaissance and Baroque eras, Spanish bibliophiles sought to create universal collections, whereas during the Enlightenment their libraries tended to represent their own particular interests as readers. The most noted example from the early Spanish Renaissance, and a figure regarded as one of the greatest bibliophiles of all Spanish history, was Hernando Colón (1488–1539), the son of Cristóbal Colón [Christopher Columbus].

Hernando Colón began to amass his collection in 1505, with the aim of gathering together all of the books thus far published in the world. By the time of his death, his library contained some 15,000 volumes, as well as an archive related to the initial European/American encounter (Fernández Sánchez 35). As José Fernández Sánchez points out, Colón created not only one of early modern Europe's first great libraries, but also one of its first bibliographies (35). His hope was to bequeath a collection that would stand as a kind of national library, although after his death many of his books were dispersed. What remained passed into the hands of the cathedral of Seville, and came to be known as the Biblioteca Colombina.[18]

The model of the humanist bibliophile in sixteenth-century Spain was Diego Hurtado de Mendoza (1503–75). During his diplomatic career in Italy he built up an extensive collection of Greek-language manuscripts and books that were eventually housed in the Biblioteca de El Escorial (Sánchez Mariana, *Bibliófilos* 36–8).[19] The greatest collection of seventeenth-century Spain belonged to the Conde-Duque de Olivares (1587–1645) and included bibliophile treasures from throughout Spain and Europe (50–2). During this period, when the Baroque aesthetic dominated Spanish and European architecture, wealthy bibliophiles housed their books in sumptuous libraries with lavish decorations and works of art that exalted the virtues of knowledge and reading (46). In the eighteenth century, Spanish bibliophiles not only became interested in works of the Enlightenment, but they also began to foment relationships with bibliophiles in countries that would soon launch a worldwide demand for Spanish books. The Valencian bibliophile Gregorio de Mayáns y Siscar (1699–1781), for example, maintained a correspondence with the German bibliographer David Clement, who made Mayáns y Siscar's collection known to the German-reading public through the publication in 1763 of his *Specimen Bibliothecae Hispano-Majansiane* [Sample of the Hispano-Mayáns library]. In this period, bibliophiles in Germany, England, and France increasingly turned to the libraries of Spain, both for their collections of universal history and culture, as well as for a literature that by the nineteenth century they regarded as a wellspring of the Romantic spirit.

Spanish bibliophilia entered its Golden Age in the nineteenth century, after the government began to expropriate rural Church property in the mid-1830s. As a result of the seizure of monastery lands and the subsequent closing of religious houses, the state took possession of great ecclesiastical libraries, and although many confiscated books eventually found a home in the Biblioteca Nacional de España [National Library of Spain] and other secular institutions, many more became available for purchase by Spanish and European bibliophiles. In addition to these books, others came onto the market as the remaining entailed estates of the nobility were disbanded and their libraries were sold off.[20]

In the course of the nineteenth century, troves of antiquarian books began to circulate through Spanish cities by way of burgeoning libraries, bookshops, and bookstalls, and as in cities like Paris, major urban centres like Madrid and Barcelona came to resemble what Alberto Castoldi calls a "spazio-biblioteca" (83) [library space]. In contrast to the closed space of the traditional library, the "city as library" was virtually boundless, not only because of the seemingly infinite number of places where one might find books housed, but also because of the constant flow of books in and out of these places as they were bought, sold, and traded. The journey of bibliophiles, moreover, became increasingly externalized, as book lovers were obliged to traverse an ever-changing cityscape in search of books. If the city was now an open library, the bibliophile became like a wanderer, a seeker, or, as Castoldi would have it, a pilgrim in a secular world on a quest for something precious, rare, and ultimately sacred (83).

The image of nineteenth-century bibliophilia crystallized during the period of Romanticism in a figure that might best be described as the Romantic bibliophile. Romantic bibliophiles were particularly drawn to rare and unusual books, and for European bibliophiles in general these were often books of Spanish origin (Fernández Sánchez 154) – as if, from the perspective of the dominant European nations of the nineteenth century, Spain were a privileged site of the rare and unusual. The difficulty of obtaining exceptional books enhanced the personal mythologies of Romantic bibliophiles, endowing them with qualities not only of individualism but also of heroism. In the lore of bibliophilia, their struggles and passions set them apart from ordinary people, albeit not always as models to be revered and emulated. Rather, because of the seemingly arcane and inward-looking world of bibliophilia, Romantic bibliophiles were often regarded as bizarre creatures whose extreme proclivities, while at times subject to ridicule and satire, were believed to border on madness. The figure of the mad bookman, or bibliomaniac, was in fact the principal prototype of the Romantic bibliophile.[21]

In their writings about books, Romantic bibliophiles often express feelings of the sublime. The notion of the Romantic sublime, theorized by Edmund Burke and Immanuel Kant in the eighteenth century and revealed in the works of a wide range of nineteenth-century European writers, is typically associated with the exalted and powerful emotions that one might experience in the presence of the grandeur of nature, not physical books – even if other cultural artifacts, like paintings, sculptures, musical compositions, and literary texts, were thought capable of eliciting such responses. In his essay on the sublime and the beautiful, Burke argues that small objects can be beautiful but not sublime, and that they can evoke love but not admiration. He writes: "The sublime, which is the cause of the former [admiration], always dwells on great objects, and terrible; the latter [love] on small ones, and pleasing; we submit to what we admire, but we love what submits to us; in one case we are forced, in the other we are flattered into compliance" (113). Yet elsewhere Burke warns against "the confounding of greatness of size with greatness of manner," that is, confusing the physical dimensions of a work of art with the quality of its execution (cxii).[22] Despite their relatively small size, physical books as works of art should therefore be no less conducive to the experience of the sublime than other forms of artistic expression. As evidenced in the writings of Romantic bibliophiles, books in fact have an irresistible power that produces the sublime emotion of what Burke calls admiration, and only when they have been possessed and lose their novelty do bibliophiles find them beautiful or merely pleasing. It is then that their passion or mania for books becomes a more sedate kind of love.

Given the distinctively Christian belief in God as the divine Word, the book in the western tradition most likely to arouse a sense of sublimity is precisely the Bible. In his essay on the theme of the sublime in Spanish neoclassical and Romantic literature, James Mandrell cites the work of Alberto Lista y Aragón, a teacher and friend of the nineteenth-century Romantic poet, José de Espronceda, who described the Bible as "el más sublime de todos los libros ... porque su autor y su objeto es el más sublime de todos, esto es, el verdadero Dios" (Lista y Aragón 21 qtd. in Mandrell 304) [the most sublime of all books ... because its author and its object is the most sublime of all, that is, the true God]. For Lista y Aragón, the Bible is sublime because of its content. Yet the physical format of the Bible, with its special bindings, paper, type fonts, and illustrations (as well as the large size of the volumes used in religious ceremonies) is explicitly designed to inspire the kind of emotions characteristic of the art, music, and literature of the sublime, including exaltation, awe, and reverence, all of which are felt by Romantic bibliophiles. Regardless of their particular attitudes towards Christianity or the Bible, Romantic bibliophiles frequently describe their bibliophilia through the vocabulary of the sublime: rapture, euphoria, and ecstasy when they obtain and hold their sought-after volumes, or misery, desolation, and despair when books are lost, destroyed, or simply out of reach.

Although Romantic bibliophiles regard books as a source of sublime emotions, most mainstream nineteenth-century commentators of bibliophilia maintain that books should be employed as a means to an end, rather than an end in itself. From the perspective of the increasingly bourgeois mindset of the period, books are of value because they make possible a knowledge of the world, which in turn can be wielded to gain mastery over it. Using books solely to cultivate a life of the mind or to achieve aesthetic pleasure in a sense contravenes the ethics of industriousness and purposiveness associated with the ideal bourgeois male, who directs his actions towards the public sphere. Romantic bibliophiles are thus often represented as effete, if not decadent, as are members of the old order of the aristocracy. As has often been noted, the majority of bibliophiles depicted in the literature of bibliophilia are men. This is not simply because throughout history more men than women have had the economic wherewithal necessary to collect books and become bibliophiles, but because the literature of bibliophilia, at least to a certain extent, aims to censure and hold in check a kind of behavior deemed inappropriate in modern males. This is clearly the case in the satires of figures like Gallardo, whose detractors ultimately treated his life as a bibliophile as worthless and absurd.

Notwithstanding their personal foibles and idiosyncrasies, many Romantic bibliophiles were practising bibliographers. Indeed, if the mid-nineteenth century marked the beginning of the Golden Age of Spanish bibliophilia, with its impassioned book collectors and ever-expanding market of old and new books, it was also, as José-Carlos Mainer remarks, "la era dorada de la bibliografía acumulativa" (91) [the golden era of cumulative bibliography]. José Luis Checa Cremades in fact correlates the nineteenth-century practices of bibliophilia and bibliography, and asserts that bibliography, as the scientific study of antiquarian books, became the necessary condition for the cultivation of bibliophilia (*El libro* 2012, 148–9). As Manuel Sánchez Mariana observes, bibliographical work was an activity in which bibliophiles without the economic means to buy antiquarian books could engage ("La bibliofilia" 68). More important, the compilation of bibliographies of the literature of a people sharing a common language formed part of the project of national consolidation underway in many European states, and advanced the burgeoning movements for political autonomy and independence in regions like Catalonia, Galicia, and the Basque Country.

If bibliographies were intended to delineate the literary and cultural contours of a nation, then new presses were launched to make the great works of the past available to a large reading public,[23] and new libraries were designed to house them. The most important library of the modern Spanish state has been the Biblioteca Nacional de España. Founded in the early eighteenth century by Felipe V, it remained under the auspices of the monarchy until 1836, when its administration was transferred to the Ministry of Governance. Since 1896 it has been housed at its current site on the Paseo de Recoletos in Madrid. In the course of the nineteenth century it developed into a truly public and national library (Fernández Sánchez 97). As Stuart Davis explains, it also "became a key source for the construction of a new nationalized identity" (*Writing* 50). Although this identity could be broadly construed to encompass the various regional identities of Spain precisely because the holdings of the library have included texts written in all the languages of the Spanish state, central libraries were gradually launched in other regions of the Peninsula. The Biblioteca de Catalunya began in 1907 as the library of the Institut d'Estudis Catalans, moving in 1940 to its present location in the fifteenth-century Hospital de Santa Creu in Barcelona. Since the 1980s most of the autonomous communities of the Spanish state have formed their own central libraries, even if, in 1986, the Biblioteca Nacional de España took on the role of "centro estatal depositario de la memoria cultural española" (50) [central state depository of Spanish cultural memory]. Although its holdings are vast and comprehensive, as self-proclaimed "gatekeeper or guardian of Spanish 'literary cultural memory'" (53), it obviously cannot and will not archive the print (and now digital) heritage of the entire population of Spain in all its diversity. For this reason, alternate archives as well as narratives attempting to represent and imagine such archives have been forged throughout the modern period.

In nineteenth-century Spain, Gallardo, Vicente and Pedro Salvá, and Hidalgo emerged as the models of the Romantic bibliophile and modern bibliographer, librarian, and bookstore manager. Yet first and foremost, they were bibliographers. As they saw it, the primary task of bibliographers was to identify books (including their provenance), describe their physical characteristics, and summarize their contents. In the late nineteenth and early twentieth centuries, bibliographers such as Marcelino Menéndez Pelayo (1856–1912) emphasized the importance of actually evaluating and analysing texts. Menéndez Pelayo is thus often considered one of the first modern Spanish scholars of Spanish literature.

Although Menéndez Pelayo criticized the work of his predecessors in the field of bibliography for what he saw as their failure to do textual analysis, traditional bibliographers clearly value content, and are often less interested in the physical aspects of books than are bibliophiles in general. Yet like many bibliophiles, bibliographers can be regarded as collectors, not of physical books per se but of titles and lists of books. Just as some bibliophiles seek to possess ever greater numbers of books, so bibliographers typically attempt to expand and develop their files and catalogues. The psychological characteristics of bibliographers are thus similar to those of many bibliophiles. What is more, these characteristics are present in bibliographers engaged not only with print but also digital media, given that the bound volume is not necessarily the primary focus of their attention.

In late nineteenth- and early twentieth-century Spain, with the advent of industrialization and the gradual advancement of literacy, books were mass produced in inexpensive formats for an ever-widening group of readers who desired not only access to traditional learning and culture but also practical information on a plethora of subjects related to contemporary life (Estruga et al. 19). Prior to the Industrial Revolution books were crafted artisanally (93) and were directed to a small coterie of readers, including aristocrats, clergy members, and women and men of letters (19). These pre-industrial books, as Pla observes, were rare and costly from the moment they were made (166), and their value only increased in the mass book-markets of the late nineteenth and early twentieth centuries. The cult of rare books practised during this period was to a certain extent a reaction against what some bibliophiles perceived as the levelling forces of modernity. Their disdain for mass-produced goods and their veneration of objects from the past, which in their minds were connected to an older and more hierarchical social order, reveals the elitist strain of some modern bibliophilia. As Willa Z. Silverman writes, "such highly symbolic commodities as fine books ... were associated with an aristocracy that ... had lost much of its political power but nothing of its cachet" (17).

As book production became industrialized in Spain, the work of publishing, printing, and bookselling was transformed into distinct professions and was often carried out by multiple agents (Mainer 96; Pérez-Rioja, *La edición* 17). Although these tasks came to be regarded by some bibliophiles as secondary to the act of writing books, for others they are often equally important. In the early twentieth century, Azorín described both writers and printers as members of a sort of priesthood capable of giving tangible form to the ephemeral world of thought and feeling. Elisa Ruiz García similarly highlights the role of the "editor" [publisher], noting that the word derives from the Latin "ēdo," which can mean "bring to light" or "give birth to" (22). Except in the case of certain contemporary artisanal books crafted in their entirety by a single person, publishers are in fact the ones most responsible for the physical format of books, and by the late nineteenth and early twentieth centuries they would determine to an increasing degree the character of bibliophile works.

Throughout the modern period, Spanish bibliophiles have prized rare books above all else. But in the late nineteenth and early twentieth centuries, some, like Uzanne in France, not only pursued already existing rarities but also began to create them, producing what they considered to be exquisitely beautiful editions. These books were rare precisely because they were almost always printed in limited numbers (Fontbona, "La bibliofília" 12). In Spain, some of the greatest accomplishments in the creation of deluxe editions and ultimately what came to be known as artists' books have taken place in Catalonia. The publications of Miquel i Planas, with their superb illustrations and designs, became models of modern Catalan book production. In them, Miquel i Planas sought both to craft beautiful books and to make available to modern readers the treasures of the Catalan literary and cultural heritage.

If Miquel i Planas was one of the leading exponents of early twentieth-century Catalan bibliophilia, Azorín was the primary Castilian-oriented bibliophile of the period and of the group of modernist writers known as the Generation of '98 (a term that he created to denote the impact on their worldview of Spain's loss to the United States in the Spanish–American War of 1898). Azorín penned hundreds of essays and journal articles on the subjects of book production, book collection, and bibliophilia. However, his meditations on books differ from those of other members of the Generation of '98, including the writer and philosopher Miguel de Unamuno (1864–1936), who represents books allegorically, and in *Cómo se hace una novela* [How to make a novel] portrays the acts of reading and writing books as metaphors for the act of living. Books in fact feature prominently in the writing of Unamuno, but, like Cervantes, he is more interested in the function of texts and discourses than in material books per se. Other early twentieth-century Spanish commentators of books, including the philosopher José Ortega y Gasset (1883–1955), reflect on the relationship of textuality to material books, and in a controversial essay titled "Misión del bibliotecario" [The mission of the librarian] Ortega y Gasset argues that given the ever-increasing number of books published in the modern period, librarians must act as a police force in order to protect readers from being overwhelmed with an incomprehensible and unmanageable number of books. In the late twentieth and early twenty-first centuries the novelists Goytisolo, Rivas, and Ruiz Zafón would react vehemently against such a viewpoint, and in several of their novels they provide a searing indictment of the efforts of totalitarian regimes to control books, often through acts of biblioclasm, in order to erase the collective memory of oppressed peoples, reconstruct historical narratives, and wield power.

During the Spanish Civil War numerous libraries and collections were destroyed in cities like Madrid, including those of the bibliophile writers and artists Vicente Aleixandre, Manuel Altolaguirre, Pío Baroja, Ramón Gaya, José Moreno Villa, and Emilio Prados (Marchamalo 17).[24] In his book on lost libraries, Jesús Marchamalo cites Villena, who recalls a conversation that he had with Aleixandre in 1975 regarding the destruction of his library. Aleixandre showed Villena a first edition of his book of poetry, *Pasión de tierra* [Passion of the earth], published in Mexico in 1932: "El libro me llamó la atención porque tenía en algunas páginas unas curiosas marcas en relieve que parecían rastros de piedrecitas o arena, como si hubiera estado en el suelo o alguien lo hubiera pisado" (qtd. in Marchamalo 17) [The book caught my attention because on some of the pages there were some curiously embossed marks that seemed like the traces of little stones or sand, as if it had been on the floor or someone had stepped on it]. These traces, formed by the detritus from the bombing of Aleixandre's library, link the volume to a particular historical moment and reveal the tremendous value of physical books, which make visible not only the words and images imprinted on them but also the events that transpire after they are produced and that transcend the lives of their owners. It might be said that Aleixandre's book is a testimony of the Spanish Civil War unlike most others, not because of its discourse but because the war itself indelibly marked it, just as it did all the human bodies scarred and damaged by the conflagration. The common fate of books and bodies during wartime became horrifyingly apparent to Aleixandre after the war, when he and the poet Miguel Hernández returned to Aleixandre's house and Hernández found lying in the rubble of the library a first edition of Federico García Lorca's poetry collection, *Canciones* [Songs], "firmado por el amigo fusilado y con la huella de una bota militar como perpetuo ex libris" (Calderón 159) [signed by the assassinated friend and with the footprint of a military boot like a perpetual ex libris].

Following the Spanish Civil War books were severely censored in Spain, and the practice of bibliophilia was at times actually subversive. Old books took on a greater value than ever before as treasure houses of traditional Spanish literature and culture. What is more, the writings of modern authors were often only available in pre-war editions, since many of them were censored. In reflecting on his youth in Francoist Spain, Nieva remarks that all the books that he read were old, and that as a result "todo lo moderno [le] venía del pasado" (131) [everything modern came to him from the past]. As Josep M. Ainaud de Lasarte observes, during the early years of the dictatorship publishers were able to elude censorship by producing books for a bibliophile clientele. He argues that censors, when confronted with deluxe editions destined for what they believed to be a small coterie of readers, were occasionally more tolerant or even oblivious to what they might otherwise have deemed seditious. Some books of literary and scientific value were thus available, albeit in limited numbers and for a restricted sector of the book market, precisely because they were "'disfressats' de llibres de bibliòfil" (66) [disguised as bibliophile books]. Under the cover, as it were, of bibliophilia, these books enriched the cultural life of the period. What is more, bibliophile books published in languages such as Catalan, Galician, and Basque helped preserve the linguistic diversity of the Spanish state, which was threatened by the regime's official ban on the public expression of languages other than Castilian.

During the early decades of the Franco dictatorship, censored books could often be found in the back rooms of bookstores and in private libraries. Bookstore owners and managers played a particularly crucial role in the dissemination of censored books, although as Josep Mengual Català notes, up until now most have received only scant praise for their daring efforts: "[A]caso convendría homenajear algún día ... a los numerosos libreros que satisfacían la curiosidad y el interés de los lectores más activos abasteciéndoles, de tapadillo, en la trastienda de obras que en apariencia eran inencontrables en España. Eran libreros y no meros vendedores de libros" (17) [Perhaps it would behoove us to pay tribute someday to the many book dealers who satisfied the curiosity and interest of the most active readers by providing them, stealthily and in the back room, with works that were ostensibly unavailable in Spain. These were "book men" and "book women," and not mere "booksellers"]. Owners of private libraries were also instrumental in maintaining Spanish book culture. One such individual was Aleixandre, whose restored library in his home in Madrid became a gathering place for several generations of Spanish poets eager for a free exchange of books and ideas.[25] Another was the Catalan editor Josep Janés, the most influential publisher of the early postwar period. In 1940, after returning to Spain from wartime exile, Janés attempted to help his fellow returnees by commissioning them to translate books and thereby providing them with much needed financial assistance. The translations remained unpublished for years, and Janés supposedly kept them in a closet behind the desk in his library. Mengual Català describes this book repository as Janés's "mítico armario" (26) [mythic closet], and based on the memoirs of Josep Miracle he suggests that in it, "según se contaba *sotto voce* y a veces medio en broma en el mundillo editorial de la época, Janés fue almacenando traducciones que sabía que la censura de ningún modo le permitiría publicar por entonces" (25) [as was told *sotto voce* and at times half in jest in the little publishing world of the period, Janés was storing translations that he knew the censors would in no way allow to be published at that time]. Despite the rigors of censorship, Janés gradually made accessible to Spanish readers the works of a wide range of foreign authors. He also advanced the production of bibliophile books in Barcelona, which the Catalan bourgeoisie cultivated in the period of the postwar, and along with book artists like Pla he helped restore the Catalan book arts movement (370–1).

The vital importance of private libraries and archives during the period of the Franco dictatorship is perhaps most clearly depicted in Prada's narrative, *Las esquinas del aire: En busca de Ana María Martínez Sagi* [The corners of air: In search of Ana María Martínez Sagi]. In this text, a narrator representing the author is struggling to unearth information on Martínez Sagi (1907–2000), a Spanish poet, journalist, feminist, athlete, and lesbian, who spent several decades in exile because of her leftist political activities at the time of the Spanish Second Republic.[26] His aim is to locate and interview her, and eventually write a book about her extraordinary life, thereby preserving for future generations not only her memory but also the memory of women like her, who were silenced and repressed under the Franco regime. In the course of his investigation, he reaches out to the poet Pere Gimferrer for assistance. Gimferrer owns a library that the narrator describes as an "alud de libros" (298) [avalanche of books] and that contains an out-of-print volume of poems by Martínez Sagi, titled *Laberinto de presencias* [Labyrinth of presences]. Gimferrer reveals that in 1970, when he and his wife were browsing in a bookstore in Barcelona, he stole the book. As he recalls, "¡[e]ra tan hermoso pecar contra el séptimo mandamiento e infringir la propiedad privada en aquellos años!" (304) [during those years it was so beautiful to sin against the seventh commandment and flout private property!]. Yet the theft of the Martínez Sagi volume was ultimately not a personal act of rebellion but, as becomes evident over time, an appropriation and safeguarding of a voice that might otherwise have been relegated to oblivion.

Prada's text highlights the potential ramifications not only of book stealing but also of removing entire libraries and archives from the reach of an ever-vigilant state. In his quest for Martínez Sagi, the narrator is guided by an elderly lesbian couple, identified as Gabriela Cuesta and Mercedes, who throughout the dictatorship maintained a secret library of books by and about women, which they had gathered before the Spanish Civil War when they directed an anarchist-inspired cultural association for women called Atenea.[27] After the restoration of democracy, they disclosed the existence of their library and made it available to the public. The anecdote is a turning point in the narrative. But it is also telling of the status of books and libraries anathematized by the Franco regime, for although many books were destroyed, others were jealously protected for posterity. The preservation of such books was particularly important for sexual minorities, whose stories – and the artifacts in which their stories were inscribed – have been largely absent from Spanish state-sponsored libraries and archives, even during periods when the governments in power have not been overtly repressive. Prada compares the library of Mercedes and Gabriela, "escindida" (261) [excised], as it were, from the social fabric, to their love for each other. In so doing, he gives renewed meaning to the metaphor so often cited by bibliophiles that books are like bodies, since in this instance the lives that books incarnate have not simply been marginalized and repressed but at times denied an ontological status altogether. The emergence into the light of day of lesbian-informed books is thus a moment of restoration and also, in a sense, an engendering of lives and experiences heretofore deemed impossible.

The censorship laws instituted at the end of the Spanish Civil War remained in effect throughout the early decades of the dictatorship, but they were loosened somewhat in March 1966 with the proclamation of the *Ley de Prensa e Imprenta* [Printing and Press Law]. As a result of this law, the number of books published on previously forbidden topics gradually rose, even though the kind of freedom of press enjoyed by most western democracies would not be achieved in Spain until the dissolution of the regime in the mid-1970s. As Kostis Kornetis explains, a politicized publishing sector began to emerge in the 1960s and make available to the reading public not only political works but also works that dealt with issues traditionally associated with the private sphere such as gender, sexuality, and the body. In Barcelona, the group of leftist artists and intellectuals known as the Gauche Divine [Divine Left] were influential in the development of a progressive press in Catalonia.[28] What is more, a new culture of books became one of the hallmarks of the burgeoning youth movement of the late 1960s and early 1970s. Kornetis cites José Álvarez Junco, who remarks on the practice of reading among young people of the period: "We read the same books, then we commented on them. We went to the cinema together and after the film discussed what we had seen. We ... went to bookshops and we went together to buy books ... or to steal books." Like Gimferrer, Álvarez Junco highlights the phenomenon of book stealing. Although the literature of bibliophilia is replete with tales of book thieves, book stealing in Francoist Spain was clearly a gesture of defiance against an oppressive system and at times even an attempt to acquire information or knowledge intentionally withheld by the regime or out of reach because of the limited economic resources of consumers.

With the end of the dictatorship and the final eradication of state censorship, the different kinds of books published increased exponentially in late twentieth-century Spain. But even though legal restrictions diminished, the economic constraints faced by writers and publishers grew, reaching a point of crisis in the first decade of the twenty-first century. In his seminal study of contemporary Spanish culture, Jonathan Snyder provides a succinct overview of the plight of opposition writers and cultural producers in the wake of the financial crash of 2008 (xi–xv).[29] Since the beginning of the twenty-first century the number of independent publishing firms and self-publishers has increased worldwide as a result of the advances in digital technology and the development of publishing software. However, in the economic environment after 2008, many mainstream Spanish publishing houses were obliged to curtail their output, and, as a consequence, writers in even greater numbers turned to self-publishing and other digital formats, including web pages, blogs, and various kinds of social networks, in an effort to showcase their work. In contrast to traditional publishers, self-publishers often support the copyleft movement, which favours the free circulation of cultural materials independent of copyright restrictions. In so doing, they challenge the monopoly held on cultural production by corporate publishers. Self-publishing can make possible new kinds of material published and new communities of readers, even if it does not always reach the desired reading public given the overwhelming amount of material available on the internet and the distribution strategies employed by self-publishers, which are often less effective than those of long-established ones. For this reason, Luis Moreno-Caballud calls for the creation of sustainable communities of cultural workers who share their needs and resources.

The crisis in publishing that took hold in early twenty-first-century Spain, although mitigated by improvements in the economy in the late 2010s, has been tenacious. In 2012, Sigrid Kraus, co-owner of the Barcelona publishing house Salamandra (which the Spanish-language division of Penguin Random House acquired in 2019), noted that "mucha gente sigue leyendo, pero está leyendo todos los libros que compró y no había podido leer, su fondo de armario, después de una época de hiperconsumo" (qtd. in Martín Rodrigo et al.) [many people continue reading, but they are reading all the books that they had bought and had not been able to read, books in the back of their closets, after a period of hyper-consumerism]. Her words were equally applicable to the COVID-19 crisis of 2020, which put added strain not only on publishers but also small bookstore owners unable to compete with the e-commerce and distribution capabilities of giant companies like Amazon. In these situations, the practice of bibliophilia did not cease, but it certainly changed. Indeed, one of the activities most commonly associated with modern bibliophilia, to wit, bookstore browsing, will likely become less frequent than in the past given the catastrophic conditions resulting from such phenomena as economic recession and pandemics, as well as the ever more efficient ways of discovering and acquiring books that digital technology has made possible and that twenty-first-century bibliophiles increasingly embrace.[30]

Outside the world of antiquarian book dealers, contemporary Spanish bibliophiles are perhaps most visible in the small, independent groups of book makers that have emerged in recent years. These bibliophiles not only seek personal fulfilment through their efforts but also aspire to a greater social good, as occurs with book collectives affiliated with the *cartonera* movement. Launched in Argentina at the time of that country's monetary crisis in the early 2000s with the publishing entity Eloísa Cartonera, the *cartonera* book makers produce hand-made volumes of quality, typically with cardboard materials collected by *cartoneros*, or cardboard scavengers. The cardboard is used to make book covers, which are hand painted, and the books are sold cheaply on the streets. As Marcy Schwartz explains in her in-depth analysis of the phenomenon, "[i]n the current media environment of increasing reliance on the internet and digital platforms, the cartonera project represents a determinedly retrogressive move ... [and] a return to bookmaking as an artisanal activity" (155). But it also provides lesser-known authors an outlet for publication while making books more available to the general reading public in times of economic crisis. It might be said, therefore, that it democratizes both book production and book consumption, even if, as Schwartz notes, its "revolutionary aesthetic ... has not truly democratized literature or entirely transformed consumer practices around books, [and] ... its impact has been more symbolic than concrete" (189). In recent years, the *cartonera* movement has spread throughout Latin America as well as to Spain and other countries around the world. Cartopiés, a Spanish collective in the Madrid district of Lavapiés, describes itself as such:[31]

> Editorial autogestionada lavapiesera, hacemos los libros de manera artesanal, uno a uno, con portadas únicas hechas con mucho amor y arte. ... Cartopiés es una cooperativa que proporciona auto trabajo y una alternativa para los escritores a las editoriales empresariales obcecadas con la valoración comercial y el lucro. Forma y contenido se abrazan en un libro que es una obra de arte total, desde el principio, hasta el final. (Cartopiés Cartonera)

> [A self-managed publisher from Lavapiés, we make books artisanally and individually, with unique covers made with love and art. ... Cartopiés is a cooperative that provides self-employment and an alternative for writers to the business publishers obsessed with commercial value and profit. Form and content are joined in a book that is a total work of art, from beginning to end.]

In its love of books, Cartopiés follows in the long history of Spanish bibliophilia. Yet the works that its members create differ from traditional bibliophile books, especially those produced as deluxe editions, because materials like cardboard are highly acidic and last only a short period of time. Their potential either to edify or give pleasure is hence more transitory than that of most books.

To a certain extent, the works created by Spanish collectives like Cartopiés share commonalities with artists' books, which are made manually by individual artists or small groups of artisans. Yet artists' books are not necessarily directed to lower income consumers and are often highly priced, as is the case with the productions of Plana. What is more, in many artists' books discursive content is subordinated to physical form, and in some instances disappears altogether, along with the traditional format of print books, the codex. Artists' books therefore oblige us to raise questions about the nature of books that are particularly germane in the age of digital books and media. As Amaranth Borsuk observes, "artists' books provide a useful touchstone for thinking about digital books because they are fundamentally interactive, tactile, and multisensory," and because users "must manipulate them to experience their full effect" (225). Artists' books nevertheless remind us of what bibliophiles have historically most valued in print books, namely, their physicality. The physicality of artists' books, like that of the *cartonera* creations and paper-based books in general, is subject to a process of change and decay, and for this reason bibliophiles find them so valuable. But unlike most print books (and clearly unlike digital books), artists' books are not necessarily intended to be read (assuming that they are read at all) but apprehended in their concrete materiality through all the senses. They might thus be regarded as the quintessence of bibliophile books.

Throughout the modern period in Spain, the practice of bibliophilia has often been an individual enterprise, but it has also made possible the development of special relationships, whether between family members or friends. The most noted example from the nineteenth century is the bibliophile bond of the father-and-son bookmen Vicente and Pedro Salvá. The family dynamics of bibliophilia have been expressed most recently in several short stories by Vicente Gómez Escámez, which portray a grandfather-grandson relationship nurtured through the management of a family bookshop (see *La huella*). A particularly touching bibliophile friendship from the post-Francoist period is that of Pla, the exemplary mid-twentieth-century Catalan book artist, and Juan José Gómez-Fontecha, a lawyer and professor of law. In a study of their letters, Anna Caballé and Francesc X. Puig Rovira reflect on the friendship that grew out of the two men's shared appreciation of the book arts and artists' books. Caballé and Puig Rovira compare their letters, which Gómez-Fontecha's wife described as the "epistolario de la Transición" (26) [the correspondence of the Transition], to those that form the basis of Helene Hanff's epistolary novel (and subsequent stage play and film), *84 Charing Cross Road* (22), about the relationship between an American bibliophile and a British antiquarian bookdealer. During the late 1970s, Gómez-Fontecha's personal library, which he kept in storage containers in the basement of his house, was stolen. As a result of the loss of thousands of valuable books, he began to decline physically, declaring that "[s]in la bibliofilia la vida no tiene sentido" (21) [without bibliophilia, life makes no sense]. But for Pla, the eventual silence of his friend was the greatest tragedy, because through him he had come to express his own love of books: "[yo] había cogido cierta adicción a nuestro diálogo y ahora me encuentro algo desconcertado, como si me hubiera suprimido el porro bibliográfico" (126) [I had formed a sort of addiction for our dialogue, and I now find myself somewhat disconcerted, as if my bibliographical high (or joint) had been taken away]. This comment, while amusing, reveals the addictiveness that some bibliophiles throughout history have felt for books. But it also suggests that books are not always the ultimate goal of bibliophilia but rather a means for fomenting and enriching human relationships.

Bibliophilia, of course, is practised not only by those who cultivate physical books but also by those who write books about books. Among the most noted book-centred narratives by contemporary Spanish authors are Ruiz Zafón's *La sombra del viento* (2001) [*The Shadow of the Wind*], Rivas's *Os libros arden mal* (2006) [*Books Burn Badly*], and Goytisolo's *El sitio de los sitios* (1995) [*State of Siege*]. For these writers the physical book is most potently a symbol of human life and in particular the human body. In representing the loss and destruction of books, they express an acute awareness of our mortality. They further convey a nostalgia for books, present in traditional bibliophiles who seek rare or ancient texts, but exacerbated in the current historical moment when for some bibliophiles, books might seem destined to disappear. In their writings this nostalgia, although initially backward looking, is reconfigured as an impetus for future change and progress. Their narratives are thus not wistful evocations of a bygone age of books but sites wherein the often-subversive discourses of other books are given a renewed relevance. More important, they remind us of the embodiedness of all texts, and affirm the perseverance of human life, however fragile our own bodies might be.

In their fictional narratives, Ruiz Zafón, Rivas, and Goytisolo depict books and other cultural artifacts that have been threatened with extinction by oppressive political regimes. Rivas and Goytisolo in particular evince what Ann Cvetkovich describes in her theorization of lesbian archives as an "archiving impulse" (269), which results from an experience of trauma and an encounter with mortality. As is the case with certain cultural artifacts, such as the AIDS Memorial Quilt, an archive can function as a memorial to the dead and thereby enable the work of mourning.[32] But it is also a means through which the living affirm themselves. If nineteenth-century bibliophiles like Gallardo, the Salvás, and Hidalgo sought to create a national archive of the Spanish people, more contemporary figures like Rivas and Goytisolo often seek to create alternate archives (albeit in the circumscribed context of their fictional writings) of peoples absent from dominant national archives, including the non-Castilian-speaking communities of the Spanish state as well as religious, racial, and sexual minorities, and in so doing empower them.

Whereas these writers limit their depiction of bibliophilia to certain works of fiction, Amat reflects on bibliophilia, books, and libraries throughout much of her written corpus. By profession a librarian, she is also an author of novels, plays, short stories, autobiographical vignettes, and essays, including studies of print and digital libraries. Unlike Ruiz Zafón, Rivas, and Goytisolo, Amat not only writes books about books but also reflects on how her life with books has actually affected her ability to write about subjects other than books, as if she were continually drawn back to her own all-consuming bibliophilia. She even goes so far as to speculate that reading and writing books are expressions of bibliophilia. Yet in the panorama of Spanish bibliophilia Amat stands out precisely because she is a woman. Given that the history of book collecting has been largely dominated by men of economic means, the practice of bibliophilia has typically been described from a masculine perspective. Amat, nevertheless, situates her development as a bibliophile in the context of gender, and comments on the distinctive ways that girls are both encouraged and hindered in their cultivation of books. What is more, she represents the lives of bibliophiles and her own passion for reading, writing, and collecting with humor and irony. In so doing, she subtly deflates the seriousness of many of her male predecessors, while reaffirming a love for books in the present age.

As the work of Ruiz Zafón, Rivas, Goytisolo, and Amat makes clear, modern Spanish bibliophilia is deeply rooted in the distinct histories, languages, and cultures of the Spanish state. But it is also bound up in the bibliophile traditions of other European countries, including Italy, Belgium, Germany, Britain, and France. In the modern period, the nation with the greatest impact on Spanish bibliophilia has in fact been France. This is due in part to the geographical proximity of Spain to France as well as the histories of the two countries, which both witnessed a flowering of bibliophilia in the nineteenth century. Yet France has led Europe in the cultivation of the book arts since the end of the eighteenth century, especially in the areas of bookbinding and printing and in the creation of deluxe editions. Although bibliophilia features prominently in all western cultures, and although many of the most prolific collectors of Spanish books have been German, British, and North American, a significant number of renowned commentators of Spanish bibliophilia have been French. French book arts and the writings of French bibliophiles have strongly influenced Spanish book production and Spanish bibliophiles' perceptions of themselves. Some, such as the Salvás, Hidalgo, and Azorín, had transformative experiences while reading French literature or simply browsing the bookshops of Paris and other French cities, and they incorporated these experiences into significant passages of their writings. Others, such as Goytisolo, actually situated parts of their book-centred narratives in France. Miquel i

Planas, although primarily focused on Catalan literature and culture, discovered the origins of the iconic tale of the murderous bookman of Barcelona through his study of French writing. Like many of his compatriots, he was steeped in the history of French book production, and his own deluxe editions reveal the inspiration of French styles. In my study, I therefore highlight these Franco-Hispanic connections, just as I do the connections between the various linguistic and cultural traditions of Spain itself.

# 1 The Legend of the Murderous Bookman of Barcelona

One of the most notorious tales in the literature of bibliomania is *La llegenda del llibreter assassí de Barcelona* [The legend of the murderous bookman of Barcelona]. This curious account of Fra Vicents, a monk turned bookseller who kills for priceless incunabula and rare editions, was first published anonymously in 1836 in a French crime journal, *La Gazette des Tribunaux*, under the title "Le Bibliomane ou le nouveau Cardillac" [The bibliomaniac or the new Cardillac].[1] Gustave Flaubert subsequently recast it as a short story titled "Bibliomanie" [Bibliomania],[2] and in his monumental study of Flaubert's life, *L'Idiot de la famille* [*The Family Idiot*], Jean-Paul Sartre used Flaubert's text to articulate what is perhaps the most rigorous philosophical theory of bibliomania to date. Variants of the Fra Vicents legend appeared throughout the nineteenth, twentieth, and early twenty-first centuries. In 1928, Ramon Miquel i Planas produced the first full-length Catalan version. His aim was to explain the origins of what he regarded as a French representation of Catalonia and recreate it in Catalan linguistic and cultural terms. Not only did Miquel i Planas translate and meld the *Gazette* and Flaubert narratives, but he also reproduced other versions of the tale together with historical and literary commentaries. His edition of the legend is exemplary of Catalan book arts in the early twentieth century, and features graphics representative of the aesthetic trends of the period. It also reveals how the practice of bibliophilia in Catalonia was used to assert the Catalan language and Catalan culture. Since the publication of Miquel i Planas's work, the legend of the murderous bookman has continued to haunt the Iberian literary imagination, resurfacing most recently in a short story by the Catalan novelist Montserrat Roig, "El profesor y el librero asesino" [The professor and the murderous bookman], and in a song by the Catalan folk singer Jaume Arnella, "El llibreter monjo" [The bookman monk]. Roig sets the narrative in post-Francoist Spain, and uses it to reflect on the phenomenon of bibliomania in the contemporary period. Arnella, in contrast, transforms the story into a work of Catalan folklore. As all these renditions of the tale make clear, bibliomania is never solely a passion for books but in fact an attitude with wide-ranging philosophical, psychological, religious, ethical, and political implications.

The historical context of the Fra Vicents tale is Spain's first Carlist War (1833–40), which resulted from a dispute over royal succession after the death of King Fernando VII in 1833.[3] The Carlists, who supported the late king's brother, Carlos, favoured absolute monarchy and the restoration of the privileges of the Catholic Church and the Spanish regions (including Catalonia and the Basque Country), which had been progressively curtailed by the Bourbon monarchy since its arrival in Spain in the early eighteenth century. The opposing group, known as the Isabelinos or Cristinos, supported the infant daughter of Fernando VII, Isabel, and her regent-mother, María Cristina. This more liberal faction favoured constitutional monarchy along with a continued centralization and secularization of the Spanish state. The liberals won the war, and María Cristina ruled until 1843, when her daughter ascended the throne and was crowned Isabel II. As an outcome, the central state further consolidated its hegemony over the Church and the Spanish regions.

During the mid-1830s, under the direction of the finance minister, Juan Álvarez Mendizábal, the Spanish government confiscated major Catholic properties, especially those entailed to rural monasteries. Through a program of *desamortización* [disentailment] carried out by Mendizábal,[4] monastic houses were closed and monks were ex-cloistered. More important, huge tracks of land were transferred from the Church to the government, and subsequently to the aristocracy and upper bourgeoisie, the social classes most economically equipped to purchase the land. As a consequence of the government policies enacted during this period and throughout much of the rest of the nineteenth century, the bourgeoisie gradually assumed a position of economic, legal, and cultural dominance in Spain. The Church, in contrast, not only lost much of its property, but also found its moral authority increasingly challenged by liberal propagandists.

In the legend of the murderous bookman, Fra Vicents is identified as a member of the Catalan monastery of Poblet, historically one of the most powerful religious houses in northeastern Spain. In July 1835, during the liberal assault on the Church, Poblet was sacked and its great library was burned. In the aftermath, Fra Vicents made his way to Barcelona and set up shop as a bookseller. In his obsessive love of books, he quickly forgot his religious calling, and in a crazed attempt to obtain the bibliophile treasures of his rivals, he became a serial murderer. Given this negative portrayal of a Catholic clergyman, the tale can easily be read as a liberal indictment of the Church. Yet to the extent that the character's secular worldview caused his downfall, it can also be regarded as a conservative corrective to an imagined threat of unbridled liberalism. In fact, Fra Vicents is a contradictory figure, representing not simply religious tradition or modernity but rather a continuity between the two. Although he is indifferent to Christian faith and morality, he is at heart an idealist, as evidenced by his blind but dogged belief in the existence of original, unique, and ultimately perfect books.

## The French Background of the Tale

Despite the absence of conclusive evidence, Miquel i Planas argues that the legend of the murderous bookman of Barcelona, although grounded in historical events and published in the *Gazette* as a real occurrence, is the literary creation of Charles Nodier (1780–1844).[5] Miquel i Planas speculates that Nodier drew inspiration from several sources: a journey he made to Spain in 1827; E.T.A. Hoffmann's short story, *Das Fräulein von Scuderi* [Miss von Scuderi] (whose protagonist, Cardillac, appears in the *Gazette* title);[6] and the announcement in London in 1829 of a recently discovered medieval incunabulum in Valencia, Mossen Lambert Palmart's *Furs e ordinacions*.[7] Miquel i Planas seemed disinclined to seek sources for the tale within Spanish literature, even though Nodier was familiar with the Spanish classics.[8] He was also unaware, as Didier Barrière has recently argued, that another French bibliographer and book collector, Francisque Xavier Michel (1809–87), might have penned the *Gazette* piece. Miquel i Planas's hypothesis nevertheless remains plausible. Not only did Nodier have a penchant for publishing anonymously or pseudonymously, but he frequently satirized the figure of the bibliomaniac in his fiction and essays. Yet even if Nodier did not write "Le Bibliomane ou le nouveau Cardillac," he became, through his book collecting and bibliographies, a significant figure in Spanish book history. In fact, Miquel i Planas regarded Nodier as the consummate bibliophile and a model that he would invoke when fashioning himself as one of the pre-eminent Catalan bookmen of the twentieth century.

During his long career, Nodier was a leading figure of the French Romantic movement, a member of the French Academy, and the most important bibliographer and librarian of his day, heading the prestigious Bibliothèque de l'Arsenal from 1824 until his death. Michel, although thirty years Nodier's junior, frequented his salon at the Arsenal in the 1830s and was admired by the elder bibliographer for his erudition, albeit not his literary talent. In 1830 Michel invented a medieval chronicle, which he titled *Chroniques françoises de Jacques Gondar* [French chronicles of Jacques Gondar]. Nodier knew that the text was a fake, but he nevertheless wrote an afterword for it on the literary features of medieval chronicles. Even though both men were complicit in this hoax, Barrière believes that Michel alone fabricated the *Gazette* piece, primarily because of its style. As he points out, Michel typically begins his narratives with a pithy and riveting introduction. In the *Gazette* tale,

> [o]n a là quelque chose de vraiment caractéristique de la manière de Michel: c'est un tempérament nerveux qui a le don des *commencements* (dans tous les domaines); il met toute son énergie, tout son talent dans les introductions de récits, pour saisir l'attention du lecteur sans aucun préambule, sans description ni portraits. (133)
>
> [we have here something truly characteristic of the style of Michel: a nervous temperament that has a knack for beginnings (in all ways); he puts all his energy, all his talent into the introductions of his stories, in order to catch the attention of the reader without any preamble, description, or portraiture.]

According to Barrière, Michel's striking introductions are usually followed by extensive dialogue, as is the case in the *Gazette* narrative. Barrière further notes that at the time of his death Michel had in his possession a copy of the catalogue of Vicente Salvá announcing the discovery of the *Furs e ordinacions*, which, according to Miquel i Planas, was the source of the non-Spanish form of the name, Vincente, used in the *Gazette*. Finally, Barrière speculates that Michel set the tale in Spain because of his own interest in the bibliographical treasures of the Iberian Peninsula that had become available to bibliographers, both foreign and local, in the wake of the disentailments of Spanish monasteries in the 1830s. Although Barrière does not claim to have resolved the mystery of the tale's origin, he hopes through his argument to have at least distanced Nodier from the hoax:

> Un chercheur qui reprendrait l'enquête un jour devrait placer Michel en premier parmi les hispanisants capables de bafouer l'éthique du journalisme pour un léger profit ou le plaisir d'un artifice littéraire. Ceux-ci n'étaient pas rares dans les années trente à Paris. L'important est surtout de blanchir Nodier, dont les multiples talents et la réputation de mystificateur lui ont valu d'être accusé de participation à plus d'affaires douteuses qu'il ne pouvait en assumer. (135)

> [A researcher who resumes the investigation should place Michel first among the Hispanists capable of flaunting the ethics of journalism for a small profit or for the pleasure of literary artifice. Such people were not rare in Paris during the 1830s. The most important thing is to exonerate Nodier, whose many talents and reputation as a hoaxer have led him to be accused of participating in more dubious affairs than he could possibly have undertaken.]

Barrière cites monetary profit and the pleasure of literary deception as possible reasons for the hoax. But as he also points out, the readers of the *Gazette* likely knew that the narrative was fictional. The inclusion of colourful details and the attempt by the author to reconstruct the psychological profile of Fra Vicents are not typical of the crime reports of the journal. According to Federico Pablo Verrié, the references that appear above the *Gazette* narrative, "Sala de los Ministros del Crimen" [Hall of the crime ministers] and "Audience Royale de Catalogne Résidant à Barcelone" [Royal court of Catalonia resident in Barcelona], sound absurdly fictional, at least to a reader familiar with Barcelona (Miquel i Planas, *La llegenda* 1951, 50).[9] As Barrière remarks, "l'indignation des critiques contre la fausseté de cette histoire est sans doute hors de propos puisque l'auteur ne faisait pas beaucoup d'efforts pour cacher son jeu d'écrivain" (133) [the indignation of critics over the falseness of this story is definitely out of line since the author makes little effort to hide his writer's game]. But he or she does conceal personal identity as well as the motive for the hoax.[10]

As Barrière suggests, Nodier perhaps did not author the *Gazette* narrative. Yet the obsessive passion for books that leads to the undoing of Fra Vicents is clearly more present in his other writings, including "Le Bibliomane," than in the writings of Michel. What is more, although in 1836 Michel had a growing interest in Spanish literature and culture, Nodier had already had direct experience of the Peninsula as well as the site of the tale, Barcelona, which he, his wife, and his daughter visited in 1827. The primary sources of information about their excursion to the Catalan capital are found in Nodier's letters to the publisher Joseph Crozet and in the biography of Nodier written by his daughter, Marie Mennessier-Nodier. In these texts Nodier comments on the violence in Catalonia prior to the first Carlist War, and Mennessier-Nodier recounts the details of the family journey. In his study of the legend of the murderous bookman, Miquel i Planas further indicates that Nodier had hoped to discover rare books and bibliographical curiosities while in Barcelona.[11] But neither Nodier nor his daughter reveal anything that might relate to the tale. In fact, the events central to the story take place not at the time of their trip in the late 1820s but in the mid-1830s, when the monastery of Poblet was sacked. Whoever wrote the story thus had some familiarity with Spanish history and politics of the period. He or she was also acutely sensitive to the attack on the monastery's ancient library, an event that was sure to have elicited in book lovers both their age-old dread of burning libraries as well as their unbridled excitement at the prospect of acquiring precious, historic books.

## The *Gazette* and Flaubert Narratives and the Sartrean Interpretation

The *Gazette* narrative begins by highlighting the library of Poblet.[12] The narrator, ostensibly a newspaper correspondent from Barcelona, describes it as "cette magnifique bibliothèque qu'un des derniers rois d'Aragon avait donnée à son couvent" (68) [this magnificent library, which one of the last kings of Aragon gave to his convent],[13] adding that after the burning of the archives of Zaragoza and the Sanctuary of San Juan de la Peña in the previous war, it was the only place where "on pouvait trouver des monuments authentiques pour écrire notre historie" (68) [one could find authentic masterpieces with which to write our history]. Throughout the text the narrator reveals a knowledge of Spanish literature and mentions certain historical and literary works that might have been housed at Poblet. The narrator nevertheless incorrectly implies that the attackers (and also Fra Vicents) stole the contents of the library: "On disait même que ceux qui avaient envahi le monastère n'avaient pas seuls enlevé les richesses littéraires qui s'y trouvaient; que don Vincente, voyant que chacun prenait, avait fait comme les autres" (70) [It was even said that those who had invaded the monastery were not alone in carrying off the literary treasures that were located there; that don Vincente, seeing that everyone was taking them, did as the others did]. But in fact, the majority of the library's books were not stolen. Nor were they destroyed in the fire that burned the library building, as the narrator suggests when referring to the "précieux débris" (69) [precious debris]. As Bernardo Morgades explains, the monks were warned in advance of the threat to the monastery, and thus packed up the contents of the library and sent it to the town of L'Espluga before the sacking took place (281–2). According to Lluís Domènech i Montaner, most of the books and documents from the Poblet library were then transferred to Madrid, where they were eventually absorbed into the Spanish National Archives (399). The narrator of the *Gazette* piece thus seems unaware of the ultimate fate of the library of Poblet.

Another curious fact, which the *Gazette* author did not likely know, was that a monk named Vicente was a member of the Poblet community at the time of the exclaustration. The monastery records, provided by Joaquín Guitert y Fontseré, describe him as follows: "P.D. Vicente Salvador, minorista, ingresado el 29 de mayo de 1832, con el P. Gatell, y profeso del 30 de marzo del 33. Era natural de Ruidoms" (*Continuación* 173) [Father Vicente Salvador, retailer, entered on 29 May 1832, with Father Gatell, and took his vows on 30 March 1833. He was a native of Ruidoms].[14] Although there is nothing in the historical records to prove that Fra Vicents was a real person, it is intriguing that a monk named Vicente once resided amidst one of the greatest collections of books in Spanish history, and that he also had the kind of practical experience that would allow a lover of books to enter retail business and perhaps become a book dealer in his own right.

Although the narrator of the *Gazette* piece is unclear about the history of the library of Poblet, he seems generally knowledgeable about the contemporary political situation in Spain. In fact, he shares affinities with both the liberal and conservative factions of the first Carlist War. In keeping with the anti-clericalism of the Cristinos, he subtly denounces the Church through his negative portrayal of Fra Vicents, and when referring to the character's nostalgia for the monastery library after its sacking, ironically comments: "La vie oisive du cloître n'était pas ce qui excitait ses douloureux souvenirs; il ne regrettait ni les rentes de la communauté ni les trente livres catalanes que payait aux bons pères le village de Poblet" (68) [The idle life of the cloister was not what provoked his sorrowful memories; he missed neither the income of the community nor the thirty Catalan pounds that the village of Poblet paid the good fathers]. The narrator, however, uses the figure of Fra Vicents to disparage not only the Church but also the liberals. Like the despoilers of the monastery, Fra Vicents steals books from the library of Poblet, and later in Barcelona, after murdering his rival, Agustín Patxot, he sets fire to his house in order to conceal his theft of the Lambert Palmart incunabulum. By juxtaposing Fra Vicents's crimes of robbery, murder, and arson with the revolutionary actions of the insurgents, the narrator implicitly denigrates the cause of the Cristinos. The text thus seems caught between the conflicting political and social perspectives of Spain in the 1830s.[15]

The murders Fra Vicents commits are nevertheless unmotivated by politics. Some of his victims are Cristinos whereas others are Carlists.[16] The people of Barcelona at first fear that the killings are the work of the Inquisition (which had been abolished only a year earlier in 1834), and as a monk, Fra Vicents is also a suspect. The police search his shop, and an officer notices what he believes is a telltale book on the Inquisition.

But when he tries to remove it from the shelf, he dislodges another volume, the Lambert Palmart incunabulum, implicating Fra Vicents as the murderer of Patxot and the most probable perpetrator of the other crimes. As the Inquisition, with its courts of terror, recedes into the past, the contemporary courtroom appears as the site of an enlightened system of justice. Fra Vicents quickly confesses his crimes, but in keeping with modern legal practice, he cannot be condemned solely on his own word. In an attempt to exonerate him, the defence lawyer reveals the existence of another copy of the incunabulum, arguing that no one would kill for a book that was not an original. Upon hearing this, Fra Vicents is overcome with anguish and rage, not, as the judge assumes, out of remorse for the murders but because his cherished book is not one of a kind. In the end, then, the illusion of the unique and the original gives way to the reality of multiplicity and simulacra.

The *Gazette* version of the tale establishes a dichotomy between being and appearance, and although Fra Vicents is a violent criminal, he is depicted as "un homme de petite taille, mais fort et vigoureux; son visage frais et rose respire la franchise et la loyauté" (79) [a man of small size, but strong and vigorous; his fresh, pink-coloured face breathed sincerity and loyalty]. In "Bibliomanie," in contrast, Flaubert makes the character, whom he names Giacomo, explicitly negative:

> Il avait trente ans et il passait déjà pour vieux et usé; sa taille était haute, mais courbée comme celle d'un vieillard; ses cheveux étaient longs, mais blancs; ses mains étaient fortes et nerveuses, mais desséchées et couvertes de rides. (132)
>
> [He was thirty, and he already looked old and worn out; he was tall, but he was bent over like an old man; his hair was long, but white; his hands were strong and sinewy, but dried out and covered with wrinkles.]

In his rendition of the tale, Flaubert eliminates most of the contemporary historical details and uses Spain merely as a backdrop for atmosphere. As a result, Giacomo represents none of the tensions and contradictions of his period, but is an incarnation of evil. Like Fra Vicents, he has abandoned God and the cloister, and sold his very soul for books. This is indeed extraordinary, since in Flaubert's narrative Giacomo barely knows how to read. Giacomo's love for books as objects in themselves thus exceeds even that of Fra Vicents.

Giacomo is enthralled by all the physical characteristics of books, especially old manuscripts: the illegible gothic letters, heavy broken binding, and dusty pages that for him exude a gentle perfume. He places his favourite volumes on the highest shelves, as though wanting to adore them from below, and he caresses his treasures while neighbours spy through his window. Gerry Max discerns a sexual element in these scenes, which he regards as both masochistic and homoerotic. Giacomo prostrates himself before books and, when gazing at a page, is drawn inexorably down to the word "finis" (which Max reads as "penis"), "that two cupids, as a sort of visual pun for testicles, adorn on either side" (15). To justify this reading, Max cites Francis Steegmuller: Flaubert had a "tendency to be obscene, profane, and scatological. In these realms he was fluent and, particularly in youth [he was fourteen when he wrote "Bibliomanie"], linguistically inventive" (xv). Not only do certain passages of "Bibliomanie" suggest a homoerotic subtext, but the whole unfolding of Giacomo's passion seems to follow the logic of homosexual deviance, as if Flaubert had inadvertently conflated the positions of both traditional Christian theology and nascent nineteenth-century sexology. Giacomo's life begins with a rejection of a divinely ordered natural world, leads to madness and crime, and ends in death.

Both Flaubert and the anonymous author of the *Gazette* piece highlight some of the "profane" aspects of the bibliomaniac's life. Sartre, in contrast, is more is interested in the overall existential and ontological dimensions of the character, and in *L'Idiot de la famille* he provides a philosophical interpretation of "Bibliomanie" and, by extension, the entire phenomenon of bibliomania. In analysing "Bibliomanie" he draws on the theory of desire elucidated in *L'Être et le néant* [*Being and Nothingness*]. Here, he defines consciousness as an anguished nothingness (the *pour-soi* [for-itself]) that exists only in relation to the being of which it is conscious (the *en-soi* [in-itself]). The for-itself not only lacks the being of the in-itself but also desires it precisely because it is nothing. Its ultimate goal, however, is not to become the in-itself, but rather to achieve the being of the in-itself while remaining conscious. This ideal unity, which Sartre calls the in-itself-for-itself, would be tantamount to Supreme Being, or God. Sartre further argues that the for-itself attempts to achieve the ideal unity of the in-itself-for-itself through acts of appropriation. In so doing, it reaches out not to the in-itself as an undefined and unmediated being but to particular objects and others. The for-itself, moreover, does not want to possess the in-itself in a relation of exteriority but rather incorporate it into itself and thereby achieve, however illusory, a sense of ontological plenitude. Although the for-itself desires a particular object, the ultimate aim of its acts of desire and appropriation is the fullness of being and, as such, the realization of the in-itself-for-itself. In "Bibliomanie," as in the *Gazette* version of the narrative and indeed all tales of bibliophilia and bibliomania, the object of desire that informs the subject's project of being is precisely a book.

In his discussion of "Bibliomanie," Sartre disparages Giacomo for treating books as static and inert objects, since in his view books are potentially instruments through which humans can effect change in the world. This is because books, insofar as they are read as texts, inevitably make readers aware of their freedom. Even if their aim is to obscure or alienate freedom, they nevertheless appeal to readers as agents capable of constituting meaning and aesthetic value. They thus implicitly posit human beings as subjects rather than objects. For this reason, Sartre claims that literature possesses an ethical dimension.

> [B]ien que la littérature soit une chose et la morale une tout autre chose, au fond de l'impératif esthétique nous discernons l'impératif moral. Car puisque celui qui écrit reconnaît, par le fait même qu'il se donne la peine d'écrire, la liberté de ses lecteurs, et puisque celui qui lit, du seul fait qu'il ouvre le livre, reconnaît la liberté de l'écrivain, l'œuvre d'art, de quelque côté qu'on la prenne, est un acte de confiance dans la liberté des hommes. (*Qu'est-ce que* 79)

> [(A)lthough literature is one thing and morality a quite different one, at the heart of the aesthetic imperative we discern the moral imperative. For, since the one who writes recognizes, by the very fact that he takes the trouble to write, the freedom of his readers, and since the one who reads, by the mere fact of his opening the book, recognizes the freedom of the writer, the work of art, from whichever side you approach it, is an act of confidence in the freedom of men. (*What* 62–3)]

Following this logic, books would appeal to Giacomo as a free agent even if he is illiterate, since their physical characteristics (bindings, pages, and print) not only inscribe the past agency of book producers but simultaneously require him as a connoisseur to render their brute materiality beautiful in the present.

Sartre nevertheless emphasizes that although Giacomo finds books beautiful, he also regards them as meaningless. Rather than appreciate books as sites of past praxis or the means through which his own praxis might be activated, Giacomo remains fixated on their "splendide matérialité" (*L'Idiot* 286) ["splendid materiality" (*Family* 276)]. Sartre recalls that as a child he himself was similarly attracted to books: "Qui n'a de semblables réminiscences? ... Si l'histoire contée n'était qu'un moyen nécessaire pour produire tant de beauté formelle?" (*L'Idiot* 285) ["Who doesn't have similar memories? ... Perhaps the story told is only a means necessary for producing such formal beauty?" (*Family* 275)]. According to Sartre, Giacomo also treasures books for their artificiality. But as he explains, n'allons pas croire qu'il apprécie en eux le travail des hommes, leur volonté de communiquer par des signes: sa perversion ... consiste à traiter ces produits d'un travail humain comme si c'étaient des fruits de la terre et, singulièrement, à nier les fins humaines en vue desquelles on les a manufacturés. (*L'Idiot* 287)

[let us not begin to imagine that he appreciates them as products of human labor, man's will to communicate by signs; Giacomo's perversion ... consists of treating these products of human labor as if they were the fruits of the earth and singularly denying the human purpose for which they were made. (*Family* 276)]

If Giacomo cuts books off from their human origins and ends, he also severs them from the natural world through a process that Sartre describes as a double negation.

Ce parasite de notre espèce vole les livres, même lorsqu'il les achète honnêtement, puisqu'il les détourne de leur office véritable et les collectionne comme des papillons. Double négation: à la Nature, il préfère ... les créations humaines à la condition de traiter celles-ci comme des objets naturels qui n'auraient pas d'auteurs et ne serviraient à rien. C'est nier l'homme dans son produit. (*L'Idiot* 287)

[This parasite of our species steals books even when he buys them honestly, since he diverts them from their true function and collects them like butterflies. A double negation: he prefers ... human creations to nature, on the condition that he can treat them like natural objects having no author and serving no purpose. This is to deny man in his product. (*Family* 276–7)]

In the hands of the murderous bookman books thus ultimately have no value whatsoever, and as such mirror the lack of value that Flaubert saw in himself and ascribed to his alter ego, Giacomo.

Sartre contends that "Bibliomanie" is grounded in the theme of jealousy – the jealousy that Giacomo feels for his book rival, Baptisto (the name that Flaubert gives to Patxot) and, by extension, the jealousy that the young Flaubert felt for his elder brother, Achille, the preferred son of Flaubert's father. Sartre finds significant the fact that Giacomo is depicted from the outset as guilty (at his trial he never denies having committed the murders), as if this were a reflection of Flaubert's own sense of insufficiency and worthlessness in his father's eyes. Endowed with a "culpabilité irréfutable" ["undeniable guilt"] and the "marque d'une infinie lacune, d'une blessure qu'un géniteur criminel leur a faite"

(*L'Idiot* 291) ["mark of an infinite abyss, of a wound that a criminal progenitor gave (them) at birth" (*Family* 281)], both Giacomo and Flaubert are victims of a cruel destiny. What is more, their miseries continually repeat themselves (Baptisto always has money to purchase the books Giacomo most covets, just as Achille is always able to obtain the father's love), and both in fact are masochists, reveling in the "volupté du douleur" (*L'Idiot* 293) ["sensual delights of pain" (*Family* 283)] and "le retour éternel des mêmes souffrances" (*L'Idiot* 293) ["the eternal recurrence of the same sufferings" (*Family* 282)]. As Sartre argues, "[l]'anomalie du jeune auteur constitue l'essence même de Giacomo" (*L'Idiot* 286) ["(t)he young author's anomaly constitutes the very essence of Giacomo" (*Family* 276)]. Yet if Giacomo and Flaubert share similar psychological temperaments, their life stories clearly follow different trajectories.

Although Giacomo destroys Baptisto, he is unable to transcend his own neurosis. Short of death, his desire remains unfilled, and he continually seeks the impossible through the acquisition of beautiful books. For Sartre, his passion is satanic: "Mais, dira-t-on, Giacomo brûle, la bibliomanie le consume. Et Satan? Ne collectionne-t-il pas les âmes?" (*L'Idiot* 289) ["But someone will say that Giacomo is burning up, consumed by bibliomania. What about Satan? Doesn't he collect souls?" (*Family* 279)]. Unlike the divine will, satanic desire is unable to create being and must attempt to appropriate it, even if always failing. It is thus paradigmatic of human desire in general. But although for Sartre all human desires have a common ontological structure, they are also all individual. What Flaubert does not provide in the case of Giacomo (and what Sartre himself attempts to elucidate through his 3,000-page study of Flaubert) is an explanation of a particular life, or how "un certain désir [est] creusé par une certaine histoire" (*L'Idiot* 291–2) ["a certain desire (is) hollowed out by a certain history" (*Family* 281)]. In contrast to Flaubert, the primary Iberian commentator of the murderous-bookman legend, Miquel i Planas, offers considerable historical and social context, and thereby makes available a nuanced portrayal of the figure of the bibliomaniac in modern Iberian culture.

## Ramon Miquel i Planas as Bibliophile and Catalanist

Miquel i Planas was drawn not only to the legend of Fra Vicents but also to Nodier, whom he assumed to be the author of the anonymous *Gazette* narrative. In a sense he regarded Nodier as a mentor and model as he developed his own career as bibliographer and publisher. In 1931 he gave a lecture on the art of book illustration at the International Salon du Livre d'Art in Paris. In his opening words he indicates that he made the journey to the French capital in devoted memory of the "inmortal bibliotecario del Arsenal" (*Ensayos* 43) [immortal librarian of the Arsenal], whose love of books led him 100 years earlier to Barcelona. Miquel i Planas thus sees his own journey as a complement to Nodier's, and the two together as a reflection of the long-standing bibliographical and bibliophilistic relationship between Spain and France.

> Permitidme, pues, que salude en todos vosotros, bibliognostas parisienses, a los dignos sucesores de Carlos Nodier, quien tuvo ... a través de sus libros, un grande amor a España y a nuestras cosas, como preludiando una futura e inquebrantable hermandad bibliofílica entre los aficionados de uno y otro lado del Pirineo. Porque preciso es que sepáis amigos de Francia, que, sin vuestros libros, nuestras propias aficiones se verían faltas de una buena parte de sus objetivos, y aun nuestra historia bibliográfica quedaría en muchos pasajes sin explicar. (*Ensayos* 43–4)

> [Permit me, then, to greet you all, bibliognosts of Paris, as worthy successors of Charles Nodier, who revealed through his books a great love for Spain and our culture, and who heralded a steadfast, bibliophilic brotherhood between book enthusiasts on each side of the Pyrenees. Because you should know, my French friends, that without your books our own efforts would have failed to achieve a good part of their objectives, and even our own bibliographical history would in many ways remain unknown.]

According to Miquel i Planas, France has played the leading role throughout Franco-Hispanic book history, discovering, as it were, Spanish book treasures and making possible the development of Spanish bibliography. Spain, in contrast, has done little to advance France's understanding of its own book history. Spain thus owes France a debt of gratitude. But it also, as Miquel i Planas's rendition of the Fra Vicents legend makes clear, owes a debt to itself, which to a certain extent he fulfills by re-appropriating the French versions of the tale and re-expressing them in the languages of Spain. Although his words pay homage to France, his overall work as a scholar and publisher asserts Spanish, and in particular Catalan, culture on its own terms.

Miquel i Planas writes most extensively on the artistic dimensions of books in his essay *El arte en la encuadernación* [The art in bookbinding]. For him, the purpose of bookbinding is to make books useable and to preserve them. But bookbinding is also what turns physical books into works of art and is itself an artistic expression. As Miquel i Planas sees it, "la encuadernación es la suprema manifestación del amor al libro" (3) [bookbinding is the supreme manifestation of the love of the book]. In his view, bibliophilia is thus ultimately a love of the physicality of books. He further remarks that the emergence of bibliophilia in the early modern and modern periods is coeval with the flowering of the art of bookbinding, and that the way a society fashions its books most clearly reveals its aesthetic values as well as its "grandes inquietudes esprituales" (16) [great spiritual concerns].

In *El arte en la encuadernación*, Miquel i Planas delineates the history of Spanish bookbinding, including the influence of Italian bookbinders of the sixteenth century and French bookbinders from the seventeenth to the twentieth centuries. As he argues, the most distinctive Spanish style is *mudéjar*, or Hispanic-Arabic, first developed by Muslim book producers in late medieval Spain.[17] Although schools of Arabic bookbinding evolved in Italy and elsewhere, the *mudéjar* style is in his view autochthonous to the Iberian Peninsula (14). What distinguishes it from earlier and later European schools of bookbinding are the graphic features, which highlight geometric forms, lace designs, and braiding. Through his writing on bookbinding, Miquel i Planas hopes to recuperate the *mudéjar* tradition and inspire contemporary bookbinders to replicate it, even though his own style of bookbinding is far more representative of *Modernisme*, including Art Nouveau and Art Deco (Mateos Pérez 63).

In a lecture at the Athenaeum of Madrid in 1922, Miquel i Planas explains his general understanding of books. Like traditional western commentators of the nature of books, he invokes a spirit/matter or soul/body dichotomy when describing them. As he sees it, a perfect book would unite these elements in absolute harmony.

> Es, en efecto, el Libro un todo completo, en el que la criatura humana se muestra creadora a su vez, supuesto que en él se reúnen un elemento espiritual, que es la obra literaria, fruto del pensamiento, y un elemento material, que es el libro mismo en su forma tangible. Libro perfecto sería aquel en que ambos elementos, cuerpo y alma, se correspondieran dignamente; en que la belleza de la obra literaria tuviera una exacta concordancia con la belleza y perfección de los componentes materiales que forman el libro, hasta el punto de que semejante conjunción constituyera una integral y perfecta obra de arte. (*Ensayos* 24)
>
> [The Book, in effect, is a complete whole in which human creatures show their creativity, provided that it unites a spiritual element, which is the literary work, the fruit of thinking, and a material element, which is the book itself in its tangible form. The perfect book would be the one in which both elements, body and soul, were in complete correspondence; in it, the beauty of the literary work would exactly match the beauty and perfection of the material components that formed the book, to the point where this conjunction constituted an integral and perfect work of art.]

Miquel i Planas further compares book creators to architects. In making books, he argues, they construct edifices in which to house texts. The cover of the book, like the façade of a building, (both of which are called "portadas" in Castilian and Catalan), is a crucial feature intended to predispose observers favourably to what lies within (*La formación* 57). Through books, moreover, the spiritual and the material are fused, and "el Pensamiento adquiere forma tangible y queda perpetuamente fijado" (*La fiesta* 7) [Thought acquires tangible form and is permanently fixed]. The manifestation of "Thought," an ideal suggestive of the Platonic Forms, occurs both in the physical structure of the book as well as in what Miquel i Planas regards as the textual content. Yet he is less interested in the truth that texts might convey than in the aesthetic pleasure that reading a beautifully crafted edition makes possible. His aesthetic appreciation of books is thus reminiscent of the bibliophilia of early and mid-nineteenth-century bibliophiles, including Nodier and even Fra Vicents, although he is clearly more self-controlled than the latter. Perhaps most significant is their shared illusion that books, once constituted, become sites of permanence and stasis. Nevertheless, unlike the bibliomaniac depicted by Sartre in his reading of Flaubert's "Bibliomanie," Miquel i Planas does not attempt to detach books from their practical ends or preclude them from effecting change in the world, precisely because so many of his publications, through their linguistic and artistic features, highlight a Catalan ethos and thereby advance the project of Catalan linguistic and cultural identity.

Both Miquel i Planas and the commentators of his life and work are keen to distinguish bibliophilia from bibliomania. Josep Rodergas Calmell in fact feels compelled to assert that bibliophiles are inherently good people, and that Miquel i Planas was a model husband, father, friend, and citizen on account of the lofty sentiments that he experienced through his appreciation of books (14). Miquel i Planas was himself perplexed that so many people regard bibliophilia as a mania, whereas other passions are considered completely normal. He blames non-bibliophiles for the negative image of book lovers – although as a matter of fact the most notorious depictions of bibliomaniacs are penned by bibliophiles. Rodergas Calmell nonetheless assures us that Miquel i Planas was "un bibliòfil normal" (4) [a normal bibliophile], who valued books for their contents and believed that their purpose was to be read rather than simply possessed. Yet if Miquel i Planas was a "normal bibliophile," he was not, according to his admirers, a typical one. Rodergas Calmell declares that the editions Miquel i Planas published during his lifetime were unsurpassed in their sumptuousness and exquisite taste (14). And as Josep M. Cadena puts it, even though

Miquel i Planas might not have been the most expert bibliophile of his day, he was by far the most enthusiastic and the one whose work had the most far-reaching impact ("Miquel" 13).

In the preface to *Contes de bibliòfil* [Bibliophile tales], a collection of French and Catalan stories of bibliophilia and one of his most beautifully crafted editions, Miquel i Planas reflects more deeply on the nature of books. He describes the experience of reading in topographical terms, as if when reading one entered a different sphere called Bibliopolis. According to José Luis Checa Cremades, a version of the term "Bibliopolis" was coined by Victor Hugo (*El libro* 2011, 200), but it was most fully developed by Octave Uzanne in *La nouvelle bibliopolis*. For Miquel i Planas, Bibliopolis is a domain inhabited by book lovers from throughout history. As he declares, all bibliophiles have two countries, their own and Bibliopolis. Through the stories of *Contes de bibliòfil* he offers to take his readers on a journey to Bibliopolis, where they will discover not only the imaginary worlds that books make possible, but also a realm in which the lives of bibliophiles like themselves are revealed. In this sense, *Contes de bibliòfil* stakes out a special province of Bibliopolis where lovers of books might come to see and know themselves.

In *Contes de bibliòfil*, Miquel i Planas reiterates the Enlightenment notion that books free humans from the "esclavatge de la ignorancia" (xlii) [slavery of ignorance].[18] But he describes books in such reverential terms that they seem tantamount to the divinity itself. In his view, books are the locus of all that is: "*Tot es en els llibres*" (xl) [*Everything is in books*]. Books, moreover, have no limits in time and space (xli). Yet even though the essence of books is temporally eternal and spatially unbounded, it expresses itself within time and space, thereby grounding the infinite. In imagining future generations of readers, Miquel i Planas writes:

> [T]indran llibres gracies als quals podran considerarse situades a igual distancia d'un passat y d'un futur remotíssims, vivint en un present com el nostre, qu'es només un instant efimer en mitg de l'eternitat. Sols el llibre dura y perdura. ... El llibre, donchs, es etern y infinit. (xlii)

> [They will have books thanks to which they will be able to regard themselves situated equal distance from an infinitely remote past and an infinitely remote future, living in a present like our own, which is no more than an ephemeral instant in the midst of eternity. Only the book lasts and endures. ... The book, therefore, is eternal and infinite.]

As the interstice of time and eternity, the book is thus like the Christ, the divinity made flesh, and as such "un veritable dò de Déu" (xlii) [a veritable gift of God]. For the believer turned secular bibliophile, the truth of the book is known not through faith but rather reading and, concomitantly, an aesthetic appreciation of the physical volume as a beautiful object. For Sartre, the acts of reading and aesthetic appreciation as Miquel i Planas envisions them would amount to an attempt by consciousness to achieve the fullness of being that it lacks, that is, the in-itself-for-itself. In fact, Miquel i Planas conceives of Bibliopolis not as a place outside of consciousness but as a site of self-consciousness where ontological fulfillment might ultimately occur. What he calls "una excursió a Bibliòpolis" (vii) [an excursion to Bibliopolis] is hence a fantasy of being, although for him this being is real, persisting by way of books through all that is ephemeral and transitory in human experience.[19]

To a certain degree Miquel i Planas's upbringing primed him for the life of a bibliophile. Although his family was what Barry Taylor calls "commercial rather than intellectual" (59), his father owned a shop that made handcrafted bookbindings as well as accounting ledgers and stationery.[20] Through exposure to the art of bookbinding, Miquel i Planas began to develop an interest in fine editions. Upon his father's death, he took over the family business, which to this day continues to produce paper products and school accessories under the trade name Miquelrius.[21] As a child, Miquel i Planas showed an interest in writing, occasionally publishing literary vignettes under pseudonyms (Ollé Pinell 70), and as an adult he continued to write fiction while advancing his career as a publisher, translator, bibliographer, and scholar of the Catalan language and literature. Overall, he published some 150 pieces, written in both Catalan and Castilian, albeit primarily in the former language. As José Porter points out, although many of his publications are reprints of old texts or translations, to a certain extent they are original works, since Miquel i Planas tended to include in them (as in the case of the *Llegenda*) his own extensive prologues and historical and critical commentaries ("La bibliofilia" 57). Antonio Ollé Pinell remarks that Miquel i Planas wanted to produce the most perfect books possible (75). According to Porter, he achieved this goal not only because he had his own press and bindery, but also because he personally supervised every step in the production of his books ("La bibliofilia" 58).

Miquel i Planas's main contributions to the recuperation of early Catalan literature include the volumes published in the series Biblioteca Catalana, launched by Marià Aguiló i Fuster in the nineteenth century, and the ten volumes of *Històries d'altre temps*. As Taylor explains, the Biblioteca Catalana was intended to parallel the Castilian Biblioteca de Autores Españoles, although unlike the latter series, it aimed not only to reprint old texts but also create deluxe editions (59).[22] Through the

*Revista Ibérica de Ex-Libris*, Miquel i Planas sought to foment the cultivation of bookplates in Catalonia and Spain.[23] In the area of bibliophilia, he published the two volumes of *Bibliofília*, which Prudencio Mateos Pérez considers his greatest contribution to the Catalan bibliophilistic movement (64). He also spearheaded the Catalan-language series, Col·lecció Bibliofília, and the Pequeña Colección del Bibliófilo, in which some of the titles of the Col·lecció Bibliofília were reprinted in Castilian (Mateos Pérez 64). In describing the aims of the Pequeña Colección del Bibliófilo, Miquel i Planas reveals own his aspirations as a book publisher.

> Con la publicación de la serie de tomitos que habrán de formar la "Pequeña Colección del Bibliófilo" trata el editor de introducir en España el libro de lujo, tal como lo conciben los editores extranjeros que buscan su clientela entre los bibliófilos y las personas de gusto delicado. Huyendo de las ediciones monumentales, esto es, colosales, que fueron para nuestro país los libros de lujo durante el siglo pasado, se ha creído que el verdadero libro de bibliófilo había de imponerse al público español por la exquisita calidad de los materiales en él empleados y por la cuidada ejecución de la obra. (*Els cent* 1–2)

> [With the publication of the series of little volumes that will form the "Pequeña Colección del Bibliófilo," the editor attempts to introduce into Spain the deluxe edition as understood by foreign publishers who search for their clientele among bibliophiles and persons of refined taste. Fleeing from the monumental, or rather colossal, editions that were for our country the deluxe editions of the last century, we believe that the true bibliophile book should be promoted to the Spanish public because of the exquisite quality of the materials used in its manufacture and the careful production of the work.]

Although Miquel i Planas uses the term "de lujo" [deluxe] to define his books, he clearly wants to distinguish them from the ostentatious works favoured by the Catalan bourgeoisie in the nineteenth century. Given their small size and apparent simplicity, some of his volumes, including the *Llegenda*, might actually escape notice as bibliophile editions. But they were, in fact, directed towards bourgeois consumers who, as a consequence of the industrialization of Catalonia, had not only acquired the economic means to purchase luxury items, but had begun to develop a taste for subtlety and understatement as signs of heightened social status.

To a certain extent the flowering of bibliophilia in modern Catalonia was a reaction to the mass production of books made possible by the Industrial Revolution. Yet it was also a consequence of the nineteenth-century endeavour to revitalize the Catalan language and culture, known as the *Renaixença* (Puig Rovira, "L'interès" 182).[24] In late nineteenth- and early twentieth-century Catalonia, books were published in both Castilian and Catalan, but, as Pilar Vélez explains, those geared to bibliophiles tended to be written in Catalan (*El llibre* 280). Publishers like Miquel i Planas in fact produced Catalan books with the explicit aim of preserving and reaffirming the Catalan literary tradition of the Middle Ages and Renaissance. By recuperating Catalan-language writing, modern Catalan bibliophiles not only validated the Catalan past but also promoted the Catalan language as a fundamental instrument of Catalan nationalism.[25] In late nineteenth- and early twentieth-century Catalonia, bibliophilia formed part of the burgeoning nationalist movement and became institutionalized through various publishing houses and cultural entities (Vélez, "D'Ivori" 148). The publications of Miquel i Planas are among the most noted examples of the Catalan bibliophilistic enterprise.

As a dedicated Catalanist, and in keeping with the tenets of the *Renaixença,* Miquel i Planas believed that the assertion of Catalan identity hinged on the recovery and practice of the Catalan language. Yet he actually came of age during the period following the *Renaixença,* as Catalanists gradually shifted their attention from the Catalan past and increasingly identified the Catalan language and culture with the modern, urban milieu of Barcelona. In fact, his career spanned the two early twentieth-century Catalan cultural movements, *Modernisme* and *Noucentisme,* each of which rejected the regionalist thrust of the *Renaixença* and sought to make Catalan culture a national culture.[26] As Albert Balcells explains, these movements represented the view that cultural autonomy could be achieved only through full political independence from the Spanish state (58). But Catalan *Modernisme* and *Noucentisme* are markedly different. Catalan *Modernisme,* for instance, possesses a Romantic strain that at times pits the artist as an individual rebel in opposition to bourgeois society. *Noucentisme,* in contrast, allies the artist with bourgeois society and its political and cultural institutions in order to advance the Catalan nationalist project. Moreover, Catalan *Modernisme,* especially in architecture, design, and the plastic arts (and also the art of bookmaking), typically highlights the decorative over the purely functional. Because Miquel i Planas occasionally satirized the *Noucentistes,* he has often been regarded as an exponent of Catalan *Modernisme.* But given his deep interest in the literature of the Catalan Middle Ages and Renaissance, coupled with his work as an "'arqueólogo-restaurador' de la lengua y literatura catalana" (Mateos Pérez 64) ["archeologist-restorer" of the Catalan language and literature], he was in many ways closer in spirit to the *Renaixença* (Vélez, "D'Ivori" 152).

Despite Miquel i Planas's identification with the nationalist thrust of late nineteenth- and early twentieth-century Catalanism, his publications reveal an aesthetic emphasis not wholly reducible to nationalism. Throughout his career, he consistently promoted the Catalan language and Catalan culture, and even in the anti-Catalan atmosphere of the Miguel Primo de Rivera dictatorship he continued to produce works in Catalan, including the *Llegenda*.[27] Yet his patriotism was matched by an equal if not greater love of the book, not merely as a bearer of national culture but as an object of beauty in itself. Despite his appreciation for what Taylor calls "the double nature of the book" as both form and content (71), Miquel i Planas's intense attention to the surface reality of books (an attitude he seemingly condemns in Fra Vicents) runs counter to essentialist expressions of nationalism and at times sets him apart from his more overtly politicized contemporaries, including those bent on modernizing the Catalan language.

In the early twentieth century, Catalan linguists and grammarians undertook a systematic process of standardizing the Catalan language. The chief exponent of standardization was Pompeu Fabra, who, in conjunction with the group affiliated with the journal *L'Avenç* and subsequently the Institut d'Estudis Catalans, wrote various texts on Catalan spelling and grammar, as well as the Institut's first dictionary of the language. Miquel i Planas, however, opposed the work of Fabra and his followers in the philological section of the Institut, giving speeches and penning polemical essays and literary pieces that denounced the version of Catalan they promoted. Manuel Llamas contends that Miquel i Planas's posthumous fame was damaged by his belligerent attitude towards the normalization of Catalan (183), although according to Cadena, the early controversies surrounding the Catalan language no longer matter, and Miquel i Planas's reputation now rests on the important work he did in preserving and disseminating the early Catalan literary tradition ("Miquel" 13). Miquel i Planas in fact differed from the *fabristas*, or followers of Fabra, insofar as he insisted on maintaining the traditional spelling and grammar of old Catalan, that is, the language as it appeared in the bibliophile books that he produced. His approach to the linguistic question was thus aesthetic. Nevertheless, he was firmly convinced that the project of Catalan nationalism would be better served through an affirmation of the traditional Catalan language and literature.

In "Contra la Reforma Lingüística" [Against the linguistic reform], a speech delivered at the Athenaeum of Barcelona in August 1918, Miquel i Planas describes the Catalan language as the most important treasure of the Catalan national patrimony. In his view, the norms proposed by

Fabra and the Institut d'Estudis Catalans pose a great threat to Catalonia because they corrupt its language and neglect its literary past. In fact, Fabra did not ignore the Catalan past, and as Thomas R. Hart explains, he "sought to create a culture that would be open to new developments and also solidly rooted in Catalan tradition" (211). But he did not want simply to restore the medieval Catalan language:

> L'ideal que perseguim no és la resurrecció d'una llengua medieval, sinó formar la llengua moderna que fóra sortida de la nostra llengua antiga sense els llargs segles de decadència literària i de supeditació a una llengua forastera. (Fabra 144 qtd. in Hart 216)
>
> [The ideal that I pursue is not the resurrection of a medieval language, but to form the modern language that would have emerged from our ancient language without the long centuries of literary decadence and subjugation to a foreign language.]

According to Miquel i Planas, Fabra privileges the everyday spoken language of Barcelona over the rich language of the Catalan literary tradition. As he sarcastically remarks, the situation would be the same if the Real Academia Española sought its model for the Castilian language in the *barrios bajos*, or working-class districts, of Madrid. Miquel i Planas believes that as a result of Fabra's reforms the literature of the Catalan past will come to be regarded as archaic, if not dead. The consequences of this will be dire, for as Miquel i Planas elsewhere maintains, a literature is what gives value to a language in the eyes of the world (*Memoria* 3). A national literature requires both a corpus and precedents, and without a "library" behind it, a language is no more than what he calls a familiar dialect for humble uses (3). The salvation of the historical language and literature of Catalonia is thus, for Miquel i Planas, a matter of national urgency.

But then again, it is also an aesthetic issue. As he sees it, the normalization of Catalan has been particularly pernicious because it has damaged the language as an instrument of beauty. One point he highlights is the preference of the reformers for the Latin "i," as opposed to the Greek "y," for the conjunction "and." He argues that the "y" was not adopted from Castilian but that it simultaneously replaced the Latin "e" in both Castilian and Catalan. (It was for this reason that he usually spelled his name "Miquel y Planas" and not "Miquel i Planas.") He also mocks the use of the middle dot between a double "l," since from his perspective it would look unattractive on the cover of a fine book: "Y pensèu en uns IDIL·LIS I BAL·LADES, també de lletres majúscules, en una portada!" ("Contra" 348) [Just imagine an IDYL·LS AND BAL·LADS, also in upper case letters, on the cover of a book!]. Although he admits that such considerations might seem petty, he ultimately fears that if the grammatical changes sought by Fabra take effect, the Catalan language will lose both its subtlety and force of expression. More important, it will cease to be beautiful.

Miquel i Planas intertwines his views of the Catalan language and bibliophilia in his satirical and fantastic novel, *El purgatori del bibliòfil* (1920) [The purgatory of the bibliophile]. In this narrative, the protagonist awakens one night to discover the Devil, dressed in a green overcoat, rummaging through his library. The Devil informs him that he approves of his bibliophilia because books lead humans to unhappiness and doubt. To corroborate this, he tells him the tale of Fra Vicents, as recounted by Antoni Palau i Dulcet. The Devil wants to make a pact with the protagonist, but before doing so he takes him on several excursions, first to two libraries in Barcelona and then to a magical land called Analefia. The inhabitants of Analefia speak Catalan, but they have no written language. Although the rulers hope to maintain this state of affairs, the protagonist inadvertently teaches the Analefians how to write, and as a result a war breaks out between the literate and the illiterate. The authorities hold him responsible for the conflict and sentence him to be burned at the stake. At the last minute, however, the Devil rescues him and spirits him back to Catalonia. There, they go to an auction of rare books, where the French representative of the American Hispanist, Archer Huntington, is about to buy the only known copy of a 1497 edition of the medieval Catalan romance, *Tirant lo Blanc* [Tirant the White], by Joanot Martorell. The protagonist is desperate to acquire the volume and keep it in Catalonia, and for this reason he finally agrees to sign a blood pact with the Devil, who gives him the money necessary to purchase the book. In the following episode the two go to a meeting of the reformers of the Catalan language. Upon hearing their plans for linguistic normalization, the protagonist launches a verbal attack against their leader, Padre Fabricio (clearly an avatar of Fabra), and denounces him for ignoring Catalan tradition and the historical ethos of the Catalan people as embodied in their language.[28] Afterwards, he returns home and opens his copy of *Tirant lo Blanc*, only to discover that it is filled with worms. As he meditates on his misfortune, a group of women ("las Maestras Bibliotecarias" [the librarian matrons]) burst into his house, and on the orders of Padre Fabricio begin to burn all of his books that do not conform to the standards of the linguistic reform movement. The protagonist then awakens from what turns out to have been a long nightmare. He regains his senses and vows that henceforth he will make the books he already possesses his "little garden of delights," and that he will never again harbor ambitions or illusions about society.[29]

This narrative, which in fact often reads like a dream, reveals many of Miquel i Planas's deepest concerns about the Catalan language, Catalan culture, and books in general. Through his attack on the *fabristas* Miquel i Planas rejects the movement to modernize the Catalan language, and through his representation of Analefia he satirizes the entire Catalan cultural establishment, which he considers intransigent and anti-intellectual. He also reveals what some, including Nuria Amat, regard as his misogyny.[30] Not only are women the agents of the worst crime that can be committed against books (biblio-pyromania), but those with feminist aspirations are mocked in the episode in Analefia. It is the Devil, however, who is the most complex figure in the narrative, for despite his ostensible evil he opens the protagonist's eyes to what from the perspective of Miquel i Planas are the hypocrisies and errors of early twentieth-century Catalan society. What is more, he allows the protagonist to cultivate his passion for books. But although the book that he funds is a treasure of Catalan culture that Miquel i Planas would surely hope to see preserved, it is, at least in its physical format, rotten. This perhaps represents Miquel i Planas's belief that only the higher truths (or *Pensamiento*) contained in material books matter, and his fear that excessive attention to the external form, as occurs in the tale of Fra Vicents, leads ultimately to failure and death. In this sense, material books are like "coins in the Devil's purse" – that is, nothing.

The images in the final episodes of the novel are particularly rich. Clearly, the incunabulum riddled with worms and the library engulfed in flames are indicative of human destruction and death. From a Freudian perspective they also suggest a sexual dynamic. In Freudian dream-theory books are believed to represent women, whereas worms are often read as symbols of repressed passions. If the protagonist's love of books entails a displaced erotic desire that has gone unfulfilled, the expression of this desire is nevertheless something he dreads, for when the librarian matrons set fire to his books, the result is mayhem. The dream depicted in *El purgatori del bibliòfil* could thus represent a terror of female sexuality. It could also reveal a fear that women might actually impede the fulfillment of his latent sexual desires. Yet more important, the indomitable power of the library matrons is a sign of their role as agents of modernity, since what they aim to destroy are precisely those elements of tradition that cannot be assimilated into the prevailing agenda of Catalan nationalism. Their modernity is indeed almost fascistic, although the protagonist chooses to align them with an oppressive past, comparing their leader, Padre Fabricio, to Cardinal

Francisco Jiménez de Cisneros, who after the reconquest of Granada ordered the burning of a vast trove of Jewish and Muslim books that he deemed inimical to Christianity.

## The Catalan *Llegenda:* Visual Innovation and Narrative Recovery

In early twentieth-century Catalonia, the bibliophile movement kindled new developments in all the graphic arts, including drawing, painting, typography, and bookbinding. It drew on the aesthetics of Catalan *Modernisme*, melding the artistic currents of the period with the values and tastes of collectors and scholars of early Catalan literature (Llamas 179). As Eliseu Trenc observes, practitioners of Catalan *Modernisme* tended to regard a work of art as a totality (121). In the case of the bibliophile editions of publishers like Miquel i Planas, this meant that the text and illustrations and indeed all the visual and tactile elements of a volume were conceived of as a unified whole. With its harmonious configuration of narrative, commentary, drawings, fonts, colour, and paper, *La llegenda del llibreter assassí de Barcelona* can be read as an example of Catalan *Modernisme*, although as Vélez argues, Miquel i Planas remained throughout his creative life more closely tied to his predecessors of the *Renaixença* than to his modernist contemporaries ("D'Ivori" 152).

The *Llegenda* is in fact less striking for the story itself, since this is an amalgamation of previous texts, than for a visual quality typical of the plastic arts. The volume is small (fourteen by ten centimetres), and as such similar in size to a breviary or pocket book (Ollé Pinell 77), formats that Miquel i Planas often preferred over the deluxe editions of his more profit-oriented peers.[31] It is printed on Japanese and pigskin paper. The three principal narratives (the *Gazette*'s, Flaubert's, and Miquel i Planas's own) are each set in different coloured fonts – red, blue, and black, but all with green headings – as if Miquel i Planas wanted to highlight the distinctiveness of the various texts while simultaneously drawing them together. The book, moreover, features eleven illustrations in black, white, and sienna brown, synthesizing the story, while also making it available in all its poignancy even to someone like Fra Vicents, who could barely read. One illustration is on the cover, one is opposite the title page, and the other nine are interspersed throughout Miquel i Planas's Catalan version of the tale. The artist D'Ivori (1890–1947) also decorated several pages with floral designs and composed the bookplate.[32]

D'Ivori was nearly twenty years younger than Miquel i Planas, and his work as a graphic designer coincided more closely with *Noucentisme* than did the career of his elder collaborator. As Vélez remarks, his graphic style actually links the aesthetic and cultural concerns of the *Renaixença* and *Noucentisme* and is thus eclectic, evincing elements of nineteenth-century neo-medievalism as well as the baroque style of certain exponents of *Noucentisme* ("D'Ivori" 149). D'Ivori was not only an illustrator of books but also, beginning in 1928, an editor of bibliophile editions. He met Miquel i Planas through the graphic artist Josep Triadó i Mayol (1870–1929). D'Ivori learned the art of drawing from Triadó, whereas his apprenticeship as a bibliophile took place under the tutelage of Miquel i Planas, who cultivated him as his direct successor as a publisher of bibliophile books (Vélez, "D'Ivori" 149).

D'Ivori, whose early work entailed illustrations for children's books, first collaborated with Miquel i Planas in 1908 in the production of *Les rondalles populars catalanes* [Popular Catalan fables]. Over the years he illustrated other publications of Miquel i Planas, including *La librería* (1921) [The bookstore], by Tomás de Iriarte; two stories in *Contes de bibilòfil* (1924), Alphonse Daudet's "El darer llibre" [The last book] and Joan Pons i Massaveu's "En Quicu dels llibres" [Quicu of the books]; and *Un libro viejo* (1926) [An old book], by Josep Feliu i Codina. According to Montserrat Castillo, D'Ivori produced his most stylistically accomplished work in his illustrations and decorations for the *Llegenda*. In composing the drawings, he first made sketches, which he subsequently filled in by using pens with coloured inks. In contrast to the colours in his illustrations for children's books, the tones are soft and subtle. The figures are represented in a variety of profiles and positions, and they are fully integrated into their surroundings. Dramatic effect is achieved through the use of shadow (see Castillo 125–8).

Whereas the illustrations within the text of the *Llegenda* depict Fra Vicents in various moments of the action, the cover drawing provides a close-up of his face and body (see figure 1). In his right hand Fra Vicents clutches a blood-stained knife, and in his left hand he cradles a book. In front of him are scattered several more books, one of which has a cross on the cover. Two drops of blood fall on the book in his hand, as if he had just committed a murder in order to attain it. As Castillo remarks, the entire image, from the character's frock coat to his long white hair to his mad expression, is evocative of Romanticism (126). As in the other illustrations of the *Llegenda*, D'Ivori eschews the aesthetics of early twentieth-century Catalan art so as to replicate the cultural context of the original narrative of the 1830s. Castillo further maintains that D'Ivori understood the passion of the murderous bookman because he himself was immersed in the world of bibliophilia and collecting (126). But the cover illustration is distinctive not only for the expression and

Figure 1. Book cover, recto. Ramon Miquel i Planas, *La llegenda del llibreter assassí de Barcelona*, Miquel-Rius, 1928. Illustration by D'Ivori. Image courtesy of Biblioteca de Catalunya.

demeanor of the character but also for the colour. Although all the illustrations of the *Llegenda* contain black, white, and sienna brown, this one alone includes green.[33] The colour green frames the image of Fra Vicents. It also appears on his face (and in particular around his eyes) and in the outline and folds of his garments, as if a green light were either shining on him or emanating from within his being. As the colour of decomposing flesh, the green hue gives him a sickly and even death-like pallor. Yet it also endows him with a diabolical quality, since green is a colour often associated with Satan. By brandishing a bloody knife over a book with a cross on its cover, Fra Vicents clearly appears satanic, a destroyer of both humans and books and implicitly the "Good Book" in which the divine essence is believed to inhere. As the cover illustration suggests, bibliomania is thus not merely a sickness or crime but an ominous manifestation of sin.

Several other illustrations make interesting use of light and the interplay between inside and outside spaces. The frontispiece is surrounded by a green and red floral design (see figures 2a and 2b). In the centre is a second frame that resembles a window from which a curtain has been drawn back. Fra Vicents appears within this second frame. He is seated in front of a stack of books and is leafing through a volume with the word *Crònica* on the cover. (This is in fact one of the books for which he murders.) His left hand is raised, as if in a gesture of surprise or delight. Behind him is an open window with a lamp on the sill that illuminates the entire scene. Overall, the illustration reveals the intimate world of Fra Vicents and draws the reader into it. Yet the lamp, with its burning flame, is particularly significant, symbolizing both the light that the narrative will shed on the character as well as his zealous passion as a bibliomaniac.

The third illustration shows a full-length Fra Vicents standing in front of his bookcase and eagerly perusing a volume (see figure 3). On a chair at Fra Vicents's side is the lamp, and behind him is an open window. Visible through the window is the window of the opposite house, from which a man and a woman spy on him. Through their gaze, Fra Vicents's ostensibly innocuous actions become noteworthy and, if not perverse, at least somehow unusual. In the fourth illustration a customer enters Fra Vicents's bookshop, and in the fifth illustration he purchases a book from him. In contrast to the second and third illustrations, this scene is illuminated by the light shining in from the outside rather than the light from Fra Vicents's lamp. In this "natural" light, which emanates from the social sphere, Fra Vicents seems to lose power. In fact, the action is dominated not by his intentions but by those of the customer, since clearly, from the expression on his face, he does not want to sell the book.

Figures 2a and 2b. 2a: Frontispiece.

Figures 2a and 2b. 2b: Title page. In Ramon Miquel i Planas, *La llegenda del llibreter assassí de Barcelona*, Miquel-Rius, 1928. Illustration and design by D'Ivori. Images courtesy of Biblioteca de Catalunya.

Figure 3. Illustration. In Ramon Miquel i Planas, *La llegenda del llibreter assassí de Barcelona*, Miquel-Rius, 1928. By D'Ivori. Image courtesy of Biblioteca de Catalunya.

In the seventh illustration Fra Vicents is depicted in a position of weakness, standing in a shadow and on the sidelines while a volume he desires is auctioned to a rival. Yet on other occasions he evinces strength, as when he murders a man or when he tears up his most coveted book and throws it in his lawyer's face at the end of his trial (illustrations 10 and 11). With regard to the symbolism of light and space, the most intriguing image (illustration 8) shows him jumping from the window of the burning house of Patxot (see figure 4). Fra Vicents had started the fire and then returned to the house to steal whatever books he could lay his hands on. As he makes his way through what the text describes as the "*sancta sanctorum* d'en Patxot" (41) [*the holy of holies* of Patxot], he is compared to a salamander slithering through the flames. He is thus by nature like the denizens of hell.[34] As the illustration reveals, when Fra Vicents jumps from the window, he is himself on fire, and flames rise from his singed coat while books fall to the street below. In the background a group of spectators silently watches. Here, the quiet flame that illuminated Fra Vicents as he privately held his own books has exploded and engulfs him, as if as a result of the consummation of sin he were now falling pell-mell into damnation. His sin, of course, is murder. But it is also his unbridled love of books as material objects.

In addition to the eleven illustrations, D'Ivori composed the bookplate for the 1928 edition of the *Llegenda* (see figure 5). Although at first glance it does not seem integral to the text, the image is actually significant. For Miquel i Planas, bookplates are essential components of books. Through them, bibliophiles establish ownership of a volume – something often more important to them than the experience of reading. In Miquel i Planas's view, bookplates should be unique, revealing the interests and tastes of book owners and not simply their names (*Los ex libris* 19). As he explains, the cultivation of bookplates came late to Spain and was initially promoted by Catalan bibliophiles and artists (*Los ex libris* 25–6). What is more, their flowering in Catalonia coincided with Catalan *Modernisme* (Vélez, "El libro" 555), forming an important part of the entire modernist movement (Puig Rovira, "L'interès" 191).

The bookplate of the *Llegenda* was nevertheless created during the period of *Noucentisme* and is plainer in style than many modernist bookplates, which are often highly elaborate and ornamental.[35] Here, a long strip of paper is loosely wrapped around a small pile of books. A dagger has pierced the strip of paper and books and joined them together. The dagger resembles the one Fra Vicents wields in the cover illustration and is thus clearly intended to invoke his crimes. But more interesting is the strip of paper, which can be taken as a symbol of the discourse of the Fra Vicents narrative. This discourse extends beyond

Figure 4. Illustration. In Ramon Miquel i Planas, *La llegenda del llibreter assassí de Barcelona*, Miquel-Rius, 1928. By D'Ivori. Image courtesy of Biblioteca de Catalunya.

Figure 5. Bookplate. In Ramon Miquel i Planas, *La llegenda del llibreter assassí de Barcelona*, Miquel-Rius, 1928. By D'Ivori. Image courtesy of Biblioteca de Catalunya.

any one publication, be it that of the *Gazette*, Flaubert's "Bibliomanie," or the subsequent renditions of the tale. In a sense, the knife functions to pin down the story, just as Miquel i Planas attempted to do by compiling and analysing the various versions of the legend and endowing them with a fixed and definitive form. Yet whereas Fra Vicents sought to attain his ideal book through theft and murder, Miquel i Planas aspired to his through the production of the *Llegenda* itself. Were one to imagine his name under the bookplate, his possession of this "book of books" might seem complete. But the space for the name is empty, an invitation to potential buyers of the volume to inscribe their names and thereby link their identities to it. Until that happens, the space remains a mute sign of the emptiness and inevitable failure at the heart of the tale and the bibliophilistic enterprise in general. Not only is the ideal book non-existent, but the dream of conjoining humans and material books is an illusion, lasting only as long as it takes to write one's own name.

Several of Miquel i Planas's personal bookplates also reflect themes and images present in the *Llegenda*. One, made by the artist, engraver, and bookplate designer Joaquim Figuerola (1878–1946), depicts a boy in front of a fruit tree. A snake coiled around the tree offers him a fruit. The design of the frame melds a modernist aesthetic with elements of the *mudéjar* artistic tradition. The letters are in the Gothic style of medieval incunabula. With his left hand the boy rejects the snake's offering and with his right hand he reaches up and picks a fruit from the tree. Beneath him is the inscription, "A bon seny, no hi val engany" [Against good sense, deceit has no purchase]. According to Rodergas Calmell, Miquel i Planas chose this motto not only as a marker for his books but also as the guiding principle of his life (6). The image, although clearly informed by Genesis, suggests a departure from conventional readings of the biblical narrative, for if the boy rejects the temptation of Satan, he does so in order to partake of the Tree of Knowledge on his own terms. An implicit message is that reading (and, by extension, books) is good, provided it is guided by the wisdom and prudence of the reader. This theme is repeated in another bookplate, which Joaquín Diéguez made for Miquel i Planas and his brother Josep (the "Germans Miquel" [Miquel Brothers]) (see figure 6). Here, the human figure is a fully grown man and under his feet is a row of books.[36] In a sense, these two bookplates stand as counterpoints to the position of Fra Vicents, who succumbs to the temptation of books without ever considering the moral consequences of the actions he must take in order to possess them.

Another one of Miquel i Planas's personal bookplates, drawn by Triadó, features two panels representing his study, surrounded by eight figures engaged in various activities with books (see figure 7). The right panel depicts part of a table, a chair, and bookshelves, while the left panel reveals the main part of the table and an open window. Several books and a tall candle have been placed on the table, and articles of clothing have been left on the seat of the chair. Books and papers are scattered elsewhere throughout scene. Clearly, this space resembles the private chamber of Fra Vicents. But whereas Fra Vicents's room was illuminated by his lamp, Miquel i Planas's study is filled with light streaming in from the outside. For this reason, his study might be regarded as outward looking, as if through reading he were opening himself up to worlds beyond and not simply to whatever sense of self he might hope to achieve through his interaction with books. Fra Vicents's window is also open, but the world outside is either darkened and empty or

Figure 6. Bookplate. By Joaquín Diéguez. Image courtesy of Biblioteca de Catalunya.

Figure 7. Bookplate. By Josep Triadó i Mayol. Image courtesy of Biblioteca de Catalunya.

obstructed by the intrusive gaze of others. The fact that Miquel i Planas is not present in the image in the bookplate is also significant, for what matters is not the bibliophile but precisely the open window to the world that, according to Miquel i Planas's conception of books, reading makes possible.

Although the visual components of the 1928 edition of the *Llegenda* were new, the narrative itself had been published many times since the first appearance of Flaubert's "Bibliomanie." Among the authors who retold it were Leopold-August-Constantin Hesse (1843), Jules Janin (1870), José de Castro y Serrano (1871), Prosper Blanchemain (1879), Andrew Lang (1881), and Albert Cim (1903).[37] Prior to Miquel i Planas's publication of the tale, the Catalan publisher Palau i Dulcet included a summary of it in Catalan in the preface to a 1916 book catalogue (*Corona* v–vi). According to Palau i Dulcet's memoirs, this was the first mention of the Fra Vicents legend in Catalonia (*Memorias* 311). Although Palau i Dulcet does not indicate how he learned of the story, he might have discovered it when Flaubert's "Bibliomanie" was republished in 1910 – a noteworthy event, given that the text had been out of print since its original publication in 1837. Palau i Dulcet in fact criticizes "Bibliomanie," which he regards as a piece of juvenilia devoid of literary merit. He also explains that after he published his summary of the legend in 1916, numerous magazines in Barcelona and Madrid reproduced it, often with elaborate graphics, until Miquel i Planas provided what he considers the definitive explanation of its origins at the hands of Nodier (*Memorias* 312). He further adds that in 1928, following the publication of Miquel i Planas's edition of the *Llegenda*, a Catalan journalist named Francisco Baget wrote several articles about the tale, having first scoured old issues of the *Diario de Barcelona*, as well as court and prison archives, in order to prove that it was fabricated (*Memorias* 461).

Miquel i Planas learned of the existence of the *Gazette* version of the legend after he published the *Contes de bibliòfil* (which features only "Bibliomanie"), as he conducted research on the history of the narrative. He published his findings in the 1928 edition of the *Llegenda* in the collection Amor del Llibre, which had been launched four years earlier. His work was not republished until 1951, shortly before his death. The editor of the mid-century edition was Federico Pablo Verrié, who chose to print the work in both Catalan and Castilian in order to make it available to a wider readership. He also changed the spelling in order to conform to the contemporary norms of the Catalan language. As he explains,

> Miquel y Planas fue durante muchos años el campeón de una escuela ortográfica personalísima que no tenía, prácticamente, seguidor alguno.

> En ese terreno ganaron la partida Pompeyo Fabra y los filólogos del *Institut d'Estudis Catalans*, y hoy, para el lector común – e incluso para los acostumbrados a nuestros clásicos medievales – el catalán que podríamos llamar de los académicos – el de Miquel y Planas – o de los Juegos Florales – el de Francesc Matheu – resulta inadmisible: produce un verdadero malestar físico, visual y auditivo. (Miquel i Planas, *La llegenda* 1951, 26–8)
>
> [Miquel i Planas was for many years the champion of a highly personalized school of spelling that had practically no followers. In this debate Pompeu Fabra and the philologists of the Institut d'Estudis Catalans won, and today, for the average reader as well as those accustomed to our medieval classics, what we might call the Catalan of the academics (of Miquel i Planas, of the Juegos Florales, or of Francesc Matheu) is inadmissible: it produces a veritable physical, visual, and auditory unease.]

This comment is significant, for not only does it clarify Miquel i Planas's legacy (or lack thereof) to the Catalan language, but it also reveals how the legend itself continues to be modified and tailored to reflect the desires and aspirations of each new generation of readers. Verrié claims that Miquel i Planas granted him permission to alter the style of the work, but because he died before authorizing him to make more substantive changes to the narrative, Verrié decided to limit his revisions to orthography, despite, as he confesses, his wish to "rehacerla del todo" (30) [rework it entirely]. After the publication of Verrié's work in 1951, Miquel i Planas's *Llegenda* went out of print and was not republished until the end of the twentieth century. Recent Spanish editions appeared in 1991, under the title *El librero asesino de Barcelona*, and in 2011, as a translation of Flaubert's "Bibliomanie," under the title *Bibliomanía*.

Despite Miquel i Planas's immense admiration for Nodier, he considers that the French writer unintentionally played a dirty trick ("una mala pasada" [*De tonterías* 8]) on Barcelona by passing off such a horrifying story as true. Through his *Llegenda* he intends to set the record straight, clarifying above all that the story is a fiction. But he also re-establishes its Catalan context. In so doing, he restores the Catalan names of the characters, places, and book titles used by the *Gazette* author. In his Catalan version of the narrative, a student from Salamanca thus becomes a student from Cervera; a priest from the cathedral of Oviedo becomes the rector of the church of La Mercè; the *Chronique de Turquie* becomes the *Crònica d'en Puigpardines*;[38] and the *Mystère de Saint Michel* is replaced by the *Furs e ordinacions* of Valencia. More important, Fra Vicents is no longer simply a monk but a former member of the monastery of Poblet. Miquel i Planas also incorporates passages from the *Gazette* narrative that relate to the Inquisition (including the episode in which the

*Furs e ordinacions* is discovered) as well as the final courtroom scene. Yet he relies more heavily on "Bibliomanie," which he considers the more literary of the two earlier texts, and thereby retains the psychological profile of Fra Vicents developed by Flaubert. Finally, by placing the *Llegenda* in both the public and private spheres, he makes possible a fuller understanding of the tale's multiple meanings.

In this more complete representation, the bibliomaniac appears as a decadent, not only for having fallen into a state of physical and moral decay, but also because of his exaggerated preoccupation with the external form of the book – even if the book as thing, with its intoxicating array of colours, textures, and scents, is inevitably "read" as a kind of discourse. But unlike the "dandy-bibliophiles" of the late nineteenth century, who paid for the production of exquisite editions of their favourite works, Fra Vicents searches for already existing rarities.[39] In his vision, the unique is discovered not in nature but in cultural artifacts. Through identification with a unique book, he hopes to acquire a unique identity of his own. Yet uniqueness is ultimately an illusion, and when a sought-after volume is at last seen, touched, known, and at times even eaten, it loses its imaginary potential to transform.[40] For this reason, his ideal self lies always just beyond him, in the next object about to be possessed.

Fra Vicents's adamant belief in an ever-elusive perfect book is ostensibly quixotic, but he is actually closer in temperament to the figure of Don Juan than to Don Quixote. Indeed, there is a promiscuity about Fra Vicents's entire passion for books. Once a book is possessed, he quickly tires of it, and a new one soon catches his eye. Yet each falls short of his ideal, not through any inherent fault of its own but because of his inability to remake himself through it. As a result, his *raison d'être* becomes the act of collecting rather than the pleasure derived from the objects collected. As his compulsiveness demonstrates, he never experiences satiety, and he is undone in the end not when a prized possession is proved to be a sham but when he realizes he will never collect again.

Despite all the mystery and intrigue surrounding him, Fra Vicents is most attracted to the simple materiality of books. But he is not a materialist in any pragmatic sense, and is instead motivated by a desire to hold at bay the inexorable changes of the material world and thereby achieve a kind of impossible stasis. As he proclaims at his trial, humans may have souls and eventually be called to God, but books (like himself, because of his rejection of the divine) will inevitably disintegrate and vanish unless everything possible is done to protect, conserve, and cherish them. In the end, then, he hinges his defence on love. What this love of books ultimately reveals, God and immortality notwithstanding, is an anguished realization of the transitory nature of the world and our own lives in the here and now.

Throughout his discussion of the tale, Miquel i Planas ostensibly assumes a traditional stance with regard to discourse. In addressing the issue of provenance, for example, he maintains a strict distinction between history and fiction, arguing that the *Llegenda* has no basis whatsoever in historical fact: "[N]o hi havía un pèl de veritat en tot aquell escrit. Era, de cap a cap, una enginyosa superxería literaria" (*La llegenda* 1928, xvii) [There was not a shred of truth in the whole text. From beginning to end it was an ingenious literary hoax]. He dismisses the possibility that the tale might be the "fruyt d'un treball colectiu" (xxii) [fruit of collective work] and as such a veritable legend. Instead, he insists that all texts are the products of individual authors, and in the case of the author of the Fra Vicents narrative "es quasi de necessitat que fós aquell nostre antich amich Carles Nodier" (xxii) [it is almost certain that it was our old friend Charles Nodier]. Like Fra Vicents, Miquel i Planas seems so steeped in the cult of individual authorship and its attendant myths of uniqueness and originality that he makes these the *sine qua non* of all writing. Yet as a matter of fact, he too appropriates the texts of others, not through the crude violence of a biblioklept or outright plagiarism, but the more indirect and subtle approach of a gentleman-scholar. Miquel i Planas indeed attributes the *Llegenda* to Nodier and the French literary tradition. But through his very intervention, the tale is imbued with his own bibliophilistic desires and intentions and becomes, albeit tentatively, Catalan.

Nevertheless, because the Fra Vicents narrative was already so widely disseminated in western European culture, it could never be regarded as a purely Catalan tale. And because of its numerous internal slippages and incongruities, it could hardly function as an instrument of Miquel i Planas's own self-fashioning as a bookman, even if the book itself is incredibly beautiful. Fra Vicents, after all, is everything that an exemplary bookman would reject. But then again, he is nothing, not only because his ideal is always beyond reach but also because his library, which provides the objective unity to his self, is in the end dispersed. Fra Vicents confesses his crimes on the condition that his library remain intact, but he is tricked and loses it anyway. Miquel i Planas and all those who tell the tale are likewise beguiled to the extent that they attempt to use the story as a means of self-affirmation, since the lesson it imparts is the impossibility of ever achieving, at least through books, a fully integrated self.

In a sense, Miquel i Planas's *Llegenda* is the antithesis of the bibliophile's ideal book: it is a copy of numerous other texts and its message is nothing short of the utter futility of book collecting. The author himself would have probably agreed that it stands as a cautionary tale.[41] Yet it also reveals how early twentieth-century Catalan aesthetics anticipated narratological experiments in multilayered discourse and consciously intertextual composition typical of late twentieth- and early twenty-first-century postmodernist writing. What is more, the tale in fact subverts the values it purports to uphold. Miquel i Planas claims to believe in the unique and the original, but his *Llegenda* exposes these as myths, thereby challenging the culture in which both the tale itself and Catalan nationalism are embedded. In the final analysis, however, social critique and nationalist politics are not Miquel i Planas's principal concerns, perhaps because in his case what Amat describes as "la nostalgia de los libros perdidos" (*Letra* 186) [the nostalgia for lost books] is not only a nostalgia for a historically suppressed culture but also a longing for a kind of ontological plenitude once dreamed of in a library.

## The Legacy of Fra Vicents

Although Miquel i Planas's version of the legend of the murderous bookman of Barcelona continues to be republished in Catalonia and Spain, there have been several reworkings of the tale, the most significant of which are the short story of Montserrat Roig and the folk song of Jaume Arnella. Roig is best known for her novels portraying the lives of women during key moments of twentieth-century Catalan history: *Ramona, adéu* (1972) [Ramona, farewell], *El temps de les cireres* (1977) [The time of cherries], and *L'hora violeta* (1980) [The violet hour]. In addition to writing many novels, she also authored numerous essays, including *Els catalans als camps nazis* (1977) [Catalans in the Nazi camps], and short stories, including the collection *El cant de la joventut* (1989) [The song of youth]. The story "El profesor y el librero asesino," penned in Catalan and translated into Spanish by the author herself, was published in 1989 in an anthology of short stories by contemporary Catalan writers. Here, Roig situates the legend of Fra Vicents within contemporary Barcelona. Although she does not typically highlight the theme of books in her writing, in this brief and at times light-hearted piece she constructs a nuanced narrative of bibliomania that reveals the legacy of past discourses of books and the continued effects that these discourses have on present-day lives.

The initial setting of the story is a meeting of a book club composed of two women, Señora Recasens and Fifí de Comanala, a young male writer, Joan Borràs, and an unnamed, middle-aged male professor. From the outset, the omniscient narrator reveals not only the characters' lack of serious engagement with books (in the first line Señora Recasens yawns and Fifí de Comanala admits to falling asleep with a book) but also the dearth of readers in Barcelona, despite the fact that for years the city had been the centre of publishing in Spain. As Borràs remarks: "Ésta es una ciudad llena de libros. Aunque dudo que haya en ella lectores" (205) [This is a city filled with books. Although I doubt that there are any readers in it]. When Señora Recasens mentions the contemporary authors Milan Kundera, Tom Sharpe, and Patrick Süskind, the professor indicates that he has not read any of them. She registers surprise, given what she assumes to be his love of books. In response, he informs her that he does not love books in themselves – "[y]o no amo los libros como objetos" (206) [I do not love books as objects] – and that after reading a volume he immediately gives it away. He then asks her if her love of books is such that it might lead her to commit a murder. She laughingly dismisses his question, and she and the other characters agree that no one in Barcelona would ever kill for a book – even if in London one might. This exchange prompts the professor to tell them the tale of the murderous bookman, Fra Vicents, whose saga forms the nucleus of "El profesor y el librero asesino."

The professor begins his account by explaining to the group the difference between bibliophilia and bibliomania. Bibliomania, he maintains, is an exaggerated passion for books and ultimately a disease. Borràs denies the existence of bibliomania in late twentieth-century society, not only because of the ever-diminishing number of readers who might covet books but also, as he speculates, because the printed text might actually soon disappear. To justify his claim, he cites the system of photocomposition and the audiobooks produced by the London-based "Talking Tape Company," adding that he submits his own manuscripts to his publisher on compact floppy discs. Although the time frame of Roig's story precedes the rise of the internet and the proliferation of e-books and e-readers, the narrative evinces a concern that new technologies, coupled with a shrinking reading public, might eventually lead to the demise of traditional books. This concern presages early twenty-first-century anxieties about the status of books, while evoking the period of Fra Vicents in the nineteenth century, when the advent of mass-produced editions was regarded by some as the end of books as inimitable and beautiful objects.

The professor's rendition of the legend of Fra Vicents replicates the composite version of Miquel i Planas in his study of the narrative. Unlike Miquel i Planas, however, the professor presents the entire episode as fact. He describes Fra Vicents as emaciated, white-haired, and hunchbacked and, as such, the Romantic prototype of the stories of Hoffmann – or, as Fifí de Comanala proposes, a kind of Christopher Lee, most likely because of the British actor's numerous roles in horror films. According to one passage, Fra Vicents feels as if those who buy his treasured books are stealing his very soul. This is significant, for it suggests that without books in his life he is nothing – an empty cipher devoid of meaning and identity.

When the professor finishes his narrative, Señora Recasens remarks that the kind of crimes committed by Fra Vicents no longer occur in a city like Barcelona, where people have ceased to value books and reading. Fifí de Comanala invites the professor to return to their future gatherings because she appreciates what she describes as his charming and true stories, in contrast to those of contemporary writers, which in her view are totally detached from reality. The irony of these comments becomes apparent after the professor leaves the group and begins to express his thoughts about the Fra Vicents legend and his own bibliomaniacal desires and intentions.

As the professor makes his way through the darkened streets of Barcelona, he reminds himself that Fra Vicents was in fact a character of fiction. He further reveals that although he told Señora Recasens he did not love books as objects in themselves, for many years he has longed to possess one particular volume, to wit, *La llegenda del llibreter assassí de Barcelona*, published by Miquel i Planas in 1928. In detailing the professor's ruminations, the narrator explains to the reader that Miquel i Planas was a bibliophile and scholar who rejected the linguistic norms of Pompeu Fabra and who made the case that Nodier anonymously published the original narrative of the Fra Vicents legend in *La Gazette des Tribunaux*, which the young Flaubert then rewrote as "Bibliomanie." Yet more important, the narrator highlights the bibliomania of the professor himself. As it turns out, he is not really a university professor but rather a teacher of Catalan, burdened with debts, who earns extra money by entertaining people with stories he passes off as true. With regard to the *Llegenda*, the narrator indicates the following:

> Había un librero de viejo en la calle de la Palla que lo tenía. Pero era un libro carísimo y aquél no quería rebajarle el precio. ¡Cuántas veces lo había sostenido entre sus manos, acariciado el papel de hilo, contemplado sus dibujos al carbón, siniestros y románticos! (212)
>
> [There was a dealer of old books in the Calle de la Palla who had it. But it was a very expensive book, and the book dealer did not want to lower the price for him. How many times he had held it in his hands, caressed the linen paper, and contemplated the charcoal drawings, so sinister and romantic!]

The professor's desire to possess a book he can ill afford, coupled with his love of its physicality, is reminiscent of the drama of Fra Vicents. But according to the narrative, the book dealer and owner of the coveted volume of Miquel i Planas is also a re-embodiment of the murderous bookman, "flaco, canoso y encorbado" (212) [emaciated, white-haired, and hunchbacked]. In Roig's short story the character of Fra Vicents is thus re-scripted as both the protagonist and antagonist of the action.

In the culminating scene, the professor enters an antiquarian bookshop and asks to see the *Llegenda*. The book dealer, however, denies his request, knowing that the professor will never be able to buy it and advising him to consider new and less costly editions. He adds that the Miquel i Planas volume is in the back room, and emphasizes that it is hidden because he has recently been robbed of many books. In this moment,

> [e]l profesor lo miró con instinto de muerte. Él era más fuerte que el librero, no hubiera sido demasiado difícil darle un golpe por detrás y, luego, introducirse en la trastienda y coger el libro. Sabía perfectamente en qué estante se encontraba. Notaba su presencia, el libro le estaba llamando. Casi le decía: «¡Tómame!» (213)

> [the professor looked at him with murderous intent. He was stronger than the bookman, and it would not have been too difficult to give him a blow from behind and then go into the back room and grab the book. He knew exactly on what shelf it was located. He could feel its presence; the book was calling to him. It was almost saying, "Take me!"]

As the professor leaves the shop, he vows that he will one day have the book. He then hears a metallic, laughing sound, and wonders whether it is the laughter of the bookman or the book itself hidden in the back room.

The fact that the professor knows where the Miquel i Planas edition is hidden suggests that he has already been in the back room and that he is thus perhaps the person who stole the bookman's missing volumes. Indeed, not only is he possibly a book thief but he is also, given his fantasy of killing the bookman, a would-be murderer. Yet what is most significant is that his ideal book is one which reveals his own bibliomania. Whereas Fra Vicents sought an incunabulum, the *Furs e ordinacions* of Lambert Palmart, which was one of the first ever published in Spain (and which for Miquel i Planas was a foundational text of the history of the region of Valencia, whose language he esteemed above all the other languages of Spain for its poetic expression), the professor seeks a rare tome that tells of a bibliomaniac's failed attempt to acquire his ideal book. In this *mise en abyme*, the professor's passion turns back on itself to the extent that he is drawn to the image, however deformed, corrupted, and tragic, of his own persona. In contrast to the murderous bookman of the legend, his desire is implicitly narcissistic, focused, as it is, on the "sinister and romantic" drawings of a man like himself. But in keeping with the logic of Sartre, the goals of the two characters are fundamentally the same. By possessing the *Llegenda*, the professor hopes to transform his existential nothingness into a thing of permanence and perfection. When he ecstatically touches the beautiful book, it is hence the impossible totality of being, or the in-itself-for-itself, that he fleetingly imagines at his fingertips.

Roig's rendition of the legend nevertheless differs from earlier versions with regard to the representation of the ideal book as well as the protagonist himself. In both the *Gazette* and Flaubert narratives, the content of the ideal book is of less importance than the belief that it is one of a kind. Like the *Furs e ordinacions*, the *Llegenda* is in fact not unique.[42] But its subject is significant insofar as the bibliomaniacal desire of Fra Vicents (albeit not his actions and outcome) mirrors that of the professor. The *Llegenda* is rare; it is beautiful; and in a sense it incarnates the professor's own essence as a lover of books. But the professor does not possess it, and the mocking laughter he hears at the end of the narrative is none other than his own inner voice reminding him that he never will – not because he lacks the money to buy it, but because as a human being he is unable ever to possess anything on an ontological level. Even if he did manage to purchase the book and take ownership of it, it could never become part of his being precisely because his being, from the existentialist perspective of Sartre, is always and only a desire for an impossible ideal. Yet in contrast to the mad bookmen of the *Gazette* and "Bibliomanie," who were undermined by external enemies (rival book dealers, magistrates, or, as Sartre argues in his reading of Flaubert, an unloving father and elder brother), the bibliomaniac of Roig is his own worst enemy. As bookman or simply as human, he is, as Sartre concludes his philosophy of consciousness in *L'Être et le néant*, "une passion inutile" (678) ["a useless passion" (*Being* 784)], that is, a being ontologically destined to fail. Although at the end of the narrative he affirms that he will one day not only possess the *Llegenda* but also "[contar] una nueva historia" (213) [tell a new story], his own story as a frustrated lover of books will likely end only with his death.[43]

Like most previous renditions of the tale, Roig's narrative not only is humorous and light-hearted in tone, but it also raises intriguing questions about the psychological temperament of the figure of the bibliomaniac and the existential and ethical implications of the practice of bibliophilia. It is not, however, explicitly political. Yet in the decades immediately prior to its publication, some of the images and scenes would have lent themselves to a political interpretation. During the

Franco period, books deemed subversive by the regime were often hidden in the back rooms of book dealers, who on occasion made them available to a clientele with left-leaning sympathies. What is more, stealing books was frequently regarded as a subversive act directed against the guardians of culture, as well as a means of obtaining information and knowledge that might aid in navigating and challenging the status quo. In Roig's story, the sought-after book is guarded by a jealous and hostile book dealer, who acts like a censor, and the professor considers robbing and possibly even killing him. But the professor is not a subversive, and his motives are not political. Rather, like the figure of Giacomo in Sartre's reading of Flaubert's "Bibliomanie," he regards books solely as beautiful objects, and thereby neutralizes whatever practical or political potential they might possess as texts. Like the general populace of Barcelona as described by Borràs, the professor and his contemporaries read little, although they remain viscerally tied to a culture of reading through their book club. Given that Roig herself was a prolific author who took on highly charged political and social issues throughout her writing career, her depiction of the characters in the story is most certainly satirical. What is more, if she expresses in it a kind of nostalgic longing, hers is a nostalgia not simply for a culture of print that might or might not be vanishing, but for the kind of politically engaged reading and writing that flourished, albeit largely clandestinely, during her formative years in Francoist Spain.

Whereas "El profesor y el librero asesino" dramatizes the quest for an impossible ideal at the heart of all the previous iterations of the Fra Vicents legend, Arnella's song, "El llibreter monjo," reduces the narrative to the more fundamental question of good and evil. Arnella composed the lyrics in the form of a *romance*, or ballad, which consists of quatrains of eight-syllable lines with minimal rhyme. By employing this type of versification, typical of the anonymous poetry of the Catalan Middle Ages, he presents the tale as if it were part of the Catalan folk heritage. Rather than the product of elite foreign writers of the nineteenth century, the story now seems to possess the qualities of a veritable legend, with its origins in the oral tradition of the Catalan people. In contrast to Miquel i Planas, who translated the tale into the Catalan language, Arnella endows it with an even more authentically sounding Catalan voice by transforming it into a folk song.

In melding the anonymous "Le Bibliomane ou le nouveau Cardillac" and Flaubert's "Bibliomanie," Miquel i Planas highlighted Catalan place names and Catalan works of literature. In Arnella's song, most of these markers have been eliminated. Fra Vicents is simply referred to as a "llibreter" [bookman] and "monjo" [monk], originally from Poblet, who sells books in the market area of Els Encants in Barcelona, and who covets the edition of *Els furs de València* that a rival book dealer buys at an auction. He has no distinctive physical features and no psychological characteristics other than "una obsessió" [an obsession] to obtain *Els furs de València* and a "mal pensament" [bad thought] about how to do so. When the judge confronts him about his crime, he responds that he regarded the murder of his rival as "ben normal" [quite normal], since the rival owned the book not "per interès" [because of interest] but "la raó simple / que tenia més diners" [the simple reason that he had more money]. Arnella's version of the tale, while not portraying Fra Vicents as good, thus implies that he faced an unjust situation. He genuinely desired a book, but a richer man bought it merely because he had the money to do so. In this context the problem is not bibliomania but rather what seems to be an arbitrary social hierarchy that impedes the fulfillment of natural human desires. Fra Vicents, however, is not an innocent victim of circumstance precisely because he employs unethical means to achieve his goal. In the final stanza the moral of the story is spelled out: "mai de mai robar cap llibre / i menys encara matar" [never, never steal any book, much less kill]. Rather than a cautionary tale about the perils of an unbridled love of books, the song is basically an injunction against robbery and murder.

In charting the history of the tale of the murderous bookman of Barcelona, one might expect to find its origins in Catalan folklore, or at least in some early-Iberian written account from which the author of the anonymous *Gazette* piece drew inspiration. But the seemingly original text of Arnella was created only after numerous retellings of the story in several countries and languages. In fact, the rendition of the tale most like a legend appears in the wake of a long literary, cultural, and historical interchange between Catalonia, France, and Spain as a whole. In this case, moreover, orality follows writing, for the song was possible only because the text had already been written.

In contrast to the previous accounts of Fra Vicents, Arnella's song ignores the overwhelming passion for books that leads to the character's crimes. It nevertheless reveals an enigmatic quality through the understatement of the lyrics and the haunting voice of the singer. Given the enormity of the Llibreter-Monjo's malevolence, the final quatrain enjoining the listener not to steal books almost begs the question why one would ever do so, much less kill someone in the process. Yet unlike the earlier narratives, which aim to explain the bookman's desire, the song presents his actions without speculating on his motivations or reflecting on the nature of his love of books. To understand these, one must return to the earlier exegeses of the legend.

Fra Vicents's love of books is perhaps most poignantly revealed through what Flaubert describes as his near illiteracy. Rather than diminish his power to value books, as most commentators of bibliomania (including Miquel i Planas) would maintain, his inability to read allows him to experience them exclusively as aesthetic objects. Unaware or even disdainful of the potential of printed material to transmit meaning, Fra Vicents regards books solely as a source of beauty. To the extent that he reads, he does so typographically, establishing contingent relations between the forms of the letters and words, rather than arranging them syntactically and thereby tethering them to the structural relations of already existing discourses. His attitude is almost playful, if not viscerally liberating, since he strips books of the intentions of others and recreates them in his imagination to fit his own bibliophilistic desires. His approach is in fact suggestive of the manner of reading proposed by the nineteenth-century poet and radical book theorist, Stéphane Mallarmé. As Gerald L. Burns writes, Mallarmé "resist[ed] the pull of language towards meaning" (224), and through the visual configuration of poetry attempted to evoke the beautiful. According to Burns, Mallarmé was particularly interested in the form of words and their potential not simply to reveal an external world of objects, but to make possible an "unfolding, typographically, of a manifold of pure activities" (229). To be sure, Mallarmé did not imagine the readers of his poems to be illiterate, but his emphasis on the visual aspects of texts allows us to discern in the bibliomania of Fra Vicents a degree of aesthetic appreciation that commentators of the legend have tended to overlook.

Rather than read his books, Fra Vicents literally skims over the surfaces of the printed pages without becoming enmeshed in their discourses or bogged down in the world that they represent.[44] In so doing, he imagines that he possesses his books and indeed is one with them. But his happiness is fleeting, and when he looks away, he experiences the anguish of his own nothingness. His quest for the beautiful, which from the perspective of Sartrean ontology is ultimately his attempt as a consciousness to attain the fullness of being that he lacks, thus ends in failure. Through failure, however, he inadvertently undermines the cult of books that modern, bourgeois culture has struggled to sustain in the wake of the dismantling of the myths of religion. As Sartre suggests in his analysis of the failure of Mallarmé's poetic project, this is because he exposes the inability of art to realize the imaginary in-itself-for-itself.[45] Commentators like Miquel i Planas blame Fra Vicents for his failure, thereby implying that if he had used the language of books to aspire to higher truths, he might have achieved the goal of ideal being. Yet what the legend repeatedly emphasizes, through Fra Vicents's futile pursuit of beautiful books, is the impossibility of grasping this being in the here and now.

Ontology notwithstanding, Fra Vicents's desperate passion for books also reveals a somewhat simpler truth: namely, that books, regardless of our love of them, do not last forever, and for this reason we are saddened. Not only do books inevitably deteriorate, but their traditional form is historically bound and may (and indeed perhaps should) be replaced by new formats. Although Fra Vicents bemoaned the fact that books lack souls capable of surviving their physical demise, in the current digital age their contents seem all but guaranteed to live on indefinitely, even if paper-based volumes cease to exist. Yet belief in an immortal soul is not enough to assuage the grief we experience in the face of death, be it of cherished loved-ones or of things like books. Fra Vicents's sorrow thus stands, despite all of the character's idiosyncrasies, as a modern-day lament not merely for the impossibility of ever finding that one perfect book, but for the passing of the age of books in general.

# 2 Bibliophiles, Bibliographers, and Bookstore Browsers

The great flowering of modern Spanish bibliophilia lasted from roughly the second third of the nineteenth century through the first third of the twentieth century. Among the noted bibliophiles of the period were Bartolomé José Gallardo, Vicente and Pedro Salvá, Dionisio Hidalgo, and Azorín. For them, as for so many bibliophiles throughout history, books were a source of both aesthetic joy and personal fulfillment. Yet to a certain extent their practice of bibliophilia was informed by Spanish nationalism, and specifically the nationalism fomented by the Castilian-speaking Spanish state. Whereas Gallardo, the Salvás, and Hidalgo participated in the national resurgence that followed the Peninsular War (1808–14) and the expulsion of the occupying forces of Napoleonic France in the early nineteenth century, Azorín, like many of his contemporaries in the Generation of '98, contributed to the national revival that arose in the early twentieth century as a response to Spain's defeat by the United States in the Spanish–American War (1898) and the final dissolution of the Spanish Empire.

In an attempt to advance Spanish nationalism, nineteenth-century Spanish bibliophiles at times worked to create comprehensive bibliographies of Spanish books, and through them help facilitate the consolidation of the Spanish book heritage within the physical spaces of archives and libraries. Archives and libraries, they believed, would in turn provide a tangible validation of Spanish culture and ultimately of Spain itself among the European nation-states. The project of national self-affirmation initiated in the early nineteenth century continued with the writers of the Generation of '98, who likewise sought to assert a distinctively Spanish ethos. But unlike their nineteenth-century predecessors, they did so not by cataloguing and archiving books but by recreating in their own writings what they believed to be an inner history or essence of the Spanish people embedded within the Spanish book tradition. Their aim was to revitalize this history and thereby render a more living archive of the Spanish experience than that found in libraries themselves. Whereas the majority of the writers of the Generation of '98 championed the Castilian-language tradition, their efforts paralleled those of writers and bibliophiles from the non-Castilian regions of Spain, who have struggled to catalogue their respective book heritages, while using their own books to give renewed life to these traditions.

Although nineteenth- and twentieth-century bibliophiles share similar experiences and goals, the discourse through which they depict bibliophilia differs. When nineteenth-century bibliophiles engage in bibliographical work, their style, as might be expected, is unadorned and objective. But when describing their subjective reactions to books, they often have recourse to Romantic tropes in order to convey the emotions that books arouse in them. These emotions are almost always intense, and can range from desire and love to fear and anguish, as evidenced in the portrayal of the murderous bookman of Barcelona. In fact, the awe that books inspire in bibliophiles of the Romantic period is suggestive of the overwhelming sense of the sublime expressed in the works of many Romantic writers and artists. Notwithstanding their accomplishments as bibliographers, it is the intensity of feeling that makes the legacy of Romantic bibliophiles so compelling, even if it is frequently a target of satire, as occurs in the writings of some Romantic bibliophiles themselves, who on occasion distance themselves from their own overwrought style and make light of it.

Like nineteenth-century Romantic bibliophiles, early twentieth-century Spanish bibliophiles regarded the cultivation of books as the wellspring of their richest emotional and spiritual lives. The writings of Azorín, however, differ from those of other bibliophiles of his period insofar as he depicts the experience of bibliophilia through a kind of verbal impressionism that uses words to represent a multisensory apprehension of books as objects. Through this approach, he not only describes books in a particular moment in time, but also attempts to imagine their ever-shifting forms across time. In so doing, he feels a connection with a whole world of readers and bibliophiles through whose hands books have passed, especially if they are old and used, and even more so if they are written in Spanish. Thus, although Azorín is less engaged in the nationalist project of figures like Gallardo, the Salvás, and Hidalgo, he is equally, if not more committed to the notion of "Spanishness" as a category of identity, and to the task of projecting this identity through his writings on bibliophilia.

The effort to affirm Spanish nationalism and identity, whether through bibliographies or libraries, was particularly difficult for nineteenth-century bibliophiles precisely because so many of the most treasured volumes of the Spanish book heritage had been plundered during the wars of the Napoleonic period and repatriated to libraries and private collections in England, France, Germany, and the Americas. The anguish that Gallardo, the Salvás, and Hidalgo feel for lost books, although evident in much of the literature of bibliophilia, arises in the specific context of war and foreign domination, and is not solely a personal or psychological phenomenon. In fact, it portends the nostalgia felt by twentieth- and twenty-first-century Spanish writers for a book tradition ravaged not by foreign military forces but by agents of repression within Spain itself. An anxiety regarding books is also present in the writings of Azorín, albeit to a lesser degree, when he expresses exasperation in Spanish state-run libraries, which in his view place excessive restrictions on the public's access to books, and Spanish bookstores, which historically discourage browsing and thereby prevent bibliophiles from engaging with books and discovering volumes with which they are not already familiar.

For Gallardo, the Salvás, and Hidalgo, the primary sites of books were in fact libraries and bookstores, and their writings are important documents of the history of these venues in Spain and abroad. At different points in their careers they either supervised libraries or launched and managed bookstores, not only in Spain but also in France and England, where they developed their personal collections and fostered the commerce and diffusion of books in society at large. Although Azorín was not a librarian or bookstore owner, some of his richest meditations on Spanish books resulted from his forays into libraries, bookshops, and book fairs. When taken together, Gallardo, the Salvás, Hidalgo, and Azorín thus provide a broad spectrum of bibliophile expression and activity during the Golden Age of the Spanish book, and of the efforts of Spanish bibliophiles to use their historic book tradition to advance the goals of the Spanish state and promote Spanish cultural identity.

## Bartolomé José Gallardo

In the words of Josefa Gallego Lorenzo, Bartolomé José Gallardo towers over Spanish book history as "el padre de la bibliofilia moderna" (216) [the father of modern bibliophilia]. He is also considered the first modern Spanish bibliographer and an enduring inspiration for subsequent generations of Spanish bibliographers. What he is most remembered for today is a two-volume work titled *Ensayo de una biblioteca española de libros raros y curiosos* [Essay on a Spanish library of rare and curious books]. This work is a compilation of the tens of thousands of *papeletas,* or note cards, that he prepared throughout his life, describing the books that he either possessed or consulted and that he hoped to use to create a comprehensive bibliography of the Spanish book heritage. In his own day, Gallardo was most famous for his all-consuming passion for books as well as the zealousness of his efforts to obtain them, which led several of his contemporaries and successors to satirize and ridicule him. His life story is in fact a site of the conflicting narratives of the relationship between humans and books that characterize modern conceptions of bibliophilia. Whereas Marcelino Menéndez Pelayo, albeit perhaps ironically, called him the patron saint of Spanish bibliophiles, José María Fernández Espino, in a decidedly less generous spirit, described him as "basura y miseria" [garbage and squalor].[1] Praised by some while denigrated by others, Gallardo played an active and important role in the political and cultural life of early nineteenth-century Spain. Through his cultivation of books, he experienced his greatest joy. But he was also racked by anguish over the repeated decimation of his library that occurred as a result of the political upheavals in Spanish society in the decades following the Peninsular War. In his essays and correspondences, Gallardo expresses an intense nostalgia for his lost books, which he implicitly relates to the nation's loss of much of its book heritage to the destruction of war and the rapaciousness of foreign book collectors. His experience as a Romantic bibliophile – impassioned, misunderstood, and ultimately tragic – thus played out against the backdrop of what from his perspective was a national tragedy that could be overcome only as Spain developed its own system of modern bibliographies and libraries.

As a bibliophile, Gallardo attempted not only to acquire new books but also to recuperate the ones he had lost and reclaim those that had been stolen from him. In fact, the most poignant and telling observations in his personal writings focus on the volumes that he no longer possessed. His greatest passion was thus not for books per se but for his own lost library. Although in the course of his lifetime he did recover some of his books, the majority remained irretrievable. Because he was unable to achieve the fulfillment through books that he so ardently desired, he was continually overcome by a sense of both bitterness and emptiness. As some of his detractors implied, Gallardo was perhaps his own worst enemy, for despite his quixotic belief that he might someday have the library of his dreams, he obstinately persisted in what could only have seemed like a futile endeavour, given the recurrent disasters that plagued his life as a bibliophile.

Although Gallardo was clearly an impassioned bibliophile, José Fernández Sánchez argues that he was first and foremost a bibliographer, who devoted his greatest attention to the description of the contents of books rather than their physical features (169). Fernández Sánchez further indicates that, unlike many bibliophiles who tend to be scrupulous in their care of books, Gallardo often wrote in his volumes and kept his library in disarray. In their appraisals of his life, most scholars in fact highlight Gallardo's efforts to create a comprehensive bibliography of Spanish books. In the early twentieth century, Milton A. Buchanan described him as "Spain's foremost bibliographer" (5), and Pedro Sainz y Rodríguez declared that "su actividad bibliográfica no ha sido superada por nadie en Epsaña" (Gallardo, *Obras* 1: viii) [his bibliographical activity has not been surpassed by anyone in Spain]. Late twentieth-century scholars continued to echo these views, with Ricardo Senabre lauding him as the "príncipe de los bibliógrafos españoles" (17) [prince of Spanish bibliographers]. Such adulations attest not only to the impact of Gallardo's bibliographical production on his contemporaries but also to the passion with which he carried out his work.

In addition to being a bibliographer, Gallardo was a prolific correspondent and an author of numerous essays and satirical tracts in which he attacked political conservatism and religious orthodoxy, engaging in what Buchanan calls "a continual warfare of pamphlets" (5). His liberal views often placed him at odds with the prevailing authorities and on occasion led to his ostracization at home and exile abroad. Gallardo's worldview was shaped by the Enlightenment. But despite the affinities he shared with the eighteenth-century French *philosophes*, he was opposed to the *afrancesados*, or Spanish emulators of French culture, and maintained that Spanish writers should seek inspiration in the Spanish classics and imitate the language of Spanish Golden Age literature. In fact, he frequently bemoaned the devaluation of old Spanish that occurred when the French language came into vogue in the eighteenth century, and he vehemently argued for its revival. As Senabre remarks, Gallardo's position on language was similar to that of the eighteenth-century Enlightenment scholar, Benito Jerónimo Feijóo (8), although like Ramon Miquel i Planas in his use of Catalan, Gallardo actually went so far as to adopt a distinctive style of spelling that was anachronistic in writers of his period.[2] If Gallardo was a political progressive and secularist, he was thus also a traditionalist in his views of language and literature and in his nostalgia for what he imagined to be an autochthonous Spanish identity. This nostalgia appears most concretely in his ruminations on bibliophilia and his own lost books.

Gallardo was born in the town of Campanario, in the Spanish region of Extremadura, in 1776. Although his parents wanted him to pursue an ecclesiastical career, as a young student at the University of Salamanca he expressed interest in the experimental sciences and studied medicine. Sainz y Rodríguez speculates that the research methods he learned in the sciences influenced his conviction that historical criticism should be grounded in a close examination of existing documentation (16). But he traces the origins of Gallardo's bibliophilia to his exposure to the library of the Colegio de San Bartolomé and the influence of one of its librarians (17), who, according to Alejandro Pérez Vidal, supported his decision not to become a physician (9). After leaving the university, Gallardo travelled in France, where he gained proficiency in French, and settled in Madrid. Following the French invasion of the capital in 1808, he joined the retreating Spanish government in its relocation to Cádiz, and in 1811 he was named librarian of the Biblioteca de las Cortes, or library of the parliament. During this period, he wrote a controversial text titled *Diccionario crítico-burlesco* [Critical-burlesque dictionary], in which he defended enlightened thinking and political reform. He was temporarily jailed for his outspokenness in the *Diccionario*, but he quickly resumed his position in the Biblioteca de las Cortes, which he held until the end of the Peninsular War and the restoration of the Bourbon monarch, Fernando VII, to the Spanish throne in 1814.

As head of the Biblioteca de las Cortes, regarded by royalists as a hotbed of republicanism and anti-clericalism, Gallardo was obliged to flee Spain in 1814 and seek refuge, first in Lisbon and then in London, where he remained until 1820.[3] His period in London was particularly fruitful. Not only did he interact with noted Spanish exiles of the period but he also met leading British thinkers, including Jeremy Bentham, as well as renowned British book collectors, chief of whom was the Hispanophile, Richard Heber. According to contemporaneous bibliophiles (including Vicente Salvá [Fernández Sánchez 161]), Heber owned the largest private library of rare Spanish books in the world, although his taste extended well beyond the Iberian Peninsula, as evidenced by the catalogues of his books that were auctioned after his death.[4] Gallardo considered Heber the greatest European bibliographer since Hernando Colón (Fernández Sánchez 161), and he marvelled at his love of books and Spanish literature:

> Un Caballero inglés (el célebre Bibliósofo E. Heber) asombro de erudición, y tan aficionado a los Injenios de España, que por un *Romancero jeneral* tuvo la bizarría de pagar diez-mil reales; entusiástico admirador de nuestro Teätro me decía por los años 1818 en Lóndres que no había parä él lectura tan sabrosa como la de una Comedia antigua Española. (*El Criticón* 2: 80)

> [An English gentleman (the famous bibliosoph Heber, esquire) an amazement of erudition and a keen enthusiast of Spanish creations, was brave

and generous enough to pay 10,000 reals for a *Romancero general*; an enthusiastic admirer of our theater, he told me in London in around 1818 that for him there was no reading as delightful as that of an old Spanish play.]

While in London, Gallardo took copious notes on the Spanish volumes housed in Heber's library and in many other private and public collections, such as those of the British Museum (Rodríguez-Moñino, *Historia* 19). He also acquired a large number of Iberian books not readily available in Spain.

Gallardo returned to Spain in 1820, at the outset of the Liberal Triennium, a three-year period of liberal government during the autocratic reign of Fernando VII, and resumed his position as librarian of the Biblioteca de las Cortes. In 1823, when France dispatched the army of the "Hundred Thousand Sons of Saint Louis" to Spain to restore the absolutist rule of Fernando VII, Gallardo moved with the liberal government, first to Seville and then to Cádiz. After the government fell, he chose not to go abroad but to remain in the country. As Pérez Vidal explains, his situation was less precarious than in 1814, when controversy over the *Diccionario crítico-burlesco* was still fresh in the minds of the authorities (39). But he did suffer brief imprisonment and internal exile until the death of Fernando VII in 1833. In the more open period that followed the reign of Fernando VII, Gallardo returned to Madrid, and in 1837 he was elected to the Cortes. Yet given his advanced age, his stint as a deputy was brief, and he retired from public life in 1841. Throughout this period, he nevertheless continued to write and to labour on his bibliography, until his death in 1852.

During his lifetime, Gallardo suffered several great losses of books. What Antonio Rodríguez-Moñino describes as his first "malaventura bibliofílica" (*Historia* 17) [bibliophile misadventure] took place in Seville in 1809, when Gallardo was forced to evacuate the city during the Peninsular War. The second loss, which Gallardo laments throughout much of his personal writings, occurred during his exile in London. Before departing from Madrid, he left many of his books in the care of his servants, who were ill advised by his friends and sold them to the book dealers known as the Brothers Orea.[5] Some were subsequently resold to the writer Juan Nicolás Böhl de Faber, who took them to Germany. Gallardo claims that Böhl de Faber promised to return them to him, but he died before he could do so. In a letter to his friend, Joaquín Rubio, dated 2 August 1839, Gallardo remarks that these books, like so many bibliophile treasures of the time, "salen de España, i salen para no volver" (Sainz y Rodríguez 332) [leave Spain, and leave never to return again]. Before going into exile, Gallardo did entrust some of his books to a bibliophile friend. Although she sent these to Gallardo, many, according to him, were stolen during shipment and never reached him in England (Rodríguez-Moñino, *Historia* 19).

Gallardo's third and greatest loss of books occurred in Seville during the festival of Saint Anthony, on 13 June 1823. On this occasion, he and the members of the Cortes were fleeing the city for Cádiz, in advance of the invading French army. During the commotion of the evacuation, a mob attacked the ship carrying the government's baggage and ransacked Gallardo's vast trove of books and papers, stealing and destroying many valuable items. Years later, Gallardo describes this event in a letter to Antonio María de Araoz, librarian of the Biblioteca Colombina, whom he unsuccessfully petitioned to restore to him several lost volumes that he thought had been acquired by the library.

> En los barcos ... iban ... mis más preziosos libros y papeles, señaladamente los trabajos literarios de toda mi vida.
>
> Todo lo perdí.
>
> ...
>
> [Q]uizá podré recobrar alguna más de tantas i tan preziosas cosas, como me robaron en el dicho día, negro y aziago para mí. (Sainz y Rodríguez, 239–40)

> [In the boats ... were my most precious books and papers, and indeed the literary works of my entire life.
>
> I lost everything.
>
> ...
>
> Perhaps I will be able to recover some of the many precious things that they stole from me on that day, so dark and fateful for me.]

By dint of a great effort, Gallardo did recover some of the volumes that disappeared in the chaos of Saint Anthony's Day, 1823. Yet his missing books and papers haunted him until the end of his life. In his writings he often reiterates the conviction that he lost everything, as in the following lament: "todo lo he perdido ... [y] nada, nada me ha quedado, sino la memoria lastimosa de todo" (*Obras* 1: 177) [I lost everything ... (and) nothing, nothing remained to me but the heartbreaking memory of it all].[6]

During the internal exile that Gallardo suffered in the years immediately following the Liberal Triennium, he describes the loss of his beloved books as a tragedy. In a letter to Rubio, dated 23 December 1827, he declares that he is "condenado á arrastrar [su] ecsistenzia lejos de Cádiz, separado de [sus] libros i [sus] amigos" [condemned to bear the burden of his existence far from Cádiz, separated from his books and his friends]; and he bemoans the life that he has come to lead: "en efecto haze años pareze estoi destinado á ser mero varón de deseos" (Sainz y Rodríguez 322) [in fact for years it seems that I am destined to be merely a man of desire]. In this vision of himself as nothing more than a desire for something unattainable, he reveals an intuition of his existential condition as well as a recognition of his failure to achieve fulfillment through the cultivation and possession of books. Prior to the events of 1823, Gallardo perhaps did find satisfaction as an owner of books. Yet given his earlier history of loss, his happiness was at best always ephemeral. In another letter to Rubio, dated 19 May 1835, he writes: "[H]e llegado en estos días á tener una amarga evidenzia: cosa qe me tiene desabridísimo. Haze años no hago más que tejer y destejer la tela de Penélope" (Sainz y Rodríguez 324–5) [I have recently come to recognize a bitter fact: something that has left me quite discouraged. For years I have done nothing but weave and unweave the cloth of Penelope]. In the context of his past, the cloth of Penelope that he weaves and unweaves can be interpreted as a metaphor for his library and, by extension, the identity that he has attempted to forge for himself as bibliophile and bibliographer. Although chance has repeatedly deprived him of his books and papers, this comment suggests that he feels almost responsible for his fate, as if he were continually undoing his life's work.

Gallardo's fourth significant loss of books occurred at the end of his career, when he retired to his farm in La Alberquilla, near Toledo. Before moving to La Alberquilla, he had arranged to have his books and papers sent ahead to his new residence; but, when he arrived, he found that the trunks carrying them had been robbed. In a letter to Rubio, dated 15 May 1846, he writes:

> [D]el tesoro inmenso de libros rarísimos, de Mss. preziosísimos, i de los trabajos literarios de toda mi vida, materiales de qe iba a levantar el edifizio jigante de mi gloria (obra no ingloriosa para la Nazion) ... todo lo he encontrado saqueado. (Sainz y Rodríguez 341)
>
> [Of the immense treasure of very rare books, very precious manuscripts, and literary works of my entire life, materials with which I was going to raise a giant edifice to my glory (and a work not inglorious for the nation) ... I found it all plundered.]

Gallardo intended to use these books and papers to complete a monumental Hispanic bibliography, which in his view would cement his legacy and provide an immeasurable service to his country. Faced with his loss and the possibility of never accomplishing his goal, he felt as if he had died: "Esto es morir" (341) [This is to die]. Gallardo rails against the "[f]atalidad lastimosa" [pitiful fate] of having spent his entire life working, while "los zánganos [le comen] la miel i la zera qe labr[a]" (341) [the parasites eat the honey and wax that he cultivates]. What is more, he blames the theft on his nephew, Juan Antonio Gallardo, whom he had entrusted with the management of La Alberquilla during his absence.[7] Gallardo in fact exaggerates the magnitude of the situation, and upon his death he left behind a plethora of books and papers. Yet as he remarks in a letter to Juan Luis de Chaves, at this stage of his life the loss of so many bibliographical treasures shattered his illusion of a "dulze i apazible" [sweet and pleasant] old age, "con muchos i buenos libros, i en una casa de campo qe es un Paraïso" (Rodríguez-Moñino, *Historia* 103) [with many good books, in a country house that is a paradise].

Gallardo writes not only about his personal losses but also the far greater loss of books that Spain suffered during the early and mid-nineteenth century. In the essay "Biblioteca Nacional de Cortes" [National Library of the Cortes] he maintains that over 2,000 public and private libraries were pillaged or destroyed during the Peninsular War. These included the libraries of numerous religious communities as well as the Biblioteca de El Escorial, which he claims lost up to half of its rare Spanish books. He also cites attacks on the Biblioteca del Monasterio de San Juan de los Reyes in Toledo, the library of the diocese of Valencia and The University of Valencia, and the Biblioteca Medinaceli and the Biblioteca Osuna in Madrid. The French plundered Spanish libraries a second time in the nineteenth century, during the invasion of 1823. Gallardo holds both the French and the Spanish *afrancesados* responsible for these tragedies. But he levels his most stinging invective against Spanish librarians that colluded with the enemy, often for monetary gain, calling them "traidores a su Rei y a su Patria" (*Obras* 2: 221) [traitors to their king and to their country]. As Gallardo notes, one positive consequence of Spain's many wars with France was in fact the creation of several great libraries, including the Biblioteca de El Escorial in the sixteenth century, the Biblioteca Real in the eighteenth century, and the Biblioteca de las Cortes in the nineteenth century. Yet the losses that occurred as a result of war and the complicity of Spanish librarians with foreign conquerors and book buyers were irreparable.

Gallardo's observations of the deleterious effect of French military incursions on nineteenth-century Spanish libraries are significant, for they reveal how through imperialist expansion one nation can actually appropriate the culture of another. The countless Spanish books either stolen by invading French forces or sold off to them by mercenary Spaniards were priceless treasures akin to paintings and sculptures. Yet they were also, given the sheer quantity and diversity of the volumes, representative of the cultural heritage of the entire Spanish people. If Gallardo regarded the loss of his personal books as a threat to his individual identity, he feared that the national identity of Spain was in even greater peril when, from his perspective, its almost four-centuries of print production began to disappear. In fact, the massive transfer of books out of nineteenth-century Iberia affected not only the Castilian-speaking population but all the linguistic communities of the Peninsula, precisely because many of the books that made their way into French, British, German, and American collections were written in languages other than Castilian. Throughout the nineteenth and twentieth centuries, Spaniards have often had to negotiate a national identity defined by foreign assumptions and prejudices about Spanish life. Ironically, Gallardo and many of the bibliophiles and scholars of his generation felt obliged to travel abroad in order to recover texts in which, from their perspective, a more authentic Spanish ethos was inscribed.

Although Gallardo frequently decries the loss of his books and the books of the Spanish patrimony, he also reveals many emotions typical of traditional bibliophiles. In a letter to Rubio, dated 4 December 1843, he speaks longingly of the collection of a recently deceased librarian, Francisco de Peralta, whose books, gathered over the course of half a century, "honrarían la [b]iblioteca del más ilustrado bibliófilo" (Sainz y Rodríguez 334) [would honor the library of the most illustrious bibliophile]. Gallardo asks Rubio to help him obtain some of these books by visiting the collection and identifying the most beautiful and finely printed and bound works. In a letter to Luis María Ramírez, dated 7 September 1843, he expresses joy at being able to touch certain volumes from which he had been separated for many years (Sainz y Rodríguez 356). And in a letter to Fernando Casas, dated 16 February 1844, he tells of the pleasure of leaving books uncut until he can appreciate them to the fullest in the privacy of his study (Sainz y Rodríguez 366). More often than not, however, Gallardo writes of the pain of losing his books, which he equates to the sorrow of losing friends. In so doing, he compares himself to Don Quixote, when he discovered that all his books had vanished. In a letter to Cayetano Barrera, dated 30 May 1843, he declares: "No se qedó más estupefacto el insigne Caballero de la Mancha, cuando buscando sus libros de Caballerías, ni libros, ni librería, ni nada encontró" (Sainz y Rodríguez 365) [The famous Knight of La Mancha was not more stupefied, when he looked for his books of chivalry and found neither books, nor library, nor anything].

Not only did Gallardo compare himself to Don Quixote, but so too did Benito Pérez Galdós, who later inhabited the house in La Alberquilla where Gallardo once resided. According to Pérez Galdós, Gallardo spent his final years "sepultado en una biblioteca, donde le devoraba, como a Don Quijote la caballería, la estupenda locura de los apuntes" (qtd. in Fernández Sánchez 165) [buried in a library, where he was devoured by the stupendous madness of his (bibliographical) notes, just as Don Quixote was devoured by knight errantry]. Yet the most extensive and most notorious comparison of Gallardo to Don Quixote is the satirical novella penned by Gallardo's friend turned nemesis, Adolfo de Castro, titled *Aventuras literarias del iracundo bibliopirata estremeño don Bartolomico Gallardete, escritas por el buen don Antonio de Lupián Zapata (La horma de su zapato)* [The literary adventures of the irascible book pirate from Extremadura, don Bartolomico Gallardete, written by the good don Antonio de Lupián Zapata (his shoetree)].[8]

Castro's text parodies the life of Gallardo, as if he were a latter-day knight-errant engaged in ceaseless battles for books; but, unlike Don Quixote, the character that Castro depicts is resentful, hypersensitive, and vainglorious. Castro asserts that as a youth Gallardo hoped one day to become a Spanish Voltaire, radically challenging the cultural foundations of traditional Spanish society. Yet through his satire, Castro diminishes the import of Gallardo's lifelong attacks on royal absolutism and religious intransigence. What is more, he mocks the love of country that Gallardo expresses in his denunciations of the foreign appropriation of Spanish books. According to Castro, Gallardo, while exiled in London, came to the preposterous conclusion that all the rare Spanish-language books held in libraries and private collections in the British capital had been stolen by Sir Francis Drake during his raids on the Peninsula in the sixteenth century. In a frenzy of patriotism, he therefore decided to reappropriate as many of these volumes as possible and restore them to Spain. But his real aim was to keep them for himself, and as a result he quickly became notorious among British bibliophiles. Just as sixteenth-century Spaniards would cry *"ahí viene el Draque"* [*here comes Drake*] when they saw English vessels approaching the Spanish coastline, British bibliophiles "decían con temerosa voz: *ahí viene Gallardete*" [would say in a frightened voice: *here comes Gallardete*] when they learned that "el iracundo estremeño iba á visitar sus bibliotecas" (18) [the irascible Extremaduran was going to visit their libraries].[9]

In perusing British libraries, Gallardo occasionally found items that he claimed were stolen from him. But according to Castro, he also stole books himself. Once, while visiting Heber, he supposedly provoked a scuffle with Heber's other guests, threw a book on a candle, and in the ensuing darkness managed to pilfer several of Heber's rare Spanish volumes. This mocking and ultimately defamatory depiction of Gallardo's behaviour in Heber's home differs from the respectful attitude that Gallardo conveys when describing Heber, whose love of books and Spanish literature he greatly admires. Although Castro makes a joke of Gallardo's interaction with Heber, their relationship, at least from Gallardo's perspective, was based on mutual esteem.

Castro ridicules not only Gallardo's actions in public but also what he imagines to be his inner life and dreams. In several episodes of his narrative, he portrays Gallardo as a somnambulist. In one scene, Gallardo dreams that criminals have come to steal his books and the drafts of what he has been writing for the glory of Spanish letters. While still asleep, he rises from his bed and begins to attack the imaginary intruders, stabbing them with an Albacete knife. The following morning his housekeeper enters his chambers and finds that the walls and chairs have been slashed, which she attributes to the work of rats and weasels.[10] In another scene, Gallardo dreams that he is in a library filled with unusual books. He begins to crave several of the volumes, and takes them and throws them out a window and into a well. The following day he looks for his own books, only to discover that the ones he purloined in his dream are now missing. Castro maintains that these nightmares reveal Gallardo's unfounded belief that thieves were continually stealing the books that he fought so hard to acquire – although they might also reveal Gallardo's own desire to steal books or even a past experience of bibliokleptomania. He further contends that Gallardo frequently changed residence in order to escape his tormentors, but that he did so in vain because he actually tormented himself with his obsession.

> Mudaba de casa, pero no de sueños: de forma que siempre iba con los trastos a cuestas huyendo de los foragidos, que lo acosaban, y él era su propio acosador y foragido. (23)

> [He changed house, but not dreams: so that he always went about with his baggage on his back, fleeing from the thieves that assaulted him, even though he was his own assailant and thief.]

Although his narrative is frequently humorous, Castro reveals what Sainz y Rodríguez describes as a kind of "monomanía persecutoria," or persecution complex, which Gallardo developed as a result of the repeated theft of his books (109). Yet whereas Sainz y Rodríguez writes sympathetically of Gallardo, Castro depicts him as ridiculous, if not implicitly malevolent. His representation of Gallardo is thus consonant with nineteenth-century European renditions of the Romantic bibliophile as an aberrant figure. The bibliophile that he portrays is nevertheless distinctively Spanish to the extent that his madness is explicitly conflated with that of Don Quixote. If Bartolomico Gallardete differs from Don Quixote, this is because he carries out his impossible battles not simply through the lens of what he has read in books but within the sphere of books themselves, either in the real libraries that he encountered in the world or in the libraries of his imagination.[11]

According to Rodríguez-Moñino, Castro was the creator of the black legend surrounding Gallardo (*Historia* 99). Yet while some of Gallardo's contemporaries, like Fernández Espino, levelled virulent charges against him, other noted nineteenth-century figures, including Menéndez Pelayo, portrayed him in the satirical vein of Castro's *Aventuras*.[12] Menéndez Pelayo in fact relates an episode in Gallardo's life reminiscent of the dream scenes depicted by Castro. As Buchanan summarizes it, "the keepers of the Chapter library of the cathedral of Toledo became weary of watching Gallardo while working in their library, and as there were no other readers, resolved to lock him up in the library each morning and examine him upon leaving in the afternoon. This method worked very well, until one day it was discovered that books were being thrown from a window and picked up by a boy who carried them to Gallardo's lodgings" (14–15). Rodríguez-Moñino, nevertheless, disputes the notion that Gallardo was a biblioklept, declaring that in all his extensive research he found no solid justification for Gallardo's bad reputation (*Historia* 30).

Most modern scholars in fact reject the negative views of Gallardo advanced during his lifetime, and in their more sober and erudite analyses they express admiration for his extensive knowledge of Spanish book history and his efforts to construct a comprehensive bibliography of Hispanic book production.[13] Satires such as those of Castro are nonetheless significant insofar as they reveal a mocking and disparaging attitude towards bibliophilia, present as far back as the Greco-Roman period in authors like Lucian of Samosata, that came to fruition in nineteenth- and early-twentieth-century European portraits of book lovers.[14] In these narratives, bibliophiles often evince characteristics typical of Romantic heroes. Not only are they driven by a grand passion that sets them apart from ordinary humans, but they also experience exalted emotions, even when they fail in their quest for books. Yet satires of bibliophiles also serve as correctives to their perceived excesses, and in the modern period they ultimately function to reaffirm accepted standards of behaviour, especially as these standards apply to the lives of bourgeois men.

In nineteenth- and early-twentieth-century satires of bibliophilia, the male bibliophile is often represented as unmasculine or childlike. In Castro's narrative, Gallardo is identified through diminutive forms of his name (Bartolomico and Gallardete), and he displays stereotypically immature behaviour, as evidenced by the "llorimicos" (45) [little whimperings] that he emits when he is disappointed and unable to obtain what he wants. In fact, he is frequently depicted as crying. Although he sees himself as a victim of crime, he disrespects the private property of others, stealing books whenever he can in order to satisfy his whims. More important, his love of books is not directed to a practical or useful goal. Indeed, his detractors go so far as to suggest that he invents his losses in order to cover up his unproductiveness as a bibliographer (Buchanan 7).

During his lifetime, Gallardo was a controversial figure not only because of his reputation as a bibliophile and bibliographer but also because of his outspoken criticism of the Spanish monarchy and the Catholic Church. His contemporaries accordingly expressed widely divergent opinions of his writings and activities. One unbiased and measured observer of Gallardo was the Russian bibliophile, Sergei Aleksandrovitch Sobolevsky, who visited him at La Alberquilla in early 1850. Sobolevsky spent a significant portion of his career in France and fomented close ties with French writers, including Prosper Mérimée. Like Mérimée, Sobolevsky was an ardent admirer of Spanish literature. In 1849 he travelled to Spain for the purpose of visiting libraries and bookstores and purchasing rare Spanish-language texts related to his primary areas of interest, Asia and the Americas. Sobolevsky documented his impressions of Spanish book culture in letters to an unnamed friend, who Joaquín del Val speculates was the French bibliophile and bibliographer, Pierre Jannet.[15] In these letters he remarks that Spain was historically one of the richest countries in the world in terms of its book heritage. He further notes that as a consequence of the wars and political events of the early nineteenth-century, most of the rare volumes once held in its monastic libraries had been relocated to the libraries and collections of northern Europe. Conversely, books held in the libraries of Spanish aristocratic households, which in his view were more appealing to bibliophiles, only occasionally entered the marketplace. He therefore tells his reader that if he hopes to assemble a Spanish-language library of his own, he should either remain in Paris or travel to London, where in three months' time he will acquire far better volumes than he would if he spent ten years searching for books in Spain. With regard to the Biblioteca Nacional de España he even goes so far as to declare that it contains "*nada, absolutamente nada*" (Sobolevsky

88) [*nothing, absolutely nothing*] comparable to the Spanish literary treasures housed in the public libraries and private collections of Britain, France, and Germany.

According to his letters, Sobolevsky spoke with Gallardo for three hours one day and for a shorter period a second day.[16] He indicates that he first heard of Gallardo from Vicente Salvá and from friends and fellow bibliophiles in Madrid, who claimed that Gallardo's familiarity with Iberian books was greater than that of anyone in the world, and who described him as an "oráculo de la bibliografía española" (110) [oracle of Spanish bibliography]. Warned that the elderly Gallardo was not receptive to visits and not particularly communicative, Sobolevsky was delighted to find him congenial and forthcoming in their conversations.

> [T]uve ocasión de admirar la ciencia variada, el ingenio fino y observador, la memoria prodigiosa de datos y de fechas, que hacen de don Bartolomé uno de los hombres más extraordinariamente dotados que haya encontrado en mis largos viajes. Ninguna de las preguntas a que yo le sometí dejó sin respuesta, ninguna de mis dudas literarias o bibliográficas quedó sin explicar, y todo ello con un conocimiento profundo y variado de cuanto concernía la materia, con una multitud de corolarios, a menudo más interesantes que el tema principal. (111)

> [I had the chance to admire his wide-ranging expertise, his fine and observant intellect, and his prodigious memory of facts and dates, all of which make Don Bartolomé one of the most extraordinarily gifted men that I have met on my long travels. None of the questions that I put to him went unanswered; none of my inquiries about literature or bibliography went unexplained; and he clarified everything with a deep and broad knowledge of the subject, and with a multitude of corollaries often more interesting than the primary topic itself.]

Sobolevsky comments on the rare volumes that Gallardo showed him and on the copious bibliographical notes that he had gathered over half a century of research. His only hope was that Gallardo would live long enough to put them all in order.

Gallardo nevertheless died before completing his life's work. What remained of his books and 140,000 notes (many of which were in fact lost in the events of 1823) passed to his nephew, who in the words of Rodríguez-Moñino "[los] dispersó estúpidamente" (*Don Bartolomé* 10) [stupidly dispersed them] among various individuals. Manuel Ramón Zarco del Valle and José Sancho Rayón obtained some of the notes and published them in the two volumes of the *Ensayo de una biblioteca española de libros raros y curiosos*. Menéndez Pelayo, who acquired others, published them in a third and fourth volume of the same series. According to Fernández Sánchez, although Gallardo's notes were of more value than his books (165), those included in the *Ensayo* relate solely to works that he owned and therefore do not constitute a comprehensive Hispanic bibliography (168). Moreover, given that nearly 200 years have passed since he first composed the material, its value has greatly diminished. Yet as Joaquín González Manzanares remarks, it is still of interest to bibliophiles and bibliographers (301).

**Vicente Salvá and Pedro Salvá**

Vicente Salvá and his son Pedro Salvá were among the most distinguished Iberian bibliographers and bibliophiles of the nineteenth century. Although Vicente achieved the greatest renown, his bibliographical work was not completed until after his death through the efforts of Pedro, and was not published until after the latter's death. The Salvá bibliography was based on the books that the father-and-son bibliophiles had amassed over the first half of the nineteenth century while living in England, France, and Spain. Unlike the bibliophilia of Gallardo, who attempted to use books to achieve individual fulfillment, Vicente and Pedro's cultivation of books made possible a powerful bond between the two men. Through their mutual appreciation of the volumes in their library they not only developed a distinctive father-son relationship, but they also enriched and deepened their friendship, which for them ultimately surpassed in importance their love of books.

Despite differing family circumstances, Vicente Salvá and Gallardo shared much in common. Both supposedly had difficult personalities, and both were outspoken liberals who were exiled during the reign of Fernando VII.[17] They were also famous figures in their day, and their lives as bibliophiles became the stuff of legend, revered by some while parodied by others. Like Gallardo, Salvá tried but failed to complete a comprehensive Spanish bibliography during his lifetime. Yet whereas Gallardo's bibliographical work was posthumously compromised by his nephew's dispersal of his books and papers, Salvá's reached fruition through his son and heir. His career was thus at least ostensibly more successful than Gallardo's, and his legacy was more lasting. In the private sphere, Gallardo frequently bared his soul in his correspondences with friends, revealing his passion for books and his obsession with those he had lost or feared he might lose. Salvá, in contrast, left less of a record of his inner life as a bibliophile. In fact, he was an entrepreneur, and he established and managed important Spanish-language bookshops in London and Paris. He was also the author of fictional texts and essays related to politics and language. Notwithstanding these accomplishments, in the oftentimes sensationalized world of bibliophilia he gained the greatest notoriety for his fabled library, "la jaula de los Salvá" (Fernández Sánchez 154) [the cage of the Salvás], which no one but he and his son could enter. What is more, he was actually regarded as a possible inspiration for the tale of the murderous bookman of Barcelona, even if he was never known to have engaged in criminal activity.

As a young man, Vicente Salvá studied Greek, Latin, and Hebrew, and for a brief period prior to the Napoleonic invasion of Spain he taught Greek at the University of Alcalá de Henares. In 1809 he married Josefa Mallén, the daughter of a French book dealer who had settled in Valencia in the late eighteenth century, and joined his father-in-law and brother-in-law in the operation of the Mallén bookstore. Because of his outspoken criticism of royal absolutism and the Inquisition, Salvá fled Spain after the restoration of Fernando VII. He returned to the country during the period of the Liberal Triennium and held political office as a deputy to the Cortes. Yet with the re-imposition of autocracy in 1823, he was forced to undergo a much longer exile, first in London and then in Paris.

As Vicente Llorens remarks in his study of the Spanish emigration to England during the reign of Fernando VII, Salvá arrived in London at an opportune moment in the history of the Spanish-language book business (90). The market for old and rare Iberian books had dramatically increased in early nineteenth-century Britain, and in the words of Nigel Glendinning, "interest in Spanish books ... became 'maniacal' towards the turn of the century, growing in the early 1800s to its fullest development in the 1820s when Spanish books and manuscripts, fleeing Spain like political exiles, deluged the London book market for a brief but brilliant period" (70). What is more, in the wake of the independence of the Spanish American colonies, Britain had begun to replace Spain as the dominant power in Spanish American commerce, and British traders were anxious to gain control over the export of Spanish-language books to the Americas (Reig Salvá 95).

Salvá capitalized on the British enthusiasm for Spanish-language books in the 1820s. Like the majority of Spanish *émigrés*, he and his family resided in the humble district of Somers Town. But in 1824, he acquired the financing necessary to launch his Librería Española y Clásica in an elegant shopping district of London, and set up business at 124 Regent Street.[18] As Carola Reig Salvá explains, Salvá's bookstore gained prestige among British bibliophiles and Spanish *émigrés*, and soon became the centre of Spanish cultural life in the British capital (99). All Spanish books published in London were showcased in the Librería Española y Clásica, and the British Museum was in fact one of its clients, using its services to acquire volumes from Spain (99). After several years, however, Salvá decided to liquidate his London book business because he wanted to create a Spanish-language publishing house in a city where products and labour were more readily available than in London (117). He chose Paris for his new venture, and moved there with his family in 1830. Soon afterwards, Fernando VII died, and most of the Spanish exiles in London returned to Spain. By that time, as Glendinning wistfully remarks, "the great years of Spanish book importation [were] over; the lively political and literary interest in Spain which the presence of the exiles had fostered was declining; the Romantic passion for Spanish ballads had passed. Salvá had moved on to Paris ... and most of the *émigrés* were gone" (91).

As Reig Salvá explains, Vicente Salvá fomented relations with a Parisian book dealer, Martin Bossange, and established a Spanish-language bookshop, the Librairie Hispano-américaine, on the premises of Bossange's bookshop at 60 rue de Richelieu. The Librairie Hispano-américaine functioned as a sort of entrepôt for books that Salvá obtained through the Mallén bookstore in Valencia and subsequently exported to Spanish America. He also reprinted Spanish-language volumes that were in high demand on the Spanish-American market. Salvá resided in Paris during the early 1830s, but after the death of Fernando VII he returned to Spain and re-engaged in Spanish politics. From his base in Valencia he continued to operate the Librairie Hispano-américaine, but he soon took over the Mallén bookstore, which he purchased from his brother-in-law. In 1847 he moved his vast collection of books from Paris to Valencia, in the hope of using it to complete his Spanish bibliography. But during a brief visit to Paris in 1849 he contracted cholera and died, leaving to Pedro the bookstores in Paris and Valencia, along with his entire library, which remained intact until after the death of Pedro in 1870.

In 1830 Vicente Salvá published a virulent diatribe against the Catholic Church titled *La bruja* [The witch]. In this text he lashes out against the Roman Curia, the primary governing body of the Church, which in his view had ignored the teachings of Christ and acted out of ambition and greed. He also challenges the power of the pope and denounces the reverence of relics as superstitious. At the outset, Salvá identifies himself as the executor of the will of a recently deceased priest. In sorting through the priest's books and papers he claims to have discovered the manuscript of a novel that the priest had written during a period of exile. In this narrative, which forms the body of *La bruja*, the priest recounts how one night while reading in bed a witch appeared to him and whisked him away on a fantastical voyage through the past and present in order to reveal to him the abuses of the Church. The witch, as Ana Rueda argues, functions like the figure of the devil in *El diablo cojuelo* [The crippled devil] of Luis Vélez de Guevara (36), providing the priest with access to the private abodes of others and thereby exposing their secret machinations and misdeeds. Although Salvá differentiates himself from his characters, their opinions are clearly his own. Like Salvá, the witch is deeply anti-clerical. What is more, the priest is a passionate bibliophile with a library containing an immense number of books on topics of interest to Salvá, such as the Castilian language. Yet *La bruja* is significant not only for its denunciation of institutionalized religion and its representation of bibliophilia but also because it foreshadows the situation in which Pedro Salvá would one day find himself. The fictional Vicente Salvá, like Pedro after his father's death and indeed like so many inheritors of libraries, is almost overwhelmed by the quantity of books that are left in his care: "No tardé muchas horas en hacerme cargo de su dinero y ropilla, por tener poco de ambos artículos; pero no sucedió lo mismo con sus libros y manuscritos" (Salvá y Pérez 6) [I did not spend many hours accounting for his money and clothing, since he had little of both; but the same was not the case with his books and manuscripts].[19] For Pedro Salvá, however, the accounting of his father's books would ultimately entail writing a bibliography.

Vicente Salvá's bibliographical work in fact began long before his death. In 1826 he printed a short catalogue of his library in London, titled *A Catalogue of Spanish and Portuguese Books, with Occasional Literary and Bibliographical Remarks by Vincente Salvá*. In 1829 Pedro republished it as *A Catalogue of Hispanic and Portuguese Books, on Sale by Vincent Salvá*. Francisco Almela y Vives notes that Vicente was embarrassed by this work, and that Pedro considered some of the entries badly written (81). As Pedro explains in the prologue to his own catalogue of the library, published after his death in 1872 under the title *Catálogo de la biblioteca de Salvá* [Catalogue of the Salvá library], Vicente began to form an index of the books in late 1848, and when he died in 1849 he had composed some 300 entries. Yet despite Pedro's intention to finish the catalogue, he waited over two years to do so because he was so grief stricken by the death of his "venerado padre [e] idolotrado amigo" (Salvá y Mallén vi) [revered father and idolized friend]. When he finally resumed the project, he realized that his father had only just started the bibliographical description of the books, including their titles, place and year of publication, and size and number of pages, but he had not actually undertaken the more substantive task of describing their contents. Pedro thus made the completion of the Salvá catalogue his final life's work.

For the most part the catalogue published by Pedro Salvá highlights books written in Castilian and the other languages of the Iberian Peninsula and the Americas. It also features texts published abroad by Spaniards and books published in Spain by non-Spaniards. These volumes were located not only in the Salvá library but also in the libraries that Pedro had visited over the course of his career, including the primary public libraries of Spain, France, and England, as well as in the collections of noted Hispanist bibliophiles such as Charles Nodier and Richard Heber. Pedro indicates that he occasionally rectifies the work done by other bibliographers including the seventeenth-century Nicolás Antonio (1617–84), albeit not with the intention of lessening the merit of Antonio's monumental *Bibliotheca hispana vetus et nova* [Old and new Hispanic library]. For model catalogues he looks to the works of contemporary British, French, and German bibliographers, whom he describes as "nuestros maestros" (xxi) [our teachers].

In the prologue to the catalogue, penned in June 1869, Pedro reveals that what motivated his project was a desire to bequeath to posterity a record of the beautiful books that he and his father had collected over the course of their lifetimes. Yet he claims that the Salvá library ultimately owed its existence to him. To justify this assertion, he cites a letter that his father sent to him in 1843, giving him instructions about the binding of certain books and the seal that they should display (see figure 8).

> Tendrá este [el sello] dos manos enlazadas; la leyenda *Biblioteca de Salvá*, y a un lado una *P* y al otro una *V*, iniciales de tu nombre y del mío, porque a ti se debe primariamente el proyecto de formarla: nunca olvidaré el día en que me dijiste que habías rehusado 550 fr. que te habían ofrecido por el *Romancero general* de 1614, porque no querías que nos desprendiéramos de él hasta tener otro ejemplar más hermoso. Entonces te di facultad para que escogieras los que más te agradasen entre los libros raros que teníamos para vender; tú los recogistes y formastes con ellos el primer cimiento de la colección. Además, has empleado tantas diligencias y conatos para adquirir las obras con que la hemos enriquecido; te has ocupado a veces en transformar un ejemplar, haciéndolo bello si era bueno, o dejándolo decente cuando antes era malo; lavándolo, quitando la tinta y las manchas, remendándolo, añadiéndole papel al margen, y hasta copiando portadas y hojas que se equivocan con las empresas. Nuestras manos deben estar unidas aquí como otro monumento de que esta Biblioteca es debida a nuestros afanes comunes, y están unidas como lo están nuestros corazones. (vi)

Figure 8. Book seal of Vicente and Pedro Salvá. In Pedro Salvá y Mallén, *Catálogo de la biblioteca de Salvá*, vol. 1, Ferrer de Orga, 1872, p. xvii. Image courtesy of Biblioteca de Catalunya.

> [This seal will have two clasped hands, the inscription "Salvá Library," and on one side a "P" and on the other a "V," the initials of your name and of mine, because the project for forming it belongs primarily to you. I will never forget the day you told me you had refused 550 francs that they had offered you for the *Romancero general* of 1614, because you did not want us to let it go until we had another more beautiful copy. So, I gave you the authority to choose the books that most pleased you from among the rare ones we had available to sell; and you took them and made them the foundation of our collection. Moreover, you employed great diligence and knowledge in acquiring the works with which we have enriched it; and you have at times taken responsibility for transforming a volume, making it look beautiful if it was in good condition, or at least making it look decent if it was in bad condition. You would wash it, remove the ink and stains, mend it, add paper to the margins, and even copy the covers and pages that were improperly printed. Our hands should be united here as testimony to the fact that this library is the fruit of our common efforts. They are united as are our two hearts.]

According to this letter, Vicente recognizes in Pedro an appreciation of beautiful books, and he entrusts him with the task of gathering together the finest volumes available and making them the basis of their collection. Pedro is clearly worthy of the undertaking, for not only does he display an ability to restore old books and recreate their original splendor but he also considers monetary gain secondary to the virtues of bibliophilia. As the seal represents, the two men are joined through the books in their collection. Whereas most bibliophiles describe the acquisition of books as an individual enterprise in which they attempt to fashion their personal identities, the Salvás use their books to provide an objective structure to their relationship with each other. On one level, their books function to unite them as partners in trade. Yet their emphasis on quality also endows their shared life with a value that it might otherwise not have had. In this sense books are neither their ultimate goal nor the site of a displaced desire for something other than books, but the means through which they develop and foment their bond as father and son and as friends.

In narratives of bibliophilia, books are often depicted as a connection between members of different generations, and when they are bequeathed from parent to child they can help mitigate the loss experienced by the survivor. Yet Pedro does not actually inherit his father's library, precisely because it was their joint possession from the outset. Although they might have competed with other bookmen in their efforts to assemble their collection, and indeed although their relationships with their peers might have borne all the characteristics of male homosociality typical of traditional male bibliophiles, their relationship with each other, as evidenced by the seal, is one of reciprocity. Unlike the hierarchical relationships of fathers and sons prevalent in patriarchal societies, their relationship is a joining together of equals akin to friendship. As revealed in the prologue to Pedro's *Catálogo*, it in fact takes precedence over their identities as individuals, and ultimately their love for each other supersedes their love of books. If Vicente and Pedro Salvá are examples of Romantic bibliophiles, they thus clearly differ from the stereotype of the bibliomaniac as portrayed in popular nineteenth-century writings on bibliophilia.

In his prologue, Pedro explicitly distinguishes himself from the figure of the bibliomaniac. He recognizes that many of his contemporary bibliophiles are obsessed with certain kinds of books and certain aspects of books, and he cites Thomas Frognall Dibdin's characterization of their proclivities as manifestations of "book madness" (xv). He notes that some purchase volumes only if they are bound in vellum or are very old or very small. He admits that he himself feels compelled to acquire multiple editions of the same works, which he justifies by explaining that his father often found it necessary to consult different versions of a single text in order to create his *Diccionario de la lengua castellana* [Dictionary of the Castilian language]. He also defends his taste for finely bound editions, a penchant he shares with many bibliophiles, arguing that quality binding helps preserve books. He concludes that if his cultivation of bibliophile books might seem extravagant, it is in the final analysis a harmless activity.

What Vicente and Pedro Salvá in fact share with bibliophiles of the Romantic period is their veneration of rare books. Yet in contrast to many Romantic commentaries on bibliophilia (including the portrayals of mad bookmen authored by Dibdin and Nodier), Pedro's discussion of rarity is measured and almost business-like. He begins by enumerating the qualities of rare books, which in his view have nothing to do with their contents. According to his ranking, the rarest are those that are known to have been published but that no longer exist in print form. As examples he cites the *Buscapié* of Cervantes (the literary hoax of Adolfo de Castro); the so-called Limousin Bible, the first Valencian version of the Bible, translated by Bonifacio Ferrer; and the first volume of Rafael Martí de Viciana's *Crónica de la ínclita y coronada ciudad de Valencia y su reyno* [Chronicle of the illustrious and crowned city of Valencia and its kingdom]. The second rarest books are those limited to one or two copies, and the third rarest books are those that only occasionally appear for sale, such as the *Romanceros* and the *Cancioneros*. His other classifications of rarity include books that have been published in limited editions; books printed on vellum or parchment; and books written in Valencian, Basque, and the native languages of the Americas.

According to Pedro, the rarest book is not the sole copy of a specific edition but the book that seems no longer to exist at all. Although a copy of such a book might one day reappear, for the time being it is only imaginary. Whereas the rarity of existing books depends on their relationship to other books in their class, the rarity of a non-existing book is an almost inherent quality, given that a non-existing book is ontologically different from those that do exist. The pursuit of a non-existing book (an absolute akin to the divine in that it seemingly transcends what is particular and finite) might be regarded as the ultimate quest of the Romantic bibliophile. Yet this quest is carried out not only in the bibliophilistic imagination but also through the bibliophile's attention to a multitude of details that existing books make evident.

One aspect of books that fascinates Pedro is the degree to which they have been used. In his view the most desired volumes are those whose pages are uncut and, in particular, those that have never been opened.

> [U]n libro está *sin cortar* o *intonso*, circunstancia muy apreciable para los bibliómanos, cuando el ejemplar se encuentra con todas sus barbas, que *tiene hojas sin cortar*, cuando este hecho prueba que las márgenes son espaciosas por haber profundizado tan poco la cuchilla del encuadernador que ha dejado testimonios de su conciencia (sin duda por esta razón los franceses dicen: *avec témoins*); y por fin, cuando noto que está *sin abrir*, es que todavía conserva las hojas unidas, y por consiguiente mayor evidencia de su belleza. (xx)

> [A book is *uncut*, or *intonso*, a characteristic much appreciated by bibliomaniacs, when the copy has all its rough edges and the *leaves are untrimmed*, and when this fact proves that the margins are spacious because they have been barely penetrated by the blade of the book binder, who usually leaves witnesses of his consciousness (without doubt it is for this reason that the French say *avec témoins* [with witnesses]); and finally, when I note that it is *unopened*, its leaves are still united and it therefore shows even greater evidence of its beauty.][20]

These unopened volumes, whose depiction is evocative of virginity as conceptualized under patriarchy, are only potentially books insofar as they have not actually been employed as such. What is more, their contents, both discursive and visual, can only be imagined. They are thus similar to the non-existing books that Pedro considers the rarest of all. For all intents and purposes, they are unknown, and in the eyes of the Romantic bibliophile they are the most sought after and ultimately the most beautiful.

The Salvás are significant figures in Spanish book history, not only because of their insightful reflections on the cultivation of books but also because of their bibliographies and bookstores, through which they made available to European readers a wide range of Spanish literary and cultural texts. If during the Romantic period British, French, and German bibliophiles regarded Spanish books as exotic objects and Spanish libraries as akin to cabinets of curiosities, through the efforts of the Salvás they came to appreciate more fully the rich literary and cultural traditions of the Peninsula, especially as expressed in the *Romanceros* and *Cancioneros*. Like Dionisio Hidalgo, the Salvás also played a pivotal role in delineating the literary and cultural contours of the Spanish nation and, to a lesser degree, those of non-Castilian linguistic groups seeking to affirm a national identity. Yet their greatest legacy, as in the case of Gallardo and later generations of Spanish bibliophiles, is their heartfelt testimony of their love of books and the example they provide of the power that books hold in the human imagination.

## Dionisio Hidalgo

Dionisio Hidalgo, although less renowned than figures like Gallardo and the Salvás, explicitly reflects on his life as a book dealer, bibliophile, and bibliographer in his brief, autobiographical narrative, "Mi biografía" [My biography].[21] According to this text, Hidalgo regards his activities as a bookman as the natural consequence of his inner inclinations, but he also reveals how the expression of his inclinations is contingent on social class and, in particular, capital. Because of his class, he receives the education necessary to become a reader and the financial resources that allow both the purchase of books, bookstores, and printing presses, as well as the leisure to conduct bibliographical research. Hidalgo's life – he was born into the rural gentry, attended a religious seminary, and eventually became an entrepreneur – in a sense delineates the transition that occurred in nineteenth-century Spain from a society controlled by the Church and aristocracy to one dominated by the interests of an urban, business-oriented middle class. Hidalgo plainly states that the key to success lies in "el trabajo y la firme voluntad de querer" (*Diccionario* xv) [work and the firm will of desire]. He thus affirms the core values of bourgeois individualism. But he also deplores bourgeois life, which in his view hinders him from dedicating himself entirely to books. Based on his experience with ruthless colleagues in the book business, he comes to abhor all business dealings and ultimately seeks refuge in what he imagines to be an idyllic realm of books. Although his attitude might seem indicative of an aristocratic or even religious temperament out of step with the bourgeois world, his effort to catalogue the Hispanic literary tradition is in fact consonant not only with the attempt of the Spanish state to further consolidate its hegemony on the Peninsula but also with the more general, bourgeois production of systems of knowledge intended to foster the advancement of capitalism. Hidalgo's text, a realist portrayal of a professional bibliographer, is hence symptomatic of its times. It also provides a balanced assessment of a life devoted to books that stands in contrast to the many sensational representations of bookmen present in nineteenth- and twentieth-century accounts of bibliophilia and bibliomania.

At the outset of his autobiographical sketch, Hidalgo indicates that his writing will, in keeping with the conventions of bourgeois realism, truthfully and rigorously depict the history of his existence. In addition to satisfying the curiosity of book lovers, it will also achieve a moral end by providing his children with an example of a worthy life. According to the narrative, Hidalgo was born in the town of Medina del Pomar, in the province of Burgos, during the period of the Peninsular War.[22] Because his father possessed a large library, books were always readily available to him, and at an early age he developed a love of reading: "Apenas había yo aprendido a leer cuando brotó naturalmente la afición que siempre me ha dominado, la lectura" (*Diccionario* xii) [I had hardly learned how to read when there naturally sprouted within me the passion that has forever dominated me: reading]. As a youngster, he eschewed childhood games and often shut himself up in his father's study, finding particular pleasure in tales of chivalry. Yet whereas as a child Hidalgo spent long hours reading alone, as an adolescent he frequented the *tertulias*, cafes, and dances of Burgos, and as a result he was regarded with suspicion in the seminary. On one occasion he received what he describes as an excessively harsh and unjust punishment. Afterwards, his parents moved the family to Valladolid, and at his father's behest he entered the university to study law.[23] During this time his love of books grew ever stronger: "Mi afición a leer ... había tomado entonces colosales proporciones" (xiii) [my passion for reading had taken on colossal proportions]. He declares that "los ídolos de [su] cariño [eran] los libros" [the idols of his love were books], and that "[e]l centro de [sus] delicias eran las librerías" (xiii) [the centre of his delights were bookshops]. In bookshops, moreover, he found himself "en [su] propio y natural elemento" (xiii) [in his own, natural element]. Through these comments, typical of nineteenth-century bibliophiles, he implies that his identity as a book lover differed from the identity he was obliged to represent in society as a student of law with a future career as a lawyer. What is more, he believes that this identity as a book lover was his true essence, and that in the right habitat it would flourish.

Hidalgo regards the acquisition and reading of books not merely as acts, freely chosen from a wide range of possibilities, but as the expression of his inner inclinations. His conception of the self thus parallels burgeoning nineteenth-century notions of human nature, especially in the domain of sexuality. In describing his experiences with books, he uses a language that at times seems even sexually coded. Upon seeing books in bookshops, for instance, he would react physically: "palpitaba [su] corazón de pura alegría" [his heart would beat with pure joy]; and when he returned home with a new purchase, he would do so "para devorar[lo], más bien que leer[lo]" [to devour (it), rather than read (it)]. Afterwards, "se revelaba en [su] semblante el contento y la satisfacción" (xiii) [his face would reveal contentment and satisfaction]. Hidalgo, nevertheless, does not interpret his bibliophilia as a displacement of sexual desire, and instead takes it at face value. Noting that his taste in books was encyclopedic and that it spanned both fiction and non-fiction, he concludes: "había nacido indudablemente para ser bibliógrafo" (xiii) [I had undoubtedly been born to be a bibliographer].

After his father died, Hidalgo moved to Madrid to begin his career as a lawyer.[24] While there, he engaged in an explicit act of self-analysis: "[M]e reconcentré dentro de mí mismo, examiné con detención mi carácter, mi genio, mi capacidad y mis inclinaciones" (xiii) [I focused within myself and carefully examined my character, my temperament, my abilities, and my inclinations]. What he discovered was that he had entered a profession "enteramente contraria a [sus] aficiones" (xiii) [completely contrary to his interests]. Despite his father's hopes for him, he was uninterested in law and had neither the temperament nor the capabilities necessary for success in the legal arena. Unlike his father, who had been tenacious in his legal affairs, Hidalgo hoped to avoid conflict with others and valued peace over material gain. He thus made the decision to dedicate his professional life to books and become a bibliographer.[25] Yet as he explains, there existed no clear career path for bibliographers in Spain in the 1830s. Not only did he lack mentors, but he did not come from a family of book dealers, and as a result he had no entrée into the major bookstores and libraries of the day.

Hidalgo made his first foray into the book business in 1838. He and a friend placed a notice in the *Diario de Avisos* announcing their desire to buy private libraries. They were soon approached by the heirs of the Conde de Salazar, who had little interest in books.[26] Hidalgo and his friend purchased the Salazar library, and Hidalgo familiarized himself with the rudiments of bibliography by memorizing the titles in the collection. In 1839 he returned to Medina del Pomar, where he sold his entire patrimony with the aim of using the profits to set up a bookstore specializing in Spanish and foreign editions. He then travelled to Brussels and Paris and fomented relations with book publishers and distributors. While abroad, he learned of the existence in Madrid of a foreign bookstore, founded by Philippe Denné, and of the owner's desire to sell it. In 1840 he purchased the bookstore, moving it from the Calle de Jardines to the Calle de la Montera, number 12, and called it "Denné, Hidalgo y compañía." He kept the name "Denné" in the sign, even though he was the sole owner of the establishment, in order to make known the provenance of the original stock, although he added to it the many books he had brought from Brussels and Paris. After acquiring the shop, also known as the Librería Europea, he considered himself the owner of a treasure so rich that he would not have exchanged it for all of the mines of Potosí (xv). He took special pride in the fact that his was one of the first Spanish and foreign-language bookshops in Spain.

Hidalgo owned the Librería Europea for five years. During this period, he played an important role in the dissemination in Spain of books written in French and other European languages. In 1840 he also launched a journal of bibliography, the *Boletín Bibliográfico Español y Extranjero* [Spanish and foreign bibliographical bulletin], to which he occasionally added catalogues of his own bookstore. Between 1840 and 1850 he published eleven volumes of the *Boletín*. Jean-François Botrel describes it as "notable y justamente famoso" (546) [notable and justly famous], and according to Juan Delgado Casado, it constituted "una auténtica y pionera bibliografía nacional española" (514) [an authentic and pioneering Spanish national bibliography]. Nevertheless, Hidalgo himself laments that while some Spanish bibliophiles and book dealers received it positively, others perceived it as an attack on their fraudulent practices and rejected it. Hidalgo maintains that his work was validated by foreigners but underappreciated and unsupported by his fellow Spaniards: "recibí de los estranjeros varias felicitaciones; de mis compatriotas, ninguna" (*Diccionario* xv) [I received from foreigners various congratulations; from my compatriots, none]. In his view Spaniards of his day were enemies of bibliography, yet they were in fact in dire need of a deeper knowledge of their own bibliographical history.

Hidalgo, nevertheless, felt optimistic about his endeavors, and in 1843 he decided to acquire a printing press and become a publisher. But he was unsuccessful, as he claims, because the persons with whom he associated were either inept or "demasiado listos" (xvi) [too clever]. For this reason he sold his business – first the printing press to two Spaniards and then the bookstore to two French book dealers, Bonnat and Jaymebon, from Bayonne.[27] As his comments reveal, Hidalgo often seems deflated by the actions and attitudes of others:

> [E]l esmero que yo ponía en cumplir religiosamente mis deberes para con los demás, ni era correspondido ni se agradecía siquiera, que se apoderó de mi ánimo el desaliento, y el hastío a los negocios sucedió al calor con que los había emprendido. (xvi)
>
> [The care with which I religiously fulfilled my obligations to others was neither reciprocated nor even welcomed, to such an extent that I felt utterly discouraged, and a boredom with business replaced the passion with which I had undertaken it.]

Although Hidalgo believed that success in business resulted from hard work and determination, he was easily demoralized. What is more, his interest in the book business was tenuous. In fact, his true passion was for bibliography and for the study that the creation of a national bibliography required. For this task he believed that God had given him "la cualidad de la perseverancia para no desmayar, y el esfuerzo de ánimo y robustez de cuerpo para trabajar sin descanso" (xvi) [the quality of perseverance not to lose heart, and the force of mind and strength of body to work tirelessly]. If he failed to accomplish all of his goals as a bibliographer, this was because of "[e]l siglo en que vivimos" (xvi) [the century in which we live], which prevented him from fully committing his life to a vocation that, while in his view necessary, brings no glory or reward. As he remarks, "he tenido necesidad de dedicarme a otras ocupaciones que me proporcionaban lo que no podía esperar en el ejercicio de mi pasión favorita" (xvi) [I have had to dedicate myself to other occupations that provided me with what I could not hope for in the exercise of my favourite passion]. Ultimately, what he blames for his unhappiness is nineteenth-century capitalist culture, as if in an earlier age he would have been free from material concerns and able to devote himself exclusively to books.

To a certain extent, Hidalgo sees himself as endowed with a nobility of spirit that sets him apart from his peers. He further expresses pride in his supposedly ancient and noble lineage and what he regards as an illustrious family reputation that his rivals in the book business have sought to tarnish. His bibliophilia is thus not simply a love of books or an effort to recover for posterity his nation's literary past, but a seemingly aristocratic gesture intended to distinguish himself from his bourgeois contemporaries, even if, given his financial situation and professional activities, he is one of them. Although the Spanish national bibliography constructed in the nineteenth century reinforced the ever-increasing centralization of the Castilian-speaking Spanish state and, by extension, the capitalist system undergirding it, Hidalgo's bibliographical enterprise at times reveals a nostalgia for an older order in which he imagined that an ideal life with books was possible. If the economic conditions of the mid-nineteenth century fostered the flowering of Spanish bibliophilia through the creation of a vast new marketplace of books and book buyers, for bibliophiles like Hidalgo these same conditions threatened to make obsolete a life lived solely for and with books.

Despite Hidalgo's tendency to idealize the past, his writing on bibliophilia is not, ipso facto, conservative, precisely because of his repeated criticism of the economic culture of his period and its negative effect on his personal well-being. In fact, his particular Romantic bibliophilia shares commonalities with what Michael Löwy calls Romantic anti-capitalism. As Löwy sees it, Romantic anti-capitalism, even when backward looking, poses a challenge to the dominant economic and social order: "The essential characteristic of Romantic anti-capitalism is *a thorough critique of modern industrial (bourgeois) civilization* (including the process of production and work) *in the name of certain pre-capitalist social and cultural values*. The reference to a (real or imaginary) past does not necessarily mean that it has a regressive or reactionary orientation: it can be revolutionary as well as conservative" (891). Given his aspirations as a bibliophile and bibliographer, Hidalgo is not interested in carrying out a full-scale critique of his society. But in his reflections on his experience in the book business, he clearly rejects the "domination of (quantitative) exchange-vale, of the cold calculation of price and profit, and the laws of the market" (Löwy 892) that have come to govern the modern commerce of books and book culture. His depiction of bibliophilia thus differs from that of Gallardo and the Salvás, since he intentionally makes visible how its practice is determined by economics and social class.

Although business pulled Hidalgo away from his bibliographical work, he was again drawn back to business activities, not only because of economic exigencies but also a desire not to "permanecer en la inacción, que está reñida con [sus] hábitos y es un peligroso escollo" (*Diccionario* xvii) [remain in inaction, which is at odds with his habits and is a dangerous reef]. For Hidalgo, being inactive does not mean being unemployed but rather unengaged in personally fulfilling activities. The "dangerous reef," therefore, is a kind of psychological malaise. To avoid this state, he returned to business, as if, despite his idealization of the solitary life of the bibliophile, what promised him greatest satisfaction was direct engagement in the social sphere. In late 1852 he moved his entire family to Paris and opened a Spanish-language bookshop, the Librería Universal Española. He also launched *El Comercio: Periódico mensual de la Librería Universal Española* [The trade: Monthly newspaper of the Universal Spanish Bookstore]. As in the past, however, he had difficulties with his business partners, on this occasion two Carlists who had sought to join resources with him in the bookstore but who ultimately defrauded him of his money, leaving him empty handed.

Hidalgo's Paris debacle not only caused him to reject business permanently but also led him to an experience of misanthropy. Nevertheless, after spending a summer recuperating on one of his wife's farms near Burgos, he returned to Madrid, and in 1855 friends helped him secure a position in the Ministry of Public Works and Transport. His duties in this new job were light, and as a consequence he was able to resume his bibliographical work. In 1857 he joined Carlos Bailly-Baillière to produce *El Bibliógrafo* [The bibliographer], in which they included works that had appeared since the suspension of the *Boletín Bibliográfico Español y Extranjero* at the beginning of the decade.[28] Between 1857 and 1859 they published three volumes of *El Bibliógrafo*. In 1859, Bailly-Baillière decided to terminate *El Bibliógrafo*, and Hidalgo re-launched the *Boletín* under the modified title, *Boletín Bibliográfico Español* [Spanish bibliographical bulletin]. At the time of the completion of his autobiography in 1864 he had brought out four volumes of the *Boletín Bibliográfico Español*. He had also begun to publish his *Diccionario general de bibliografía española* [General dictionary of Spanish bibliography].[29]

In the prospectus for the *Boletín Bibliográfico Español*, Hidalgo explains that Spain lacks a fully developed and methodically ordered bibliography. What the nation requires, and what he aims to provide through the *Boletín*, is a regularly published periodical that will list all of the Spanish books, pamphlets, and newspapers as they appear on the market in addition to books from the Spanish past. The *Boletín* will therefore typically include sections for new Spanish publications, Spanish works from the seventeenth and eighteenth centuries, and Spanish works prior to the seventeenth century, as well as foreign works, engravings, lithographs, maps, music, and announcements. Hidalgo argues that because of the absence of a rigorous and comprehensive bibliography, Spain has been held in low esteem by other European nations that measure the value of a civilization precisely by its literary and cultural accomplishments. The creation of a proper bibliography is thus a patriotic endeavor that will place Spain on the level of other European countries and give proof to the entire world that Spaniards are not as "atrasados en las ciencias, la literatura y las artes como se cree generalmente" (*Boletín* 1: 1) [backwards in the sciences, literature, and arts as is generally believed]. Hidalgo's comments on the subject of bibliography are significant, for they suggest that the development of a Spanish and specifically Castilian-language bibliography in the nineteenth century was not only an affirmation and assertion of Castilian-language writing but also a defensive reaction by those identified with the Spanish state to a European perception of Spain as culturally deficient. Although for Hidalgo this perception was unjustified, given what he describes as "la gloria de nuestra patria" (*Boletín* 1: np) [the glory of our fatherland], in his view Spaniards were responsible for the situation because they had failed to cultivate the science of bibliography.

In the prologue to the first volume of his *Diccionario*, Hidalgo explains that he differs from most bibliographers of his time, who believe that a proper bibliographical entry should include extensive biographical information on the author and critical commentary on the text. Rather than biography or criticism, Hidalgo wants to provide his readers with "los productos del genio del hombre" (vii) [the products of man's genius], not through a discussion of their literary or scientific merits, which are subject to "diferentes y encontradas opiniones de los hombres" (viii) [differing and conflicting opinions of men], but through a description of "las condiciones materiales del libro] (viii) [the material conditions of the book]. His goal is to assist readers in identifying and locating books either for consultation or acquisition. As Delgado Casado points out, Hidalgo's bibliographies are thus more similar to twentieth-century bibliographies than to those of his peers, whose works, according to Fernández Sánchez, are for all intents and purposes "bio-bibliografías, con abundantes digresiones" (199) [bio-bibliographies, with abundant digressions]. In nineteenth-century Spain, bibliographical writing was typically regarded as a form of literary criticism, which Menéndez Pelayo describes as "juicio *estético* y ... apreciación *histórica*" ("De re" 66) [*aesthetic* judgment and *historical* appreciation]. Menéndez Pelayo insists that "la crítica ha de ser la primera condición del bibliógrafo" [criticism must be the first concern of the bibliographer], and he bemoans the tendency of some practitioners of the period to focus solely on "los accidentes externos del libro" (66) [the external accidents of the book]. In his view,

> [P]roduce ciertamente triste impresión la lectura de muchos catálogos bibliográficos, cuyos autores para nada parecen haber tenido en cuenta el valor intrínseco de los libros, fijándose sólo en insignificantes pormenores propios más de un librero que de un erudito. (66)
>
> [Reading many bibliographical catalogues leaves a very sad impression, since the authors seem not to have taken into account at all the intrinsic value of books, focusing solely on insignificant details in a way more typical of a book dealer than a scholar.]

For Menéndez Pelayo, such bibliographers are nothing more than "acarreadores y faquines de la república de las letras" (67) [bearers and porters of the Republic of Letters].[30] Nonetheless, he speaks quite favourably of Hidalgo, and affirms that he has done much to advance nineteenth-century Spanish bibliography (68). Although Hidalgo was not of the old school of "bio-bibliographers," his bibliographies were in fact more informative and useful to many readers. For this reason, Fernández Sánchez concludes that he was Spain's first professional bibliographer (200).[31]

In contrast to Fernández Sánchez, Delgado Casado goes so far as to assert that Hidalgo was exclusively a bibliographer: "No investigador, amante de los libros, bibliotecario, bibliófilo o librero; exactamente bibliógrafo" (512) [Not a researcher, a lover of books, a librarian, a bibliophile, or a bookman; but specifically a bibliographer]. To be sure,

Hidalgo's ultimate vocation was bibliography. Yet his autobiographical narrative also reveals a deep-seated bibliophilia, evident in his recollections of the libraries and bookshops of his youth, and his passion for bibliography is in fact an expression of it. Like bibliophiles, he is most interested in the material conditions of books (their physical properties as well as the details of their publication, provenance, and location) rather than what is conventionally understood as their content. What is more, through his bibliographical lists he generates an immense collection of books in schematic form, in which the number of volumes catalogued ultimately takes precedence over reading, or at least reading in any in-depth fashion. Hidalgo's bibliophilia in a sense even borders on bibliomania: he is an insatiable collector of titles, and his goal, through documentation, is nothing less than the gathering together of the entire Hispanic print tradition.

Hidalgo concludes his autobiographical narrative by expressing satisfaction with the life he has led thus far as a bibliographer, although he notes that despite his appeal that greater attention be paid to bibliography, "todos [lo] han oído con la más glacial indiferencia" (*Diccionario* xviii) [everyone has heard him with the most glacial indifference]. Nevertheless, when he died on 11 October 1866, he left behind a considerable corpus of bibliographical material. In addition to his early bibliographical publications, he edited all of the issues of the *Boletín Bibliográfico Español* contained in the first six and a half volumes of the journal, and he published the first volume of his *Diccionario*.[32] He expresses contentment that through this work he has been able to offer his services to the nation, and he maintains that he has done "lo que hasta ahora no [ve] que nadie haya realizado, porque falta comunmente entusiasmo y laboriosidad" (xviii) [what until now he sees that no one has achieved, because of a typical lack of enthusiasm and dedication]. By devoting himself to bibliographical work he believes that he has fulfilled the mission for which he came into the world, and he has spent what he regards as the most valuable part of his life classifying and ordering books. His experience as a bibliographer has thus been similar to that of a librarian, if not a national librarian.

In *The Library at Night*, Alberto Manguel argues that a national library is often conceived of as a means through which a society achieves a sense of national identity and collective self-definition (294). As Hidalgo imagines it, a national bibliography performs an analogous function. Although it does not make available the discursive content of printed texts, it makes visible the contours of national identity through its guide to a nation's books. The national identity traced through Hidalgo's bibliographies is almost exclusively Castilian-speaking, even if it draws into its scope works written in other Iberian and European languages. It encompasses all fields of human knowledge, but it emphasizes those regarded as distinctively Hispanic, including literary, historical, philosophical, and religious writings from nineteenth-century Spain and the Spanish Middle Ages and Golden Age. For Hidalgo, this ever-evolving bibliographical corpus would provide the foundations of a Spanish national identity as well as his own sense of self. Whereas most bibliophiles forge their identities through the acquisition of books, Hidalgo constructs his through a nationalist enterprise that transforms him into an arbiter of the Spanish national heritage. To be sure, his mission has been to write a national bibliography. Yet given his youthful craving to devour books and thereby incorporate them into himself, his objective has also been to realize the identity of ideal bookman towards which his inclinations have always pointed him. At the end of his autobiography Hidalgo seems assured that he has attained his goals. He has written the Spanish bibliography he dreamed of, and he now enjoys the "recompensa [que] ... nadie puede arrebatar[le]" (*Diccionario* xviii) [the reward that no one can take away from him].

**Azorín**

Azorín was a consummate bibliophile and, of all the writers of early twentieth-century Spain, the one who wrote most extensively on the subject of bibliophilia and the role of books in private life and the life of his generation. An iconic member of the Generation of '98, Azorín produced literary texts that have often been regarded as representative of the cultural crisis that Spanish intellectuals experienced during their country's transition to full modernity. Over the past 100 years his texts have been continually republished and taught in Spanish literature programs throughout the world. Azorín's writings on books, however, have received less critical attention, perhaps because many of them appeared in periodical form in newspapers in Spain and Argentina and have rarely been reprinted.[33] This is a glaring editorial lacuna given that Azorín, according to Roberta Johnson, considered himself first and foremost a journalist (19). In response to this omission, in 2014 Francisco Fuster García published a compilation of Azorín's most significant commentaries on books, some of which had not been available to readers for decades. This volume, *Libros, buquinistas y bibliotecas: Crónicas de un transeúnte: Madrid-París* [Books, used-book dealers, and libraries: Chronicles of a passerby: Madrid-Paris], along with other texts of Azorín, including *Un pueblecito: Riofrío de Ávila* [A little town: Riofrío de Ávila], provide insight into his conception of books; but they also, as Andrés Trapiello remarks in his prologue to Fuster García's collection, constitute a veritable self-portrait of Azorín as bibliophile (Azorín, *Libros* 6).[34]

In his introduction to Azorín's writings on books, Fuster García cites a passage in which Azorín explains how books can operate as a substitute for life. They do so in two ways: by "interposición," that is, by positioning themselves between reality and our experience of reality, and by "suplementación," that is, by supplanting our personality and leading us to see ourselves differently from the person we are (Azorín, *Libros* 11). Both of these processes relate to texts, or the discourses encountered in books through the act of reading. In his lifelong meditation on books Azorín typically focuses on the function of discourse and the consequences of reading. But he also ponders the nature of books as material objects and their role in his life as a bibliophile. As he suggests, material books do not necessarily alter his perception of reality but rather draw him into deeper contact with things, with others, and with himself. In fact, there is a tension in Azorín's writings about books. At times he reveals an explicit desire to escape from books and a contemplative life of reading in order to engage more directly with the world. Yet to a certain extent his engagement with the world occurs precisely through his relationship with books, not only as a reader but also as a seeker of print matter. His quest for books is a quest for life, and through his continual forays into bookshops, bookstalls, and libraries, he discovers a more authentic self – not an essentialized identity that readers often discern in his literary portrayals of eternal return, but rather a sense of freedom that is a wellspring of happiness as well as a means of experiencing a bond of commonality with his fellow human beings.

Azorín never fully dissociates his love of books from a love of reading, and in a fashion typical of traditional commentators of bibliophilia he maintains that true bibliophiles read, whereas false ones merely collect (*Libros* 151). Thus, despite his attraction to bound volumes he privileges ideas over matter: "por encima de la materia, están las ideas" (36) [above matter, are ideas]. In his reflections on book production he exalts printing above other trades and envisions both typographers and writers as practitioners of a sacred art and members of a kind of priesthood: "Que haya siempre en las artes del escribir y del imprimir el pensamiento de un sacerdocio" (37) [May there always be in the arts of writing and printing the notion of a priesthood]. Through their craft, typographers perform an act of transubstantiation, transmitting to the printed page "la niebla sutil del pensamiento" (37) [the subtle mist of thought], and thereby giving physical expression to the transcendent.[35] Yet not only do they make manifest a transcendent reality, but they also save it from oblivion, and as a consequence of their efforts "[n]ada se pierde en el Universo" (37) [nothing in the universe is lost]. The upshot is that without typographers and, by extension, the myriad of human agents whose work brings books into being, something potential in the universe would remain unrealized and ultimately cease to exist. This fear of loss – resulting perhaps from an intuition of mortality at the heart of all creative enterprises – informs much of the modern discourse of bibliophilia and imbues it with a nostalgic and wistful tenor. In Azorín's writing, however, the depiction of bibliophilia is more often than not filled with positive emotion and a sensation of peaceful excitement.

In his reflections on bibliophilia, Azorín criticizes Spanish attitudes towards books, arguing that, in contrast to the French and other national groups, Spaniards are not prolific readers. Nor are Spanish publishers particularly interested in books as works of art. The creation of fine books, he maintains, requires a knowledge of architecture and painting (45). It therefore depends not only on printers but also painters, sketch artists, and decorators, whose goal is to render something beautiful, original, and different from other already existing books. As Azorín sarcastically remarks, the art of books is far removed from the world of the typical Spanish publisher, who is satisfied to "cargar un carro de papel y enviarlo a la imprenta" (45) [load up a cart with paper and send it off to the press]. Azorín in fact blames Spanish publishers for not fomenting in Spain a greater connoisseurship of books. But he also expresses dismay at what he perceives to be a more widespread decline in the book arts: "El arte, tan sencillo, tan bello, de colocar trazos negros en una página blanca – de colocarlos armoniosamente – está en sus postrimerías" (144) [The art, so simple and so beautiful, of placing black marks on a white page – and of placing them harmoniously – is in its dying days]. What is significant in these observations is that Azorín ultimately envisions books as aesthetic objects with a beauty independent of their discursive content. This is not surprising, given his own creative expression, which numerous scholars have compared to the visual arts, and specifically the plasticity of his distinctive prose style, which Gayana Jurkevich rightly characterizes as painterly ("A Poetics" 284).

Despite the aesthetic dimension of the material book, Azorín devotes a large portion of his discussion of bibliophilia to the subject of reading. In his view, the books we read in youth profoundly alter the way we see the world in later life: "Y así las cosas, esas cosas que nosotros hemos conocido y palpado en nuestra niñez, tendrán ahora, en la edad madura, lo que sin eso no tendrían" (*Libros* 81) [And so things, those things that we knew and touched in our childhood, will now have, in our mature age, something that they would not otherwise have had].[36] Reading, nevertheless, affects not only our perception of the world but also the world itself in its ontological nature.

> Las cosas por sí valen poco; las cosas no son más que las cosas. Les hace falta, para vivir, tener ambiente espiritual. Sin ese ambiente, sin esa sutil atmósfera, las cosas no son nada. Y la atmósfera espiritual de las cosas la dan los pensamientos que los libros hacen nacer en nosotros; pensamientos acerca de nuestro destino, acerca de la muerte, acerca de nuestra situación en el Universo. Ése es el ambiente moral que da precio a las cosas. Unas páginas de alguno de los libros que yo quisiera ver en todas las bibliotecas infantiles, unas páginas de fray Luis de Granada o del otro fray Luis, hacen, como si fueran un fulminante, que las cosas adquieran de pronto una profunda significación que antes no tenían. Hacen que las cosas sean las cosas. (81)

> [Things in themselves are worth little; things are no more than things. They lack the spiritual atmosphere necessary to live. Without this atmosphere, without this subtle aura, things are nothing. And the spiritual aura of things is given to them by the thoughts that books bring to life in us; thoughts about our destiny, about death, about our place in the universe. This is the moral atmosphere that gives value to things. The pages of some of the books I would like to see in all children's libraries, pages from Fray Luis de Granada or the other Fray Luis, act as if they were detonators, and through them things immediately acquire a profound meaning that they did not have before. They make things be things.]

In this passage, Azorín initially suggests that things in themselves are no more than brute objects. But he then declares that until readers endow them with a quality of spirit or thought derived from reading, they are nothing. In so doing, he not only privileges ideas over matter but actually implies that matter exists only insofar as it is known. In his view, humans thus seem to be the ultimate creators of both meaning and being. Through human agency, and more specifically through acts of perception made possible by reading, things paradoxically become what they are.

At first glance Azorín's comments on reading might appear radically idealistic. As E. Inman Fox remarks, Azorín's writing is filled with descriptions of the things that he encounters in his personal and social milieu; however, what he actually portrays are not things in themselves but ideas about things that he has internalized through reading. Fox therefore concludes that Azorín's art is fundamentally "anti-realista y anti-realidad" ("Azorín" 22) [anti-realist and anti-reality].[37] Azorín's comments on reading might also seem elitist, for a potential corollary is that those who do not or cannot read are unable to discern reality with nuance or possibly even know the world at all. Yet elsewhere in his reflections on books Azorín advances an entirely different position, asserting that those who do not read are more directly engaged with reality than those who do. What is more, he does not base his depictions of material books on images of them contained in other books, or how he might have imagined them while reading books about books, but rather on his own direct experience as a bibliophile.

In one essay on reading, Azorín identifies three levels or degrees of culture. The first is achieved through reading many books, the second through reading only a few, and the third through things themselves. In this context, he argues that those who do not read or who are illiterate often have a deeper understanding of the world than do the most erudite scholars (191). What we should study, then, are not books but life itself: "[S]abemos que ni los libros ni la ciencia nos enseñarán nunca el misterio de las cosas" (190) [We know that neither books nor science will ever teach us the mystery of things]. If reading is not the prerequisite of knowledge, then we must, as Arthur Schopenhauer put it, learn the art of not reading, or at least the art of reading more judiciously, as we approach death and our time in the world grows ever shorter (Azorín, *Libros* 119).

Azorín, nevertheless, has tremendous difficulty not reading. In one moment, he wants to flee books, but in another he is drawn inexorably back to them. He gives the example of going to a house in the Valencian countryside in the hope of spending a long period of time not reading.

> Huimos, por unos días, de la vorágine ciudadana y del acoso de los libros. Los libros llenan allá nuestra estancia. Los libros son como un bebedizo embriagador que nos enajena e impide la visión directa de la vida. Ahora aquí, en la soledad y en la esquivez, vamos a prescindir de la lectura y a contemplar, de día, las montañas, los árboles, la fuente que fluye. ... No vamos a leer. (*Libros* 219)
>
> [We fled, for several days, from the vortex of the city and from the assault of books. Books fill our room there. Books are like an intoxicating potion that distracts us and impedes our direct vision of life. Here now, in solitude and seclusion, we will dispense with reading and contemplate, by day, the mountains, the trees, the spring that flows. ... We will not read.]

Regardless of his best intentions, Azorín's desire for books remains overwhelming, and he begins to search the house for something to read, furtively opening a locked cupboard, like a curious child or a criminal about to commit a crime (220). Inside, he discovers "un libro encuadernado en pergamino" [a book bound in parchment]. He then muses: "Está en nuestras manos nuestro enemigo. ¿De veras enemigo? Si es enemigo, ¿por qué, sin querer, lo acariciamos tanto?" (221) [Our enemy is in our hands. Is it really our enemy? And if it is an enemy, then why, without wanting to, do we caress it so much?]. Although Azorín is delighted to read the text, *David perseguido* [David pursued], by Cristóbal Lozano, what initially enthralls him is the physical aspect of the volume. As in so many narratives of bibliophilistic desire, he seemingly makes the material book the object of deeper longings – be they longings for an ontological or spiritual fulfillment, or longings of a more personal nature that he might not fully recognize or even want to acknowledge: "El proceso psicológico desde el hallazgo del libro hasta su lectura, por la noche a la luz de un velón, dulce luz de aceite, sería largo de contar" (221) [The psychological process from finding the book to reading it, by night in the light of an oil lamp – sweet oil light – would take long to tell].

What is most intriguing in this anecdote is not the possible motivation behind Azorín's desire for books but rather the way a particular book brings him into intimate contact with the world and others. The book is in fact the focal point of the entire scene and the object around which all the other elements of the description are organized – the country fields, the night sky, the house, the furniture, and the items stored in the cabinet, with their musty odours and memories of the past. It also reminds Azorín of all the hands that once touched these things. Yet despite the book's over-determining presence, there is something absent in the description, for although we see in our mind's eye "un libro encuadernado en pergamino," we do not experience what Azorín himself experiences "en el proceso" [in the process]: the colours, textures, and scents of the pages and binding that fill his senses even before he begins to read. Azorín's narrative thus suggests that not everything is reducible to discourse and that our ideas about reality do not completely delimit our experience of it. Indeed, what is lived most profoundly seems precisely to be that which is not said.

In many of his commentaries on reading, Azorín reiterates the notion that books are inescapable, and in *Un pueblecito*, in an apostrophe directed to the eighteenth-century clerical writer Jacinto Bejarano Galavis y Nidos, he actually compares them to a prison.

> Leer: ése es nuestro sino. Tú crees que las montañas, esas montañas de Ávila que te cierran el paso, son las que te tienen aprisionado. ¡Ah no, querido Galavis! La prisión es mucho más terrible. La prisión es nuestra

> modalidad intelectual; es nuestra inteligencia; son los libros. ... De los libros somos prisioneros todos nosotros. Vivimos con ellos en comunión íntima y constante; a ellos amoldamos nuestro espíritu; sobre ellos fabricamos nuestros amores, nuestros odios, nuestras fantasías, nuestras esperanzas; un ambiente especial nos envuelve con nuestros libros. ... Y un día, cuando queremos romper este ambiente y esta marcha de nuestra vida; cuando queremos lanzarnos a gozar de otros aspectos del mundo, de otros distintos sabores de las cosas, vemos que no podemos. (593)

> [Reading: that is our destiny. You think that the mountains, those mountains of Ávila that block your path, are what keeps you imprisoned. Oh, no, dear Galavis! The prison is much more terrible. The prison is our intellectual condition; it is our intelligence, it is books. ... We are all prisoners of books. We live with them in intimate and constant communion; we mould our spirit to them; from books we construct our loves, our hatreds, our fantasies, our hopes; a special atmosphere envelops us through our books. ... And one day, when we want to break through this atmosphere and the course of our lives; when we want to launch out and enjoy other aspects of the world and savor things differently, we find that we cannot.]

This special atmosphere, which elsewhere, according to Azorín, endows reality with meaning and brings it to life, is not merely a "bebedizo embriagador" but, like the waters of Lethe in ancient Greek mythology, something that functions ultimately to conceal the world from us. The fact that we have been moulded through our reading makes the task of seeing beyond books all the more difficult. Not only is our way of perceiving the world constructed through books, but so too are we ourselves.

Azorín's life with books is nevertheless not always portrayed as problematic – and even when it seems most fraught, it is depicted with fondness insofar as he clearly loves the books that he also feels constrain him. What is more, his experience as a reader is not entirely the same as his experience as a bibliophile. In his reflections on bibliophilia he comments on bibliophiles who regard book collecting as a sport as well as those who have a mania for books and are drawn to them in the way that an alcoholic is drawn to drink. In describing this type of bibliophile, he begins by identifying the writer, Pío Baroja, as having caught the virus of bibliophilia. But he subtly draws himself into the portrait.[38]

> Ya a ciertas alturas, el libro llega a ser lo que el alcohol [es] para el beodo; no se puede salir de casa sin volver llevando consigo un volumen; no podemos pasar por delante de un puestecillo o de una librería, sin ponernos incontinenti a revolver libracos y echar mano enseguida a

> la faltriquera. ¡Terrible pasión! Luego, ya nuestro el volumen, hojeado ligeramente, pierde su encanto. Y ya estamos pensando en otro que esta mañana, o ayer, o hace dos días, hemos visto en tal tienda. (*Libros* 115)
>
> [At a certain stage of the game, the book becomes what alcohol is for the drunkard; one cannot leave the house without bringing back a volume; we cannot pass in front of a little stall or bookshop without losing all control and rummaging through the old tomes and immediately reaching into our pocket. What a terrible passion! Then, after the volume is ours and we have leafed through it a bit, it loses its charm. For we are already thinking of another that this morning or yesterday or two days ago we saw in some store.]

This figure is like the bibliomaniac, the Don Juan of book lovers, whose greatest pleasure is the act of acquiring the desired book, not the book itself.

In articulating his theory of bibliophilia Azorín posits three classes of bibliophiles. The first consists of connoisseurs who desire incunabula, deluxe editions, and rare and unique copies of books. They pay large sums of money, but they seldom read what they purchase. The second category of bibliophiles is comprised of individuals who buy more modest, contemporary editions of literary classics with the specific aim of reading them. The third group, in contrast, intentionally seeks out books by second rank or totally unknown writers. These bibliophiles, with whom Azorín most closely identifies, are drawn to the works of lesser-known authors precisely because they are more likely to contain "el verdadero espíritu de un pueblo" (111) [the true spirit of a people]. For Azorín, the ideal book is thus not the most finely crafted or erudite volume but the one that makes him feel most bonded with others. Moreover, his sense of connectedness is achieved not only through reading but also through contact with the materiality of print matter itself. In reflecting on the materials that arrive daily in his mail, he experiences a quiet joy while pondering the sites of their origin.

> Todos los días, a una hora misma, sobre nuestra mesa de trabajo sea depositado un paquete denso de cartas, periódicos, libros, revistas. Libros y revistas que exhalen el grato olor a tinta reciente. Castilla y Europa. (Vasconia y Europa; Cataluña y Europa.) (*Un pueblecito* 533)
>
> [Every day, at the same hour, a dense packet of letters, newspapers, books, and magazines is deposited on our work table. Books and magazines that exude the pleasant odour of fresh ink. Castile and Europe. (The Basque Country and Europe; Catalonia and Europe.)]

In another essay Azorín distinguishes between bibliophiles not by the kind of books they read but by the way they read. Whereas some bibliophiles read in order to learn, and thus choose their books according to a certain project of study, others read merely for pleasure and are more spontaneous in their selections: "Y el lector, el lector libre, el lector caprichoso, lo que desea es leer entregándose al libro, leer desinteresadamente, leer sin propósito de aprender nada" (83) [And the reader, the free reader, the fanciful reader, what he desires is to read by surrendering himself entirely to the book, to read disinterestedly, to read without intending to learn anything]. Azorín calls these book lovers "bibliófilos andariegos" [wandering bibliophiles], "bibliófilos callejeros" [roaming bibliophiles], "bibliófilos aventureros" [adventurous bibliophiles], and "bibliófilos ocasionales" (83–5) [occasional bibliophiles]. They know all the particularities of their books, including their origins and histories, just as, according to Azorín, peasants know the location of the best sources of water for irrigating their fields. They therefore seem to grasp something essential about books that most readers miss. Although they might be avid readers themselves, their relationship with books is ultimately not intellectual but visceral.

In describing what he considers the ideal bibliophile, Azorín highlights the total perception that bibliophiles have of material books.

> [Este] bibliófilo vive intensa y amorosamente con sus libros. Las manos, los ojos, el olfato y el intelecto se hacen una piña con el volumen. El fluido nervioso del bibliófilo impregna las páginas del libro. Lleva este bibliófilo el volumen en el bolsillo y lo va apretando amorosamente contra su persona. El libro así tratado, así querido, debe sentirse también solidaridad con su dueño. (84)

> [This bibliophile lives intensely and lovingly with his books. Hands, eyes, smell, and intellect join together with the volume. The nervous fluid of the bibliophile impregnates the pages of the book. This bibliophile carries the volume in his pocket, and presses it lovingly against his body. The book, when treated and loved like this, must also feel solidarity with its owner.]

Azorín's bibliophiles read their books, but they also approach them through senses not typically associated with reading, such as smell and touch. (Indeed, they are at times like readers of braille, since they do not rely entirely on the sense of sight to perceive books.) To the extent that they employ the body, the mind, and the senses in their experience of books, they are capable of new and richer kinds of knowledge. In a manner reminiscent of Góngora and the surrealists, for example, they discover that even "[l]a humedad o la sequedad del libro tienen sus colores especiales" (84) [the dampness or dryness of the book have their own special colours]. What is most noteworthy, however, is the bonding that occurs between bibliophiles and books. According to the metaphor of impregnation, bibliophiles give something of their essence to material books, and as a result books come to life and become aware of their human proprietors. This occurs not when bibliophiles read but rather when they apprehend books in their totality. In this passage Azorín actually goes further than when he suggests that we re-envision and transform reality by endowing it with ideas we derive from reading. Here, a metamorphosis takes place through an almost physical osmosis between bibliophiles and books.

Azorín in fact depicts the book as a living creature ("cual si fuera [un] organismo vivo" [91] [as if it were a living organism]). In so doing, he expresses a secularized image of the so-called living book, or sacred scripture of Christian tradition. He also reiterates the more commonplace notion of the book as a friend or companion. Our most immediate and most likely reaction to these views of books is to interpret them metaphorically: the book is not a living organism, but we often treat it as if it were. Yet Azorín reveals an intriguing intuition, not that books are literally alive or have some spiritual or transcendental essence, but rather that the duality we typically distinguish between humans and things is illusory. Both humans and things are composed of the same basic elements, and on the physical level our relationship with material reality is grounded not in difference but similarity. Because we interact with books in multiple ways (through "[l]as manos, los ojos, el olfato y el intelecto"), books are thus the locus of one of our most textured experiences of things.

If books, as Azorín has said, can be obstacles that isolate us from the world, they are nevertheless part of the world itself. Reading should thus be undertaken not only as a way of knowing the world but also as a way of being in the world. Through a more visceral interaction with books, readers can achieve a richer appreciation of reality as well as a heightened consciousness of their own freedom. Although passive readers often find their identities and perspectives "supplanted" by those that they encounter when reading, Azorín's bibliophiles experience their greatest authenticity and happiness when cultivating books. As an example, he describes a bibliophile for whom "[l]a lectura ... era ... algo más que una simple lectura: había *sentido* el libro; había vivido con él" (159) [reading ... was ... something more than a simple act of reading: he had *felt* the book; he had lived with it]. In fact, many of the volumes in this bibliophile's possession were tattered and broken, yet his life was bound up with them in an intimate and heartfelt way. One day he inherited a small but magnificent library of deluxe editions of learned works that he could never have afforded. But instead of joy at his windfall, he felt a vague sadness.

> Aquellos libros espléndidos no eran los que le habían acompañado durante toda su vida. Los otros, los vagabundos, los callejeros, representaban para él la libertad, la independencia de espíritu, la sensibilidad espontánea y viva. (159)

> [Those splendid books were not the ones that had accompanied him throughout his entire life. The other ones, the vagabond books, the street books, represented for him freedom, an independence of spirit, and a sense of spontaneity and life.]

Because of their form and content, the books in his new library seemed immovable, solemn, and dogmatic, whereas his old ones reminded him of a life that he longed to recover.

> Y lentamente, sin poderlo remediar, el buen bibliófilo volvía las espaldas a sus espléndidos libros y se encaminaba a los puestecillos de las ferias en busca del volumen aventurero. (160)

> [And slowly, without being able to help it, the good bibliophile turned his back on his splendid books and headed for the little stalls of the book fairs in search of the adventurous volume.]

For this bibliophile, not only was the procurement of a new volume an experience of freedom but the book itself, precisely because of its ordinariness, made him feel bonded with a greater swath of humanity than did the erudite editions in his inherited collection.

According to Azorín, the freedom of bibliophiles is expressed through their acquisition of books and reflected back to them through their personal libraries.[39] In formal libraries managed by the state and Church (and indeed in many private libraries) books are arranged in terms of established categories of knowledge. Yet as Azorín recognizes, this affects the meanings that the discourses of books convey. Although readers might be inclined to regard individual books as discrete sites of meaning, Azorín suggests that meaning arises through an interplay of discourses within a given space. In formal collections this space is demarcated by the way books are organized on shelves and juxtaposed with one another. The potential meanings generated through reading are thus determined by the overarching logic of the library. Whereas in formal libraries "[l]a seriedad se impone a todo" (82) [seriousness is imposed on everything], in the libraries of Azorín's ideal bibliophiles the randomly ordered books remain "traviesos, arriscados, desenvueltos" (82) [playful, spirited, free], like the bibliophiles themselves.

More often than not, Azorín's ideal bibliophiles discover their books by accident and purchase them without any specific plan of reading in mind. Once they take them home, they place them on their shelves haphazardly.

> En el extremo opuesto de sabios almacenes de libros se hallan las bibliotecas reducidas y formadas al azar. Nada en ellas es sistemático. Ni siquiera existe catálogo de los libros que en sus anaqueles reposan. Los libros han ido viniendo aquí por casualidad. El dueño de la biblioteca es un bibliófilo andariego que a lo largo de su vida ha ido reuniendo unos millares de volúmenes. (83)
>
> [At the extreme opposite of wise warehouses of books are to be found the more modest libraries formed by chance. Nothing in them is systematic. There is not even a catalogue of the books that rest on their shelves. The books have come here by accident. The owner of the library is a wandering bibliophile, who throughout his life has been gathering thousands of volumes.]

This wandering bibliophile, a seemingly casual yet intense reader, collector, and guardian of books, is the clearest self-portrait of Azorín himself. As Johnson indicates, Azorín was methodical in his own reading habits and took careful notes in the margins and front and back covers of his books (18). Yet his method of acquiring books was more often than not spontaneous. According to Checa Cremades, Azorín was in fact a *bouquineur*, or casual browser of bookshops, and his bibliophilia was "ante todo una bibliofilia no premeditada[,] ... una bibliofilia sin programa" ("Azorín" 336) [above all an unpremeditated bibliophilia, ... a bibliophilia without a program].[40]

Azorín's criticism of formal libraries extends to specific institutions, including the national libraries of both Spain and France. In a satirical piece, he describes the bureaucracy of the Biblioteca Nacional de España and what he considers the excessive amount of paperwork that patrons must complete in order to gain access to books (*Libros* 69–72). He also bemoans the fact that patrons are prohibited from reading items they take into the library, and he cites with bemused surprise an occasion when he was actually told he was not allowed to read his newspaper there. Just as Azorín finds certain libraries inimical to reading, so too does he disparage library catalogues. In his view, library catalogues represent order, discipline, and authority, and they are anathema to the "ameno vagabundeo" (151) [pleasant wandering] of true bibliophiles.

He reiterates his conviction that true bibliophiles would never have catalogues of their own libraries, although he does experience pleasure in reading bibliographies as a way of apprising himself of the existence and contents of books (200–4). Reading bibliographies might seem like a substitute for reading books, but bibliographies are in fact printed volumes (Azorín cites Manuel F. Miguélez's *Catálogo de los códices españoles de la Biblioteca de El Escorial* [Catalogue of the Spanish codices of the Library of the Escorial], which totals over several hundred pages), and through them bibliophiles can also express their love of books.[41]

In one of his most nuanced reflections on bibliophilia, Azorín depicts the annual book fair of Madrid, at a time when it took place on the Paseo del Prado, next to the Botanical Garden. As if commenting on a painting, he invites his readers to contemplate the various components of the setting. Although he mentions books only briefly, he integrates them into a larger, natural landscape, and in so doing uses them to crystallize his entire philosophical worldview.

> A los viejos libros madrileños del otoño, se asocian los centenarios cipreses del Jardín Botánico y la perspectiva luminosa, infinita, de la llanura manchega. Vamos caminando, por el Botánico abajo, en busca de los libros. Contemplamos las bellas fuentes que están puestas a mitad del paseo. El agua cae en un fleco deshilachado de las anchas tazas; cae el agua dulcemente, como sin querer; cae como los días de nuestra vida; la verán caer otros paseantes que en otros tiempos se dirijan, igual que nosotros, en busca de un volumen viejo; la han visto caer otros hombres, en lo pretérito, cuyos afanes, cuyos dolores, cuyas alegrías, se han disuelto ya en la lejanía. (*Un pueblecito* 531–2)

> [We associate the old Madrid books of autumn with the century-old cypresses in the Botanical Garden and the luminous and infinite panorama of the Manchegan plain. We go walking, down along the Botanical Garden, in search of books. We contemplate the beautiful fountains located in the middle of the paseo. The water falls from the wide cisterns, like frayed threads of fabric; the water falls sweetly and as if inadvertently; it falls like the days of our lives; it will be seen by other passersby, who in other times will set out like us in search of an old volume; it was seen falling by other men in the past, whose ambitions, sorrows, and joys have now dissolved into the distance.]

In this scene, books are juxtaposed with symbols of mortality (the cypresses in the garden) and immortality (the infinite plain on the horizon). The most prominent image, however, is the water flowing from the fountains. Azorín explicitly compares it to the temporal movement of our lives. In this endless flux – of time, of water, and of the passersby at the book fair – Azorín finds permanence in the volumes that he and others like him across the generations continually seek. Yet not only do books provide bibliophiles with a refuge from the ineluctable passage and dissolution of time, but the scene itself, as painted by Azorín, hypostatizes their ephemeral lives and grounds them in being.

In this vignette, books can be interpreted as examples of *sinfronismo*, a term coined by José Ortega y Gasset in his essay, "Azorín: Primores de lo vulgar" [Azorín: Exquisite vulgarity of the commonplace].[42] In contrast to synchronism, which indicates the simultaneity of distinct actions and lives, *sinfronismo* refers to the recurrence of the same action or the reincarnation of the same spirit in different times. But whereas in novels such as Azorín's *Doña Inés* this reincarnation occurs in humans,[43] in the description of the Madrid book fair it takes place in the books that objectify the human spirit. According to the passage, the bibliophile does indeed reappear throughout history, but it is through books that the spirit of bibliophilia is contained and reflected back to the spectator. In her analysis of the function of ekphrasis in *Doña Inés*, Jurkevich notes that in the text's elucidation, "literature's diachronic movement is temporarily subverted by the synchronic and self-reflective ekphrastic moment which 'spatializes' the text as it arrests its linear progression" ("Azorín's" 41). In his depiction of the Madrid book fair, Azorín performs a similar gesture of spatialization, not only by transforming the scene into a word picture but also, more subtly, by tethering this word picture, along with the fluid world that it distills, to the image of a book.

According to Azorín, the majority of books at the Madrid book fair are of little bibliographical or literary value, and he is struck by the enormous quantity of volumes that are poorly bound and carelessly printed on cheap paper. He maintains, however, that all the books capture moments from human lives – not only of their writers but also those who have read or touched them during the course of their existence. Books, Azorín muses, represent human thought, and although some formulate elaborate ideas, others are expressed "sencilla y limpiamente, con la sencillez y la limpieza de una fuente en la montaña" (*Un pueblecito* 534) [simply and clearly, with the simplicity and clarity of a mountain spring]. Writers in the small towns and hamlets of Castile have penned such books for centuries, but most of these authors have been forgotten and their works have been lost. One autumn morning, while browsing the stalls of the book fair, Azorín discovers a volume that in his view reveals a pure heart and humble spirit. Like the flowing water of the fountains, its discourse seems alive, albeit fleeting. Yet it is embodied in material form, and Azorín is able to hold it, thereby experiencing a somatic connection with its author, Bejarano, and, by extension, all the anonymous and now vanished authors of the past.

Bejarano was a Dominican cleric from Seville, who in 1791 published a book titled *Sentimientos patrióticos o conversaciones cristianas* [Patriotic feelings and Christian conversations].[44] This text formed the basis of *Un pueblecito*, which in turn was the inspiration for Ortega y Gasset's essay "Azorín: Primores de lo vulgar." Azorín incorporates elements of Bejarano's work into his own narrative, highlighting the earlier writer's observations of the life of Riofrío de Ávila, as well as his engagement with the eighteenth-century French Enlightenment. Like Azorín (and indeed many of the members of the Generation of '98), Bejarano revered the Castilian people and their traditions and customs; and yet, again like Azorín, he was also receptive to the cultural advances of other European countries. According to Ortega y Gasset, the figure of Bejarano depicted in *Un pueblecito* can be read as a fictional self-portrait through which Azorín expresses some of his most profound intuitions of time and identity. It is also an example of *sinfronismo* insofar as both Bejarano and Azorín appear to incarnate similar worldviews (Pérez Gracia).

Azorín presents Bejarano as a writer who shares his own aesthetic sensitivity and penchant for simple and clear prose. As indicated in much of his writing on books, Azorín disparages obtuse and ornamental language because he believes that it interposes itself between readers and the world and precludes a direct apprehension of reality. He thus cites Bejarano's affirmation that "[l]a claridad ... es la primera calidad del estilo. ... El estilo es claro si lleva al instante al oyente a las cosas, sin detenerle en las palabras" (*Un pueblecito* 544) [clarity ... is the primary quality of style. ... Style is clear if it brings the listener immediately to things, without causing the listener to pause on the words]. Azorín reiterates: "Retengamos esa máxima fundamental: *Derechamente a las cosas*" (544) [Let us keep that fundamental maxim: *Directly to things*]. The goal of Azorín, which books can prevent but also, if precisely written, make available, is the world in all its material reality. This is achieved through books as a window into the world as well as an immanent presence in the world itself.

Azorín forges his life as a bibliophile not only in Spain but also France, and some of the books that most influence his views of bibliophilia are French. Many of his essays on bibliophilia and books relate to his experiences in the bookshops and libraries of Paris, and in particular the bookstalls that line the River Seine. (It is for this reason that Fuster García subtitles his collection *Crónicas de un transeúnte: Madrid-París* and displays on the cover and throughout the volume old photographs of the sites in Paris that Azorín frequented.) Azorín often invokes the book culture of France, including its distinguished history of producing, marketing, and cultivating books, in an effort to expose the deficiencies of Spanish book culture and to press for its improvement. He appreciates French deluxe editions because he perceives in them an aesthetic restraint. In French fine books (as in the prose of Bejarano) "todo es sencillo, sobrio y correcto" (*Libros* 26) [everything is simple, sober, and correct]. In contrast, Spanish fine books are often marred by a "lujo pesado, chillón y tosco" (26) [heavy, gaudy, and vulgar luxury]. What Azorín most values in both the form and content of books is thus a simplicity of style.

According to Azorín, France in the early twentieth century led the world in book production (although the quality and quantity of its output was adversely affected by the First World War), and in Spanish bookshops of the period French-language volumes often outnumbered Spanish-language publications. Azorín admires the bookshops of France because bibliophiles are always welcome to enter and browse, even if they have no intention of making a purchase. In Spain, in contrast, the bookshops seem hermetically sealed and are guarded by their proprietors as if they were sacred temples (110). Azorín identifies the inability of Spanish bibliophiles to browse as the greatest impediment to the book trade in Spain (113). Not only are the conditions for the circulation of books more propitious in France, but the French also tend to treat books better than do Spaniards, and when used books move from private ownership back into the Spanish marketplace, more often than not they are torn, stained, and patched (143). Finally, the French have a greater appreciation of old books, which Azorín regards as a barometer of culture (143).

In a passage reminiscent of his depiction of the Madrid book fair, Azorín portrays the entire city of Paris as a kind of immense emporium of books.

> En París hay infinitas librerías; por todas partes se ven libros. La primavera en París es la estación más adecuada para el paseo lento, distraído, meditativo; la temperatura es clemente; el cielo, como casi siempre en París, nos muestra su ceniza, los árboles expanden su follaje en el ambiente dulce. Vayamos recorriendo los puestos de libros viejos a lo largo de los malecones del Sena. El río se desliza manso, de color acerado; entre la fronda de los copudos plátanos entrevemos lo gris del cielo. Tomamos un libro de un tabanco, lo hojeamos y lo volvemos a dejar. Alguna vez compramos un volumen que nos incita a la lectura. (170)

> [In Paris there are infinite bookstores; you see books everywhere. Springtime in Paris is the most suitable season for strolling slowly, distractedly,

> and pensively; the temperature is mild; the sky, as almost always in Paris, is ash coloured, and the trees spread their foliage into the soft air. Let us look through the stalls of old books along the quays of the Seine. The steely-coloured river flows gently; through the canopy of the thick plane trees we catch a glimpse of the grey of the sky. We take a book from a stand, leaf through it, and put it down. Sometimes we buy a volume that incites us to read.]

In contrast to the Madrid book fair, Azorín's image of the Paris book-scape is muted, as if there were less light present. The river and the sky are grey, and the sky itself is largely concealed by the foliage of the trees. In contrast, the Madrid book fair is illuminated by a brilliant autumn sun. Yet in both settings what draws the attention of Azorín are the books themselves, which ground the temporal movement of humans and nature and endow it with permanence. In recalling his wanderings through the bookstalls of the Seine, he highlights a volume that not only reflects his temperament as a writer and thinker (as Bejarano's text likewise does) but also embodies aspects of his life as a bibliophile (145–50). This book is titled *Le Journal d'un bouquiniste* [The journal of a used-book dealer].

Azorín does not reveal whether he discovered *Le Journal d'un bouquiniste* in Paris or learned of its existence through a catalogue or bibliography. Although he was initially unfamiliar with the author, Charles Dodeman, and the publisher, Tancrède, he was able to secure a copy of the text through the efforts of his editor in Spain. Azorín relished *Le Journal d'un bouquiniste* because it afforded him insight not into the fabled world of French bibliophilia but rather the life of a bibliophile of the people and the bookstalls of the Seine, which have attracted the attention of bibliophiles like Azorín for generations.[45] Dodeman's memoir is replete with vignettes of Paris booksellers as well as anecdotes regarding the plethora of used books that passed through his hands. He speaks tenderly of books as having an almost impish spirit, disappearing when you want them most and reappearing as if by magic. But he also leads Azorín to reflect on what he regards as a crisis in the used-book trade. The Paris bookstalls, Dodeman remarks, are besieged by an ever-growing number of book hunters, and the quantity and quality of desirable volumes is continually diminishing. According to Azorín, the situation is the same in Madrid, where the possibility of stumbling upon bibliophilistic treasures has become less and less likely over the course of his lifetime. This fear of the unavailability of books haunts much of the history of bibliophilia, and the perceived scarcity of books contributes greatly to their value and allure. Yet for Azorín, books are not merely coveted possessions but the site of one of his most profound engagements with reality. Were they to become unattainable or actually disappear, then a whole dimension of his world would vanish.

Azorín's reading of the little-known Dodeman text stands in sharp contrast to his commentaries on famous French writers, such as Marcel Proust. Both Azorín and Proust are preoccupied with the significance of time, and much of their creative output is a quasi-autobiographical depiction of their efforts as artists to achieve a sense of ontological plenitude in the midst of the temporal flux of life. Both, moreover, reveal a passion for books, although only Azorín identifies himself explicitly as a bibliophile. In a brief essay titled "El arte de Proust" [The art of Proust], Azorín highlights the French writer's attempt to re-experience past sensations and in so doing save them and himself from oblivion.[46] As Proust explains in his reflections on bibliophilia in *Le Temps retrouvé* [*Time Regained*], books might in principle help him achieve this goal, but because of their materiality they ultimately hinder him. What interests him most are not books of renown or quality editions but rather the actual volumes he read as a child, since through these he might be able to recover something of the lost essence of his past. Yet he fears that material books would prevent access to this essence, which now exists only immaterially in his mind.

> Et si j'avais encore le *François le Champi* que maman sortit un soir du paquet de livres que ma grand-mère devait me donner pour ma fête, je ne le regarderais jamais; j'aurais trop peur d'y insérer peu à peu mes impressions d'aujourd'hui jusqu'à en recouvrir complètement celles d'autrefois, j'aurais trop peur de le voir devenir ... une chose du présent. (466)

> [And if I still possessed the *François le Champi* which Mamma unpacked one evening from the parcel of books which my grandmother was to have given me for my birthday, I should never look at it; I should be too afraid that I might gradually insinuate into it my impressions of today and smother my original impressions beneath them, that I might see it become ... a thing of the present. (288–9)]

Proust clarifies that if he were a bibliophile, he would appreciate the "beauté indépendante de la valeur propre d'un livre" (465) ["beauty ... independent of the intrinsic value of a book" (286)] that is instilled in it by its previous owners. Yet because he would limit his acquisitions to editions of books that he himself had once read and cherished, this quality would come solely from him. For Azorín, in contrast, the quality that books and things possess beyond their contingent materiality results from the intervention of many human agents. In a noted passage of *Doña Inés,* in which he describes the ancient wool industry of Segovia, he emphasizes the countless hands of workers that over the centuries have given value to the wool:[47]

> En todo el ámbito de la ciudad, y en sus contornos, desde siglos atrás y a través de todas las mudanzas, millares y millares de manos se mueven incesantes. Son manos varoniles, manos femeninas, manos de adolescentes, manos de niños; son manos de jóvenes, manos de viejos; son manos huesosas, manos puntiagudas, manos regordetas. El inmenso y afanoso enjambre de manos. (754)
>
> [In the entire area of the city and its surroundings, and for many centuries and through so many changes, thousands and thousands of hands have moved incessantly. The hands of men, the hands of women, the hands of adolescents, the hands of children; the hands of the young, the hands of the old; bony hands, pointed hands, fat hands. The immense and arduous swarm of hands.]

In the case of books, including the beloved volume of Bejarano, what matters most to Azorín are the hands of those who once held them. His fundamental question as a bibliophile thus points not only to himself but also to others: "¿Qué sabemos las manos que han vuelto las páginas de este pobre libro?" (*Un pueblecito* 534) [What do we, the hands that have turned the pages of this poor book, know?].[48]

These hands, which evoke the lives of countless other people, are perhaps the ultimate aim of Azorín's bibliophilia and indeed his entire vocation as an artist. He discerns them not only in putatively great works of literature and deluxe editions but, more often than not, in ordinary books written and read by ordinary people: "Lo que nos atrae ahora es lo mediocre" (*Libros* 174) [What attracts us now is the mediocre]. To acquire books with the "cierto encanto" (174) [certain charm] of the commonplace, he turns to the bookstalls of the Cuesta de Moyano and the quays of the Seine, as well as the multitude of used bookshops of Madrid and the many cities of his lifelong peregrinations. These "librerías de lance" are modest and even poor establishments, but their walls are covered from top to bottom with books of all genres and all periods of history, and they put to shame the more prominent antiquarian bookstores whose only aim is profit (166).[49] It is in the volumes of used bookshops that Azorín discovers a sort of intra-history of the Spanish people and humanity.[50] As an artist-writer he attempts to grasp this intra-history through his painterly depictions of bibliophiles and books. Yet he also does so through a discursive repetition that characterizes his scores of essays on bibliophilia.

In his writings on bibliophilia, Azorín extols the virtues of reading while simultaneously expressing a desire to shift his attention away from books and focus more directly on the world around him. His identity as a bibliophile nonetheless remains constant throughout his life, and his love of books, both as texts to read and objects to treasure, never wanes. What is more, he continually ruminates on his life with books, and in many of his essays he repeats his observations and depicts similar images of bibliophiles in similar situations. In so doing, he does not retell the same narrative but rather fashions, from different angles and perspectives, an increasingly rich and nuanced self-portrait. The picture he paints is of someone who seeks a deep and essential communion with humans and things, both now and across time, and who prizes freedom and spontaneity above all else. The privileged site of his self-fashioning, if not in all of his writings then at least clearly in his essays on bibliophilia, is the book. Through books, and in particular used books, Azorín feels connected to a multitude of human actors including writers, readers, and all those engaged in the production and dissemination of print matter. But he also discovers in the books he reads and collects a mirror of his own humanity. For a professional writer, this might seem surprising, since writers are often inclined to take their own writings as the most tangible manifestation of their actions and lives. But Azorín, in the spirit of humanitarianism, is drawn more powerfully to the books and lives of others. What remains for us as Azorín's posthumous readers are not the books that he so fondly describes in his writings on bibliophilia (and which we are likely only ever to perceive through his distinctive lens) but his own books, as well as those of bibliophiles like Fuster García, which so exquisitely recapture the writings and images of Spain's "little philosopher" and giant of books.[51]

# 3 Lost Books and Textual Restitution

Whereas the preceding section focused primarily on non-fictional writings of nineteenth- and early twentieth-century Spanish bibliophiles, including autobiographies, correspondences, and essays, this part highlights three full-length contemporary narratives about books: Carlos Ruiz Zafón's *La sombra del viento,* Manuel Rivas's *Os libros arden mal,* and Juan Goytisolo's *El sitio de los sitios.* These texts draw attention to books that have been lost, stolen, or destroyed, and characters who attempt either to find or restore them. All, moreover, contain elements of mystery. As in the nineteenth-century "roman de livres" [novel of books], theorized by Stefano Lazzarin, the mystery of books depicted in these contemporary Spanish narratives relates to questions of identity. Yet unlike traditional novels of bibliophilia, they emphasize not only the personal identities of bibliophiles but also cultural, political, and national traditions that have been attacked and suppressed, including those of Catalonia and Galicia during the Francoist period. In *La sombra del viento, Os libros arden mal,* and *El sitio de los sitios,* the process of recovering and reconstituting these traditions is particularly arduous, since they have been embedded in books that either no longer exist or exist only in mutilated form as a result of military and state-sponsored acts of biblioclasm. Like many late twentieth- and early twenty-first-century Spanish writers, Ruiz Zafón, Rivas, and Goytisolo regard the Spanish Civil War and the subsequent terror of the Francoist state as the overdetermining trauma of modern Spanish history. The memory of this trauma lingers long after the end of the war and the dictatorship, and haunts their writings about books. In *El sitio de los sitios,* moreover, Goytisolo conjoins Spain's historical trauma with the trauma suffered by the Muslim peoples of the Balkans during the wars of the 1990s and the destruction of the National and University Library of Bosnia and Herzegovina.

In the book-themed narratives of these authors, books (and, by extension, libraries, bookstores, and book repositories) represent cultural, political, and national traditions, such as those of Republican Spain, Catalonia, and Galicia, as well as individual lives. Although some of the books depicted endure, they are all susceptible to physical assault, and among the most poignant and disturbing images are those of burning bindings and pages, eerily redolent of the immolation of human flesh. Scenes of biblio-pyromania, however, not only bear witness to historical events involving books and people, but they also suggest that discourses, as Michel Foucault argues in *L'Archéologie du savoir* [*The Archaeology of Knowledge*] and *La Bibliothèque fantastique* ["Fantasia of the Library"], cannot be constrained by the apparent unity of material books. Yet if for these writers the trope of the library on fire alludes to the uncontainable dynamic of discourses, it more powerfully evokes histories of murder and genocide. The anxiety that they express over the destruction and loss of books reflects a concern in contemporary Spanish society, and indeed in societies worldwide whose book heritage has been threatened, that a past worth remembering and maintaining will be forgotten. It also reveals a more deep-seated anguish that all humans experience when confronted with the reality of death.

Although these narratives highlight the destruction of books, they also envision at least a partial restitution of them. In several key scenes of *Os libros arden mal* and *El sitio de los sitios*, the attempt to repair charred and damaged books is compared to acts of sewing. As James Raven reminds us, the word "text" derives from the Latin word "texere" (13) [to weave], and the words "book" and "text" are often used interchangeably. Just as discursive texts are metaphorically woven together with words, material books are traditionally bound together with threads, and paper pages can even appear to have been sewn, depending on the papermaking process.[1] Through visual images of weaving, Rivas and Goytisolo subtly evoke the palpable dimension of books as well as their distinctiveness from one another. Each volume has, so to speak, its own texture, which bibliophiles feel both emotionally and physically, and which reminds them of their own unique embodiedness. The project of restoring books that for all intents and purposes have been destroyed requires tremendous imagination and ingenuity.

In some instances, the vestiges of bookplates and marginalia can be useful in the restoration of damaged books. They also remind readers of the other hands through which books have passed. According to Rivas's narrator, a knowledge of the provenance of books is often as significant as their textual content, for it allows present-day readers to feel a connection with readers of the past (even if this connection is sometimes negative, as when Goytisolo's narrator reads marginalia denigrating groups of people with whom he identifies). As Evelyne Ender and Deidre Shauna Lynch remark in their discussion of Andrew M. Stauffer's study of the marginalia in the books of poetry of Felicia Hemans, "the printed text marked with handwritten traces reverberates across time and suffuses ... readerly experiences with what is best defined as an aura" (12) – that is, with what Walter Benjamin describes as a "strange weave of space and time" that allows spectators (and here readers) to intuit the world in which a work of art was first made (518). The lives of former readers are present not only in the traces of what they intentionally inscribe in books but also in what they inadvertently leave behind, such as sweat, tears, saliva, and DNA in general. Ruiz Zafón, Rivas, and Goytisolo do not reflect on the physicality of books from a scientific perspective, or on the methods of proteomics employed by researchers such as Pier Giorgio Righetti and Gleb Zilberstein in their analyses of old books, manuscripts, and other documents.[2] But like Azorín, they do suggest that books have a natural life that is discernable to those who interact with them.[3]

As in much of the literature of bibliophilia, the narratives of Ruiz Zafón, Rivas, and Goytisolo are male-centred, although *El sitio de los sitios* clearly challenges the dynamics of heterosexual patriarchy. The texts of Ruiz Zafón and Rivas depict characters who recreate genealogies of fathers and sons in the wake of war and dictatorship. But whereas the father figures in *La sombra del viento* are fictional, those in *Os libros arden mal* are largely historical, including the Galician president of the Spanish Second Republic, Santiago Casares Quiroga. In contrast, the narrator of *El sitio de los sitios* establishes bonds of commonality with a wide range of individuals who have been historically repressed within Spain and Europe because of their sexuality, race, or religion. Despite these differences, the figures that Ruiz Zafón, Rivas, and Goytisolo hold up for emulation all cultivate books, either as dissident writers, readers, or collectors, and all are in some way rebels who challenge the prevailing social order of their societies.[4]

## Re-imagining the Spanish Past: Library Fantasies in Carlos Ruiz Zafón's *La sombra del viento*

Carlos Ruiz Zafón's blockbuster novel, *La sombra del viento* (2001) [*The Shadow of the Wind*] forms part of a long tradition of Spanish books about books.[5] Yet it not only reflects on the nature of books, but also attempts to recover a lost past, expunged at the time of the Spanish Civil War. In so doing, it seeks to re-establish a genealogy of parents and children, and specifically fathers and sons, that were shattered during the conflict. Although the books highlighted in the narrative are imaginary, they function as the means through which the past is recovered and the relationship between the self and the other is forged. In *La sombra del viento*, reading is thus an act of memory and an expression of intersubjectivity and, as such, the driving force of identity-formation. In its representation of the Spanish Civil War and its aftermath, the text is decidedly anti-Francoist, although it subtly depoliticizes this history. Ruiz Zafón suggests that the value of literature results neither from a political engagement with society nor from what he regards as the narcissistic reflexivity of postmodernism, but rather from the ability of an author to tell a good story and thereby provide readers with a vehicle of escape from quotidian reality. In fact, he advocates a return to what he calls the classical narrative.[6] Ultimately, *La sombra del viento* reaffirms the centrality of storytelling in human culture, and, given its immense popular appeal, will possibly stand as the most widely read Spanish book about bibliophilia of all time.

In its representation of books and texts, *La sombra del viento* depicts a fluidity of discourses that material books are unable to contain. As Michel Foucault argues in *L'Archéologie du savoir*, both the material book and the *oeuvre*, the ostensibly self-contained text, are illusory unities of knowledge. The apparent material unity of a book, he maintains, is "une unité faible, accessoire, au regard de l'unité discursive à laquelle il donne support" (*L'Archéologie* 36) ["a weak, accessory unity in relation to the discursive unity of which it is the support" (*The Archaeology* 23)]. What is more, "l'unité discursive" ["discursive unity"] is never "homogène et uniformément applicable" (36) ["homogenous and uniformly applicable" (23)]. In fact,

> C'est que les marges d'un livre ne sont jamais nettes ni rigoureusement tranchées: par-delà le titre, les premières lignes et le point final, par-delà sa configuration interne et la forme qui l'autonomise, il est pris dans un système de renvois à d'autres livres, d'autres textes, d'autres phrases: nœud dans un réseau. ... Le livre a beau se donner comme un objet qu'on a sous la main; il a beau se recroqueviller en ce petit parallélépipède qui l'enferme: son unité est variable et relative. (36)

> [The frontiers of a book are never clear-cut: beyond the title, the first lines, and the last full stop, beyond its internal configuration and its autonomous form, it is caught up in a system of references to other books, other texts, other sentences: it is a node within a network. ... The book is not simply the object that one holds in one's hands; and it cannot remain within the little parallelepiped that contains it: its unity is variable and relative. (23)]

*La sombra del viento* recognizes that discourses, especially in epochs of historical transition such as post-Francoist Spain, are fluid. Nevertheless, it attempts to shore them up, first within the materiality of the book, and then within its political and gender narration of the past that echoes the official ethos of the contemporary Spanish state: a liberal democracy that pays lip service to the left while diffusing radical praxis, and a male-dominated society that reasserts its legitimacy through an increased sensitivity to women and homosexuals.

In a manner reminiscent of Miguel de Unamuno's *Niebla* [Mist], *La sombra del viento* seeks to establish authorial control (and in this case also reader control) over discourses that seem to operate of their own volition. The pivotal event depicted in the text is an encounter between a reader and a book. But it is also, following Foucault, an encounter between books themselves. In *La Bibliothèque fantastique*, Foucault proposes that Flaubert's *La Tentation de saint Antoine* [The temptation of saint Anthony] marks a turning point in the history of the book, and more important in the history of the imaginary, which hereafter (at least among certain western readers) is limited to the domain of the printed word. No longer is the imaginary discovered in the external world of nature but solely in texts. Yet if the imaginary lies "en attente dans le document" (*La Bibliothèque* 9) ["dormant in documents" ("Fantasia" 90)], it is actualized through the act of reading. Foucault situates the world of the imaginary not simply in the materiality of the book or the mind's eye of the reader, but in a depersonalized zone that he describes as "l'interstice des redites et des commentaires" (9) ["the interstice of repetitions and commentaries" (91)] and "l'entre-deux des textes" (9) ["the interval between books" (91)]. He calls the imaginary "un phénomène de bibliothèque" (9) ["a phenomenon of the library" (91)], which, through progressive readings, "s'étend entre les signes, de livre à livre" (9) ["grows among signs, from book to book" (91)]. For Foucault, *La Tentation de saint Antoine* differs from previous texts in that it is linked to a network of past books that it self-consciously interpolates.[7] Not only does its existence depend on these books, but it also opens a space in which they can continue to exist and circulate. What is more, although it recovers them, it both reveals and conceals them through its own textual organization. Foucault goes so far as to call *La Tentation de saint Antoine*

> le livre des livres: elle compose en un "volume" une série d'éléments de langage qui ont été constitués à partir des livres déjà écrits, et qui sont, par leur caractère rigoureusement documentaire, la redite du déjà dit. (26)

> [the book of books: it unites in a single "volume" a series of linguistic elements that derive from existing books and that are, by virtue of their specific documentary character, the repetition of things said in the past. (105)]

With its appearance, he declares, "[l]a bibliothèque est en feu" (10) ["(t)he library is on fire" (92)]. This "fire," a dynamic that in the wake of the psychoanalytic theorization of Julia Kristeva is commonly referred to as intertextuality, destroys the illusion of the self-contained book and opens up a kaleidoscopic world of books about books.

Like *La Tentation de saint Antoine*, *La sombra del viento* presents itself explicitly as "un livre fait de livres" (Foucault, *La Bibliothèque* 27) ["a book produced from other books" (Foucault, "Fantasia" 105)]. But it also imagines books as a primary site of remembrance and, by extension, a process of identity-formation that memory makes possible. The text thus melds the acts of reading, remembering, and self-fashioning. In the introductory chapter a child, the narrator and protagonist, Daniel Sempere, awakens one morning screaming because he can no longer remember the face of his mother, who died during the Spanish Civil War. Daniel's widowed father attempts to calm him, promising that he will remember her for the two of them. Yet the father immediately realizes that this is insufficient consolation, for what Daniel has begun to lose is not simply the memory of his mother but a sense of self rendered through a personal past. Without a past, Daniel will become nothing, a mere shadow in the wind. His father therefore provides him with a means of acquiring a past, taking him, as his own father had taken him years before, to a place called El Cementerio de los Libros Olvidados [The Cemetery of Forgotten Books].

El Cementerio de los Libros Olvidados is a magical space, evocative of a long line of literary libraries, including those of Jorge Luis Borges and Umberto Eco.[8] Like an impossible cemetery of everyone who ever lived, it contains all the books ever written but forgotten. In keeping with the spirit/flesh dichotomy of Christian tradition, each is imagined as having a dormant soul (the story), endowed by its writer and former readers and now waiting to be revivified by a new reader. According to custom, first-time visitors must choose a book and promise to keep it alive forever. As Daniel's father puts it, Daniel must adopt one. Although books are like dead people awaiting resurrection, they are also like the unborn in Georgette Leblanc's *L'Oiseau bleu* [*The Children's Blue Bird*], anticipating the moment when they will be brought into the world. Daniel's father cannot restore to him his dead mother, and instead makes available to him a book that will function as both surrogate parent and child. Through it, Daniel will come to develop a new and larger past than the one he feared losing, and a new and larger sense of self than he was heretofore capable of imagining.

Daniel chooses a volume, titled *La sombra del viento*, and in so doing chooses a past through which his identity will coalesce.[9] As he wanders the labyrinthine corridors of El Cementerio de los Libros Olvidados, he remarks that "tras la cubierta de cada uno de aquellos libros se abría un universo infinito por explorar" (*La sombra* 12) ["between the covers of each of those books lay a boundless universe waiting to be discovered" (*The Shadow* 6)]. He imagines himself as a free agent, and indeed almost a god, whose act of reading will breathe life into the passive materiality of the book. Yet precisely because the book is boundless (not as a space of unlimited reader self-fulfillment but because textual signs continuously refer to other signs of signification and therefore can never be fully contained), it will elude him. What is more, he will in a way become its object, formed as it were by the discourses that through his act of reading become entrenched in his psyche. As an adult, Daniel idealizes this process, as if the particular meanings of the text he selects were themselves irrelevant.

> [P]ocas cosas marcan tanto a un lector como el primer libro que realmente se abre camino hasta su corazón. Aquellas primeras imágenes, el eco de esas palabras que creemos haber dejado atrás, nos acompañan toda la vida y esculpen un palacio en nuestra memoria al que, tarde o temprano – no importa cuántos libros leamos, cuántos mundos descubramos, cuánto aprendamos u olvidemos – vamos a regresar. Para mí, esas páginas embrujadas siempre serán las que encontré entre los pasillos del Cementerio de los Libros Olvidados. (14)

> [(F)ew things leave a deeper mark on a reader than the first book that finds its way into his heart. Those first images, the echo of words we think we have left behind, accompany us throughout our lives and sculpt a palace in our memory to which, sooner or later – no matter how many books we read, how many worlds we discover, or how much we learn or forget – we will return. For me those enchanted pages will always be the ones I found among the passageways of the Cemetery of Forgotten Books. (8)]

The book Daniel randomly chooses as a child thus becomes the logic of his entire life as an adult.

Within the introductory chapter of the Ruiz Zafón text, the plot of Daniel's book is briefly summarized.

> La novela relataba la historia de un hombre en busca de su verdadero padre, al que nunca había llegado a conocer y cuya existencia sólo descubría merced a las últimas palabras que pronunciaba su madre en su lecho de muerte. La historia de aquella búsqueda se transformaba en una odisea fantasmagórica en la que el protagonista luchaba por recuperar una infancia y una juventud perdidas, y en la que, lentamente, descubríamos la sombra de un amor maldito cuya memoria le habría de perseguir hasta el fin de sus días. (13)
>
> [The novel told the story of a man in search of his real father, whom he never knew and whose existence was only revealed to him by his mother on her deathbed. The story of that quest became a ghostly odyssey in which the protagonist struggled to recover his lost youth and in which the shadow of a cursed love slowly surfaced to haunt him until his last breath. (7)]

As Daniel gradually learns, this story is based largely on the life of its author, Julián Carax. By internalizing it, Daniel will make it, in schematic form, his life story as well. Although the paternity of Daniel's father is never called into question, and although what Daniel initially sought to recover was his lost mother, he now begins a quest for a second father in the person of the mysterious Julián. Henceforth, reading functions to construct, or rather reconstruct, Daniel, deflecting his desire for his mother onto a father figure with whom he will come to identify. In this scenario, the Ruiz Zafón text replicates the Freudian paradigm of the Oedipal crisis. What is significant is that this crisis is "resolved" expressly through reading. In fact, if Daniel's destiny is heterosexual masculinity, this has less to do with his own natural inclinations or the direct influence of his parents than it does with the discourses he encounters while growing up. Furthermore, the bifurcation of the father figure parallels a dichotomization of texts as books and discourses and, by extension, human beings as bodies and souls. From his biological father Daniel receives first a body and then a book, whereas from Julián he is infused with a narrative that will endow his life with meaning. A patriarchal genealogy of both the flesh and the word is thereby affirmed – albeit in strictly secular guise.

Although they share the same titles and similar characters, Julián's and Ruiz Zafón's texts are not identical. Moreover, the former is presented only periphrastically in the aforementioned plot summary. The Ruiz Zafón reader is led to assume that Julián's text reiterates the life of the figure Daniel comes to discover through detective-like investigation. But even this is only implied. As a matter of fact, Julián's text never appears within the Ruiz Zafón text, but instead haunts it as an ever-possible displacement of meaning and disintegration of unity: "Paso a paso, la narración se descomponía en mil historias, como si el relato hubiese penetrado en una galería de espejos y su identidad se escindiera en docenas de reflejos diferentes y al tiempo uno solo" (14) ["Step by step the narrative split into a thousand stories, as if it had entered a gallery of mirrors, its identity fragmented into endless reflections" (7)].[10] The Ruiz Zafón text is thus not a simple meta-text because the text reflected on (Julián's) does not exist as a discrete entity but only in multiplicity, and then always at a distance. This phantom text, a sign of the fluidity of discourse and the instability of identity, is nevertheless held at bay by the overarching Ruiz Zafón text, which strives to reaffirm discourse as a system of fixed signs and a means of achieving a fixed self. It does this through a peculiar conflation of traditional literary realism (including the gothic novel, the detective novel, and the serial novel) with the narrative self-consciousness and parody of postmodernism.

As a child, Daniel is enthralled by Julián's novel, but Juilán is a second-rate writer whose books are published only through the subventions of an anonymous friend. If Julián's text follows his life, then his life must resemble a kind of soap opera (whose banality, ironically, Daniel despises), because it is indeed melodramatic, if not highly convoluted and improbable. Born in Barcelona at the turn of the twentieth century, Julián grows up believing he is the son of a hatter, Antoni Fortuny, and a French mother, Sophie Carax. When he is a teenager, one of his father's customers, a wealthy industrialist named Ricardo Aldaya, takes him to live with him and enrolls him in a prestigious high school. Julián becomes close friends with Ricardo's son, Jorge; a future priest, Fernando; a leftist intellectual, Miquel; and for a time, the son of the school's caretaker, a demented boy named Francisco Javier Fumero, who later becomes his and Daniel's nemesis. Julián also falls in love with Ricardo's daughter, Penélope. The two have an affair and decide to elope, but the father foils their plan, and when he learns that Penélope is pregnant, locks her away and leaves her and her baby to die. He does so because Julián is in fact his son, and the relationship between Julián and Penélope is incestuous. Julián never discovers the truth of his relationship with Penélope, and spends years in Paris working as a piano player in a nightclub and writing on the side. In 1936, Jorge visits Julián in Paris and informs him that Penélope had been forcibly prevented from marrying him – although he does not actually tell him how or why she died. Julián then kills Jorge in a duel, returns to Barcelona in a rage, and in a kind of suicidal frenzy tries to obliterate all the existing copies of his books, starting a fire in a warehouse where they are stored and burning himself almost beyond recognition.[11] When Daniel eventually appears on the scene, Julián is living in hiding with a woman, Nuria Monfort, the former secretary of Julián's publisher and the daughter of the keeper of El Cementerio de los Libros Olvidados. Julián knows that Daniel possesses the only remaining copy of any of his books, and stalks him and his friends in an effort to appropriate and destroy it.

In certain ways, Daniel's life parallels Julián's. As a child, Daniel has a best friend and quasi-brother, Tomás, and as an adolescent, Daniel falls in love with Tomás's sister, Beatriz. Tomás and his family oppose their relationship, especially when they suspect that the two are having an affair. The present, however, does not repeat the past. Daniel and Beatriz eventually marry, and the anger that their love for each other initially instills in Beatriz's family dissipates. In further contrast, Julián has a rather large group of teenage friends whereas Daniel's primary companion is a middle-aged man, Fermín, an assistant in his father's bookshop. Daniel first discovers Fermín living on the street – a victim of the Franco regime and specifically of the torture perpetrated by the then police-chief of Barcelona, Fumero. Daniel and Fermín gradually become a detective-team, attempting to unravel the mystery of Julián. But their efforts are continually thwarted by Fumero, driven mad by an incestuous mother whom he murdered and by his rivalry with Julián for the love of Penélope. Although one-dimensional in his evil, Fumero is a pivotal character in the text. Not only does he terrorize Julián, Fermín, and Daniel (and in the climactic moment actually shoots Daniel), but he seemingly incarnates all the ills of modern Spanish history, switching political allegiance from left to right as the tide of the Civil War changes so as always to be in a position of power over others and engaging in acts of torture. But if Fumero is wantonly cruel, he is also emblematic of how the Ruiz Zafón text depoliticizes history, transmuting the violence of the war into a personal vendetta rooted in psychological trauma, and in the process laying the blame (perhaps inadvertently, although not without profound implications) on the only major working-class character.

In the complex and intertwining plots of Julián and Daniel's lives, the period from 1936 to 1939 is pivotal. In 1936 Julián supposedly disappears and Daniel is born, and in 1939 Daniel's mother dies. Throughout much of the Ruiz Zafón text this period marks a kind of rupture, leaving Daniel with no past and Julián with no future. Both are like ghosts – even though this is only immediately apparent in the person of Julián. After the fire he is transformed into a nameless and faceless spectre furtively wandering the darkened streets of Barcelona. He first approaches Daniel's blind friend, Clara, who touches a face she describes as a mask of leather. Later, Daniel encounters him in the night, and when he holds up a match, discovers a face with no nose, lips, or eyelids: "Su rostro era apenas una máscara de piel negra y cicatrizada, devorada por el fuego" (60) ["His face was nothing but a mask of black scarred skin, consumed by fire" (56)]. Daniel imagines this faceless figure, which watches him on his balcony from the street below, as diabolical – an irony insofar as the protagonist of Julián's novel is stalked in a similar fashion by the Devil himself. All of these details, presented in the opening chapters of the Ruiz Zafón text, suggest that the mystery of Julián is linked to the great crisis of modern Spanish history, the Civil War. Not only does Julián lose his identity in a violent conflagration at the outset of the Civil War, but, during the repressive period that follows, he is perceived as a monster and ultimately an embodiment of evil. Through association he thus seems to represent the Spanish Republican past, severed from the national project of the present yet not entirely vanquished, for he continues to haunt the survivors and in particular Daniel.[12] Julián and Daniel are in fact drawn to each other. Without Daniel (the Spanish present), Julián (the Spanish past) will irrevocably die. Conversely, without Julián, Daniel will lack the historical foundation necessary for the creation of a future of his own. Julián and Daniel are poised on opposite sides of a historical divide of such depth that rapprochement seems impossible. Yet their union (along with the union of the texts in which they are embedded and the generations they represent) is the implicit promise of the entire Ruiz Zafón narrative.

On the level of plot, Julián and Daniel do unite. But the rupture caused by the Civil War is not sutured, at least not in a way that permits an expression of a plurality of political and cultural meanings. Rather, like Julián's text, it is elided within a larger narrative that attempts to close off the proliferation of meanings. This elision, despite the text's anti-Francoist stance, is in a sense consonant with Francoism itself. From an epistemological standpoint, the period of the war not only marks a temporal fracture in Spanish history but also the beginning of a containment of meanings, loosened through democracy and incipient revolution, within the homogenizing master narratives of Francoist ideology. This reigning-in and subsequent erasing of divergent meanings often continues in the ostensibly liberal texts of the post-Franco Transition, which seek not necessarily to forget the past through an act of *desmemoria*, or "unremembering," but to normalize it in the pan-European context. Although liberal in its negative depiction of Francoism and in its general attitude of inclusiveness, the Ruiz Zafón text effects a subtle closure of meanings that short-circuits its initial affirmation of the heterogeneity of discourse, neutralizes the still potent politics of the past, and reinstates a male order.

When Julián first visits Don Ricardo's mansion, he discovers an immense library within "una gran sala cuyas paredes estaban tejidas de libros desde el suelo al infinito" (206) ["a large room whose walls were a tapestry of books, from floor to ceiling" (208)]. This room can be read as a metaphor for the *Sombra* text itself, which weaves together a plethora of fictional and historical narratives from the Hispanic and western traditions. The first line, "Todavía recuerdo aquel amanecer en que mi padre me llevó por primera vez a visitar el Cementerio de los Libros Olvidados" (9) ["I still remember the day my father took me to the Cemetery of Forgotten Books for the first time" (3)], parallels what is perhaps the most famous first line in modern Spanish-language literature, in Gabriel García Márquez's *Cien años de soledad* [*One Hundred Years of Solitude*]: "Muchos años después, frente al pelotón de fusilamiento, el coronel Aureliano Buendía había de recordar aquella tarde remota en que su padre lo llevó a conocer el hielo" (59) ["Many years later, as he faced the firing squad, Colonel Aureliano Buendía was to remember that distant afternoon when his father took him to discover ice" (1)]. Daniel's descent into El Cementerio de los Libros Olvidados – as in Borges's "La biblioteca de Babel," "una gigantesca biblioteca de geometría imposible" (11) ["an immense library of seemingly impossible geometry" (5)] – evokes the journeys of Odysseus and Dante into the afterworld, and even Christ's harrowing of hell. But if the tale is to be, as these lines suggest, a magical journey of epic proportions, it will also have a light-hearted side. During the initial conversation between Daniel and his father, the latter flashes "una sonrisa enigmática que probablemente había tomado prestada de algún tomo de Alejandro Dumas" (10) ["a mysterious smile probably borrowed from the pages of one of his worn Alexandre Dumas romances" (4)]. This reference to Dumas is multilayered and, in light of what follows, is a likely nod to the most immediate precursor of the Ruiz Zafón text, Arturo Pérez-Reverte's *El club Dumas, La novena puerta* [The club Dumas, the ninth gate], which rearticulates many elements of Dumas's work. The lesson of both novels is that books are valuable, not because of what they tell us about the world or ourselves, but because they lead us to dream, and in so doing free us from the constraints of the real. Through their own example, moreover, they exalt storytelling over style, thus blurring conventional distinctions between highbrow and lowbrow writing.[13] In a way they are both heirs to *Don Quixote*, preoccupied, as they are, about the relationship between how we read and how we live. But like *El club Dumas, La novena puerta*, *La sombra del viento* is also a mystery in which the protagonist struggles against seemingly diabolical forces and, like the reader depicted in Unamuno's *Cómo se hace una novela* [How to make a novel], is obliged to recognize that reading itself might be a life-and-death undertaking.

These and numerous other intertexts are explicit within *La sombra del viento,* as if Ruiz Zafón were anxious to flaunt the Romantic conceits of originality, like the young Daniel and his friend, who were "dispuestos a escaparse a través de mundos de ficción y sueños de segunda mano" (34) ["eager to escape into worlds of fiction and secondhand dreams" (29)]. But this cannibalization of other texts, like the more specific cannibalization of Spanish history, is not entirely innocent, even if all writing is ultimately intertextual. Although *La sombra del viento* regards fiction as a vehicle of escape, it also seems nostalgic for a kind of writing in which good triumphs over evil. Yet the happy endings it depicts might leave some readers nostalgic for oppositionality, for it tends to foreclose change while imagining a transcendence of issues still pertinent in Spanish society at the time the novel was written.

A telling example is the story of the gay Don Federico, who is humorously described by a friend as "[un] estimado vecino que tanto ha contribuido al enriquecimiento y solaz de esta barriada en su rol de relojero" (151) ["a well-loved neighbor who has so greatly contributed to this community's enrichment and solace in his role as watchmaker" (150)]. Don Federico, nevertheless, has a compulsion to go out at night "disfrazado de mujeruca" (154) ["dolled up as a tart" (153)] and dressed in a flamenco gown and a wig. On one occasion, he is arrested by the nefarious Fumero and forced to spend a night in jail, where the other inmates abuse him. The next morning, he is dumped on his doorstep with "tres costillas rotas, contusiones múltiples y un desgarro rectal de libro de texto" (158) ["three broken ribs, a large number of bruises, and an uncommonly severe rectal tear" (159)]. Don Federico is thus not only beaten but also raped. All of his neighbours, including Daniel, his father, and their friends, show great concern for Don Federico's suffering, and a team of neighbourhood women takes turns caring for him. In reflecting on the situation, Don Federico's friend, Merceditas, calls the perpetrators of the abuse "evil"; but Fermín contends that evil requires forethought and that Don Federico's assailants acted on instinct, spontaneously attacking someone they perceived as different from themselves. Eventually, Don Federico recovers, and in the end he and Merceditas become a couple – even though local gossips insist that, "de tarde en tarde, don Federico hace alguna escapadilla de picos pardos ataviado de faraona" (476–7) ["every now and then, Don Federico goes out on a binge, dressed up as a Gypsy queen" (485)].

Although a minor character in the text, Don Federico, through his name, inevitably invokes modern Spain's most renowned homosexual figure, Federico García Lorca. Since the Spanish Civil War, García Lorca has been regarded almost universally as a martyr to Francoism, and in recent years has been claimed as the prototypical victim of homophobia. His death is one of the most famous lacunae in Spanish Civil War history, the meaning of which several generations of literary and cultural historians have struggled to reconstruct. In a sense, García Lorca's life and writing embody the difference (whether his own homosexual difference or the ethnic and gender difference of many of his characters) that according to Fermín motivates all violence. If Francoism sought the violent erasure of difference through the murder of García Lorca and untold numbers of others, the Ruiz Zafón text seemingly reaffirms difference through the depiction of Don Federico. In so doing, it attenuates the terrible history of mid-twentieth-century Spain. But the upshot is problematic. Unlike García Lorca, Don Federico is not killed. Furthermore, his abuse is perpetrated not by Francoist agents (who arrest both the historical and fictional figures) but by common criminals (or, as Fermín puts it, "[e]l imbécil o cafre" [155] ["(a) moron or a lout" (155)]) whose actions result from ignorance rather than premeditated evil. The Ruiz Zafón text hence subtly shifts the narrative of Don Federico away from the political and ethical contexts of most narratives of García Lorca's life. Here, the malefactors are in a way even exonerated because they lack the conscience necessary for moral choice. They also seem an aberrance in Spanish society, since all the other characters are portrayed as extraordinarily sympathetic to the plight of Don Federico and tolerant of homosexuals in general. This might be read as a fantasy or possibly a means of enabling a historically marginalized group, were it not for the way Don Federico is ultimately absorbed – albeit with a wink to the reader – into a heterosexual framework. In fact, the Ruiz Zafón fiction does not affirm the difference so brutally destroyed in the life of García Lorca, but instead dismisses it, for here it is simply reduced to an amusing anecdote.

The worldview of *La sombra del viento* is expressed by Daniel, who is not only a character in the novel but also the first-person narrator. What is more, although he initially depicts himself as a reader of texts, in the end he reveals that he is also the writer of the overarching *Sombra* narrative. Like his identity as reader, his identity as writer is formed through multiple avatars of the father-son relationship. Just as his father makes available to him a book that will become the formative reading experience of his life, so too does he give him a talismanic pen, once supposedly owned by Victor Hugo, that will endow him with the power of a writer. In the course of this tale of improbable coincidences, Daniel learns that the pen previously belonged to Julián, and finally he returns it to him, thereby restoring Julián's artistic powers. In a way, Daniel plays the role of father by bringing Julián back to life as a writer. Yet Daniel not only provides Julián with a means of recreating himself, but also makes him the subject of his fiction and even names his son after him.

> Mientras escribo estas líneas sobre el mostrador de la librería, mi hijo Julián, que mañana cumple diez años, me observa sonriente e intrigado por esa pila de cuartillas que crece y crece, quizá convencido de que su padre también ha contraído esa enfermedad de los libros y las palabras. (475)
>
> [As I write these words on the counter of my bookshop, my son, Julián, who will be ten tomorrow, watches me with a smile and looks with curiosity at the pile of sheets that grows and grows, convinced, perhaps, that his father has also caught the illness of books and words. (483)][14]

Daniel's gift to Julián thus does not diminish but rather enhances his own ability to write, for if he did not give life to the past that Julián represents, he would in fact have nothing about which to write. And in giving life to the past, he also generates a future, incarnated in his own book and son, whom he will subsequently take to El Cementerio de los Libros Olvidados to begin the whole process anew.

In *La sombra del viento*, the dynamics of reading and writing are played out in father-son relationships: Daniel and his father, Daniel and his son, and Daniel and Julián. Because of the absence of the mother figure (Daniel's mother is dead from the beginning and little Julián's mother, Beatriz, although the object of Daniel's affection throughout much of the text, is on the sidelines at the end), the father-son relationship becomes a primary site of desire. This desire might seem incestuous, even though the text deflects incest onto other family configurations, including the real and quasi-real sister-brother relationships of Penélope and Julián and Beatriz and Daniel, and the relationship between Fumero and his mother. (It is interesting, and perhaps not surprising given the text's overall erasure of the mother figure, that only the relationship between Fumero and his mother is pathologized.) What attracts the Ruiz Zafón father and son figures to each other is, as Leo Bersani theorizes of the homoerotic, not a desire to fulfill an inner lack through the incorporation of difference but a narcissistic desire that seeks in the other what one already is.

> The aim of desire grounded in lack is the filling of the lack through the incorporation of difference. The desire in others of what we already are

> is, on the contrary, a self-effacing narcissism, a narcissism constitutive of community in that it tolerates psychological difference because of its very indifference to psychological difference. (150)

Bersani imagines this desire as constitutive of a gay community of equals. In the homosocial world of the Ruiz Zafón text, male erotic desire turns toward the female. Yet male-male desire remains an impetus of self-realization that leads, even in the ostensibly vertical relationships of fathers and sons, to a kind of equivalence of the self and the other.

Intersubjectivity as depicted in *La sombra del viento* is in fact clearly informed by gender difference. When, for instance, Daniel and Beatriz make love for the first time, he throws himself on her, "en busca de sus labios, convencido ya de que el canibalismo era la encarnación suprema de la sabiduría" (300) ["searching her lips, convinced by now that cannibalism was the supreme incarnation of wisdom" (304)]. This passage is telling of how the male strives to incorporate female difference (and, at least figuratively, consume her in the process) in an effort to achieve the fullness of selfhood. In contrast, Julián and Miquel actually switch identities at a critical moment in their lives. Although in doing so Miquel saves Julián by allowing himself to be killed, neither "cannibalizes" the other but instead maintains a respect for the other's self-integrity. As the Julián-Daniel relationship further reveals, in male-male pairings the other is like a mirror in which each seeks an image of himself. If, as according to Jacques Lacan, the young child first discovers an ideal body unity in the "mirror stage," and if this experience becomes "la souche des identifications secondaires" (*Écrits* 94) ["the root-stock of secondary identifications" (*Écrits: The First* 76)], then "[c]'est dans l'autre qu'il retrouvera toujours son moi idéal" (*Le Séminaire* 429) ["(i)t is in the other that he will always rediscover his ideal ego" (*The Seminar* 282)]. In the Ruiz Zafón text, this process, as enacted between males, is reciprocal, and the identities that appear, however fleetingly, tend toward similitude. If the other is a means of self-fashioning, he is thus also, to extrapolate from Bersani, the locus of "a seductive sameness" (150).

In the Ruiz Zafón father-son relationships the other is imagined not only as a mirror but also a book. On the one hand, Daniel initially reads the book of Julián's life as "una galería de espejos" (14) ["a gallery of mirrors" (7)] in which the self is simultaneously constituted and fragmented. Julián, on the other hand, regards the child Daniel as "una nueva página en blanco para volver a empezar aquella historia que no podía inventar, pero que podía recordar" (434) ["a blank page on which to restart a story that he could not invent but could remember" (444)]. Although Daniel has an intuition of the instability of identity,

Julián holds that identity is somehow fixed, albeit vexingly absent. In response to the dull Jorge's statement that "[l]os libros son aburridos" ["(b)ooks are boring"], Julián declares that "[l]os libros son espejos: sólo se ve en ellos lo que uno ya lleva dentro" (207) ["(b)ooks are mirrors: you only see in them what you already have inside you" (209)]. Reading is therefore a narcissistic enterprise. What is more, although the book is an avatar of the other, the other is conflated with the subject and as a result ceases to appear as other. The reciprocity promised through male-male bonding and expressed across books thus leads to a kind of solipsism that Julián and Daniel both achieve when they transform themselves into writers. As Julián once remarked, a book, like all stories, is really "una carta que el autor se escribe a sí mismo" (434) ["a letter the author writes to himself" (444)]. If this is the case, then the other, as Carmen Martín Gaite's *El cuarto de atrás* [*The Back Room*] suggests, is no more than a pretext necessary for an assertion of the self.[15]

In a final intertextual reference, this time to Unamuno, Daniel receives a copy of a book from a Boris Laurent, titled *El ángel de brumas* [The angel of mists]. Daniel realizes that this is the work of Julián, writing under a pseudonym, and that he has succeeded in regenerating him as a writer. The angel of the title, from the perspective of Julián the writer, is Daniel, whose action has restored him to life – although Julián could similarly be viewed as an angelic presence in Daniel's life, saving him from Fumero and providing him with the story through which he will come to forge his identity. The "ángel de brumas" might also be interpreted as a metaphor for discourse. In *La sombra del viento*, discourse seems inseparable from the materiality of the book – for, as the keeper of El Cementerio de los Libros Olvidados makes clear, if the book were to disappear, then so too would the story. Yet a spirit-body dualism haunts the text, and discourse at times seems to function like a quasi-divine agent (the "ángel"), breathing life into the brute matter of bodies and books. Although the image of mist in Unamuno's *Niebla* represents the inchoateness of human reality independent of discourse, in the Ruiz Zafón text the "ángel de brumas" represents discourse as a life-giving force. For both Unamuno and Ruiz Zafón, one exists only in and through discourse as mediated by the other (authors, readers, fathers, sons, lovers, etc.). But whereas Unamuno regards the discourse of the other as a potential threat to the ontological stability of the self, Ruiz Zafón sees it more simply as a gift of life. It is this, more than anything else, that accounts for his happy ending.

In Unamuno's world there are no real winners, and as the character Augusto Pérez declares, all – including the character, the author, and the reader – must die (*Niebla* 284). The Ruiz Zafón text, in contrast, holds up the promise that through reading and, by extension, through reading as an act of remembering, a kind of immortality can be achieved. This premise – that according to Julián "existimos mientras alguien nos recuerda" (171) ["we exist as long as somebody remembers us" (172)] – is presented in the text as an article of faith. Yet it begs the question of the motives of memory. Although one might choose to rescue the past from oblivion through an act of generosity, as this text demonstrates one also remembers in order to provide oneself with a foundation necessary for self-realization. Memory is thus not disinterested, but is informed by the concerns of the present. Here, the political past of the Civil War and its aftermath remains, if not forgotten, at least obscured by the past as articulated in the narrative. What is at stake is not the ontological status of the past – whether it is real or imaginary – but how the text's take on the past bears on the present. In *La sombra del viento*, the Civil War past is depicted as a tragedy (of broken families and a splintered society) that is transcended in the Francoist period through a patriarchal reordering of society. This telling of the past might be true. But the idealization of patriarchy is also deeply conservative.

According to press reports at the time of publication, the Ruiz Zafón text nonetheless enjoyed stunning commercial success, and its international appeal led to what Xavi Ayén called "[e]l fenómeno Zafón" [the Zafón phenomenon]. Implicitly, the text recognizes its power to attract readers and the revenue they generate. As Nuria explains to Daniel, Julián's *Sombra*, although initially a financial flop, found its stock suddenly rise when Julián's life and Spanish history took a dramatic turn in the late 1930s: "La enigmática fuga de Julián de París tras un sangriento duelo y su rumoreada muerte en la guerra civil española habían conferido a sus obras un valor de mercado que nunca hubieran podido soñar" (432) ["Julián's mysterious flight from Paris after a bloody duel and his rumored death in the Spanish Civil War had conferred on his works an undreamed-of market value" (442)]. The Ruiz Zafón text capitalizes on Spain's great twentieth-century story, the Civil War, but as a "book about books" it also highlights Spain's cultural commonality with Europe as a whole. In fact, "el fenómeno Zafón" is a symptom of Spain's "Europeanization" in the era of the European Union in the early 2000s. But it also effects a subtle "Hispanicization" of Europe as well.

This tension between Europe and Spain is played out in the relationship between books and the city of Barcelona. In a way, books seem entirely disengaged from place: "Nos acomodamos en torno a la mesa que había en la trastienda, rodeados de libros y de silencio. La ciudad dormía y la librería parecía un bote a la deriva en un océano de paz y sombra" (183) ["We settled down around the table in the back room, surrounded by books. The city was asleep, and the bookshop felt like a boat adrift in a sea of silence and shadows" (185)]. The Ruiz Zafón text itself seems to float through a sea of intertexts. But it moors itself, figuratively speaking, within the concrete context of Barcelona. As the site of El Cementerio de los Libros Olvidados (a place "[q]uizá tan viejo como la misma ciudad" [12] ["(p)erhaps as old as the city itself" (6)]), Barcelona is mythologized as the repository of all the books ever written and in a sense as the nexus of all discourse. Although its place in the world of letters was obscured by war and dictatorship, the city has managed to reassert itself, and as Daniel notes, "hay días en que me parece que la luz se atreve cada vez más, que vuelve a Barcelona, como si entre todos la hubiésemos expulsado pero nos hubiese perdonado al fin" (476) ["there are days when I feel that a certain brightness is tentatively returning to Barcelona, as if between us all we'd driven it out but it had forgiven us in the end" (484)]. Yet if Barcelona is forgiving, it is further imagined as capable of enchanting, not only its inhabitants but also, as European "Zafonmaniacs" would surely agree, a much larger reader audience as well: "Esta ciudad es bruja. ... Se le mete a uno en la piel y le roba el alma sin que uno se dé ni cuenta" (470) ["This city is a sorceress. ... It gets under your skin and steals your soul without you knowing it" (480)]. Surreptitiously, then, the text draws European and international readers into the Iberian ken. It may depoliticize the Spanish past, but it fits squarely within the cultural politics of post-Francoist Spain.

As Ruiz Zafón's critics (e.g., Ayén) note, "el fenómeno Zafón" occurred first in the word-of-mouth reports of early readers and only subsequently in mainstream media and academia. If this phenomenon, like Foucault's "phenomenon of the library," reiterates and refashions the Ruiz Zafón text and in the process the multitude of texts that inform *La sombra del viento*, it also, as Foucault has remarked of *La Tentation de saint Antoine*, reveals how texts themselves function as the locus of fantasy. According to the fantasy depicted in *La sombra del viento*, life is a struggle between good and evil in which the former always triumphs. Its more subtle fantasy – which we have all likely once believed – is that the nurturing love of a parent not only is real but also endures forever. *La sombra del viento* does not resurrect the dead parent – Daniel's mother and, by extension, all the dead parents of the Spanish Civil War remain gone despite the quixotic attempt to "read" them back into existence. Yet it nevertheless creates the illusion of a safe haven in the father-son relationships it imagines. That literature provides a safe haven is perhaps the most fantastic of all fictions. But it is one that *La sombra del viento* most stubbornly, and most effectively, sustains.

## Biblioclasm, Bibliophilia, and the Tenacity of Memory in Manuel Rivas's *Os libros arden mal*

Manuel Rivas's epic saga, *Os libros arden mal* (2006) [*Books Burn Badly*], which spans over one hundred years of Galician history, takes as the seminal event of modern Galicia the book burning carried out by the Falangists (the Spanish fascists) on the docks and on the Praza de María Pita in A Coruña on 19 August 1936. At the outset of the Spanish Civil War, the Falangists confiscated books from the city's libraries, worker societies, and private collections, including those of the Spanish Prime Minister Santiago Casares Quiroga. By destroying them, the Falangists intended to eradicate what they deemed to be their subversive content and also, as in the case of the books of Casares Quiroga, to expunge the identity of their owners from the Galician and Spanish collective memory. In *Os libros arden mal*, Rivas portrays the biblioclasm wrought by the Falangists as a trauma that haunts postwar Spanish history. Like the bodies of the victims of war and dictatorship, the majority of burned books disappeared in the wake of the conflagration. Yet some survived the flames, albeit in mutilated form, and were transmitted to subsequent generations. In *Os libros arden mal*, Rivas delineates what he imagines to be the history of these surviving volumes. He thereby provides a textual space for the restitution not only of lost books but also lost lives and ultimately lost time.

In *Os libros arden mal*, Rivas depicts images of sewing, threads, and cloth to illustrate his effort to weave seemingly disparate texts into a distinctively Galician discursive tapestry. If the war rent asunder the Galician cultural fabric, Rivas's narrative undertakes the arduous task of repairing it by drawing together a plethora of literary threads and attempting to restore the warp and woof of Galician history. *Os libros arden mal* thus forms part of the struggle for historical memory carried out in recent years by writers and cultural workers throughout Spain. According to Javier Gómez-Montero, the text represents the collective unconscious of the city of A Coruña, which was repressed by war and dictatorship, but which continues to manifest itself through the remains of the burned books that haunt subsequent generations of the city's inhabitants.[16] As Eugenia R. Romero argues in her application of Pierre Nora's theory of *lieux de mémoire* [sites of memory] to Rivas's earlier narrative, *En salvaxe compaña* (1993) [In savage company], the primary memory-site of *Os libros arden mal* resides not in the novel itself but in its readers, who perform the ultimate "act of memory, and who must give meaning to all of the images" (305).[17] In *Os libros arden mal* the most potent images are of books, and when readers begin to reconstitute these images and their attendant discourses, they become, as Romero explains, "part of the social frameworks that created them" (305) and, by extension, part of Galicia's national and international cultural heritage.

The overriding metaphor operative throughout *Os libros arden mal* is that books are like human bodies, and that books that have been destroyed are like humans who have been killed. As Gillian Silverman argues in her study of the relationship between books and bodies, readers have historically engaged in fantasies of communion with characters, authors, and fellow readers (2). Yet in so doing, they imagine a fleeting consubstantiality not only with human others but also with books themselves, which take on a kind of human corporeality. Rivas extends the notion of books as bodies to suggest that if bodies can die and subsequently be exhumed, then so too can books. The task of "biblio-exhumation" that he undertakes in *Os libros arden mal* parallels the efforts carried out in Spain in recent years by the descendants of the victims of Francoism (often buried anonymously in mass graves) to disinter their family members and give them proper burials. But whereas the bodies of the dead cannot be brought back to life except through memory, some books that have been buried can in fact be resurrected, both figuratively and literally. As Marcy Schwartz explains in the case of post-dictatorship Argentina, books deemed subversive were on occasion buried by owners fearful of reprisals by the regime and later dug up (191).[18] These books mirror the lives of the disappeared who have been revivified through the work of cultural memory. But they are also restored in the flesh, as it were, and in the case of the books depicted by Rivas, help advance the project of Galician linguistic and cultural affirmation short-circuited by the Franco regime.

The burning of books at the port of A Coruña in August 1936, narrated in the sixth chapter of *Os libros arden mal*, informs the entire narrative.

> Isto, as piras de libros, non forma parte da memoria da cidade. Está a suceder agora. Así que isto, o arder dos libros, non ocorre nun pasado remoto nin ás agochadas. Tampouco é un pesadelo de ficción imaxinado por un apocalíptico. Non é unha novela. Por iso o lume vai lento, porque ten que vencer as resistencias, a impericia dos incendiarios, a falta de costume no arder dos libros. A incredulidade dos ausentes. Vese que a cidade non ten memoria deste fume preguiceiro e renitente que se move na estrañeza do ar. Mesmo ten que arder o que non está escrito. (*Os libros* 59)

> [The book fires are not part of the city's memory. They're happening now. So this burning of books isn't taking place in some distant past or in secret. Nor is it a fictional nightmare thought up by some apocalyptic. It's not a

novel. This is why the fire progresses slowly, because it has to overcome resistance, the arsonists' incompetence, the unusualness of burning books. The absentees' incredulity. It's obvious the city has no memory of this lazy, stubborn smoke moving through the air's surprise. Even what's not been written has to burn. (*Books* 34)]

What does it mean that the event is happening "now"? To be sure, it is occurring in the present moment of the narrative, on 19 August 1936. In this moment the spectators would have no memory of any similar event, either real or fictitious, so they would be unable to interpret what they see through any particular historical or literary lens. But on the date in question most potential spectators were in fact absent from the scene, and for this reason most initial readers of Rivas's text have no knowledge of the historical event itself. Thus, for them it is also occurring in the present moment, through their act of reading. Although what they are reading is ostensibly a novel (*Os libros arden mal*), the narrative voice reminds them that the event they are observing is not a novel or a fictional nightmare, despite their incredulity or the incredulity of earlier witnesses. Here, then, we approach the interstice of knowledge and imagination, for while certain twenty-first-century individuals (including Rivas himself) possess a memory of the event (whether through direct experience or the memories of others), most will only ever accede to it through Rivas's literary reinvention. To suggest that this truth might ultimately be fictional does not mean that it is not real, but rather that objective truths that have for all intents and purposes been erased from the collective memory can only be known insofar as they are recreated. What Rivas attempts to bring back to life is not simply the memory of the particular volumes destroyed in August 1936 but the human intentions inscribed in them and, by extension, all of the lives now gone that the material books once mediated – be they those of writers, readers, owners, borrowers, bibliophiles, biblioklepts, or book handlers in general.

The book burning depicted in *Os libros arden mal* represents not only the murder of human beings at the hands of fascist forces during the Spanish Civil War but also the destruction of the Second Republic itself. One volume, titled *A enciclopedia da carne* [The encyclopedia of meat], is pulled from the fire and thrown into the air by the Falangist officer overseeing the cataclysm, perhaps, as the narrator remarks, because he imagines that a treatise on "carne," or flesh, must contain lascivious depictions of sex and orgies.

Cando o tomo chega á fin da caída, o falanxista dálle con disimulo unha patada no canto coa biqueira da bota. Ao abrirse, entre unha nova erupción de charamuscas e fume e as primeiras apalpadas das chamas, a pegada visual de que o que xorde a dobre páxina é un mapa peninsular coas provincias marcadas en cores. É un efecto demasiado causal, un descoido da punta da bota, que a propia mirada se apresura a corrixir. Non, non son as provincias de España. Vese axiña que se trata, en realidade, da ilustración do despezamento dunha vaca. O lombo, o solombo, o xarrete, a croca, o redondo, a agulla, a tes, a faldra. (60)

[When the volume reaches the end of its fall, the Falangist gives it a little kick on the corner with the toecap of his boot. As it opens, with a new eruption of smoke and cinders and the first flames, what meets the eyes is a two-page map of the peninsula with the different provinces shown in colours. The effect is too causal, an accidental jerk of the book, which the eyes hasten to correct. No, they're not the provinces of Spain. It soon becomes obvious it's really an illustration of the different parts of a cow. Loin, sirloin, hock, coccyx, rump, rib, brisket. (35)]

The juxtaposition of images in this passage suggests that Spain has been, or is about to be, butchered. The narrative voice directly guides the metaphor, indicating that while at first glance the illustration appears to be a map of the country, it in fact depicts a cow, albeit one whose synthetic unity as a living creature has been carved up into contingent, physical parts, or slabs of meat. Despite the initial prurience of the Falangist, who thought it a "mágoa non terlle botado unha ollada" (60) ["shame not to have had a peek" (35)] into a book about flesh, the image of the dismembered animal is a sinister reminder of the brutalization and murder of untold numbers of Spanish Loyalists of the period, including the wife of the local Republican governor, a librarian whose breasts were slashed and who was raped and tortured to death.

The comparison of books to flesh continues throughout the episode. As living flesh, books are not only manufactured products but also, as the character Vicente Curtis explains, natural entities. Curtis is a boxer known as Hercules, the name of the classical hero as well as the lighthouse at A Coruña harbour whose light shines from an open volume sculpted in its insignia. According to Gómez-Montero, the sculpture of this book was removed during the Francoist period (413). Significantly, the character with the name most closely tied to the figure of the book in the Galician public imaginary is the one who reflects most directly on the natural and regenerative essence of books.

Vicente Curtis decatouse de que nunca antes pensara de onde viña a materia da que estaban feitos os libros. Non, non pensaba agora nas ideas, nas doutrinas, nos soños. Sabía que os libros tiñan que ver coas árbores. Que

> había unha relación. Que dalgún xeito se podería dicir, e a medida que andaba cara ás fogueiras avanzaba en precisión, poderiamos dicir, si, que os libros procedían da natureza. Mesmo non sería incorrecto dicir, nin dicir de máis, que os libros eran un enxerto. (65)
>
> [Vicente Curtis realised he'd never wondered where the material books are made of came from. No, he wasn't thinking about ideas, doctrines and dreams. He knew that books had something to do with trees. There was a relation. It could be said somehow or other – and as he walked towards the pyres, he clarified his thoughts – that's right, we could say that books come from nature. It might not even be false or exaggerated to say that books are a kind of graft. (38)]

The notion of the book as a graft is intriguing. Through an act of grafting, a tree is reproduced. As an "enxerto," its life is "inserted" or "introduced" into the cast of pages, dust cover, and binding. As suggested by the English word "graft," a derivative of the Greek word "graphein" [to write], the process culminates when ink is inscribed on paper through an act of writing. Books as grafts are thus not clones of trees but rather hybrids through which trees and human intentions are conjoined in a new form. As living creatures, they resist the assault to their being wrought by fire, producing "o cheiro lúgubre e aflixido das cousas que non queren arder" (66) ["the mournful, afflicted smell of things that (don't want to) burn" (39)]. The upshot is that books are not passive; they do not give up easily and they desire to live. To the displeasure of the fascists of the 1930s (and without doubt to the relief of subsequent generations of readers), books do burn badly: it is difficult to dispose of them, and many ultimately persist. Herein, then, lies the optimism of *Os libros arden mal*.

In the book burning of 19 August 1936, the Spanish Nationalists aimed to destroy not only individual volumes but also whole libraries. The most important library depicted in Rivas's narrative is that of Casares Quiroga, the prime minister at the time of the Nationalist uprising against the government of the Second Republic. As a native of A Coruña, a founder of the Autonomous Galician Republican Organization, and a consummate bibliophile, Casares Quiroga was particularly vilified by the Nationalists. By destroying his library, the finest private collection in the city, they hoped to eradicate him from the Spanish collective memory and expunge at least that aspect of his identity that as a reader and collector he had forged through books. Casares Quiroga's love of books began when he was a child and would await with excitement the packages of books that his father had ordered from abroad, many of which were prohibited or impossible to find in Spain: "un dos intres máis felices da súa infancia era abrir os paquetes 'que traía o mar'" (76) ["one of his happiest childhood memories was opening the packages 'brought by the sea'" (47)]. The Falangist officer supervising the book burning is particularly keen to seize Casares Quiroga's books, as if in doing so he were capturing not only one of his possessions but the man himself.

> Olla con deleitación a marca xenuína da peza, o sinal distintivo, o ex-libris que coincide coa sinatura do propietario.
> Si señor, bo traballo. Un auténtico *Casaritos*! (66)

> [He pores over the guarantee of authenticity, the distinguishing mark, the ex-libris that matches the owner's signature.
> "Yes, well done. It's a genuine Casaritos!" (39)]

Casares Quiroga's distinctive signature on his bookplates, "Santiagcasares Qu," is like a drawing through which the Falangist can grasp "o retrato do home" (76) ["the portrait of the man" (46)]. Casares Quiroga's books are thus like grafts, and when destroyed, something of Casares Quiroga's own essence vanishes. Not only is his library subject to a "despezamento" (60), or "dismemberment," heretofore linked to the Second Republic and its supporters, but all his possessions, including even his fingerprints, are obliterated. Yet as *Os libros arden mal* makes clear, it is Casares Quiroga's books that convey his most intimate self, and some of these actually survive.

At one point during the book burning a young Falangist, Paralelepípedo (so-named because of his delight in attempting to pronounce the word when one of his comrades referred to the assembled books as parallelepipeds) picks up a volume with the name Federico García Lorca on the cover, glances inside, and throws it with hatred onto the pyre. Although he has never read anything by García Lorca, he remembers jokes depicting him as "García *Loca*," or "García Drag Queen," and as one of the "maricas roxos" (83) ["red queens" (52)]. He then picks up another book, García Lorca's *Seis poemas galegos* [*Six Galician Poems*]. He hands it to his boss, Ricardo Samos, and with a look of disgust on his face asks him: "Este marica tamén escribía en galego?" (84) ["Did this faggot also write in Galician?" (52)]. Samos is intrigued by the book, a thin volume on whose cover appears an illustration of the scallop shell of Saint James the Apostle and the words "Prólogo E. B. A. Editorial Nós. Compostela" (84) ["Foreword E. B. A. Nós Publishing House. Compostela" (52)]. The image of the scallop shell, the quintessential emblem of historic Galicia, sets this volume apart from the other books highlighted in *Os libros arden mal*. The editorial information is also significant. Nós was founded by Ánxel Casal Gosenge, a proponent of Galician language and culture and the last Republican mayor of Santiago de Compostela. Both Casal Gosenge and García Lorca were assassinated on the same day as the book burning, 19 August 1936. As the narrator remarks, as if in anticipation of Rivas's own text,

> [s]e alguén, algún día, escribise esta historia da queima de libros na Coruña podería engadir unha anotación non gratuíta. Ánxel Casal e Federico García Lorca foran asasinados aquela mesma madrugada. O editor galego nunha cuneta, á saída de Santiago, en Cacheiras, e o poeta granadino no barranco de Víznar, en Granada. Sobre a mesma hora e a mil quilómetros de distancia. (86–7)

> [(s)hould somebody ever write a history of the burning of books in Coruña, they could add a non-gratuitous detail: Ánxel Casal and Federico García Lorca were murdered that same morning. The Galician publisher in a ditch outside Santiago, in Cacheiras, and the Granadine poet in the gully of Víznar, Granada. At about the same time, six hundred miles apart. (54)]

These horrific killings are not an absurd coincidence, given that Casal Gosenge and García Lorca both opposed the Nationalist uprising. Although in their work as publishers and writers they typically emphasized different causes, at least on one occasion they collaborated through the *Seis poemas galegos* text. The simultaneity of their murders and the book burning corroborates the commonality of humans and books suggested earlier in the chapter. Yet the episode also reveals a key difference precisely because Samos does not destroy the copy of the *Seis poemas galegos* but instead keeps it. In *Os libros arden mal*, the attitude of the Nationalist characters towards books is in fact complex, for while their express goal is to destroy them, they also save some works, and in so doing make them available to posterity despite their intentions.

Samos himself harbours a secret love of books. He explains to Paralelepípedo that García Lorca spent time in Galicia with his theatre company, La Barraca, and that he made many friends in the region. After Paralelepípedo gives Samos the *Seis poemas galegos*, the book begins to dance in his hands, perhaps because it is on fire and he cannot hold it without burning his skin, or perhaps because it comes to life, as it were, when he recites verses from one of the six poems:

> Cabelos que van ao mar
> onde as nubes teñen o seu nidio pombal. (84)

[Locks that go out to sea,
where the clouds their glittering dovecot keep. (52)][19]

These verses are taken from the "Canzón de cuna pra Rosalía Castro, morta" ["Lullaby for Dead Rosalía Castro"]. In this piece, a poetic voice meditates on the dead Castro in her grave beneath the grass, "a negra fonte dos teus cabelos" (García Lorca 564) [the black spring of your locks]. Castro's locks, albeit moldering in the earth, also rise up in the poem like the ashes of the burning books or even birds. (In the same passage in *Os libros arden mal* the burning books are explicitly compared to birds that have come down from trees [the physical progenitors of print material] and fallen into a trap of men [*Os libros* 83, *Books* 51].) In the poem, Castro's locks waft out to sea, blown by a wind that "muxe como unha vaca" (564) [lows like a cow] (a potent echo of the dismembered animal and broken lives depicted earlier in the book-burning episode) and carries them to a celestial sanctuary in the clouds. In *Os libros arden mal*, the upshot is that books can and do have an afterlife. Initially, Samos has Paralelepípedo throw the *Seis poemas galegos* onto the book pyre, where it lands on top of another volume and thereby escapes immolation. Samos then considers picking it up, which he attempts to justify by telling Paralelepípedo that the initials on the cover might prove useful, most likely for tracking down more anti-fascists. But he really wants the book because it might someday become a rarity: "A primeira edición dos *Seis poemas* acadaría o valor dun pergameo medieval" (87) ["A first edition of the *Six Poems* would be as valuable as a medieval parchment" (54)]. Samos's knowledge of literature coupled with his desire to possess books of value clearly reveals a deep-seated bibliophilia.

Samos expresses interest in many books, including the Bible. He specifically asks the groups of soldiers tending the book fires to keep an eye out for editions of the New Testament. He informs Paralelepípedo that the volume he is seeking has a dedication in it: "*A Antonio de la Trava, o Valente de Fisterra*" (89) ["For Antonio de la Trava, the valiente of Finisterra" (56)]. At the end of the chapter, Paralelepípedo has found the book and hidden it under his blue Falangist shirt. As he reflects on the possible importance of the work, he feels a slap on his back, and another Falangist, named Ren, asks him what he is concealing. Paralelepípedo tells Ren that it is a novel: "Unha desas francesas. Para ler no escusado" (159) ["A Frenchy to read in the toilet" (107)]. But Ren demands that he hand it over to him, and the book, the most important in *Os libros arden mal* insofar as it links the entire timespan of the narrative, thus temporarily passes into the hands of the fascists.

The provenance of this New Testament is revealed in the second chapter of *Os libros arden mal*. Here, a historical figure, the Englishman George Henry Borrow, recalls to a stepdaughter how in 1836, 100 years before the book burning, he was almost shipwrecked one night in a storm off Cape Finisterre, Galicia. But because of a sudden burst of lightning the ship's crew was able to see the rocky coastline and save the vessel. Borrow, a member of the British Bible Society, had gone to Spain for the purpose of propagating the New Testament. He subsequently recounted his activities in the country in a book titled *The Bible in Spain*. Borrow's sojourn in Spain coincided with the first Carlist War. While there, he was captured by liberal Cristino soldiers, who thought he was a Spaniard and leader of the conservative Carlists.[20] He might have been executed, but Antonio de la Trava intervened and declared that he was an Englishman because of his ability to translate the English words "knife" and "fork" into Spanish. As a token of his appreciation, Borrow gave De la Trava a copy of the New Testament, which he dedicated to him.[21] Afterwards, he made his way to Madrid, set up a bookshop, and printed 5,000 Spanish-language editions of the New Testament. At one point he was arrested and forbidden to continue his work. From his decidedly Protestant perspective this was because

> [o]s papistas non querían que o pobo lera o Evanxeo! O vaticano asignou a España o papel de verdugo. Sempre afastaron a xente da palabra de Deus. Era algo escandaloso, mais do que no se falaba. No país máis católico do orbe, a xente tiña medo de mercar as Sagradas Escrituras. Podías ver como lles tremían as ventas do nariz cando eu lles puña un libro nas mans. Estaban a cheirar o lume da Inquisición. (23)

> [(t)he Papists didn't want the people reading the Gospel! The Vatican assigned Spain the role of butcher and always kept the people apart from the Word of God. A scandal that was never talked about. In the most Catholic country in the world, people were afraid to buy the Holy Scriptures. You could see their nostrils quivering when I put a book in their hands. They could smell the flames of the Inquisition. (7)][22]

This passage, appearing at the outset of *Os libros arden mal*, links the burning of the books in 1936 to the fires of the Inquisition, which destroyed not only persons and books deemed inimical to Catholicism but also, as the juxtaposition of the Holy Scriptures and the smell of flames suggests, to the annihilation of the Word of God. If the pages of the Bible reek of the Inquisitional fires, then the institution of the Inquisition stands guilty of having killed living people as well as the living God made incarnate in the Word. The work of the fascists in 1936, although ostensibly intended to obliterate their political adversaries, thus forms part of a long tradition of Spanish biblioclasm, and in *Os libros arden mal* libricide is equated with both homicide and deicide.

In the chapter following the book burning, titled "O enterro dos libros" ["The Books' Burial"], a municipal gardener, Polca, and other conscripts are ordered to rake up the ashes and charred volumes and bury them. Polca notices some of the book burners rummaging through the debris and kicking "aos ósos dos libros" (162) ["at the bones of books" (109)]. Among them is Samos, who continues to search for Borrow's New Testament. Polca reflects on the strangeness of the scene and the task that he and his fellow workers are about to undertake. None of them really knows how to handle the remains of burned books because none has ever encountered such objects before. As Polca observes: "o que hoxe ardía era o tempo. Diso si que me decatei. No dixen nada, mais penseino. ... [A]rde o tempo. Non as horas, nin os días, nin os anos. O tempo" (164) ["What was burning today ... was time itself. I realised that. I didn't say anything, but I thought it. ... [T]ime is burning. Not hours or days or years. Time" (111)]. Polca's comment regarding the burning of time is multilayered. On one level, what is destroyed is time as it has been depicted in the books. When this time is lost, so too is a plethora of past worlds, be they real or imaginary. As Polca realizes, the book fires also affect the future, and for him the experience he might have had by reading if the books had not been burned: "Os libros todos que non lin ... están a arder" (164) ["All the books I never read ... are burning" (111)]. The burning of the books thus results in the loss of a potential future. Yet on a deeper level, the burning of time is also a metaphor for the destruction of life itself insofar as the act of living is always temporal. With this metaphor Rivas alters the traditional spirit/matter dichotomy present in Borrow's Christian conception of the Bible as the physical medium through which the Word of God is expressed. What Rivas suggests is not that books and humans are fundamentally spiritual in nature, but rather that they are temporal agents and as such dynamic. Through their biblioclasm the fascists (as well as their Inquisitorial forebears) attempt to suppress the potential of books to effect change. They thus reduce them to the status of inert matter: "cinza," "pel torrada," "papel contraído" (165) ["ash," "toasted skin," "shrivelled paper" (112)]. In a final gesture of desecration, they urinate on them. Some books, however, including the *Seis poemas galegos* and the New Testament of Borrow, are saved, and as a result they connect the time of the past and the time of the future and remain vital.

Following the book burning and burial, *Os libros arden mal* traces its narrative of books through the characters Samos and Police Inspector Ren, as well as several of their contemporaries and children including Tomás Dez, Alfonso Sulfe, and Gabriel Samos. Dez is a professional censor, and for this reason he is intimately tied to books and print material in general. He is also a sadist, holding his Loyalist lover, Luis Terranova, as a virtual slave. (Eventually, Terranova leaves him, and Dez has him severely beaten, after which Terranova's closest friend, Curtis, arranges for Terranova to leave the country.) In a dream Dez finds himself driving through the night in search of archives and libraries in an effort to ferret out and expunge all his own pro-Nazi writings. But everything he encounters in the dream is pro-Nazi, and the trail of his writings is unending. His friend Samos upbraids him for aligning himself so directly with Nazism, and when Dez levels the same charge against him, Samos reminds him that he tempered his own political views by aligning them with Catholicism. But what Dez says to Samos about words is most significant.

> Non é tan doado manter a raia as palabras. Son como cascudas, como ratas. Andan polo subsolo, polos sumidoiros, entre as tumbas. Son como insectos. Como bacterias. Aos homes é doado pararlles os pés, mais non é tan doado poñerlles couto ás palabras. Os silencios, as pausas, son parte da linguaxe. (222–3)
>
> [It's not so easy to keep words in line. They're like cockroaches or rats. They live underground, in sewers, among tombs. They're like insects. Bacteria. It's easy to stop men in their tracks, but it's not so easy to contain words. Silences, pauses, are part of language. (158)]

According to Dez, language survives even when silent. The image of words living underground in sewers and tombs and proliferating like rats, insects, and bacteria evokes the books burned, urinated on, and buried in a place we later learn is called "the field of the rat." It also suggests that the language of these books will continue to have agency in succeeding generations despite the destruction of the books themselves. Although Dez wants to erase his own words, which would eventually put him at odds with the Francoist dictatorship (in the waning years of the Second World War the regime began to distance itself from Nazism), his dream also reveals a fear that the discourses opposed to totalitarian ideology present in many of the burned books might undermine his position in society. In his dream, with its "noite de horas viscosas, de reloxo a derreterse" (223–4) ["night of sticky hours, of a melting clock" (159)], reminiscent of the surrealist paintings of Salvador Dalí, he stands before the pyres of books burned in 1936. But when he and Samos attempt to articulate the event, the dream suddenly ends. As the narrative voice explains,

> [a] simple mención á queima dos libros esluía o cadro. Todas as personaxes enmudecían. Desaparecían. Dábase por clausurado o pesadelo. Non houbera unha consigna específica. Non se xuntaran adrede para decidir o silencio perpetuo nin tampouco xurdira como iniciativa nunha xuntanza. Simplemente, a queima deixara de existir. O pacto de silencio acadaba tamén o subconsciente. (224)

> [(t)he mere mention of burning books dissipated the scene. All the characters fell silent. Disappeared. The nightmare was officially over. There was no specific instruction. They hadn't assembled on purpose to agree on perpetual silence, nor had it been suggested at some meeting. The burning of books had simply ceased to exist. The pact of silence applied to the subconscious as well. (159)]

Just as in his waking life Dez censors the language of the regime's political opponents, in his dream he represses the memory of the crime of the book burning whenever it begins to assert itself. The memory rises up from his unconscious like rats, insects, and bacteria from the underground. In a sense, these creatures are the discourses of the books and, by extension, the books themselves in disguised form. By pressing the Freudian paradigm that Rivas makes explicit in the passage, one might say that books for Dez are not really objects of disgust and revulsion, as they first appear to be, but objects of desire that he does not want to recognize as such. His secret, like that of the other Falangist characters in the *Os libros arden mal*, is precisely his bibliophilia – a passion he shares with some of the regime's greatest perceived enemies, including Casares Quiroga. But after being burned, the books also function like spectres of the destroyed lives of the Spanish Civil War that haunt both Francoist and post-Francoist societies in spite of the official project of forgetting.

The past exerts its power not only in dreams but also in waking moments through actions that individuals seem unable to control. Samos, who in the postwar period becomes a prominent Francoist judge, has an immense library that contains remnants of the books burned in 1936. As a collector he is primarily interested in Bibles, and he describes his library as a resting place for the items he has gathered over the years in his search for copies of Old and New Testaments. When he visits his library, he seems almost unconsciously drawn to one particular volume.

> A memoria ás veces anda ao seu, pensou o xuíz. Cando te dás de conta, sen querer, tes nas mans un libriño cos cortes queimados que estaba alí, na recámara. Podía ir na procura doutros, doutras xoias de bibliógrafo que tamén andan por alí, edicións inglesas con dourado nos cortes ou debuxos en acuarela, marabilla dos impresores de Albión. Mais no, cando se decatou, o que fixera a memoria das mans fora ir onda aquel libriño dos cortes e recantos queimados co símbolo da vieira no centro da portada, o libriño dos *Seis poemas galegos*. Coas cousas que pasaron, xusto tiñan que ir morrer ese día o poeta e o editor, o 19 de agosto, o día da queima. (353)

> [Memory sometimes does its own thing, thought the judge. By the time you realise, without wanting to, you've a book in your hands from the alcove, with burnt edges. He could have gone in search of others, other bibliographical jewels that were in there, English editions with gilt edges and watercolours, wonderful editions. But no, by the time he realised, what the memory of his hands had done was pull out the little book with burnt edges and the symbol of a scallop shell in the centre, the little book with the *Six Galician Poems*. The way things happened, both poet and publisher had to go and die on that day, August 19, the day they burnt books. (257)]

As this passage suggests, memory is not a voluntary act performed by the person remembering but an agent in its own right. In this case the thing remembered, García Lorca's book of poetry, acts on Samos and perhaps even prompts him to feel a slight sense of regret. What seems to disturb him is not the coincidence of the deaths of the poet and the publisher but the very fact that they died. As he recalls, their deaths occurred in conjunction with the book burning, as if all three events were interrelated – which indeed they were, since all three resulted from the concerted efforts of the Falangists. But Samos subtly shifts responsibility for what happened. In fact, the question is not why García Lorca and Casal Gosenge "tiñan que ir morrer" (353) ["had to go and die" (257)] on a certain day in August 1936, as if they had a choice in the matter, but why the forces of Samos had to kill them, and also destroy the books.

The memory of the García Lorca volume occurs in the context of a conversation between Samos and Ren, Samos's primary purveyor of Bibles and old books. Samos's lifelong goal is to obtain the copy of the New Testament with Borrow's inscription, which he does not know Ren already possesses. When Samos asks Ren if he has been able to locate it, Ren lies and says that he has not. Ren then advises Samos to forget the Borrow Bible, and informs him that he is seeking for him a book by an Irish writer, most likely James Joyce's *Ulysses*. The reference to *Ulysses* is not incidental, for both *Ulysses* and *Os libros arden mal* are structured around a single day. Although *Os libros arden mal* spans over a century, beginning in the early 1880s with Borrow's recollections of Spain and ending in the mid-1990s with the disclosure of the existence of Borrow's Bible, the events of one day, 19 August 1936, inform the entire narrative and provide a kind of thematic unity to the plethora of disparate voices and perspectives that permeate the text. The disunity of these voices and perspectives is in fact the result of the rupture that occurred in Spanish society during the Spanish Civil War. This rupture functioned not only to destroy but also disperse the discourses of the burned books, like threads of a fabric that has been torn apart. The image of torn fabric and the attempt to mend it appears in several key passages in Rivas's narrative.

The summer of 1936, when the war began and the books were burned, is described through an image of fabric that is at once nostalgic and horrific: "un fermoso verán cosido a balazos" (96) ["a beautiful summer, sewn with bullets" (60)]. Here, bullets do not stitch together the tapestry of summer but rather pierce it with holes. Repairing the damage (to the fabric of summer as well as the fabric of society as a whole) will require an act of reweaving. In a later chapter, this act is depicted as a work of creation, even though the same threads of the torn fabric will be used. In a key episode, a character named Silvia is charged with mending a cape of King Alfonso XIII that the city officials of A Coruña plan to give to Franco when he visits the city:

> Silvia explicou que ía ser unha tarefa case imposíbel. Só servían os fíos da propia peza. Unha cirurxía delicadísima. Máis que atopalos, tería que inventalos un por un para reconstruír o urdido. (530)
>
> [Silvia explained how the task was almost impossible. She could only use the garment's own threads. An extremely delicate operation. Rather than finding them, she would have to invent them one by one in order to reconstruct the warp. (388)]

The seemingly contradictory task of inventing something in order to find it is in fact the task undertaken by Rivas and by a society whose book heritage has been ravaged. Although Silvia's labour might at first glance seem unrelated to books, Rivas elsewhere establishes a parallel between books and fabrics. As the narrator reveals, Casal Gosenge's wife was a clothing designer named María Miramontes, whose skill with a needle made his book printing enterprise possible. On one occasion, visitors actually observed that "a modista e as costureiras estaban a coser libros" (121) ["the designer and seamstresses were sewing books" (79)]. If books are made by sewing together both the threads of the binding and the words of the discourse (indeed, Borrow himself is reported to have read scripture "co aceno severo de quen está a enfiar a agulla da eternidade" (19) ["with the severity of someone threading the needle of eternity" (5)]), then the recovery of the lost books of 1936 will be achieved when they are stitched back together – as they are, to a certain degree, through Rivas's text itself. In the process, the warp and woof of Galician history will be resutured, and the texture of lost time will be restored.

Within the narrative of *Os libros arden mal* many of the lost books of 1936 are salvaged for posterity by Samos's son, Gabriel, who acts as a sort of liaison between the pre-Francoist past and the post-Francoist future. There is in this family a genealogy of bibliophilia beginning with Samos's father, from whom Samos believes he inherited a passion for book collecting, and continuing with Gabriel, who is unable to resist the allure of his father's large and recondite library. Many of the books in Samos's library in fact once belonged to Casares Quiroga, and as Gabriel secretly reads them, he begins to recuperate a dimension of the world of their former owner. Gabriel is made aware of Casares Quiroga's connection to his father's collection by his father's friend, Sulfe, a professor and, since childhood, bibliophile, who regards his books as his most valued property. During a visit to Samos's house, Sulfe recalls their shared interest in books and a conversation they once had after the war when Samos spoke of some interesting volumes that he had obtained "polo azar da historia" (401) ["by a stroke of fate" (294)]. These books include *Le Nu de Rabelais* [The nude of Rabelais], a collection of erotic images of women by the nineteenth-century French painter Jules-Arsène Garnier. Samos denies any knowledge of this book or any conversation he had with Sulfe about books in general. A change in his tone of voice makes Gabriel, who is present in the room, realize that the matter in question is deadly serious. Sulfe also mentions Herman Melville's *Moby Dick* and a first edition of Benito Pérez Galdós's novel, *Lo prohibido* [*The Prohibited*]. Sulfe then adds that these books originally belonged to Casares Quiroga. As Gabriel listens (his father now nervously recognizes his presence in the room), he begins to feel on his hands the texture of burned books, which he has previously held in his father's library.

> Lembraba como un saúdo, como unha consigna, a sinatura de Santiag-casares Qu. E logo, a medida que pasaba as follas, un recendo exasperado a fume e ser humano. (405)
>
> [He remembered the signature like a password or greeting: Santiagcasares Qu. And then, as he turned the pages, an exasperated scent of smoke and human beings. (297)]

Samos claims to know nothing about Casares Quiroga's library, and when Sulfe asks him if the New Testament of Borrow, which Samos has always coveted, managed to escape the flames, Samos makes Sulfe leave his home. Sulfe knows that he will never be invited back. Nevertheless, what Samos hoped Gabriel would never find out has now been revealed by one whose mission it is to teach: to wit, the existence of the books that survived the fires of 1936 and the identity of one of their former owners, Casares Quiroga.

After Sulfe's visit, Samos implies that he made Sulfe leave because he is a biblioklept, even though he himself is one of the greatest biblioklepts of the entire novel. Samos then recommends that Gabriel go outside and amuse himself and not spend his time indoors reading, lest he become another Sulfe. The thought of becoming another Sulfe fills Gabriel with a mixture of excitement and guilt, and after Samos departed, he went straight to his father's study, "[s]ubiu a escaleira e alí, no recanto dos queimados, procurou *O prohibido* de Galdós" (407) ["(c)limbed the library steps and there, in the zone of charred remains, sought out *The Prohibited* by Galdós" (298)]. Gabriel is mesmerized not only by the books Casares Quiroga possessed but also by his personal papers, which Samos evidently appropriated as well at the time of the book burning. Many of these date from Casares Quiroga's youth, and through them Gabriel begins to identify with the former statesman and thereby create for himself a role model different from the one provided by his father. He is thus emblematic of the postwar generation of readers, discovering a hidden and prohibited past, albeit one that is also still potent and alive.

> Fora atopando as postais, as cartas. Tiña o propósito de repasar todos os libros do que xa chamaba as cuadrículas dos Queimados. Había case sempre sorpresas, notas, citas, versos e as postais de Durtol. Non todos o eran, mais os que si tiñan a pegada do lume facían de marcas. Identificábase co que dicía a sinatura, co que escribía aquel mozo. ... O día en que atopou a foto no interior dunha edición inglesa de 1895 dun libro de Wells, *A máquina do tempo*, sentiu, si, unha alegría arqueolóxica. Era unha foto de mocidade. (418)
>
> [He'd come across postcards, letters. He aimed to go through all the books in the zone of charred remains. There were almost always surprises, notes, quotations, verses, postcards from Durtol (a sanatorium where the young Casares Quiroga convalesced from tuberculosis). They weren't all like this, but those that were burnt acted as bookmarks. He identified with what the signature said, what this young man wrote. ... He felt archeological joy the day he found a photo inside an English edition of a book by Wells, *The Time Machine*, dated 1895. It was a photo from his (Casares Quiroga's) youth. (306)]

Unlike Casares Quiroga, Gabriel is not ill and institutionalized, but he is somewhat handicapped because of a stutter, and he is isolated within the confines of the house of his judgmental and authoritarian father. He will eventually be cured of his stutter through writing. He will then be able to rearticulate (or, as it were, reweave) the discourses dispersed in the wake of the book burning and buried within his father's library. Insofar as the burned books function as bookmarks, they allow Gabriel to stake out and map the discursive terrain of the library. His apprenticeship with language as a means of written expression takes place precisely when he reads the books and papers of Casares Quiroga. By reading them, he in a sense travels back to the time of Casares Quiroga's youth, but he also draws Casares Quiroga forward in time to the present. The acts of reading and subsequently writing thus serve as Gabriel's "time machine," which in the context of *Os libros arden mal* is imagined less as a vehicle for time travel than it is a means for recovering lost time and bringing it once again to life.

As a child, Gabriel was often silent out of fear of being mocked by his classmates. In school he was sometimes able to speak, but on other occasions he would become stuck on the same syllable for minutes. Yet he experiences a radical change when he takes up typing, and in the process his voice literally and figuratively becomes unstuck. As an adolescent, Gabriel begins to practise typing on an old iron Hispano-Olivetti. For a time, his typing is the closest approximation in his milieu to the act of making books. When once he is unable to type, he goes back to handwriting and composes imaginary postcards for Casares Quiroga in Durtol Sanatorium. It is, nevertheless, through the typewriter that he creates his own voice and learns to express himself freely, and he soon becomes a compulsive writer. It is with Gabriel, then, that the long silence in the text, wrought through the book burning of 1936, begins to break.

Through Sulfe, Gabriel learns not only of the connection between his father's library and the library of Casares Quiroga, but also of an anecdote from classical literature that nuances the relationship of the book burning of 1936 to the narrative of *Os libros arden mal*. Sulfe explains to Gabriel the origin of the word "colophon." A colophon, he tells the young boy, is the end of something, and specifically a section at the end of a book containing its final notes. As the word is generally understood, a colophon provides facts about a book's production. Colophon is also the name of the island where the ancient Greek fortune teller, Calchas, ended his days. Calchas, according to Sulfe, invented the Trojan horse (although in literary tradition Odysseus actually conceived of it and Calchas endorsed the Greek strategy to use it to penetrate the walls of Troy). To a certain extent Calchas was thus responsible for the fall of Troy to the Greeks. But Calchas was himself given a prophecy that he would die when he met a more powerful fortune teller, which happened on the island of Colophon. Gabriel asks what this other fortune teller foretold, but Sulfe does not know. Some say Calchas died of shame when he lost a contest with the fortune teller, whereas others maintain that he died of laughter when the prediction about his death was at first not fulfilled. Regardless of the variations of the legend, the Rivas text implies that the individual who made possible the sacking of Troy was in a sense brought to justice in a place called Colophon. In light of this interpretation, *Os libros arden mal* might itself be regarded as a sort of colophon, where the crime of the book burning is revealed as such, and a certain justice, at least in the literary imaginary, is achieved.

As a colophon, *Os libros arden mal* focuses less on the production of the books burned in 1936 than on their destruction and subsequent reproduction in its own pages. The role of Calchas nevertheless remains elusive, even if several of the characters instrumental in the book burning, including Samos and Ren, might be compared to him. Through a biblical anecdote in *Os libros arden mal* the image of the destroyer takes on larger, even apocalyptic dimensions. In a chapter titled "Unha 'festa sagrada'" ["A Sacred Feast"], which replicates a chapter from an unpublished book by a fictional writer, Héctor Ríos, called *Unha historia dramática da cultura* [*A Dramatic History of Culture*],[23] the Nazi jurist Karl Schmitt (admired by Samos and honoured by the Franco regime in 1962) speaks of an enigmatic figure in Paul's Second Letter to the Thessalonians known as the *katechon*. According to Paul, the Second Coming of Christ will occur only after the Antichrist is revealed. The *katechon* functions to restrain the Antichrist, so for Christ to reappear, the *katechon* must be removed. Yet according to Ríos, Schmitt assumed the role of the *katechon* through his ideology and in so doing performed a sacred task.

> Hai un poder ou persoa (*ho katechon*) que frea a chegada do "impío" (*ho anomos*), que o "mantén a raia." Aquel que se atribúe o papel de *katechon*, e é o caso de Schmitt, estaría cumprindo unha misión providencial, sagrada. (549–50)

> [There is a power or person (*ho katechon*) who prevents the arrival of the lawlwess one (*ho anomos*) and restrains him. Anyone who assumes that role, as is the case with Schmitt, is performing a sacred, providential mission. (402)]

Ríos's interpretation thus differs from Paul's, since the action of the *katechon*, by restraining the "lawless one," or Antichrist, in fact impedes the Second Coming of Christ. But Ríos offers another possible interpretation:

> Cómpre dicir que na apocalíptica cristiá hai outra corrente: o disfrace máis perfecto, acabado, do "impío" sería o de presentarse como *katechon*. (550)
>
> [Though there is another school of thought, which says the lawless one's most successful disguise would be to present himself as the *katechon*. (402)]

If the *katechon* were the lawless one disguised as a force intended to restrain the lawless one, then the *katechon* would itself be the Antichrist operating in a fashion that thwarts the Second Coming rather than expediting it. This notion of the *katechon* could easily be read as a metaphor for Francoism, at least from a leftist perspective, insofar as Francoism explicitly presented itself in religious terms as a crusade to save Spain from "godless communism." (As the narrative reminds us, Franco, after all, was "Caudillo de España pola graza de Deus" (552) ["Caudillo of Spain by the grace of God" (404)].) But what this "divinely ordained power" wrought was in reality an obstruction and postponement of the dream of social justice. In the political symbolism of *Os libros arden mal*, the *katechon* (whether in the guise of Franco, the Spanish jurists who gave legitimacy to his regime, or the Falangist biblioclasts) is the force of reaction that destroyed the books in 1936, ostensibly in order to save the Spanish people from their pernicious influence. But as the previous metaphors regarding books as avatars of life make clear, this force ultimately destroys life itself – albeit until the life depicted in and through the books is re-imagined in Rivas's own text.

The books stolen from the collections of Casares Quiroga, burned on the pyres of the A Coruña dockyards, and locked away in Samos's library are symbolically restored to their rightful heir, Casares Quiroga's daughter, María Casares, the renowned Franco-Hispanic actress who spent most of her life in exile in France. The restitution takes place in the 1990s, when Gabriel calls on her at her residence on the Rue Asseline in Paris. He brings with him a random sample of books with her father's signature on them.

> As obras que traía no foran escollidas polo seu valor, nin literario nin bibliográfico. Deixouse levar polo desexo da man. Os primeiros libros que el lera de entre os que tiñan as marcas do lume. O comenzo da súa instrución secreta. Pensaba contarlle a historia da resistencia dos libros de Panadeiras, 12. Moitos caeran. Mais algúns sobreviviran ao lume, á humidade do calabozo, aos ladróns do pazo de Xustiza. Os libros que levaba tiñan outra

cousa en común: a estilosa sinatura de Santiago Casares, como un retrato caligráfico elegante e dandi. Una sinatura antropomórfica. (700–1)

[The books he'd brought had not been chosen for their literary or bibliographical value. He'd let his hand pick them out. The first books he'd read in the section of charred remains. The start of his secret induction. He planned to tell her how the books from 12 Panadeiras Street had resisted. Lots had fallen. But some had survived the flames, the dampness of the dungeons, the robbers in the Palace of Justice. The books he'd brought had something else in common: Santiago Casares' stylish signature, an elegant calligraphic portrait. Anthropomorphic. (515)]

Gabriel also brings lists of all the books confiscated from Casares Quiroga's library, but they are incomplete: "faltan os desaparecidos e queimados. Os libros defuntos" (700) ["disappeared, burnt books, deceased books, had not been included" (515)]. When he arrives at María Casares's home, she is at the theatre, performing in *King Lear* in the title role. He realizes that this is probably for the best, as she would have been suspicious of the son of a Francoist judge arriving unannounced with a box of books. The narrator explains that María Casares in fact already possesses some of her father's books, which she needs to keep close by: "Gustáballe como pesaban. Ese peso das laxes, de arcas. Contiñan todos os outros. Todos os libros defuntos de Panadeiras 12" (704–5) ["She liked the way they weighed like arks or flagstones. They contained all the others. All the deceased books from 12 Panadeiras Street" (518)].[24] Before departing, Gabriel takes three volumes from his suitcase and leaves them for her with the return address of 12 Panadeiras Street and a stamp of a ladybug. Through this gesture a connection is established between the streets of two cities and, by extension, between the community of Loyalist exiles abroad and the Spanish homeland, and between the pre-Francoist past and post-Francoist present.

In the final chapters of *Os libros arden mal*, the characters Samos and Polca, now elderly and infirm, find themselves in the same hospital room. Polca recalls the book burning and the horror that he and his fellow workers experienced as they raked away the charred remains: "Traballamos con angazos e era como rabuñar a pel, descubrir as carnes. Houbo xente que vomitou, que botou as tripas fóra. Despois de tapalos, baixo os pés, eu notábaos bulir" (717) ["We worked with rakes, it was like scraping away the skin, revealing flesh. Some people vomited, chucked their guts up. After we'd covered them, I could still feel them bubbling under my feet" (528)]. Samos is anxious to know if Polca possesses the Borrow Bible. Polca "rakes" through his memories and through past time, just as he raked through the cinders of the books, and out of fear of Samos he lies and says that he does have it: "Matábame alí. Eu ben vin que era quen de facer unha barbaridade por un libro. Mesmo polas Sagradas Escrituras, mira ti, era quen de matar" (721) ["He could have killed me then and there. I could see he was capable of such a barbarous act for the sake of a book. Capable of killing for a copy of Scripture" (531)]. But ever since the book burning, the Borrow Bible has been in the possession of the Falangist officer who oversaw the event, Ren.

In the end, the aged Ren takes the Borrow Bible to Samos, but Gabriel receives it in place of his ailing father.[25] Ren identifies the book by showing Gabriel the dedication dated 1837: "*A Antonio de la Trava, o Valente de Fisterra*" (739) ["*For Antonio de la Trava, the valiente of Finisterra*" (544)]. He also presents Gabriel with an original copy of *Ulysses*. Gabriel thumbs through the book to see if it contains an ex libris. Ren seems indifferent to the matter of bookplates, but Gabriel insists that an ex libris would make the volume more valuable. Ren maintains that it is already of incalculable value. Yet Gabriel wants to know exactly how incalculable its value is: "'Canto de incalculábel, Ren?' ... 'Canto?' repetiu Gabriel" (741) ["'How much is incalculable, Ren?' ... 'How much?' asked Gabriel again" (545)]. *Os libros arden mal* ends with this potent question. Obviously, what concerns Gabriel is not the issue of the books' origins, or whether the Borrow Bible and Ren's first edition of *Ulysses* are authentic, but rather the identity of their previous owners. If for Ren the value of a book is incalculable because it is one of a kind, for Gabriel it would be incalculable because of the unknown number of hands (including those of Casares Quiroga) through which it passed, and because of the effects that seeing, touching, and ultimately reading it might have had on others' lives.[26] The Borrow Bible is particularly significant in this regard, since according to Christian tradition it is a "living book" with a divine essence irreducible to its material form. But in fact, all of the books immolated in the biblioclasm of 1936 were "living books" to the extent that they inscribed human intentions that could potentially and continually be reactivated through reading and aesthetic appreciation. Both the tragedy that some disappeared, as well as the miracle that others survived, are incalculable precisely because the value of all lives, whether of individuals or the generations of victims of war and dictatorship, are immeasurable. The ironic question that Gabriel poses to the old Falangist therefore has no answer.

Nonetheless, what is also immeasurable is past time, which is not lost, despite Polca's initial vision, but ever "present" – both spatially, in the mind's eye of the reader of *Os libros arden mal*, and temporally, insofar as the past and the future can only be known and imagined from the perspective of an existing consciousness. Like books, time in *Os libros arden mal* endures, and in the final chapter of restitution, when the Borrow Bible finally enters the ken of both Gabriel and the reader, the narrative voice speaks of "un tempo que non marchaba, un presente que recordaba" (738) ["(a) (t)ime that didn't leave, a present that remembered" (543)]. The memory work carried out in *Os libros arden mal* hence reconstitutes a Galician past but, more important, creates a living, Galician present. Yet the book also evinces an intense nostalgia for books themselves. This is because Rivas conceives of books not merely as symbols of human beings but as objects of value in their own right. *Os libros arden mal* aims to rectify a seemingly incalculable historical crime, which it distills into a horrific act of biblioclasm. But in so doing, it also makes visible a love of books that transcends political ideology and nationalist affiliation. It is thus ultimately a poignant and even tender meditation on bibliophilia.

### The Besieged Library of Sarajevo and the Marvelous Power of Literature in Juan Goytisolo's *El sitio de los sitios*

Juan Goytisolo was not a prolific collector of books, in part because he spent much of his adult life moving between Spain and the two countries that he inhabited as an expatriate, France and Morocco. As revealed in several of his narratives, however, he was deeply interested in material books and in the ways that they embody texts. In *El sitio de los sitios* (1995) [*State of Siege*], as in his earlier narrative *Las virtudes del pájaro solitario* (1988) [*The Virtues of the Solitary Bird*], he demonstrates how the histories and voices of vulnerable peoples (especially ethnic, religious, and sexual minorities in western societies) are contingent on their expression in books, and are therefore susceptible to manipulation, distortion, and silencing when the material formats of books are either altered or destroyed. He is particularly attentive to pages, type fonts, and bindings, as well as the instruments often employed to vandalize books such as ink, paste, erasers, razors, scissors, and paper cutters. He also highlights objects that readers have traditionally used to access books including library cards, catalogues, shelves, and ladders. What is more, he shows how books are perceived through all the senses. He frequently evokes the smell of books, and in *El sitio de los sitios* he conjures forth what is perhaps their most pungent odour, which they emit when they are burned. He even imagines their taste, as in a scene depicted in both *El sitio de los sitios* and *Las virtudes del pájaro solitario,* when San Juan de la Cruz purportedly ate the heretical pages that he had written in order to prevent them from being seized by the officials of his order. For Goytisolo, the key component of books is paper, which can be seen, touched, smelled, tasted, and (when pages are turned) heard. Like Ruiz Zafón and Rivas, Goytisolo in fact envisions paper as akin to human flesh, given its fragility and transitoriness, as well as its capacity to embody memory.

Within the narrative framework of *El sitio de los sitios*, Goytisolo attempts to reinscribe and in a sense re-archive books that have been destroyed, and in so doing restore to living memory the intentions of the human beings who produced and cherished them. However, he focuses his attention not solely on books themselves, as do Ruiz Zafón and Rivas in their depictions of the volumes obliterated during the Spanish Civil War and the right-wing and anti-Catalan and anti-Galician regime that followed, but on a particular library – the National and University Library of Bosnia and Herzegovina, located in the city of Sarajevo. Prior to the Bosnian War of the 1990s, the Sarajevo library was the primary archive of the literary and cultural heritage of the Muslim inhabitants of the Balkan Peninsula. Like incipient national libraries of the nineteenth century (including those of both the Spanish state and the Spanish regions), it focalized the nationalist aspirations of a people and provided a tangible expression of a shared identity, which in the case of the Bosnian Muslims, or Bosniaks, was not only cultural and linguistic but also religious and ethnic. For Goytisolo, the devastation of the Sarajevo library by more powerful state actors was an outcome of the long history of the marginalization and oppression of the Bosnian Muslims and ultimately an integral component of the program of genocide perpetrated against them.

In *El sitio de los sitios*, Goytisolo fictionalizes the destruction of the Sarajevo library, an event that he previously recounted in *Cuaderno de Sarajevo: Anotaciones de un viaje a la barbarie* [Sarajevo notebook: Notes from a journey to barbarism]. Goytisolo published *Cuaderno de Sarajevo* after his visit to the city in 1993, where he and the American writer Susan Sontag had observed the tragedy of the siege. *Cuaderno de Sarajevo* and *El sitio de los sitios* are deeply interwoven, and certain passages from the former are repeated verbatim in the latter, especially in the description of the attack on the library. Unlike *El sitio de los sitios*, the style of *Cuaderno de Sarajevo* is ostensibly journalistic, and the volume contains photographs by the war photographer Gervasio Sánchez. Alison Ribeiro de Menezes, however, characterizes it as a hybrid text that combines the narrative of Goytisolo's journey with committed war journalism (219), and María Soledad Silvestre discerns in it elements of a chronicle, an essay, a *testimonio*, a diary (with handwritten marginalia), and a novel (4).

In *Cuaderno de Sarajevo*, Goytisolo draws parallels between the Balkan wars in the 1990s and the Christian reconquest of Muslim Spain in the late Middle Ages.

> Los acontecimientos que desde fines de 1991 ensangrientan la ex Federación yugoslava y amagan extenderse a toda la Península balcánica presentan demasiadas similitudes con lo acaecido en España unos siglos atrás como para que podamos ignorarlos. (112)
>
> [The events that since the end of 1991 have bloodied the former Yugoslav Federation and show signs of extending to the entire Balkan Peninsula reveal too many similarities with what happened in Spain several centuries ago for us to be able to ignore them.]

Goytisolo expressly compares the destruction of the Sarajevo library to a notorious episode that occurred in 1499 in the wake of the reconquest of Granada. In a fanatical attempt to extirpate all remnants of Islam from the Iberian Peninsula, Cardinal Francisco Jiménez de Cisneros ordered the burning of over 5,000 Arabic manuscripts at the city's Bibarrambla Gate. As Goytisolo ironically remarks, the Sarajevo biblioclasm happened precisely at the moment when Spain was celebrating the five-hundredth anniversary of the first Iberian-American encounter of 1492, the year in which the reconquest of Granada was completed and the final eradication of the Muslim and Jewish peoples and cultures of the Iberian Peninsula began. He thus links the modern Balkan tragedy to the centuries-old oppression of European Muslims and Jews, and in so doing implies that Europe's historically Christian nations continue to harbour prejudice and animosity towards their non-Christian minorities, as evidenced not only by the actions of the Bosnian Serbs, but also by the inadequate response of the larger European and international communities to the plight of the Bosniaks.

The bombardment of the National and University Library of Bosnia and Herzegovina took place during the siege of Sarajevo on the night of 25–26 August 1992, and was carried out by the Bosnian Serb Army. Since the end of the Second World War, the National and University Library had been housed in the Vijećnica, the former city hall of Sarajevo, constructed at the height of the Austro-Hungarian period in the late nineteenth century. Goytisolo identifies the library by name and makes specific reference to the building's "fachadas neomorescas de la época austriaca" (*El sitio* 77) ["neo-Moorish façades dating back to the Austrian era" (*State* 66)].[27] During the siege of Sarajevo many other cherished cultural institutions were destroyed, including the Oriental Institute, shelled on 18 May 1992. As a consequence of this attack, thousands of Arabic, Persian, and Hebrew manuscripts and Ottoman documents were lost (Riedlmayer 7). Yet the decimation of the National and University Library, with its more than 1.5 million volumes and 155,000 rare books and manuscripts (7), was the most tragic of the biblioclasms of the Bosnian War.[28] As András Riedlmayer revealed at the time of the conflagration, "[t]hroughout Bosnia, libraries, archives, museums and cultural institutions have been targeted for destruction, in an attempt to eliminate the material evidence – books, documents and works of art – that could remind future generations that people of different ethnic and religious traditions once shared a common heritage in Bosnia" (8). In his view, this was not part of a simple conflict between political adversaries but instead "a crime against humanity and a violation of international laws and conventions" (9–10).[29]

In *El sitio de los sitios*, Goytisolo articulates a plethora of shifting voices that at times echo those expressed in his other autobiographical and fictional texts.[30] At the outset of the narrative a Spaniard arrives in Sarajevo during the siege of the city and checks into a hotel room. While there, he observes from a crack in the wall a woman making her way down a street. As he watches her, she is struck by a mortar shell and killed, and during the night he too seems to be killed when a projectile explodes in his room. The following day he is reported missing. An army commander initiates an investigation of the case, but he is unable to locate a body and thereby determine whether the man actually died or disappeared, although he does find writings in a valise in the man's room. These characters subsequently meld into numerous other characters, including Goytisolo himself, "el autor de *Coto vedado*" (38) ["the author of *Forbidden Territory*" (32)]; a gay poet with the initials JG (who might be Goytisolo, or a poet interned in a mental institution at the time of the Spanish Civil War, or a man named Eusebio, who appears in various guises in several of Goytisolo's novels and who perhaps represents one of his uncles);[31] the British writer and orientalist, Sir Richard Francis Burton; San Juan de la Cruz; a Muslim mystic and poet named Ben Sidi Abú Al Fadaíl; a scholar engaged in research on Ben Sidi Abú Al Fadaíl; a figure called the Defecator (who might be the Muslim mystic and poet in question and who seems to inhabit an immigrant quarter in contemporary Paris); a librarian and Hispanist; and many, many others.[32] At times, the text teases the reader into imagining that there is a single, overarching character ("nuestro protagonista" [67] ["our protagonist" (57)]) or "un narrador omnisciente" (73) ["an omniscient narrator" (63)]. But as the narrative makes clear, "[e]l narrador no es fiable y parece tender al lector una serie de trampas en las que inevitablemente cae antes de advertir que ha mordido el anzuelo y sido arrastrado al punto adonde le querían llevar" (74) ["(t)he narrator is not trustworthy and appears to lay a series of traps for the reader into which he inevitably falls before he realizes that he has taken the baited hook and been brought to the exact point where he was intended to be" (64)].[33] In fact, in commenting on the papers of the missing Spaniard, the army commander concludes the following:

> Los anacronismos y absurdidades contenidos en ellos embrollan todavía más el lance increíble de la desaparición del autor. Su lectura despojaría a mis ya inconsistentes informes de su pálida sombra de verosimilitud: todo el caso se transmuta en ficción y yo mismo en personaje ficticio! (75)
>
> [The anachronisms and absurdities contained in them make the disappearance of the author an even more incredible occurrence. The reading of them would have robbed my already inconsistent reports of even their pale shadow of verisimilitude: the entire episode becomes fiction and I myself a fictitious character! (64)]

At every turn, *El sitio de los sitios* seems to undermine its credibility. Nevertheless, even if the army commander (and indeed all the figures and voices that appear and speak) is but "un ente ficticio, un ser de papel" (84) ["a fictitious being, one who exists only on paper" (71)], the destruction of the National and University Library of Bosnia and Herzegovina, depicted midway through the narrative, did in fact happen at a specific moment in history and resulted in the destruction of a huge number of real books. Although it might be said that this event now exists only on "paper," that is, through the medium of *El sitio de los sitios* and the multitude of other representations of the siege (and, by extension, through the memories of the readers and consumers of these representations), the text never once doubts that the biblioclasm occurred.

As Genaro J. Pérez observes, the fragmentation of the narrative voice in *El sitio de los sitios* is redolent of the effects of the bombardment of Sarajevo during the siege of the city (402). What remains are like pieces of a puzzle that readers must reassemble (403), especially, as David Conte explains, since the text provides no final resolution (or *deus ex machina*) that might clarify the seemingly countless enigmas that it presents (117). Both Pérez and Manuel Hierro regard the disappearance of the mysterious Spaniard as central to the narrative. For Pérez, the missing cadaver represents the lack of authorial control in the text (402), whereas for Hierro, the text itself comes to "ocupar el *sitio* del cadáver" (146) [occupy the *place* of the cadaver]. Yet another entity that disappears in *El sitio de los sitios* is precisely the library. Comparable to the unitary voice that the cadaver might have enunciated when it was a living human being, the library, through the consolidation of discourses within books and other reading materials, and through the organization of these items on shelves and in catalogues, possessed a certain cohesiveness that was rent asunder in the biblioclasm. In a sense, then, *El sitio de los sitios* also occupies the space of the destroyed library. On one level, it seems devoid of meaning (the library that it evokes has been eviscerated). But on closer inspection, it makes visible through the narrative ken the charred books and rubble of discourses that remain in the wake of the siege. *El sitio de los sitios* does not reconstitute all these books and discourses, but through its disjointed and overlapping utterances it manages to salvage at least some from complete oblivion.

The state of siege indicated in the title of the narrative (literally either "the siege of sieges" or "the site of the sieges") is directed squarely against the National and University Library of Bosnia and Herzegovina. The term "state of siege" in fact typically describes an effort by a government or military force to restrict the free movement of people within a particular site, such as a building, a city, or a country. Often, it is a prelude to an act of aggression aimed at either conquering or destroying a community. As depicted in *El sitio de los sitios*, the inhabitants of the city of Sarajevo are clearly under assault. So too are the Bosniaks as a whole, as well as other historically oppressed and minoritized groups with whom Goytisolo identifies in much of his writing, including homosexuals, persons living with AIDS, Jews and Muslims in Europe, non-European immigrants in Europe, and political and religious dissidents in general. Yet the most explicit target in *El sitio de los sitios* is precisely the National and University Library of Bosnia and Herzegovina.[34] This library is a place wherein a culture is embodied. When "sitiado," or "besieged," it is surrounded and attacked, and its books are destroyed. As a result, the culture inscribed in them becomes placeless and, for all intents and purposes, non-existent insofar as it loses its material foundation. (One could also say that it becomes "stateless" since it is deprived of the larger social and political apparatuses through which national cultures are sustained.) Without a material foundation, this culture, the narrator fears, will ultimately be forgotten, and he thus bemoans the annihilation of the library as a veritable "memoricidio" (67) ["memoricide" (57)].[35]

The destruction of the National and University Library of Bosnia and Herzegovina is the pivotal moment of *El sitio de los sitios*. The narrator regards the event as worse than the death of a loved one insofar as it led to the obliteration of both his life's work as a researcher and "[e]l alma de la ciudad" (95) ["(t)he soul of the city" (81)]. As he explains, among the treasures consumed in the flames were countless manuscripts and treatises on history, geography, travel, philosophy, theology, grammar, astrology, chess, and music. The goal of the assailants was to "barrer la sustancia histórica de esta tierra para montar sobre ella un templo de patrañas, leyendas y mitos" (95–6) ["leave no trace of the historical substance of this country so as to build on it a temple of lies, legends, and myths" (81)]. This historical substance is in fact the collective memory of the Bosniaks as inscribed in the paper of the books in the library.[36] In reflecting on the cataclysm, the narrator recalls the utterance of a medieval Andalusian poet and philosopher to the judges of the Inquisition, when they ordered his life work to be burned: "'Aunque queméis el papel, no podréis quemar lo que encierra porque lo llevo en mi pecho'" (96) ["'Although you may burn the paper, you will be unable to burn the message written on it because I bear it within my heart'" (81)]. Yet what heart, the narrator asks, "podría abarcar la memoria de un pueblo entero?" (96) ["has room enough to contain the memory of an entire people?" (81–2)].[37] As he sees it, no single person could possibly internalize a collective memory, and for this reason libraries and archives are essential to the survival of cultures. He further implies that although memory differs ontologically from paper (or the poet's "heart"), it is inseparable from it, and when paper (and bodies) disappear, so too does the human past and, by extension, human identity. What the smoke from the burning library thus reveals is genocide: "Un humo tan espeso como el de las chimeneas de los campos de exterminio: historia esfumada en silencio, cielo cubierto de densas, ennegrecidas nubes alimentadas con las pavesas de nuestra extinción" (96) ["A smoke as thick as that rising from the chimneys of the death camps: history reduced to silent spirals, a sky covered with dense clouds blackened by the cinders of our extinction" (82)].

The narrator presses the equivalence of paper-based books and flesh when he cites a Jewish scholar and colleague of his, who declares: "'ya conocen, por desgracia, en su propia carne lo que nos cupo vivir cuando nos refugiamos aquí con el tesoro del *Haggadah*. Ahora somos iguales en la desposesión y desgracia'" (97) ["'You now know, alas, in your own flesh, what fell to our lot to live when we took refuge here, bringing with us the *Haggadah*. Now dispossession and misfortune have made us equals'" (83)].[38] In the context of this passage the word "flesh" refers to the books burned during the siege of the National and University Library of Bosnia and Herzegovina and to the meanings inscribed in them, which constitute the essence of the narrator's life and also, to the extent that he identifies with larger social groupings, the essence of the Bosnian Muslims. During the immolation, what vanished with the pages of the books was precisely this essence, which was uprooted and torn out, leaving nothing but emptiness in its wake. The narrator thus speaks of "la desolación interior, descuaje de la razón de ser, saqueo y aventamiento de nuestra memoria" (97) ["our inner desolation, the shattering of our reason for being, the sacking of our memory now scattered to the four winds" (83)].[39] The extirpation of essence results in a sort of gap or hole in being, configured in the narrative by the hollowed-out shell of the library building: "Hoy, la Biblioteca a la que ofrendé lo mejor de mi vida conserva únicamente la estructura hueca de sus cuatro fachadas ornadas de columnas, arcos de herradura, rosetones y almenas" (96) ["Today all that is left of the library to which I offered up the best of my life is the hollow shell of its four façades decorated with columns, horseshoe arches, rose windows, and crenels" (82)]. This gap will gradually yet only tentatively be filled in through the imagination of the narrative voices and, by extension, through Goytisolo's own project of historical recovery in *El sitio de los sitios*.[40]

The narrator of *El sitio de los sitios* is as concerned about the pernicious alteration of books as he is about their ultimate destruction. He describes reading a collection of poems titled "Zona Sotádica" [Sotadic Zone].[41] The text's emphasis on homosexuality enthralls him and, as he puts it, "[lo] incendia y abrasa" (84) ["inflames (him), sets (him) afire" (72)]. He quickly discovers, however, that the book has been tampered with by censors.

> Una rápida ojeada al mismo permite concluir que fue censurado: una de sus páginas, arrancada de cuajo; otras, recortadas con tijeras. Los versos de dos poemas – pues se trata de un poemario – aparecen tachados con tinta de estilográfica al punto de resultar ilegibles. A trechos, en los márgenes de la plana escrita o en lo que queda de la página emborronada, hay apostillas de lectores ofuscados o del iracundo censor: "rojo," "sinvergüenza," "degenerado," "judío," "maricón" y otros epítetos y frases denigrantes. (85)
>
> [A quick look through it justifies the conclusion that it has been censored: one of its pages has been torn out altogether, others cut to pieces with scissors. All the verses of two poems – for the notebook in fact consists of a collection of poems – are so full of ink stains that they are illegible. In places, in the margins of the written text or in the blanks left on the pages with the ink stains, there are notes left by enraged readers or the wrathful censor: "Commie," "rotten bastard," "degenerate," "kike," "queer," and other insulting epithets and phrases. (73)]

These words in fact evoke a passage in *Las virtudes del pájaro solitario,* when the narrator of that narrative at last finds in the library of a distant land the books he has been seeking:

> los ejemplares que buscas ... incluyen numerosos fragmentos tachados, páginas arrancadas de cuajo en un santo arrebato de violencia, hojas cuidadosamente despojadas de toda idea molesta mediante la realización oportuna de cortes selectos con tijeras, navajas y guillotinas
>
> borrones y manchas de tinta oscurecen la comprensión de pasajes esenciales, glosas y vituperios de hiena bardaje judehüelo ensucian la nitidez de los márgenes ... (109–10)

> [the copies that you are looking for ... prove to have many obliterated fragments, pages ripped out wholesale in a holy access of violence, others carefully stripped of any disquieting idea through an appropriate selection of deletions by scissors, excisions by razors and guillotining by paper cutters
>
> blots and ink stains obscure the comprehension of essential passages, glosses and vituperations of hyena sodomite stinking Jew dirty the clean margins ... (103–4)]

In their effort to re-imagine the world, Goytisolo's narrators are more stymied by the incursions into books of these discourses, aimed at repressing or eliminating ethnic, religious, and sexual alterity, than they are by the mere destruction of books themselves.

Whereas the narrator of *Las virtudes del pájaro solitario* finds volumes "mutilados al punto de resultar ilegibles" ["so badly mutilated as to be illegible"] and others in which "el original ha sido reemplazado ... hoja por hoja con exposiciones doctrinales ortodoxas y comentarios anodinos" (110) ["the original has been replaced page by page with orthodox doctrinal explanations and trite commentaries" (104)], the narrative voice of *El sitio de los sitios* ultimately becomes a sort of human book in which the ghosts of the library gain a new lease on life. In contrast to the library portrayed in *Las virtudes del pájaro solitario,* "[una] necrópolis inmensa de libros condenados a la aniquilación y el olvido" (123) ["an immense necropolis of books doomed to annihilation and oblivion" (115)], the library in *El sitio de los sitios* is reborn through the narrator and his various avatars. As a colleague of the narrator declares, "[l]a Biblioteca no ha ardido en vano, [y] [s]us pavesas cayeron en tierra fértil" (114) ["(t)he library has not burned down in vain, (and) (i)ts ashes have fallen on fertile ground" (96)]. This fertile ground is in fact the creative imagination of the downtrodden of the world and their indomitable ability to generate discourses and express their voices: "el arma perenne y sutil de los débiles: la dispersión seminal de sus voces, las variantes infinitas de la palabra!" (115) ["the eternal and subtle weapon of the weak: the seminal dispersion of their voices, the infinite variants of the Word!" (97)].

Even prior to the destruction of the library the narrator appears not only as a reader but also as an embodiment of texts. In reminiscing on his years spent reading, he describes himself and his colleagues as "ficheros vivientes" (104) ["living index card files" (88)].[42] As such, they possess a knowledge of the location of the books in the library before they are destroyed, as well as their essential contents. Although they have ostensibly internalized less than did the Andalusian poet previously cited (or the exiled intellectuals in Ray Bradbury's novel, *Fahrenheit 451*, who memorized entire volumes in order to recreate them after all the books in the world were burned), they recall enough to reimagine and regenerate them. In their effort to reinscribe the discourses dissipated in the ashes of the besieged library, the narrator compares the survivors of the biblioclasm to medieval scribes.

> Víctimas de este sitio medieval, tan parecido al que sufrieron los albigenses, decidimos responder, por nuestra cuenta, con la astucia, también medieval, de la diseminación de textos, cuando una gloriosa pléyade de amanuenses, memorialistas, intérpretes, monjes de escasa virtud y desbocados goliardos dispersaban por los monasterios y centros de saber de la época teorías, escolios, sophistimata, interpolaciones y apócrifos que minaban las certidumbres y dogmas de la Iglesia, la eterna aspiración del poder a centralizar el pensamiento a fin de reducirlo y domesticarlo. (111)
>
> [Victims of this medieval siege, so like the one endured by the Albigensians, we resolved to fight back on our own by means of a stratagem that was also medieval: the dissemination of texts, for in that period a glorious coterie of copyists, clerks, interpreters, monks of scant virtue, and wayward young scholar-poets distributed throughout the monasteries and centers of learning of the era theories, commentaries, sophistic arguments, interpolations, and apocrypha that undermined the certainties and dogmas of the Church, the eternal aspiration of power to centralize thought in order to render it toothless and tame. (93–4)]

As depicted in *El sitio de los sitios*, the recovery of discourses lost in the biblioclasm at times seems miraculous. In one of his roles as a hotel clerk, the narrator suggests that the man who checks into the room at the beginning of the narrative is the Muslim mystic and poet, Ben Sidi Abú Al Fadaíl. When the library is attacked, the narrator is supposedly in the process of writing a dissertation on this figure. As he inspects the room after the siege, he discovers a collection of poems titled "Astrolabio" ["Astrolabe"]. The poems from this text, along with those from "Zona Sotádica," form the appendix of *El sitio de los sitios*.[43] The narrator asserts that the verses of "Astrolabio" are in fact ones that he previously transcribed and included in his dissertation. He exclaims: "Cómo expresar mi emoción cuando hojeé su contenido? Era como si me estuviera leyendo a mí mismo!" (101) ["How to describe my emotion as I leafed through the pages of it? It was as though I were reading my own work!" (86)].[44] The narrator's voice subsequently shifts to that of a friend who expresses what he thinks has happened, to wit, that the Muslim holy man, who has been dead for several hundred years, has returned from the grave and brought with him his writings. He thus rapturously proclaims: "Lo que perdí en el incendio de la Biblioteca ha vuelto a mis manos!" (105) ["What I lost in the fire at the library has been returned to me!" (90)].

The text, of course, never clarifies if this restitution occurs, or if the narrator in one of his many guises has re-imagined and rewritten the poems, or if the poems have rewritten themselves or been reinscribed through some ever-recurring hypostatization of the divine Word. At times, the narrative voice suggests that humans are not agents of discourse but rather the means through which discourses articulate themselves, and possibly even the means through which God is made manifest in the world. In a passage reminiscent of the experience of the narrator's various avatars, including that of San Juan de la Cruz, he declares:

> Todas las teofanías o imágenes censuradas a lo largo de mi vida familiar, educativa y castrense irrumpen en la tiniebla de la celda con el fulgor del apoderamiento: el verbo me conjuga. (84)
>
> [All the theophanies or images censured throughout my life at home, at school, in the army burst into the darkness of my cell with the blinding light of empowerment: the Word conjugates me. (72)]

The narrator wonders if these are visions of a higher reality and if their light will endure after he commits them to paper. What is more, to the extent that the Word "conjugates" him (be it the Word as God or simply discourse writ large), he is inflected in a particular way and thereby takes on a distinctive identity. Yet whatever particularity or distinctiveness he feels is in fact transitory, and even if the discourse (or divinity) that he expresses someday rematerializes, it will not do so through his own unique and mortal body. Similarly, if the books destroyed in the siege of the library are eventually restored, they will not be the very same books (new paper or other media, after all, will be required to reconstitute them), and the experience of reading them will be at least slightly different from the experience of reading the original volumes.

Throughout the narrative the narrator plays with the question of the authenticity of texts. Just as there existed in Christian tradition a Pseudo-Dionysius the Areopagite, so too perhaps there exists a Pseudo-Ben Sidi Abú Al Fadaíl or a Pseudo-JG who penned the texts that he is seeking. For the narrator, the alteration and falsification of these texts is as much a threat to him as is their actual destruction. When reading, he feels like "una mosca atrapada en la urdimbre de una finísima telaraña textual" (130) ["a fly trapped in a very finely woven textual spiderweb" (109)]. As he sees it, texts can be traps to the extent that they are manipulated in ways that adversely affect people like him. In fact, he and his cohorts are also manipulators of texts: "[somos] a la vez investigadores, cuentistas, poetas, falsarios y manipuladores de textos" (145) ["we are at once investigators, storytellers, poets, forgers, and manipulators of texts" (121)]. Yet ultimately, they are pawns of more powerful manipulators.

> [V]íctimas de un asedio que años atrás hubiéramos juzgado impensable, nos hemos convertido en personajes de una Historia impuesta[.] Alguien – los señores de la guerra y sus cómplices – escribe el argumento y nos maneja como títeres desde su atalaya! La realidad se ha transmutado en ficción: el cuento de horror de nuestra existencia diaria! (145)

> [(V)ictims of a siege that a few years back we would have considered unthinkable, we have turned into characters of a history forced upon us[.] The lords of war and their accomplices are writing the script and manipulating us like puppets from their vantage point high above us! Reality has been transmuted into fiction: the horror tale of our daily existence! (121)]

As in Rivas's *Os libros arden mal*, the image of the "urdimbre" [warp and woof] of textuality is central to the narrator's vision not only of texts but also of books in general. For just as discourses are metaphorically woven together to form texts, the material components of books are literally woven together to form pages and bindings. To a significant degree, the "warp and woof" of books, that is, the particular way that they embody texts, is what traditional bibliophiles most value. The narrator of *El sitio de los sitios*, however, regards textual embodiment as a trap akin to a spider's web in which unsuspecting readers might be devoured and die – just as they might have been killed on the night of the library bombardment, when the missiles shattered the metal framework of the roof and transformed it into what looked like "una monstruosa telaraña" (96) ["a monstrous spider-web" (82)].[45] The narrator's comments in fact reveal his anxiety towards both books and bodies, given that both are subject to decline and decay. Although the malicious intent behind the devastation of the National and University Library of Bosnia and Herzegovina might seem to be his overarching concern, the mere fact that books and bodies can be destroyed in the first place is what seems to unsettle him most.

In the final segment of the narrative before the appendix of poems, the narrator finds himself charged by an editor with the task of gathering together in some coherent fashion the texts and voices that remain in the wake of the bombardment. Only he, the editor insists, has the ability to "trabar los apartados heterogéneos, [e] ... imaginar la arquitectura y diseño" (159) ["weave together heterogeneous elements, (and) ... reconstruct the overall architecture and design" (133)]. As "weaver" and "architect" he thus seems primed not only to reconstitute the lost texts and books but also to rebuild the decimated library edifice. Through his actions he "assembles," "polishes," "fits and groups together," "parcels out," "ties up loose ends," and "eliminates obtrusive loops and frayed edges." In so doing, however, he simultaneously weaves and unweaves: "al ligar uno de ellos [cabos sueltos], aflojas y deshaces el lazo de otro, [y] ... tejes y destejes, y lo ganado en un día se pierde el siguiente" (160) ["when you tie one thread in, you loosen and undo the link with another, [and] ... as you weave and unweave, what you have gained one day is lost the next" (133)]. His undertaking, he concludes, is Sisyphean (if not also like that of Penelope at her loom), and try as he might, he ultimately distances himself from the "book" and from the "encargo apremiante de recopilarlo y fabricar una novela al uso, un presentable y bien hecho producto de mercado" (160) ["urgent task of compiling the material at hand and making of it a conventional novel, a presentable, well-made market product" (134)]. This book, a seemingly impossible volume comprising all the texts lost in the biblioclasm, might in fact be read as a representation of the library insofar as the library was the site wherein these texts were once organized and housed. It is also suggestive of an ideal narrative that Goytisolo perhaps attempted to elucidate over the course of his writing career, perhaps even of *El sitio de los sitios* itself.

As the narrative of *El sitio de los sitios* makes clear, the task of recovering anything from the library fire is overwhelmingly daunting. Some books and manuscripts of incalculable value do in fact survive unscathed, but they often end up in street stalls in impoverished districts of the city and are sold for a pittance of their actual worth. They are then smuggled out of the country (frequently with the connivance of local police officers), and once abroad are resold at astronomically high prices to collectors unconcerned with the history of their provenance and indifferent to the plight the Bosniak people. They are thus permanently severed from the community that for centuries cultivated them. What is more, they no longer function as repositories of cultural memory or as instruments of cultural survival in the face of war and genocide. Instead, they take on a monetary value that corresponds solely to their perceived rarity. They become, so to speak, bibliophile books, and as such are similar in their fate to the countless number of books repatriated from Spain to northern Europe and the Americas in the nineteenth and early twentieth centuries.[46]

Nevertheless, one tangible book that is neither buried in the ruins of the National and University Library of Bosnia and Herzegovina nor held hostage by some foreign collector is precisely *El sitio de los sitios*. Although *El sitio de los sitios* was written after the destruction of the library and was hence never part of its holdings, it clearly reproduces certain aspects of the besieged books. It might even be thought of as a sort of facsimile of the original collection, albeit a decidedly impoverished one given the inability of one book (or one heart, as the Andalusian poet would have it) to encompass the memory of an entire people as contained in a library. But as the narrator affirms, a text can also confound and deactivate the power of oppressors: "Víctimas de la brutalidad de la Historia, nos vengábamos de ella con nuestras historias, tejidas de ocultaciones, textos interpolados, lances fingidos: tal es el poder mirífico de la literatura" (138) ["Victims of the cruelty of history, we took vengeance on it with our histories, woven out of ambiguities, interpolated texts, fabricated events: such is the marvelous power of literature" (116)]. In *El sitio de los sitios*, Goytisolo wields this "marvelous power of literature" to respond to the tragedies of both the Bosnian War and the human condition as he lived it.

# 4 Nuria Amat and the Persistence of Books

The Catalan writer and librarian Nuria Amat is perhaps the consummate Spanish bibliophile of the contemporary period. Her written corpus ranges from essays in the field of library science to autobiography, narrative fiction, and theatre. Her ruminations on bibliophilia are perspicacious as well as humorous. Like so many Catalan bibliophiles throughout history, she reflects on the confluence of the Catalan and Castilian languages and traditions in her intellectual formation, and explains why in her case Castilian came to dominate.[1] But in contrast to the majority of male bibliophiles, she also interrogates the gender dynamics of bibliophilia, especially as played out in her childhood family. In so doing, she highlights how her interactions with books over the course of her lifetime as reader, collector, and librarian have affected her ability to write and have moulded her perception of herself and the world. Amat expresses her love of books in the context of both print and digital media, and she has authored several watershed studies of electronic libraries and book digitalization. Ultimately, she affirms the value of digital technology as a means of making the contents of print collections available to library users, yet remains herself viscerally tied to physical books, which she regards as essential to her sense of identity.

## The Writer-Librarian and the Library Effect

Throughout her numerous publications Amat meditates on her life as a bibliophile and on the effect that being a librarian has had on her writing. At the end of the essay "Escritores que lloran, bibliotecarios que aúllan como lobos" [Writers who cry, librarians who howl like wolves], delivered as a speech at the Biblioteca Nacional de España on 29 February 1996 and published in *Letra herida* [The wounded letter] in 1998, she outlines a letter to Umberto Eco in which she describes her fellow-librarians' opinion of her as "una pseudoescritora, una farsante literaria, una chapucera de la escritura, pésima bibliotecaria y una plagiaria" (195) [a pseudo-writer, a literary fraud, a botched stylist, a terrible librarian, and a plagiarist]. Amat imagines that Eco would advise her to consider such an accusation an honour, but she claims (somewhat disingenuously given her long and successful career) that she would prefer simply to remain unnoticed. As the essay reveals, however, the accusation (notwithstanding the attack on her immense skills as a librarian) is at least in some sense true. Amat explains that her life with books has made her unable to produce a conventional narrative, and that whenever she writes, she is inevitably drawn back to the subject of books themselves.[2] This, she maintains, results from what she calls "el efecto biblioteca" (190–5) [the library effect]. In keeping with postmodernist aesthetics, she writes self-reflective and self-mocking texts that are on the one hand autobiographical (she continually reflects on her life with books), but on the other hand anti-autobiographical insofar as a life lived through books, as she sees it, resists textual inscription and grounding in physical volumes. Whereas traditional autobiography attempts to render a fixed self, Amat's writing discloses a series of competing and unresolved identities – she is at once Catalan and Spanish, her father's daughter and her own woman, a keeper of books and a producer of books, and an amalgamation of discourses and a free agent. Amat depicts a nostalgia for lost books, which is ultimately a nostalgia for a self that never really existed. But hers is also a nostalgia for the dead, for books not only beckon us with the promise of personal self-fulfillment, but they also echo the lives of those now gone, making the loss of cherished books, as her books make clear, almost as unbearable as death itself.

Amat's mother died when Amat was a child, and her apprenticeship as a bibliophile took place under the tutelage of her bibliophile father in the space of his huge personal library, which consisted primarily of books written in Catalan. Amat regards this library as an extension of her father. But it also represents her mother: "La biblioteca de mi padre es algo así como decir (casi) la esposa de mi padre. O puede ser que mi madre muerta se haya transformado en una especie de biblioteca viva" (149) [My father's library is, you might say, something (almost) like my father's wife. Or it could be that my dead mother was transformed into a kind of living library]. Amat associates both her father and her mother with the bibliophile life. But insofar as the memory of the mother is displaced onto the contents of a library, she is passivized (as in fact she must be because she is dead) and appears solely through the objects that the father uses to pursue his own particular ends as a reader and cultivator of books. Amat herself becomes objectified in her relationship with her father, not through a conventional feminization of her body but paradoxically by identifying herself with his books, which function as the incarnation of the mother and, by extension, the feminine. Amat's story is in a sense that of a girl who came to think she was a book: "En la biblioteca del padre la niña se sentía menos huérfana, más parecida a los libros que al resto de las niñas con madre pero sin libros en la casa" (178) [In the father's library the girl felt less like an orphan and more like the books than like the rest of the girls with a mother but without books in the house]. And even as an adult, "la escritora duda de si ella es una escritora o bien un libro" (184) [the writer wonders if she is a writer or rather a book]. To a certain extent, this tension of identities occurs because of her dual role as subject and object in relation to her father.

As a child of the library, Amat does not occupy a conventionally feminine space, but she comes to play a conventionally feminine role as caretaker, not of her father per se but of the primary objects through which he expresses himself: books. Amat, nevertheless, resists this role. She is assisted in part by the only adult woman present in her childhood home, her own caretaker, the Castilian-speaking Dominica. By class and occupation, Dominica is locked into a role of subservience vis-à-vis Amat's father, but by introducing Castilian into the household she makes available to Amat a means of distancing herself from him. According to Amat, Dominica subtly imposes her language on the entire household: "El poder invisible de Dominica es asombroso y al final todos acabamos hablando en castellano" (153) [The invisible power of Dominica is astonishing, and ultimately, we all end up speaking Castilian]. This is not Dominica's intention, and as a matter of fact the triumph of Castilian among Amat's family members has less to do with the influence of a humble servant than the power of the recently triumphant Francoist state. But through her language Dominica provides Amat with a refuge that the Catalan library of her father cannot. Amat writes that Castilian is

> [l]a única lengua que me reconoce en la noche, la única que me responde cuando llamo. El idioma fiel que nunca me traiciona como me engañó en su día el idioma abandonado de mi madre. Por eso yo hablo con la voz de Dominica. (152)

> [the only language that recognizes me in the night, the only one that responds to me when I call. The faithful language that never betrays me, as once did the abandoned language of my mother. For this reason, I speak with the voice of Dominica.]

Amat hence acquires a voice distinct from her father's (and from the co-opted voice of her mother) through which she will attempt to construct an independent identity. Ironically, she is empowered by an individual with no power of her own, even if Dominica's native language is that of the historically dominant Spanish state.

Although Castilian is not her only childhood language, Amat comes to use it as her primary language of self-fashioning. In her view, all writers are obliged to express themselves through a language that is in some ways foreign to them – and even more so if they are women (134). As she puts it,

> [e]scribo en secreto en este idioma áspero, difícil, y bastante inconfortable. Un idioma que voy haciendo mío a medida que crece mi escritura. El idioma que poco a poco consigue separarme del idioma incomprensible de mi madre. (131)
>
> [I write in secret in this harsh, difficult, and quite uncomfortable language. A language that I make mine to the extent that my writing grows. The language that little by little manages to separate me from the incomprehensible language of my mother.]

Amat not only begins writing in Castilian, but slowly builds up a Castilian-language library comparable to her father's Catalan-language library. Her library – both the physical books that she amasses and the distinct literary world that gradually fills her mind – becomes a source of jealously for her father: "Se siente celoso de mis libros secretos" (160) [He feels jealous of my secret books]. If her father instilled in her a passion for books ("Mi padre me transmitió [o contagió, según se mire] la manía libresca" [171] [My father transmitted to me (or infected me with, depending on how one looks at it) the obsession for books]), he seemed to do so in order to keep her bound to him. She, however, wants to direct this passion away from him. What is more, she eventually tires of her role as caretaker: "la bibliotecaria se cans[ó] de vigilar y cuidar la biblioteca del padre" (181) [the librarian tired of guarding and caring for the library of the father]. But the price that she pays for freedom is high, for although her father has always assured her that when he dies, he will leave her his library, in the end, despite her years of service, he leaves it to her brother, claiming that he is better equipped financially to maintain it. Her father's promise, "[c]uando yo muera, tú heredarás la biblioteca" (178) [when I die, you will inherit the library], is predicated on the condition that she remain the dutiful daughter – although even if she had done so, he might likely have favoured his son anyway.[3]

Amat ceases to take care of her father's library, but as a librarian she continues to tend the books of others:

> La bibliotecaria, entonces, trabajó horas infinitas en bibliotecas particulares cuyos propietarios parecían estar muertos. Horas infinitas desempolvando libros y todo por esa dedicación neurótica hacia la desaparecida biblioteca del padre. Bibliotecas particulares de abogados, médicos, y políticos que habían heredado las bibliotecas de sus respectivos padres y que no sabían qué hacer con ellas; bibliotecas difuntas, bibliotecas insulares, rancias y oxidadas como cementerios abandonados. (185)
>
> [So, the librarian worked for endless hours in private libraries whose owners seemed to be dead. Endless hours dusting off books, and all because of that neurotic dedication to the vanished library of the father. Private libraries of lawyers, doctors, and politicians who had inherited the libraries of their respective parents and who did not know what to do with them: dead libraries, closed-in libraries, rancid and rusty like abandoned cemeteries.]

Books, in this sense, are like the detritus of finished lives, akin to cadavers. They may remind us of the now departed, but they are also, Amat implies, a burden, something that must be disposed of, something better left to the professionals of the death industry, be they morticians or, in this case, librarians.

Although Amat initially hoped to free herself from her father's books, she now feels nostalgia for them. This nostalgia, which characterizes her entire writing enterprise, is directed not only at lost objects (the physical books have been dispersed and are gone) but also at an absence, for her father's library stood as a reminder of her dead mother as well as a filial identity that Amat herself never wholly embodied. Amat suggests that her writing, and indeed all writing, is a search for a non-existent mother, and more precisely an ideal other through which one might experience a fullness of self. As a child, Amat tries to constitute this other not in her father but in herself as an incarnation of her mother. She does this first in relation to her father's library and ultimately through writing: "Así es como voy construyendo mi cuerpo de escritora. Me disfrazo de madre y, gracias a esa ropa de palabras, consigo verla por un instante en el espejo. Es una suerte de destello" (148) [So it is that I go about constructing my writer-body. I disguise myself as mother, and thanks to that garment of words, I manage to see her for an instant in the mirror. She is a sort of sparkle]. This sparkle in the mirror – the longed-for ideal other – is not necessarily illusory, yet it cannot be held because the narrator, so it seems, is part of an ever-moving discourse. For if the mother is a sparkle, she also appears in "[u]n punto y aparte en el espejo" (148) [a period and tab in the mirror]. The movement from the "period" to the "next paragraph" is in fact the locus of the lived-trajectory of the narrator. Her nostalgia, therefore, is not simply a turning back to the past but an inexorable and continuous movement away from it. It is, to use the language of existentialism, the narrator's anguished recognition of herself as forever removed from the past and hence from any fixed essence.

In writing "sobre su realidad más inmediata: la nostalgia de los libros perdidos" (186) [about her most immediate reality: the nostalgia for lost books], Amat attempts not only to recover something lost but also to trace the impossibility of ever achieving an ontological stasis. On the one hand, she wants to affirm a kind of realism – that a text is like a mirror capable of holding the world (and the writer as a part of the world) within its grasp. But on the other hand, she seems fixated on books themselves, and try as she might to write a conventionally realist narrative, turning her narrative gaze outward (or back on herself), her texts inevitably reflect on books themselves. Books, she concludes, have contaminated her ability to write (188). As a consequence of "el efecto biblioteca," her writing is never more than a caricature of what she intends.

> Los escritores bibliotecarios como ella, cuando quieren escribir novelas, escriben únicamente sucedáneos de novelas, y lo mismo ocurre cuando tratan de escribir un ensayo, un relato o una conferencia como puede ser ésta. La escritora con estigma de bibliotecaria quiere escribir una conferencia y le sale un relato a la vez que una parodia de conferencia. Y también, la escritora maldita cuando escribe un relato tiene como resultado algo parecido a una autobiografía que es a su vez parodia de relato. (191)
>
> [Librarian writers like her, when they want to write novels, write only substitute novels, and the same thing happens when they try to write an essay, a text, or a lecture like this one. The writer with the stigma of librarian wants to write a lecture and what comes out is a text that is a parody of a lecture. What is more, the cursed writer, when she writes a text, ends up with something like an autobiography that is in turn a parody of an autobiography.]

This comment suggests that the original is Amat herself – the autobiographical subject. Yet she has already told us that her identity has never existed in any fixed form. Her writing, therefore, cannot be a parody as an imitation of the real but must instead be understood as a gesture through which the real is generated – fleetingly, evanescently, and at a distance.[4] If, in the etymological sense, parody is a performance that occurs alongside the principal narrative (*para ōidē*), here it is the means, and for all intents and purposes the only means, through which the self is even imaginable.

For Amat, the library is both a material entity (her father's library, her own library, and the various libraries in which she has worked during her career as librarian) as well as a metaphor. Not only does she compare the library to a mother, a family, a monastery, a cemetery, a tomb, and the universe (193), but she compares other spaces, such as cities, to libraries. In keeping with her compatriot-writer Ruiz Zafón, she identifies her native Barcelona with books, describing it as "[l]a ciudad de las palabras" (163) [the city of words], "un país literario" (164) [a literary country], "[u]n aparador libresco" (165) [a shop window of books], and "[u]na biblioteca viva, herida y luminosa" (165) [a living, wounded, and luminous library]. This is not merely a recognition on her part of the great literary tradition of Barcelona but an example of how her library experience has conditioned her to see the world. In her case the library functions as a master paradigm informing all that is. In her reflections she in fact seems to depict the relationship between the library and the world not simply as one of similitude but at times even one of immanence.[5] For Amat, memory, and indeed the entire life of the mind, is a vast and recondite library. Her "biblioteca interior" (176) [interior library], a secularized version of the interior castle of Santa Teresa de Jesús, lies buried deep within her own solitude. It is a "biblioteca ... de lo más heterodoxa e inespecífica" (176) [library of the most heterodox and unspecific]. More important, it is the foundation of her writing and the place where she hears her own voice speak: "Allí es donde la voz me habla" (176) [There is where my voice speaks to me]. This voice, winnowed from all she has read and imagined, is what she struggles to express through writing.

Amat maintains that the library is inescapable. When she begins writing, she tries to avoid anything related to libraries. But the library always returns: "allí está otra vez, provocadora como una ventana abierta al vacío, la biblioteca de siempre con sus escritores vivos o muertos y sus bibliotecarios ciegos o asesinos" (192) [there it is again, defiant like a window open to the void, the library as always, with its living or dead writers and its blind or murderous librarians]. According to this passage, the library stubbornly persists, like a fortress of being in a universe of nothingness. What is more, Amat implicitly aligns herself with the most famous librarian in the history of the Spanish-language world, the blind Jorge Luis Borges, as well as the most notorious bibliophile of the Iberian tradition, the legendary murderous bookman of Barcelona. Yet Amat is not exclusively bound to libraries of the past or to the one that she knew as a child. As she explains in *El ladrón de libros y otras bibliomanías* (1988) [The book thief and other bibliomanias], the changing library profession obliged her to change direction, and although she might have preferred to remain a traditional librarian ("bibliotecaria sacerdotisa del templo, rata de bibliotecas" [38] [priestess librarian of the temple and library rat]), she eventually chose to specialize in document technology. In so doing, she has become a spokesperson for both traditional print libraries as well as the virtual libraries of the digital age, while remaining steadfast in her love of physical books.

## Digital Technology and Book Fever

What Amat calls "el efecto biblioteca," or the effect that her lifelong cultivation of books has had on her effort as a writer to give tangible expression to her inner self, is intensified in the age of digital technology. Yet she also recognizes the tremendous utility of digital documents and electronic or digital libraries.[6] In the essay *La biblioteca electrónica* (1989) [The electronic library] she begins to formulate a vision of the twenty-first-century library and the changing role of librarians in the digital age. She notes that until the late twentieth century, knowledge was primarily stored and disseminated through paper-based books and documents. But because digital documents are more efficient and economical (in part, as she points out, because they do not require paper and physical space), they have become the dominant format for storing and disseminating knowledge. In *La biblioteca electrónica*, Amat does not address how digital media might actually be used to create knowledge or how digital products might themselves be the objects of aesthetic appreciation. Rather, she focuses on the digital library as a service that provides easy access to information: "Todo invita a la confirmación de que las bibliotecas son efectivamente servicios de distribución de la información" (177) [Everything leads to the conclusion that libraries are basically information distribution services]. To gain access to information, digital-library users are not obliged to enter the physical space of a library or interact with librarians in person. They do, however, require a digital literacy different from the kind of literacy necessary to navigate traditional libraries. As Amat suggests, the primary activity associated with the digital library is in fact not reading, in the conventional sense, but searching.[7]

As evidenced in *La biblioteca electrónica*, Amat is enthusiastic about the impact of digital technology on library users and library professionals. In the age of digital technology, libraries have been not only despatialized but also, to a certain extent, deinstitutionalized. They are thus available to a wider range of users than are traditional libraries, provided, of course, that users have access to technological instruction and electronic devices. Amat is intrigued by how digital technology will allow library users to intervene in the texts they access and thereby assume a more active role as consumers of information. Given the prestige associated with technological expertise, she further contends that in the twenty-first century, society will no longer regard librarians as mere functionaries but as specialists trained in the workings of a science. Even though digital technology might be perceived as a threat to the existence of traditional libraries, in her view it clearly enhances the careers of librarians and revolutionizes their work.

> La famosa frase de Lancaster: La biblioteca está muerta. Larga vida al bibliotecario, es, desde luego, impactante. Creo, sin embargo, que este proceso tecnológico inevitable beneficia sin duda a la profesión. (183)

> [The famous statement of Lancaster, "The library is dead, long live the librarian," is, of course, troubling. I nevertheless believe that this inevitable technological process will without doubt benefit the profession.][8]

Despite the warnings regarding "the death of the library," Amat predicts that for the foreseeable future print and digital technologies will coexist and augment each other, and that libraries as repositories of physical books will remain.

Although Amat regards digital technology as beneficial to the library profession, it nevertheless exacerbates the frustration that she often feels as a writer. She expresses this most poignantly in an early short story, titled "El laboratorio de lo imaginario" (1989) [The laboratory of the imaginary], in which she depicts a young author's attempt to write a narrative at a time when writers were just beginning to use computers.[9] The protagonist, Alejandra, declares at the outset that she is suffering from an unrelenting fever, a symbol of her overpowering desire for an ontological fulfillment that in her view is possible only through the medium of texts and books.[10] She further indicates that in order to write she must have an intermediary that will function as both a vehicle for her voice and an instrument for expressing its tone. She initially regards the ink that she applies to blank paper as a mirror of herself. But she quickly realizes that she requires an object that will provide greater distance between herself and her reflection and will function like another self through which she will be able to hear her own echo. This object, which she calls a machine, is in fact a computer. With her computer, Alejandra is able to "leerse a sí misma por vez primera" (*La biblioteca fantasma* 49) [read herself for the first time]. In so doing, she experiences relief from the fever. Yet when reading the printed pages of her text she also feels as if she were beginning to die, since what appears to her most alive are the pages themselves. As she progresses in her work, the text gains importance, and rather than reflect her, as she originally thought it would, she imagines that she now reflects the text. Eventually, the text takes on a life of its own, recreating itself and thereby revealing to her that what matters most is actually the way that the text is generated through the computer. Although the text seemingly embodies her ("por primera vez sintió el placer de sentirse cuerpo en el texto" [51] [for the first time she felt the pleasure of feeling that she had a body in the text]), she finds that she wants someone else to engage with her work as well. She therefore joins an electronic-library club through which she will be able to share her work with other writers.[11]

Alejandra considers the system of electronic publication preferable to that of print publication because of its speed and efficiency. Yet if the printed text seems alien to her, the text on the computer screen is almost uncanny: "Aquel texto luminoso le resultaba tan extraño como un sueño que inútilmente intentase recordar al despertarse" (56) [That luminous text turned out to be as strange as a dream that she might futilely attempt to remember after waking up]. Alejandra nevertheless continues to write, and her computer becomes her "otro yo" (57) [other self] and the centre of her life. Her writing, moreover, is subsumed into a vast electronic labyrinth that seemingly transforms the entire world into a kind of "literatura ambulante" (59) [mobile literature]. Yet gradually, Alejandra's views of digital writing change, and she comes to regard the program that makes possible the publication of her narratives as "el traidor más cruel de su causa literaria" (60) [the cruelest traitor of her literary enterprise]. This is because it uses the material that she and the members of the electronic-library club upload into the system to compose texts in the manner that it sees fit. It assigns these texts a byline, and as a result Alejandra sees her name on works that "el monstruo mecánico" (63) [the mechanical monster] has in fact created. In order to free herself from this digital demiurge and tyrant, Alejandra sells her computer, which she compares to a "vulgar trituradora de textos" (63) [vulgar garbage disposer of texts]. But when she does so, the fever from which she had achieved respite returns in all its intensity.

In "El laboratorio de lo imaginario," Amat reveals an anxiety that in the age of digital technology humans will lose both their agency and their individuality. Digital technology will not only do the work of humans but, through a kind of artificial intelligence (the narrator actually refers to the machine as having a brain [61]), it will also be able to create art. On the positive side, humans will be relieved of the anguish that Alejandra temporarily holds at bay by relinquishing to her computer the freedom to act of her own volition. But in doing so, they will lose something of their humanity, as evidenced by Alejandra's failed attempt to use her computer to give expression to her own distinctive voice.

After inscribing her intentions on paper, either through ink or through her computer printer, Alejandra can literally feel a dimension of herself by holding the pages in her hands and focusing her eyes on the handwritten and printed words. But the texts on the computer screen are more evanescent, and even if they can be retrieved after the machine is shut down, they do not have the tangibility that Alejandra seeks to experience through writing. More important, as a result of the machinations of the program, the texts that Alejandra ultimately reads are less a reflection of her unique inner world than of the design and contents of the program itself. Although traditional writers might feel similarly alienated by the interventions of editors and publishers, what Alejandra finds most disconcerting is the seeming anonymity of the digital world that mediates her writing, as well as her own inability to maintain a sense of connection with the final written product.

Alejandra initially achieves a sort of embodiment through print. Yet to the extent that her writing is digitalized, she experiences not only a loss of this objectivity but also, as her texts slip away from her, a waning of the subjective self that she seeks to express through them. What "El laboratorio de lo imaginario" intriguingly suggests is that the disappearance of physical books in fact entails a concomitant disappearance of texts, at least as these have appeared in traditional print formats. She thus shares concerns with critics of digital technology including Virgile Stark, who remarks sarcastically that according to proponents of digitalization "le texte ... doit être évacué avec le livre" (185) [the text must be left behind along with the book]. Digital technology, of course, does not threaten the existence of texts per se, even if it erodes the perceived unity of texts and, by extension, the personal identities that humans attempt to forge through them. But for bibliophiles like Amat and Stark, it does clearly lead to a diminution of traditional reading and writing practices, and of the kind of intellectual and aesthetic enrichment that these practices make possible.[12]

## The Return to the Library

Although in her professional life as a librarian Amat extols the advantages of digital technology, she remains powerfully drawn to physical books and the physical structures that house them. Over the course of her career she describes many real and imagined book collections. Yet it is her own personal library that continues to function as her primary site of self-discovery and as the means through which she seeks to express her identity.

In the volume of essays titled *Escribir y callar* (2010) [To write and be silent], written some twenty years after *La biblioteca electrónica* and "El laboratorio de lo imaginario," Amat describes her library, and in an intriguing passage reveals that she now keeps it in her underground garage. Her neighbours find this strange, not simply because garages are designed as a place for cars, but because in their view cars are preferable to books insofar as they provide humans with a sense of protection against the world and dignity in the eyes of others. Indeed, books have often been thought to serve the same purpose. Yet whereas cars are silent and indifferent to their owners, Amat's books, as she sees them, are potentially alive. Although they have acquired "el color vainilla del papiro" (56) [the vanilla colour of papyrus], and although they inhabit a space evocative of a tomb, a miracle occurs when "manos inquietas y faltas de consuelo deciden abrir uno de los volúmenes y descansar en ellos" (27) [troubled and disconsolate hands decide to open one of the volumes and rest on them]. In this moment, when Amat holds a book in her hands, it comes to life and begins to speak to her. In so doing, it paradoxically brings her to life as well.

The books in Amat's library are a testament to her reading life and also a means through which her past as a reader is kept alive.

> Tengo una biblioteca para ser. Una biblioteca como lazo atávico a mi tradición lectora. No crea nadie que la biblioteca es mi lugar de muerte y encierro. Tiene más de manicomio que de necrópolis. (58)
>
> [I have a library in order to be. A library like an atavistic link to my reading tradition. Let no one think that my library is a place of death or enclosure. It is more like a madhouse than a necropolis.]

What Amat's library makes atavistically reappear are not only the voices that she discovers in her books (and through them the lives and worlds of those who wrote them) but also the girl that she once was when she first read them. Her library thus provides a kind of tangible unity to the discrete moments of her past as a reader and bibliophile. It also draws her into fantasy worlds beyond her immediate milieu. For this reason, she compares her library to a madhouse and her obsession with reading to madness. As she puts it, her library

> se va pareciendo cada vez más a la biblioteca imaginaria de la novela *Auto de fe* de Elias Canetti. Cueva del intelectual fantasma, encerrado y perdido

> entre sus libros. Sumido en su locura libresca. ¿No decía Cervantes que los muchos libros terminan por volvernos locos? (56)
>
> [seems more and more like the imaginary library in the novel *Auto-da-Fé* by Elias Canetti. The cave of the intellectual phantom, shut away and lost among his books. Immersed in his book madness. Did Cervantes not say that with many books we will end up going mad?]

If Amat's library draws her back to her reading past, it also, through "el efecto biblioteca," destabilizes her sense of self. Yet she concludes that this is ultimately a tremendous boon: "su mejor recompensa es haber hecho de [ella] varias personas" (58) [its greatest reward is having made of her many people].

Amat contrasts the space of her personal library in her basement garage with the library of Michel de Montaigne, located in the tower of his family home, the Chtâteau de Montaigne. Montaigne spent the final twenty-one years of his life ensconced in his library tower, surrounded by some 1,500 books. While there, he composed his monumental *Essais* [Essays]. Amat wonders if he could have accomplished this task if he had not been situated within the setting of his library. Scholars of Montaigne have in fact studied the influence on his writings not only of the books contained in his library but also the maxims and paintings displayed on his library walls.[13] Amat, for her part, does not comment on the particulars of his library space but instead contrasts its physicality with the virtual reality of digital libraries. She suggests that only by isolating himself within a physical building containing physical books was Montaigne able to create the intellectual context and engage in the extended contemplation that made his philosophical production possible.

> ¿Se puede aislar uno en el vacío del ordenador como se encerró Michel de Montaigne en su biblioteca? Harto y fatigado de las corrupciones de los políticos, el escritor francés se retiró a leer, pensar, reelaborar conocimiento, mirar al hombre y la naturaleza y escribir sobre todo ello. (75)
>
> [Can one isolate oneself in the emptiness of a computer in the way that Michel de Montaigne shut himself up in his library? Fed up and exhausted by the corruption of politicians, the French writer retreated to read, think, re-elaborate knowledge, regard man and nature, and write about it all.][14]

In contrast to Montaigne, Amat does not live in her library, nor is her interaction with books limited to the physical volumes in her collection. Because her computer "[le] abre la puerta a una infinidad de bibliotecas" [opens the door (for her) to an infinity of libraries], "[su] biblioteca es ahora todas las bibliotecas del mundo" (75) [(her) library is now all the libraries of the world]. She thus imagines that, unlike Montaigne's library in his castle keep, her personal library in her basement garage is "recelosa de que [ella] navegue por la otra" (74–5) [suspicious when (she) navigates through the other one], that is, through the digital library. This attitude of suspicion, which she attributes to her books, in fact reveals her own apprehension that digital libraries might someday replace traditional print libraries.

If Amat identifies with Montaigne, a bibliophile of the sixteenth century, this is also because in her view present-day society regards book lovers and owners of libraries as anachronistic and at odds with prevailing social norms: "Mi biblioteca es una provocación a un sistema que tilda de personaje sospechoso a cualquier individuo propietario de una biblioteca" (57) [My library is a provocation to a system that brands as a suspicious type any individual owner of a library]. According to Amat, library owners reject the ethos of contemporary culture and the quest for immediate gratification.

> Hay algo de desafío en esta forma de acumular tesoros decadentes, despreciados por la sociedad de consumo que valora la supuesta utilidad y la moda de los objetos modernos por encima del patrimonio intelectual o de conocimiento que puedan proporcionarnos. (56–7)
>
> [There is something defiant in this way of accumulating decadent treasures, scorned by a consumer society that values the supposed utility and fashion of modern objects beyond our intellectual patrimony or the knowledge that they might provide.]

Amat, as she has previously indicated, appreciates the usefulness and effectiveness of digital technology, but she believes that books offer the possibility of more textured and extended intellectual and emotive experiences.

> La pantalla electrónica refleja el vacío del mundo. Es decir: el no mundo. Por el contrario, la biblioteca es una caja reproductora de muertes y melancolías, un hogar donde sólo pueden sentirse a gusto las personas que deseen un conocimiento más profundo sobre el mundo y sobre nosotros mismos. (57)
>
> [The electronic screen reflects the void of the world. That is to say, the non-world. On the contrary, the library is a mechanism that reproduces death and melancholy, a home where only people who desire a more profound knowledge of the world and ourselves can feel at ease.]

Amat thus reaffirms the pre-eminence of print over digital media and the traditional culture of reading over the new reading practices that digital technology makes available.

Amat speculates that a digital library might potentially provide library users with access to the knowledge amassed in all the libraries of the world. In her view, however, knowledge is useless unless we make it our own, which we are able to do most easily through the acquisition of print matter (75). She therefore regards the libraries of our choosing as preferable to the virtual libraries that come to us through the click of a computer mouse or the public and institutional libraries of print volumes that we do not own. Indeed, the notion of ownership seems crucial to her, as if the physical books that we possess are somehow more closely tied to our identities than are books accessed digitally or books owned by others.

As Amat explains, not only is her personal identity bound up with her library but her relationship with her books and, by extension with herself, is fraught with contradiction. If, as she declares, she both loves and hates libraries (26), this is because she both embraces and resists the identities that she has achieved through books. These identities, however, are tentative: "¿Soy libro? ¿Obra? ¿Mujer? ¿Madre? ¿Novela?" (56) [Am I a book? A work? A woman? A mother? A novel?]. As she has asserted on various occasions, her identities are in fact inflected by gender and language. In *Escribir y callar* she reveals that by reading books written by men and women, she has come to take on masculine and feminine identities. And by reading books written in many languages (Catalan, Castilian Spanish, the Spanish of the Americas, French, and English), her linguistic (and hence cultural) identity is "híbrida" [hybrid], "bastarda" [bastard], "mestiza" [mestizo], and, above all, "libresca" (68) [bookish]. As she grows older, she at times feels inhibited by the identities that she has achieved through reading, and she imagines that by reconfiguring her library she might free herself from them and experience other modes of being: "Ahora cuando tal vez ya me he convertido en libro y, de forma algo maniática, me dedico a ganar espacio para libros futuros desechando los pobres volúmenes que no sirven" (25) [Now, when I have perhaps become a book, I attempt, in a somewhat maniacal fashion, to make space for future books by discarding the poor volumes that are no longer useful]. But her passion for books remains unabated.

Amat's lifelong reflections on bibliophilia and her experiences as a bibliophile writer and librarian reach a sort of climax in her narrative *Todos somos Kafka* (1993, republished in 2004) [We are all Kafka], in which she imagines talking with Walter Benjamin and Italo Calvino, her two ideal mentors of bibliophilia. In a chapter titled "La biblioteca imperfecta" [The imperfect library], she fantasizes that night has fallen and that she has sought refuge in a house eerily reminiscent of Benjamin's library. She encounters Benjamin and engages him in a conversation about books, libraries, and writers. She remarks that she has been seeking a library of books whose authors were all mad and that the collection of Benjamin might be just such a library. Benjamin, however, asserts that all writers of significance are mad since they are all bibliomaniacs, even if they express their bibliomania solely by writing books.

> Porque en todo escritor que se precie, solía decir Walter Benjamin, hay escondido un bibliómano impenitente, aunque su bibliomanía sea tan débil que no vaya más allá de la larga tarea de escribir un libro, vista la imposibilidad de procurárselo de otro modo. (191–2)

> [Because in every writer of value, Walter Benjamin used to say, there is hidden an inveterate bibliomaniac, even if his bibliomania is so weak that it does not go beyond the lengthy task of writing a book, given the impossibility of obtaining it for himself in any other way.]

As the conversation of Amat and Benjamin suggests, writers of books are motivated both by a desire to acquire books and by a belief that the books most easily possessed are the ones that they write, precisely because these are more intimately tied to their own inner selves. The ideal book would in fact be the one that we imagine we have become. When Amat asks herself, as she does on numerous occasions, if she is a book, she thereby reveals not only an uncertainty about her identity but also a deep-seated longing to achieve the ontological plenitude of body and spirit that book lovers typically seek through books.[15]

If writing a book is an expression of bibliomania, then so too is the act of reading one. Indeed, it is through reading the texts of others and in a sense becoming them that Amat experiences the kind of madness that she associates with books. In a chapter of *Todos somos Kafka* titled "La estantería hipotética" [The hypothetical bookshelf], she finds herself in the library of Calvino. Calvino tells her that his books are unique because there are no copies of them anywhere else in the world. What is more, they cannot be reproduced or even imitated. By reading them, Amat imagines that she will be able to quell her seemingly insatiable desire for books.

> Me ataca la necesidad de leerlos. Si consigo leerlos, conseguiré también repetirlos. Si consigo leerlos, llegaré a ser la lectora de libros únicos e irrepetibles. Algo me dice también que si los leo me sentiré colmada de

> lecturas. Un libro que mate las ganas de leer libros. Eso es el libro único. (199)
>
> [The need to read them attacks me. If I manage to read them, I will also manage to repeat them. If I manage to read them, I will become the reader of unique and unrepeatable books. Something tells me that if I read them, I will feel saturated with readings. A book that kills the desire to read books. That is the unique book.]

But the unique book does not exist, and Amat's desire to read is never satisfied. The upshot is that bibliophilia, whether carried out through reading, writing, or the mere act of book collecting, is an impossible project of self-realization, even if, for bibliophiles like Amat, it is what ultimately makes life worth living.

# 5 Miquel Plana and the Book as a Work of Art

Bibliophiles not only seek rare and beautiful books, but they also create them. One of the most accomplished creators of bibliophile books in the contemporary period is Miquel Plana (1943–2012). Plana's productive career follows in the tradition of the modern Catalan book-arts movement, fomented in the early twentieth century by figures like Ramon Miquel i Planas. In keeping with his predecessors, Plana envisions books as texts to be read according to conventional reading practices as well as objects to be appreciated for their aesthetic qualities. However, many of his creations share characteristics with what theorists of the book arts call "artists' books," and at times seem closer in their conception to the plastic arts than to traditional bibliophile books, which usually maintain the form of the codex and highlight the printed text. In fact, the works of Plana meld elements of traditional bibliophile books and artists' books, and for this reason they stand in a class of their own. What is more, given that they were produced in the historic moment of transition from print to digital culture in the late twentieth and early twenty-first centuries, they might even be regarded as the culmination of the history of the Spanish book as a discrete physical object.[1]

In the late nineteenth and early twentieth centuries, Catalan publishers attempted to recover the literary treasures of the Catalan past and make them available to Catalan readers in deluxe editions. Volumes such as those of Miquel i Planas, with their distinctive bindings, typefaces, layouts, and illustrations, are regarded as masterpieces of Catalan *Modernisme* and have been long sought after by Spanish and international collectors. Although intended to preserve and transmit the Catalan cultural heritage, they have been valued not only for their discursive content but also their physical format. Yet despite their distinctive artistic features, they remain codices. They thus fit squarely within the ambit of bibliophilia, reflecting and appealing most powerfully to the sensibilities of those who love books.

In contrast to traditional bibliophile books, twentieth-century artists' books experiment with the structure of books. According to Johanna Drucker, they differ from the so-called *livre d'artiste*, a genre first appearing in late nineteenth-century France that provided a forum for artists to showcase their talents through illustrations and designs. As Drucker explains, the *livre d'artiste* was fomented by the art dealers Ambroise Vollard and Daniel-Henry Kahnweiler, whose publications represented works by Georges Rouault, Pablo Picasso, and others (2). Drucker argues that although the *livre d'artiste* typically "interrogates the conceptual or material form of the book as part of its intention, thematic interests, or production activities ... the standard distinction between image and text, generally on facing pages, is maintained in most [of them]" (2–3). In terms of its physical format, the *livre d'artiste* is hence less radical than twentieth-century artists' books.

Whereas traditional bibliophile books are produced under the direction of publishers who coordinate the work of writers, artists, bookbinders, engravers, typographers, and many others, artists' books are typically fashioned by individuals (Guillén Ramón and Pascual Buyé 257) and tend to be independent, personal creations. In artists' books, moreover, discursive content is often secondary to physical form. For this reason, they might seem more similar to sculptures than books (Urbani García 266), and they have in fact been more widely cultivated by artists than bibliophiles (Puig Rovira, "Miquel" 138). Yet as Drucker makes clear, artists' books have historically been linked to political activism, for example during the periods of Dada and surrealism, in part because they are often not tied to mainstream publishing houses but rather independent presses (5).

Like his early twentieth-century predecessors, Plana seeks to produce aesthetically pleasing volumes, and although he experiments with the traditional form of the book, he continues to use paper as his basic medium. Pilar Vélez thus identifies him as the most recent scion in a long lineage of distinguished Catalan book-producers, whose work, she declares, marks the end of the era of modernist Catalan bibliophilia, albeit not the end of Catalan or Hispanic bibliophilia itself ("Miquel Plana [1943–2012]" 10).

> [L]a concepción [de Plana] del libro de tirada reducida, papel escogido, ilustraciones de calidad, cuidada tipografía ... continúa en la línea que recoge Ramón Miquel y Planas a principios del siglo XX como continuador de los hombres de la Renaixença, y después del Noucentismo, del

> editor Gili i Roig, de Ramon de Capmany, de la casa Horta y más cercano a nosotros, como principal ejemplo, el grabador y editor Jaume Pla, cada uno con su singularidad y su personalidad característica, evidentemente. ("Miquel Plana: Un fenómeno" 19)
>
> [(Plana's) conception of the book of a limited print run, choice paper, quality illustrations, and careful typography ... follows in the line taken up by Ramon Miquel i Planas at the beginning of the twentieth century as a continuation of the men of the Renaixença, and afterwards by Noucentisme, by the publisher Gili i Roig, by Ramon de Capmany, by the Casa Horta, and closer to us, as a primary example, the engraver and publisher Jaume Pla, each, obviously, with his own unique individuality and personality.]

Whereas early twentieth-century producers of bibliophile books brought to their volumes the talents of artists other than themselves, Plana often does the artwork for his own books. What is more, he maintains control over every aspect of his projects, from conception to production. Some scholars therefore consider him primarily a creator of artists' books. Josep M. Pujol, for instance, notes that the most salient feature of his books is not their technical perfection (as is the case with bibliophile books) but rather their artistic formulation (as is the case with artists' books) ("Miquel" 157). Yet in Joaquim Molas's view, Plana carries to fruition the goal of *Modernisme* to synthesize the book arts and the plastic arts (140), or, as Pere Macias i Arau et al. put it, to conjoin the world of the image and the world of the text (18). Indeed, most scholars regard Plana as a bibliophile who ultimately draws together the traditions of both bibliophile books and artists' books. As Vélez concludes, he is not an artist who occasionally dedicates himself to books but rather a producer of books dedicated to bibliophilia ("Miquel Plana: Un fenómeno" 20).

Plana's works share similarities with the "obra-libro," or "bookwork," theorized by Ulises Carrión (1941–89). Carrión is one of the most innovative book theorists and artists from the Spanish-speaking world. Born in Mexico but active in Amsterdam during his mature years, he highlights the materiality of books and rejects the notion that books are simply bearers of words, even if they do have textual dimensions. Bookworks, he conjectures, are neither containers of texts nor pieces of plastic art that for all intents and purposes have lost the appearance and function of books. Rather, they occupy a space on a book spectrum halfway between traditional books and artists' books. Unlike traditional books, they do not document a reality outside of themselves. Yet unlike artists' books, at least as sometimes conceived, they cannot take any form whatsoever (for instance, a block of marble sculpted in the shape of a book), and they do not require special installation or lighting for display. In fact, they can be touched and held and stored on bookshelves. What makes bookworks distinctive is the central role of the artist in every phase of their production. Carrión further believes that traditional books are in a process of dying out, and in *El arte nuevo de hacer libros* [The new art of making books] he declares: "[C]reo ... que todo libro existente eventualmente desaparecerá. Como resultado de una catástrofe final o victimazados por la tecnología o por un proceso de auto-aniquilación, no lo sé. Pero desaparecerán" (109) [I believe that all existing books will eventually disappear. As the result of a final catastrophe or the victims of technology or a process of self-annihilation, I don't know. But they will disappear]. In keeping with the metaphor of Ruiz Zafón, he goes so far as to describe libraries, both literal and figurative, as cemeteries. For some book theorists, his words might seem prescient in the age of digital technology. But for scholars like Amaranth Borsuk, his notion of bookworks is significant precisely because it inspires us to reflect on the materiality of books in general (146).

The creations of Plana, like the bookworks theorized by Carrión, are not merely bearers of words, and the written text is but one aspect of them. In many, however, the written text is of paramount importance. For this reason, they resemble books historically created for bibliophiles, which often couch texts in distinctively beautiful or unusual physical formats. Yet Plana participates in the creation of his works at each stage of execution, and in this sense embodies the kind of book artist that Carrión champions. In fact, he even exceeds Carrión's model of the book artist insofar as he carries out most of the labour with his own hands. Carrión would likely characterize Plana's works as "una totalidad" [a totality], or "el libro como un todo" (139) [the book as a whole], given that they convey the intentions of an individual artist as inscribed in matter at a particular time and place. He might even conclude that like bookworks, they are not doomed to extinction, and that they alone retain "la posibilidad real que tienen los libros para sobrevivir" (146) [the real possibility that books have for surviving].

In contrast to Carrión, Plana was neither an intellectual nor a theoretician of books but rather an artist (Fontbona, "Miquel" 41). He was nevertheless exposed to the book arts at an early age, working as a youngster at the Gràfiques Olot in his hometown of Olot, in the province of Girona, and later studying at the Escola de Belles Arts d'Olot, where he learned engraving techniques. In 1972, after some fifteen years in the printing business, he changed direction and began designing his own books and launching several series including El burí i la ploma [The burin and the pen] and El tòrcul i les lettres [The etching press and letters]. As Domènec Moli notes, this was a particularly auspicious moment for Plana to embark on a career as an artist ("Miquel" 11). Not only did the Franco dictatorship end in the mid-1970s, and with it decades of censorship, but Catalan culture and the Catalan language underwent a renaissance, which Plana himself helped foment through his bibliophile creations.

As exemplified in the volume *Tècniques: Reverberacions gràfiques* [Techniques: Graphic reverberations], written by Pujol and illustrated by Plana, Plana employs numerous methods of graphic design including wood engraving, lithography, zincography, offset engraving, and photoengraving. Although he values traditional approaches to engraving, he also adopts more contemporary strategies to the extent that they allow him to create the kinds of volumes he desires (Jou et al. 93). In so doing, he moves beyond the practices of the luminaries of early and mid-twentieth-century Catalan bibliophilia. Plana scrupulously seeks out materials through which he can best express his aesthetic vision, yet unlike earlier bibliophiles he also occasionally uses items traditionally deemed inappropriate for fine books, such as cardboard (Monturiol and Pujolàs 9). He thereby reveals an openness to change and experimentation in a field of production and connoisseurship that has often exalted tradition.

Plana clearly differs from the makers of traditional bibliophile books through his use of colour. In contrast to many of his predecessors, he eschews black and white and muted colours in general, and employs a greater spectrum of pigments and more intense hues in both his typography and illustrations. To increase colour intensity, he often uses linocut, a procedure similar to woodblock printing, whereby an image is carved in relief on a sheet of linoleum, covered with ink, transferred to paper, and printed. The colours in Plana's books are evocative of the chromatic paintings of the school of German artists associated with Die Brüke, who were among the first to advance the use of linocut. Yet according to Antoni Monturiol and Magda Pujolàs, they are also similar to those of the illuminated books created at the time of the invention of printing in the West (15). Plana's adoption of modern techniques thus allows him to create bibliophile works of classic beauty.

Like traditional producers of bibliophile books, Plana recognizes that, after the text itself, paper is perhaps the most important element of a volume (Puig Rovira, "El paper" 87). To achieve the colour tones he desires, he rejects couche, or coated paper, because its glossy surface absorbs less ink, and instead uses an uncoated, rough paper that is more absorbent (88). In fact, the texture of paper affects not simply the typography of a book but the entire process of intaglio, through which images are impressed onto the pages. Paper is hence key to the overall aesthetic appeal of books. As Plana proceeds in his career, he ceases to work with commercially manufactured paper and adopts an artisanally produced paper more similar to that of earlier generations of book production. In his books, he also tends to use a thick paper akin to the canvases of traditional paintings.

It is in the area of binding, however, that Plana's creations differ most noticeably from traditional books. Some, in fact, are actually not bound at all, and thus lack what is generally considered the over-defining characteristic of the book.[2] In the case of *En defensa de la lletra: Vint-i-sis apologies per vint-i-sis literats* [In defense of the letter: Twenty-six apologies by twenty-six literati] the pages are contained within the case of the book cover, but they are not attached to it, either through thread or glue. Although readers can remove them all at once, each sheet, which has been folded to make four pages, can be separated from the entire set. Within each folded sheet, moreover, there is an illustrated letter on another piece of paper. There is thus no book in the traditional sense but rather the components of a book, which readers can assemble as they choose. The cover case nevertheless creates an external unity to the extent that it houses the loose sheets.

Plana's book covers often endow his works with emotions and tones, depending on how they are perceived and interpreted by readers, and as Aitor Quiney observes, they can even function as the protagonists of his books (78). The cover case of *En defensa de la lletra* is a plain red, perhaps indicative of Plana's passion for the physical beauty of letters that the text expresses, and the title is indicated on the first loose-leaf page of the content material. Yet with many of his other books, the cover design clearly reveals both the subject and the tenor of the discourse. An obvious example is *Barcelona 1888–1992: Vista per vuit escriptors, i il·lustrada amb aiguaforts per vint artistas* [Barcelona 1888–1992: Seen by eight writers, and illustrated with etchings by twenty artists] (see figures 9a, 9b, and 9c). The front and back paper cover of this volume, made from an etching by Plana, highlights the landmarks of the city of Barcelona, with its urban and natural spaces, in bright yellow, orange, pink, blue, and green. The exuberant chromatic configuration depicted on the cover heralds the celebration of Barcelona expressed in the book, and the texts and illustrations that follow trace the flowering of the modern city, from its entry into the international imagination with the Universal Exposition of 1888, to its transformation into a world metropolis with the Olympic Games of 1992.

Figures 9a, 9b, and 9c. 9a: Book cover, recto.

Figures 9a, 9b, and 9c. 9b: Paper cover, recto.

Figures 9a, 9b, and 9c. 9c: Paper cover, verso. Miquel Plana, *Barcelona 1888–1992: Vista per vuit escriptors, i il· lustrada amb aiguaforts per vint artistas,* Miquel Plana, 1991. Illustrations by Miquel Plana. Images courtesy of Biblioteca de Catalunya.

Like book covers, typography also conveys meaning and emotion. As Núria Puig i Borràs argues, different type fonts in works such as *En defensa de la lletra* transmit different emotional sensations, given that some appear heavy, aggressive, and serious while others seem light, gentle, and playful (12). Still others appeal to readers through their ostensible imperfections. In principle, readers experience the feelings generated by the typography prior to reading the text. Yet the letters themselves, as many of the twenty-six contributors to *En defensa de la lletra* remark, also evoke images and thoughts and possibly even deeply seated psychological and cultural memories. These experiences of emotion and meaning differ not only according readers but also the particular volume read, since each is individually crafted and therefore subtly distinct from all the others of a particular edition.

*En defensa de la lletra* is in fact one of Plana's most accomplished productions, and one of which he was most proud (Moli, *Colofons* 29). The twenty-six apologies for the twenty-six letters of the alphabet were composed by twenty-six different Catalan authors, and the illustrations of the letters were designed by Plana and printed through lito-offset. According to Josep M. Fonalleras, *En defensa de la lletra* shares similarities with the volumes of Oulipo (Ouvoir de littérature potentielle [Workshop of potential literature]), a group of experimental French writers who came together in the 1960s and formulated a project to create new textual formats and refashion the structures of the traditional book (71).[3] In the introduction to *En defensa de la lletra*, titled "Rigorosament literal" [Rigorously literal], the editor Modest Prats reflects on bibliophile books and, by extension, Plana's work itself. Each section of Prats's essay begins with a letter, in the order of the alphabet.

Prats describes books as a "jardí secret" [secret garden], where "tot és quietud i joia" [all is tranquility and joy], and where "pots jugar sense exhaurir mai les combinaciones possibles" [you can play without ever exhausting all the possible combinations] of the letters. It is a site where "fas i refàs constantment el món" [you constantly make and remake the world]. This *locus amenus* seems initially to be a fantasy of the world of discourse, which is fluid and ever changing, and which humans freely refashion as they please. But it is also, given Prats's emphasis on the work's physicality, evocative of the world of books depicted by bibliophiles. In the "univers de la cal·ligrafia" [universe of calligraphy], "passes dolçament la mà sobre els relleus daurats de les capitals i endevines, pel gruix i la textura, els colors" [you pass your hand sweetly over the golden surface of the capitals and divine, by the thickness and texture, the colours]. Through a kind of synesthesia, where one form of sensory perception crosses with another (here tactile and visual), Prats discerns the colours of the letters by touching them. In fact, the colours of a book do possess a tactile dimension insofar as they are composed of ink that has been inscribed in paper. This dimension, moreover, varies according to the quality and quantity of the ink and the degree of its absorption. Yet Prats's encounter with Plana's book is evocative of the poem "Voyelles" [Vowels], by the French Symbolist poet Arthur Rimbaud, in which each vowel is associated with a particular colour.[4] It is also reminiscent of the insight expressed by the twentieth-century Portuguese artist José Escada, who declared that a painter is one "who sees the world well," and that "seeing well can only be done by one who imagines what is evident."[5] As with so many bibliophiles, including Plana himself, Prats's perception of books entails all of his senses and fantasy, and thus differs from the act of reading as conventionally understood.

Plana's corpus of books includes texts by classic and modern Catalan, Spanish, and international authors. Two, with poems by the Catalan poet Narcís Comadira and illustrations by Plana, represent religious and philosophical themes in some ways indicative of Plana's own vision of books. In the poem "Rèquiem," Comadira expresses melancholy and doubt in the face of death. In the poem "Triomf de la vida" [Triumph of life], in contrast, he reveals a faith in life beyond death. However, as he explains in the prologue of the volume containing "Triomf de la vida," he wrote the poem some seven years earlier, shortly after composing "Rèquiem." He now distances himself from the exuberant optimism of "Triomf de la vida," describing it as naive and simplistic.

In "Triomf de la vida," Comadira imagines a union of the material and spiritual worlds and affirms that together they form part of the divine: "El triomf de la vida és tal ... que el món i l'ànima formen part ... de la divinitat" (*Triomf* 10) [The triumph of life is such ... that the world and the spirit form part ... of the divinity]. The site of this union, in keeping with the Christian notion of God as the Word, is language, and specifically what Comadira calls the "Nom" [Name]. He synthesizes his message in the poem's final stanza.

Jo en el Tot, en el Nom
que encercla tot impuls
generós, recobrant-me.
Trobant-me en tu i en tots,
en el Tot i en el Nom
que comprèn i ens comprèn,
que ens afirma negant-nos.
Nom reclòs en el Nom,

extasiat del Nom,
Nom, amor pur del Nom,
Nom, cristall del seu Nom. (51)

[I in the All, in the Name
that encircles every impulse
that is generous, recovering me.
Finding me in you and in everything,
in the All and in the Name
that comprises and contains us,
that affirms us by denying us.
Name enclosed in the Name,
enthralled by the Name,
Name, pure love of the Name,
Name, crystal of its own Name.]

These verses evoke a mystical conception of the transformation of the finite self within the infinite All. As in the poetry of Santa Teresa de Jesús and San Juan de la Cruz, the experience of negation is paradoxically one of affirmation, just as death, from the Christian perspective, renders life eternal. Here, the All, or God, is equated with the Name, although the identity of the Name is not explicitly stated. As depicted in "Triomf de la vida," the Name is not only imminent ("reclòs en el Nom") but also transcendent insofar as the word "extasiat," derived from the Latin roots "ex" [out from] and "stare" [to stand], suggests a standing outside of oneself. The "ecstasy of the Name," to paraphrase Comadira's verse, would presumably occur when the Name is expressed through speaking or writing, or when it is made manifest in a book, the "cristall del seu Nom."

Comadira's representation of language and, by extension, the book has a long history in Christian culture and is perhaps most succinctly articulated by the narrator of Dante Alighieri's *La divina commedia* [*The Divine Comedy*]. When, after having traversed hell, purgatory, and paradise, he finally achieves the beatific vision, he perceives the divinity as an eternal light and also as a book that draws together all that is scattered and dispersed throughout the universe. This book in a sense binds the divine essence and renders it visible to the pilgrim poet as he gazes into the light.

Nel suo profondo vidi che s'interna,
legato con amore in un volume,
ciò che per l'universo si squaderna. (639)

[I saw in its abysmal deep immersed,
Together in one volume bound with love,
What is throughout the universe dispersed. (416)]

In his prologue to "Triomf de la vida," Comadira rejects the quest for the divine, or what the poet Gabriel Ferrater once described as the temptation of the ineffable (*Triomf* 11). He admits that in the poem he formulated an idealist conception of language, "com si 'Nom' no fos un nom" (11) [as if the Name were not a name], that is, as if it were not solely material. What is more, he attributes the inspiration for his idealism to Plana, whose life and work he continues to revere.

Comadira declares that the ostensibly positive vision of "Triomf de la vida" originated in Plana, and that the superbly crafted edition of the poem owes its existence entirely to his confident and determined attitude towards life in general and book production in particular. He lists what he regards as Plana's exemplary attributes and concludes that, without them, "el llarg viatge de la matèria a l'esperit" (9) [the long journey from matter to spirit] could never be accomplished. In reflecting on this journey, Comadira elides the religious context of the life trajectory depicted in the poem. Yet he maintains a belief that books somehow unite matter and spirit, endowing the former with life while rendering the latter both tangible and permanent. The belief in this ideal is made possible in part by the arresting visual qualities of Plana's books, as well as, in certain cases, their sheer size. Indeed, as the numerous eulogies composed in the wake of Plana's death suggest, the almost defiant presence of his bibliophile creations provide at least an illusion of human endurance in the face of mortality.[6]

Most readers of Plana's books are first captivated by the striking covers and illustrations, and by the innovative and unusual formats. Yet one of the most significant features of his books are in fact the colophons, situated at the end of the texts. In contrast to book covers, which traditionally indicate book publishers, colophons highlight the names of printers. Colophons are thus especially important in bibliophile volumes, since printers are often the ones most responsible for the physical aspects of books.

Many of the colophons in Plana's books were designed by Moli, one of Plana's primary graphic artists, and are brought together in *Colofons de Domènec Moli en els llibres de Miquel Plana* [Colophons of Domènec Moli in the books of Miquel Plana]. In an essay in this volume, Albert Corberto traces the history of colophons in western printing, which in the decades following Gutenberg typically provided more information about books than book covers did. Eventually, however, book covers grew in importance, and by the seventeenth century colophons came to be regarded as vestiges of manuscripts and gradually disappeared. The use of colophons was revived in the late nineteenth century in editions inspired by the British Arts and Crafts movement. In the twentieth century, colophons often included both a descriptive text and a design or image, thus adding to a book's aesthetic appeal while drawing the text to a close.

According to Mireia Sopena, Plana transformed the traditional colophon into a work of art (v). As "metagràficas" (v) [metagraphics], his colophons not only convey information about the production of his books but also indicate their distinctive themes and features. Some are in fact complete poems and can be read as independent pieces of writing. Together, they reveal Plana's aspirations and achievements as a maker of fine books.

Several of the colophons designed by Moli replicate the conflation of religion and bibliophilia implicit in Comadira's poetry and present throughout the history of western bibliophilia. One, in a volume dedicated to Plana, Lluís Jou, and Jaume Pla, reformulates the Jesuit motto, "Ad maiorem Dei gloriam" [To the greater glory of God], and depicts the three Catalan book artists as having dedicated their lives to the "major glòria del llibre" (Moli, *Colofons* 36) [greater glory of the book]. In so doing, it implies that God and books are on the same plane. The colophon in the volume *Nocturn* (2004) [Nocturne] features a poem by the poet and artist Albert Ràfols-Casamada (Moli, *Colofons* 37). This poem traces two genealogies of textuality, one leading from God to discourse (God made humans, humans produce poets, and poets produce poems) and another leading from God to the material book (God made the wind, the wind led to the invention of windmills, windmills made possible paper, and paper made possible books). In this idealist conception of texts, both discourse and material books have their origin in God, and both thus share a common ontological foundation. Discourse, moreover, is not superior to the medium through which it is conveyed, as traditional Christian injunctions against bibliomania would have it; in fact, the trajectory delineated in the poem ends with books, as if they were the ultimate goal of divine creation.

The colophon in the volume *Haikús de primavera* [Haikus of springtime] is itself expressed in the form of a haiku (Moli, *Colofons* 42). Like traditional Japanese haikus, it is related to a season of the year through the reference to springtime in the title of the collection. Although it does not follow the classical pattern of three verses of five, seven, and five syllables, it does replicate a key feature of traditional Japanese haikus by juxtaposing two images separated by a caesura – albeit not a *kireji*, or cutting word, but a comma. The first part depicts thought, which is transformed into poetry and subsequently the haiku, and the second part depicts drawing, which is transformed into legend and subsequently the book. There is an implied correspondence between thought and drawing, poetry and legend, and the haiku and the book. In both cases, moreover, there is a distillation of the general and the abstract (poetry and legend) into the specific and the concrete (the haiku and the book). The upshot is that haikus and books are similar insofar as they are both simple in form yet infinitely rich in interpretative and aesthetic possibilities. Whereas the poem of Ràfols-Casamada represents the book as the ultimate goal of divine creation, this piece posits it as the culmination of the human creative processes of thought and imagination, while simultaneously aligning it with the new life associated with the birth of spring.

The poems in these colophons synthesize Plana's conception of books. The colophon of *Tècniques*, in contrast, looks forward to the future of book production, even if the volume itself is a retrospective of the methods of graphic design that Plana practiced over the course of his career: "la història de les tècniques gràfiques sortosament no s'exhaurirà mentre la curiositat no traeixi els humans" (Moli, *Colofons* 44) [the history of graphic techniques will fortunately never be exhausted as long as curiosity does not betray humans]. Although Plana did not live long enough to employ digital technology to any significant degree, this observation suggests that he would have both expected and welcomed the new ways of producing books that digital technology has made possible, provided that he were always able to express his own individual vision as an artist. As his corpus of works makes clear, Plana deeply cherished traditional forms of book production. Yet like so many bibliophiles throughout history he also sought to achieve through books something distinctive and ultimately unique. Technologies that foment this aspiration – whether old or new – would thus certainly have inspired him.

In an essay in the volume *Miquel Plana: Arquitecte del llibre, 1943–2012* [Miquel Plana: Architect of the book, 1943–2012], composed after Plana's death, Moli recreates a dialogue between him and Plana that in a sense functions as a colophon to Plana's life (see Moli "2015"). In this interchange, Plana reflects on his entry into the world of books. As a young man he imagined this world as a rarefied domain of authors, publishers, artists, printers, and bibliophiles, but he quickly came to regard it as his natural home. With hindsight, he regrets not having made more affordable editions of some of his works that he believes would have been of interest to a wide range of readers. Given the limited print run and high cost of his books, however, most are now only available to the general reading public through a few select libraries in Spain. Like the majority of volumes created expressly for the bibliophile market, they are thus largely inaccessible to contemporary bibliophiles, who are more often than not obliged to access books in less expensive print editions or in digital formats. In fact, books like Plana's might ultimately cease to be produced one day. Yet if his abiding intuition about books proves true, readers will always desire formats that lend themselves to aesthetic appreciation and make possible a holistic experience of reading through all of the senses.

# Colophon

In my discussion of *Os libros arden mal* I have argued that Manuel Rivas imagined the island of Colophon, and by extension his own narrative of book burning by Francoist forces during the Spanish Civil War, as a site where justice might be achieved. My own notion of a colophon, however, is closer to the traditional use of the term as a designation for information cited at the end of a book regarding its production. Yet whereas traditional colophons typically include the name of the printer and the printer's emblem, in my colophon I want simply to comment on how I came to undertake my project.

The long answer to this question would likely entail a reflection on my entire life with books. The short answer begins with an experience that I had at the end of the 1990s, when I inherited a 7000-volume library from one of my graduate school professors, Oreste F. Pucciani, along with a cache of letters from his decades-long friendship with Simone de Beauvoir. Shortly after Pucciani's death, I wrote about these letters and the relationship between him and Beauvoir in an article in the journal *Simone de Beauvoir Studies*, titled "Les adieux irréversibles" [The irreversible farewells]. In this piece, I explained that I had known of the existence of the letters for many years before Pucciani's death, but that I only found them after sorting through hundreds of boxes of books that the executor of Pucciani's estate had left for me in a storage facility in Culver City, California. In the box containing the letters were several items clearly of special significance for Pucciani, including the Austrian passport of his late life-partner, the fashion designer Rudi Gernreich. Gernreich and his mother had escaped from Europe in the late 1930s and made their way to Los Angeles as Jewish refugees. The cover of the passport was emblazoned with a swastika and a large red "J." Also in the box was an old leather-bound copy of Andrew Lang's *The Library*, which I quickly read. What struck me was Lang's description of the difficulty of selling the books of a deceased friend, which I found myself obliged to do, given the huge number that Pucciani had left me. In musing on a "day of doom and of general clearing out" (13), Lang writes that "[s]elling books is nearly as bad as losing friends," and that "life has no worse sorrow" (15). Lang's book not only verbalized for me what I was feeling at the moment but also, unbeknown to me until later, provided the initial inspiration for my own book about books, precisely because in *The Library* I discovered the narrative of the murderous bookman of Barcelona.

I had a second experience of inheriting books when, several years after Pucciani's death, my mother died, leaving me a large, albeit less extensive library that contained many of her parents' books.

Because of these two almost concurrent inheritances, my life was inundated with books, and as a result I began to reflect on the materiality of books in ways that I had not done throughout my years as a reader and professor of literature. In pouring over my newly acquired treasures, I was particularly impressed by the phenomenon (at once marvelous and painful) of the name and notations of former readers inscribed in the books, as well as the seeming permanence yet fragility of the bindings and pages.

With regard to my mother's books, both the volumes themselves and the order in which they were arranged on her bookshelves and reading table conveyed to me her former intentions and therefore seemed almost sacred. Through her library, I thought, I was better equipped to maintain a cohesive memory of her identity and past. Among her books were some that had originally belonged to my grandfather, whom I had never known, and some of these dealt with Marxist philosophy and politics. The majority of my grandfather's Marxist-themed books, however, had been destroyed by my widowed grandmother who, at the height of the Red Scare in the early 1950s, felt compelled to burn them in the backyard incinerator rather than leave them behind for others to find when she moved to a retirement residence.

Although I had long known of this event in my family's history, I only grasped its enormity after the death of my mother, as I became aware of the dearth of tangible traces of my grandfather. I thought of the anguish that my grandmother must have suffered for obliterating what were among her husband's last remaining effects. I also tried to imagine her conflicting emotions on the day after she burned the books, when she discovered that a mother cat had delivered a litter of kittens in the incinerator and sheltered them in the still warm remains of the books.

By reflecting on this event, I came to understand narratives of book burning, such as those of Rivas and Goytisolo, from a personal perspective. I also recognized how fraught my own family's story was, since our act of biblio-pyromania was carried out not by a hostile army or state but by someone who determined (whether rightly or wrongly) that her very safety depended on destroying a library. And finally, I comprehended something of the bibliophile's dream of ideal or inimitable books, which for me were precisely the ones that I inherited from those that I loved, or would want to have loved, had we been fortunate enough to coincide in the world.

# Notes

## Introduction

1 The episode of the book burning is recounted in Part 1, chapters 6–7 of *Don Quixote*. For studies of the passage, see both Baker and Eisenberg.
2 Raven distinguishes between the "history of the book" and "book history." Whereas the history of the book explores "the technical and even symbolic developments of books as material objects," book history "take[s] books as evidence of broader types of human activity in the past," that is, histories other than the history of books themselves (8).
3 Collins argues persuasively against the view that "reading books and viewing electronic media are mutually antagonistic experiences" (*Bring* 14).
4 As Borsuk points out, "the term *book* commonly refers interchangeably to both medium and content" (xi). It can also refer to a part of a larger work, such as a Book of the Bible (Raven 32).
5 I have chosen to use the Catalan spelling of Ramon Miquel i Planas's name, given his lifelong passion for Catalan literature, culture, and language, although he himself typically used the Castilian form, "Ramón Miquel y Planas."
6 One of the earliest treatises on bibliophilia is *The Philobiblon*, written by Richard de Bury, in 1345. Raven asserts that the word "bibliomania" was first used in England, in 1719, by Myles Davies (38–9). One of the earliest treatises on bibliomania is Louis Bollioud-Mermet's *De la bibliomanie* (1761) [On bibliomania]. Throughout the nineteenth and twentieth centuries countless texts have appeared on the subject of bibliophilia and bibliomania.
7 Porter stands out for his categorizations of bibliophiles and bibliophile practices, which according to Yeves Andrés, run into the thousands (14). See, for instance, Porter, *Los libros*. Yeves Andrés remarks that bibliophiles

typically value beauty, rarity, and a particular theme or subject (10). Some, like Estruga et al., argue that anyone who loves books should be regarded as a bibliophile (18), whereas others, like Pla, insist that bibliophilia refers to the love of a particular kind of book (165–6).

8 This description from Elena Pita comes from an article titled "Bibliófilos y especuladores" [Bibliophiles and speculators], which was published in the Spanish newspaper *El Mundo* on 28 February 1999.

9 According to Sedgwick, homosociality makes possible an expression of male-male desire and bonds men in a patriarchal system. It does not diminish masculinity but is in fact constitutive of it. Homosocial desire, moreover, is not usually expressed through homosexual acts, which are carefully policed in the typical homosocial settings of military units, sports teams, fraternities, etc. For a full discussion, see *Between Men*.

10 Like many male bibliophiles of the modern period, the nineteenth-century Scottish writer and folklorist, Andrew Lang, speaks of the "sport of book hunting," and in a humorous anecdote he reveals the aggressive and sometimes hostile relationships among book collectors: "But, when we think of the sport of book-hunting, it is to sales in auction-rooms that the mind naturally turns. Here the rival buyers feel the passion of emulation, and it was in an auction-room that Guilbert de Pixérécourt, being outbid, said, in tones of mortal hatred, 'I will have the book when your collection is sold after your death.' And he kept his word" (18).

11 According to Weiner, bibliophiles are solely interested in the contents of books, whereas bibliomaniacs usually do not read and are merely voracious collectors (217–18). In delineating the psychosexual symptoms of bibliomania, he notes that bibliomaniacs are less drawn to the visual aspects of books than they are to their tactile features. As he remarks, "'To fondle' a book appears repeatedly in the literature on books" (221).

12 Crypto-Judaizers were Jewish converts to Christianity who continued to practise Judaism in secret. The Inquisition was particularly tenacious in its efforts to identify and persecute these individuals.

13 Théodore's love of books, however, is neither evil nor simply shallow, as a conventional religious interpretation would have it, and is in fact subtly subversive. As Steinmetz remarks in his discussion of the story, all notions of depth (and, by extension, all transcendental values) are contested, and only the surface, "qui n'est pas le superficiel" (20) [which is not the superficial], matters. The serious attention that the bibliomaniac pays to the surface level of reality, although punished in "Le Bibliomane" and in most renditions of the Fra Vicents legend, unsettles Nodier through its apparent disregard for traditional religious belief.

14 Carrión Gútiez notes that what is sometimes considered the finest quality book ever produced in Spain, the *Conjuración de Catilina y la guerra de*

*Jugurta*, by the Roman historian Cayo Salustio Crispo, was published by Joaquín Ibarra y Marín in 1772 with the understanding that it would never likely be read ("Encuadernación" 65).

15 Writer and book artist Charles Alexander exhorts us to focus not solely on the written texts of books but on all their visual features: "Read the size of the page and the size of the book, read the fonts used, read the margins allowed, read the covers, read presence and absence, read the text and not the text" (37).

16 Not all personal libraries provide or sustain a sense of personal integration and continuity. Gikandi, for example, cites the experience of Ariel Dorfman, who thought that the library he left behind in Chile after the Pinochet coup would restore his tie to his former self and homeland when he returned from exile and recovered it. But, as Gikandi writes, "when he finally returns to Chile to be reunited with his books, he realizes that his library no longer anchors him to his natal spaces or imaginary homeland; on the contrary, it reminds him of the impossibility of *retour* – the classical return to native lands" (15). For a full discussion, see Dorfman.

17 Borges's most noted writings on libraries include the essay "La biblioteca total" [The total library] and the short story "La biblioteca de Babel" [The library of Babel]. Eco's most extensive narrative on the subject of books and libraries is the novel *Il nome della rosa* [The name of the rose].

18 A partial catalogue that Colón compiled of his library, titled *Libro de los epítomes* [The book of epitomes], disappeared shortly before his death in 1539. The volume was discovered in 2019 in the Arnamagnaean Manuscript Collection at the University of Copenhagen. It is of particular value because it contains summaries of books in Colón's original collection, some of which no longer exist. Just prior to its discovery, Edward Wilson-Lee published a biography of Colón titled *The Catalogue of Shipwrecked Books: Christopher Columbus, His Son, and the Quest to Build the World's Greatest Library*.

19 In his exhaustive historical overview of Spanish bibliophilia in *Bibliófilos españoles*, Sánchez Mariana identifies the most illustrious Spanish bibliophiles and book collectors from the medieval period to the end of the nineteenth century, when the cultivation of Spanish books reached its apex.

20 These watershed events in the history of the Spanish book paralleled a similar process initiated in France during the French Revolution, when the great libraries of the Church and the nobility were seized by the state. In England, in contrast, large numbers of old books began to move into the public sphere during the period of the Reformation, when Catholic monasteries were closed and their libraries dispersed (Raven 40).

21 The literature of bibliophilia is filled with tales of bibliophiles gone mad. References to madness appear in the titles of many commentaries of

bibliophilia, from Thomas Frognall Dibdin's *Bibliomania, or Book Madness* (1811), widely disseminated during the period of Gallardo and Vicente Salvá, to the more recent study of Basdenes, *A Gentle Madness*, and Eric Graeber's collection of book narratives, *Magic and Madness in the Library*. In her recent discussion of bibliophilia, Elisa Ruiz García maintains that true bibliophilia entails a desire to possess books, and that this desire at times borders on the irrational (19).

22 Boulton indicates that this passage appears in an anonymous letter likely penned by Burke. He further explains that although Burke "emphasizes 'magnitude' as an element in sublimity," he also maintains that "'[d]esigns that are vast only by their dimensions, are always the sign of a common and low imagination'" (cxii; Burke 76).

23 In the nineteenth century, bibliophiles created new associations and publication series with the aim of making available fine editions of the masterpieces of Spanish literature. These included the Biblioteca de Autores Españoles (1846–80) and the Sociedad de Bibliófilos Españoles (1866–1918). The series Biblioteca Catalana was created in 1870, followed in the early twentieth century by such entities as the Societat Catalana de Bibliòfils (1903–12) and the Associació de Bibliòfils de Barcelona (1944). The Librería de Bibliófilos Españoles founded in Madrid in 1875 by the Galician bookman, Bernardo Rico, launched a series of bibliophile editions titled Pequeña Colección del Bibliófilo, which Miquel i Planas directed in the 1920s. In the twentieth century, important series of books aimed specifically at bibliophiles include the volumes of the Colección de Opúsculos para Bibliófilos, published by Castalia in the late 1940s and early 1950s under the imprints "Ibarra" and "Gallardo."

24 For a discussion of the bibliophile editions of the work of the poets of the Generation of '27, see Checa Cremades "La vanguardia."

25 Aleixandre called his home Velintonia, after the name of the Madrid street on which it is located, Wellingtonia (the name of a species of sequoia). According to Calderón, five generations of Spanish poets frequented Aleixandre's library, including members of the Generation of '27, the Generation of '36, the immediate postwar generation, the Generation of '50, and the group known as the Novísimos (504). During Aleixandre's lifetime, a reproduction of a portrait of the Baroque poet, Luis de Góngora, hung on the wall of the library above the sofa where Aleixandre usually sat. The house is now empty and in need of restoration. The only trace of the painting is a slight indentation in the wall. For images of the house and commentary, see www.youtube.com/watch?reload=9&v=L2Es3IMuII0.

26 Prada draws the title of his book from a poem by Martínez Sagi titled "Voz perdida" [Lost voice], first published in the collection, *País de la ausencia* [Land of absence]. He reproduces it in its entirety in *Las esquinas* (547–8).

27 In *Las esquinas*, Prada melds history, biography, autobiography, and fiction. Thus, although Martínez Sagi is a historical figure, and although the bulk of the depiction of her life is factual, some elements of the text are fictional. In his analysis of the narrative, Pérez Bowie nevertheless clarifies that Gabriela and Mercedes are historical people when he describes them as "procedentes del universo real" (372) [arising from the real universe].

28 According to Alberto Villamandos, the term Gauche Divine was "coined ironically in French by a journalist in 1967 in order to emphasize paradoxical leftist elitism." The majority of the so-called *divinos* [divine ones] hailed from the Catalan bourgeoisie. Some of the left-leaning publishing houses founded by individuals associated with the Gauche Divine were Anagrama, Tusquets, and Lumen (Villamandos).

29 The most acute period of the Spanish financial crisis lasted from 2008 to 2014. As in other western nations, it was provoked by a housing bubble, but in Spain the situation was exacerbated by a debt crisis that ultimately overwhelmed the economy. The government reacted by imposing draconian austerity measures, which in turn incited a powerful anti-austerity movement known as the *movimiento 15-M* [15-M movement] or *movimiento de los indignados* [movement of the outraged].

30 On 23 March 2020 the Spanish daily newspaper *ABC* declared matter-of-factly (albeit with seeming prescience for the long run): "Las librerías están cerradas, pero puedes seguir comprando libros" (Martín Rodrigo) [Bookstores are closed, but you can keep buying books].

31 Lavapiés is an ethnically diverse district of Madrid known in part for a famous cultural centre housed in an old tobacco factory, La tabacalera de Lavapiés. This is a neighborhood-run venue, where members of the local community can exhibit artistic works and engage in cultural interchange.

32 The AIDS Memorial Quilt is the largest work of community-made art in the world, commemorating the lives of those who have died of AIDS. As of 2020, it contained over 50,000 panels.

**Part I: The Legend of the Murderous Bookman of Barcelona**

Some material in this section previously appeared in the following article: "The Legend of Fra Vicents in European and Catalan Culture." *Symposium: A Quarterly Journal in Modern Literatures*, vol. 56, no. 3, 2002, pp. 123–33.

1 "Le Bibliomane ou le nouveau Cardillac" was published in *La Gazette des Tribunaux* 3465 (23 October 1836). Simplified versions were printed in *Le Constitutionnel* on 24 October 1836 and in *Le Voleur* 60 (31 October 1836). Surprisingly, no critics have ever mentioned the *Constitutionnel* piece or considered it a possible source for later writers. In the case of Fra Vicents

and other characters, I have chosen to use the Catalan version of their names.

2 "Bibliomanie" was first published in a Rouen literary journal, *Le Colibri*, on 12 February 1837. The story was not reprinted until 1910. Miquel i Planas thought this was the year of its original publication.

3 The second Carlist War took place from 1846 to 1849, and the third Carlist War took place from 1872 to 1876.

4 In fact, there were several programs of *desamortización* during the nineteenth century, including one in 1810 during the Napoleonic occupation, and another in 1823 under the liberal regime of General Rafael Riego.

5 Like Miquel i Planas, Guitert y Fontseré regards the tale as fictional (*Poblet* 41), but he also suggests that the novelist Fernando Patxot y Ferrer might have authored it (38). Although Patxot y Ferrer writes in *Las ruinas de mi convento* [The ruins of my convent] about an ex-cloistered monk during the first Carlist War, his character is decidedly more positive than Fra Vicents.

6 Cardillac, the protagonist of *Das Fräulein von Scuderi,* is a silver-plater who, like Fra Vicents, murders in order to recover the treasures (here, jewellery rather than books) that he has grudgingly sold. The two stories are nevertheless structured differently. Whereas *Das Fräulein von Scuderi* is a mystery, with the title character playing the role of sleuth (Christopher A. Lee sees it "as an important forerunner of the detective story" [72]), the *Gazette* version of the legend follows a journalistic format, clarifying early on the identity of the murderer.

7 According to Miquel i Planas, the *Furs e ordinacions fetes per los gloriosos reys de Aragó als regnicols del regne de Valencia* (1482) [Edicts and ordinances made by the glorious kings of Aragon to the rulers of the kingdom of Valencia] was announced in the catalogue of Vicente Salvá. Miquel i Planas speculates that the author of the *Gazette* piece named the character after Salvá but mistakenly translated the English "Vincent," on the catalogue's cover, as "Vincente" (rather than the Castilian "Vicente"), further evidence that this author was not a native of the Iberian Peninsula.

8 Daniel-Henri Pageaux notes that sales from Nodier's library in 1827, 1833, and 1844 contained numerous Spanish titles (183). Albert Kies highlights the presence of *Don Quixote* and a collection of medieval Spanish ballads (227).

9 Verrié argues that the anonymous *Gazette* piece is stylistically similar to the writing of Prosper Mérimée. He agrees with Miquel i Planas that Mérimée did not pen it because in his other writings he always correctly spells the protagonist's name as "Vicente" (Miquel i Planas, *La llegenda* 1951, 296). But he wonders if Nodier, through rivalry with Mérimée, imitated his style in order to parody him (290).

10 Barrière discusses the real case of a German pastor, Johann Georg Tinius (1764–1846), a bibliomaniacal thief and murderer. Although his actions are similar to those of Fra Vicents (he commits multiple murders in order to obtain the money necessary to purchase books), Barrière is unaware of any French press report of Tinius's story prior to 13 September 1842, when *La Quotidienne* published an anonymous article titled "Un bibliomane deux fois assassin" [A bibliomaniac two times murderer]. He nevertheless speculates that German friends of Michel might have related to him the account (135). See also Castoldi (75). The contemporary German writer, Klaas Huizing, wrote a novel on Tinius's life titled *Der Buchtrinker* (1994) [The book drunkard].

11 Nodier also expresses a desire for Spanish books through his character, Théodore: "Il approuva cependant l'intervention française dans les révolutions d'Espagne. 'C'est, dit-il, une belle occasion pour rapporter de la Péninsule des romans de chevalerie et des *Cancioneros*'" (*Le Bibliomane* 29) [He nevertheless approved of the French intervention in the Spanish revolutions. "It is," he said, "a wonderful occasion for bringing from the Peninsula novels of chivalry and *Cancioneros*"].

12 Poblet is often referred to as the Escorial of Catalonia because it was the burial place of the Aragonese royalty before the union of Aragon and Castile. In 1835 its library comprised some 19,472 books, 385 codices, and 250 manuscripts (Vilarrubias 75). The collection was housed in two sections. One contained the priceless volumes of Don Pedro Antonio de Aragón y Fernández de Córdoba – not a king, as the *Gazette* narrative indicates, but a seventeenth-century nobleman who spent ten years as ambassador and viceroy in Italy, where he acquired the bulk of his library. The other section held the books, codices, and manuscripts of the order, as well as ecclesiastical and historical works (Morgades 181). At the time of the first Carlist War, the monks of Poblet supported and even fought for the Carlists (Balaguer 273).

13 References to the *Gazette* version of the tale are drawn from Miquel i Planas's 1928 edition of the *Llegenda*.

14 The reference appears in a history of Poblet that Guitert y Fontseré published in 1955. In this study he makes no mention of Fra Vicents. However, in a book that he published in 1937 on the various legends associated with Poblet, he relates the tale of the murderous bookman. But surprisingly, he contends that at the time of the sacking there was no monk at the monastery named Vicents or Vicente (*Poblet* 41).

15 Although the anti-clericalism of the *Gazette* narrative is not typical of Nodier, the implicit political conservatism is. Generally considered a traditionalist in both politics and religion, Nodier opposed the French Revolution, along with most of the eighteenth-century *philosophes*, and

went so far as to proclaim that religion, not revolution, regenerates society (Setbon 59).

16 The political position of Nodier's Théodore in "Le Bibliomane" is also ostensibly ambiguous. He is regarded as both a Carlist and a liberal. But in fact, he is interested only in books and is oblivious to politics.

17 Miquel i Planas also discusses *mudéjar* bookbinding in the essay *El arte hispano-árabe en la encuadernación* [Hispanic-Arabic art in bookbinding].

18 When citing Miquel i Planas's writing in Catalan, I maintain his distinctive use of the language, which differs from contemporary standard Catalan.

19 Miquel i Planas emphasizes this through verbal repetition. The book not only "lasts" ("*dura*"), but it also "endures" ("*perdura*") or "lasts through" time and space.

20 In Miquel i Planas's semi-autobiographical text *La novel·la d'un bibliòfil: (Diàlegs de llibres)* (1918) [The novel of a bibliophile: (Dialogues on books)], the protagonist (who, according to the prologue, voices Miquel i Planas's conception of books) remarks that when he was a youngster books were always available to him in his father's bindery. He also describes himself as having been a timid, sickly, and extremely near-sighted boy. He speculates that if he had had better sight, he would have devoted himself to other activities. But instead, he spent his childhood and youth voraciously reading.

21 See www.miquelrius.com/.

22 For a thorough discussion of Miquel i Planas's Catalan publications, see Taylor.

23 Only four volumes of this journal were published. They appeared in Barcelona from 1903 to 1906 and were printed by Víctor Oliva (Pérez-Rioja, "Los exlibirs" 549). As Pilar Vélez explains, the high cost of production that resulted from the superb graphics led to the journal's early demise ("El libro" 556).

24 As Joan Ramon Resina explains, the term *Renaixença* "derives from the title of a journal that, from 1871 to 1905, promoted the recuperation of the high-cultural uses of the Catalan language" ("The Catalan" 470).

25 Jordi Castellanos nevertheless speaks of a tragic split between culture and the market, and points out that in late nineteenth- and early twentieth-century Catalonia the bourgeoisie tended to promote Castilian-language books because of their greater market value. In his view, the bourgeoisie thus became the enemy of its own culture (13). At a time when Catalan literary publications (both historical and contemporary) might have helped foster a national identity, as national literatures did in other countries (8–9), they became, in turn-of-the-century Catalonia, "peces d'art" [pieces of art] destined for consumption by what Castellanos describes as a small group of snobs (13). During this period the number of

Catalan readers was also still small. In this regard, Castellanos cites Miquel i Planas's observation in 1906 that the quantity of materials published in Catalan was disproportional to the actual number of Catalan readers (16).

26 According to most literary chronologies, Catalan *Modernisme* (roughly 1888–1911) and *Noucentisme* (1906–23) overlap. (As a starting point for *Modernisme*, Resina cites both 1888, the year of the first Universal Exposition of Barcelona, and 1890, the year in which the painters Ramon Casas and Santiago Rusiñol jointly exhibited their paintings in the Sala Parés of Barcelona ["Modernism" 513]). Valentí Fiol indicates that *Noucentisme*, rather than Catalan *Modernisme*, corresponds more closely with general Spanish Modernism (17). But as Resina further clarifies, "[w]hereas the *modernistes* sought the guidance of modern, that is, northern European cultures, *Noucentisme* reactively privileged the Latin South" ("*Noucentisme*" 534). In so doing, it aimed to recuperate the artistic ideals of classicism. For a thorough discussion of Catalan *Modernisme*, see Epps.

27 During the Primo de Rivera dictatorship (1923–30), the Catalan language was repressed, although, as Balcells explains, the publication of Catalan newspapers and books was tolerated in censored form (85).

28 Other texts in which Miquel i Planas criticizes the linguistic reform movement and satirizes cultural and political trends in early twentieth-century Catalonia include the speech "La tirania filològica i l'actual decadència literària de Catalunya" (1921) [Philological tyranny and the current literary decadence of Catalonia], and the novels *La novel·la d'un bibliòfil* and *Les confidències d'en Joan Bonhome* (1918) [The confidences of John Goodman].

29 The experience of the protagonist of *El purgatori del bibliòfil* reveals a clear distinction between bibliophilia and bibliomania. In both his waking state and his dream, the protagonist expresses a love of books, but in his dream, his bibliophilia is carried to the point of hysteria and thus what might properly be called bibliomania.

30 According to Amat, traditional male bibliophiles and bibliomaniacs tend to be misogynist (*El ladrón* 66). As an example, she cites Miquel i Planas, who claimed that the love of books was superior to the love of women (67).

31 Ollé Pinell cites the adage from Miquel i Planas's *Els cent aforismes del bibliòfil* [The hundred aphorisms of the bibliophile], which reads: "Llibre xich sempre'm ve a punt, perchè puch durlo al damunt" (77) [A small book always works well for me, because I can carry it with me at all times].

32 D'Ivori's birth name was Joan Vila i Pujol. As Cadena explains, when he was young, his friends began calling him "D'Ivori" because of his ivory-white complexion ("Joan" 24). He eventually made "D'Ivori" his pseudonym and used it to sign most of his art works.

33 The colours green and red also appear in the floral designs on the book's fly pages. But in contrast to the illustrations, these drawings, as well as

the floral figure above the bookplate, are more baroque in style (Vélez, "D'Ivori" 30).

34 Salamanders have long been associated with fire. Because they often live in rotting logs used for firewood and are thus often seen emerging from burning embers, many ancient peoples believed that they were born from fire or were at least resistant to it. Augustine writes in *The City of God*: "If we may trust the reports of workers in the field of natural phenomena, the salamander lives in fire. ... What further evidence, then, do we need to prove that human bodies suffering the penalty of eternal pains ... burn without being consumed?" (21.4).

35 The Museu Nacional d'Art de Catalunya in Barcelona houses a collection of nearly 10,000 bookplates. The modernist bookplates by the artist Alexandre de Riquer i Ynglada form a significant part of the museum's overall modernist holdings. The museum also has a large collection of bookplates by Triadó, many of which reflect the aesthetics of *Noucentisme* (Quílez i Corella 215). For further discussion and reproductions of the bookplates in the Museu Nacional d'Art de Catalunya, see Quílez i Corella 212–19.

36 Miquel i Planas describes Diéguez's style as an adaptation of modern aesthetics to the Spanish Plateresque style of the late medieval and early Renaissance periods, which itself drew on the *mudéjar* tradition (*Los ex libris* 23).

37 These writers all based their versions of the tale on the narratives issued in the Paris newspapers in the 1830s. Hesse's was featured in a Leipzig journal devoted to books and manuscripts, *Serapeum*, vol. 22, 30 November 1843, pp. 337–43. Janin included his account in *Le Livre*, Paris, Plon, 1870, pp. 120–7. Castro y Serrano published his sketch of Fra Vicents in *Cuadernos contemporáneos*, Madrid, Fortanet, 1871. Blanchemain's was printed in the second volume of Éduoard Rouveyre's *Miscellanées Bibliographiques*, Paris, 1878–80, pp. 32–41. Lang's appeared in his book, *The Library*, London, Macmillan, 1881, pp. 54–6. Cim discusses the case of Fra Vicents in four texts: *Amateurs et voleurs de livres*, Paris, Daragon, 1903; *Le Livre*, Paris, Flammirion, 1905; *Le Livre contemporain*, Paris, 1906; and the article "Le Libraire assassin: Un terrible amateur de livres; les hommes sont mortels; les livres ne le sont pas," *Touche à Tout: Magazine des magazines* (January 1908): pp. 76–9. The Fra Vicents incident is also mentioned in an article titled "Bibliomanie" in *La Grande Encyclopédie*, vol. 6, Paris, Société Anonyme de la Grande Encyclopédie, 1892, p. 643.

38 In the edition of the *Llegenda* published in 1951, Verrié replaces the *Crònica d'en Puigpardines* with the *Llibre de les nobleses del reis*, since by this time there were three known manuscripts of the former text and only one of the latter (Miquel i Planas, *La llegenda* 1951, 194).

39 In Huysmans's *À Rebours* [Against the grain], the dandy-bibliophile Des Esseintes spends a considerable sum of money to amass a collection of books of incomparable beauty. But unlike Fra Vicents, he is also a voracious reader. Fra Vicents, in contrast, is more adamant in his passion, ignoring everything, including his physical appearance and health, for books.

40 As bibliomaniac, Fra Vicents is also a bibliophage and even a biblioclast. Such ostensibly destructive acts as eating or breaking books are perhaps his most radical modes of possession.

41 The events depicted in the tale may also have led to the formulation of one of the most famous maledictions ever pronounced on book thieves: "For him that stealeth, or borroweth and returneth not, this book from its owner, let it change into a serpent in his hand and rend him. Let him be struck with palsy, and all his members blasted. Let him languish in pain, crying aloud for mercy, and let there be no surcease to this agony till he sing in dissolution. Let bookworms gnaw his entrails ... and when at last he goeth to his final punishment, let the flames of Hell consume him forever" (Rabinowitz and Kaplan 30). Like the legend of Fra Vicents, this anonymous curse is associated with a Catalan monastery – not Poblet, but Sant Pere de les Puel·les in Barcelona. If its origins are ever identified, it may in the end provide a historical source for the tale.

42 In 2012, World Cat listed seventeen copies of the book in libraries throughout the world. It was also available in several antiquarian bookstores. In that year, I myself purchased the four hundred and twenty-fifth copy of the five hundred twenty-five volumes published in 1928. I paid 150 euros, or at the time roughly USD$195, at the Librería Sánchez in Barcelona. Albeit expensive, the book was considerably less valuable than the one Roig describes. What is more, the man and woman who sold it to me were not sinister-looking ghouls but pleasant and genial. They in fact owned two copies of the *Llegenda*, one of which had a large red blot on it that they were certain was ink. Although I was tempted to acquire what looked like a blood-stained edition of my own favourite story of murder and mayhem, I took their advice and bought the clean edition.

43 "El profesor y el librero asesino" not only explicitly incorporates the *Gazette*, Flaubert, and Miquel i Planas texts, but also points to several contemporary narratives of desire, possession, and books. The reference to the German novelist Patrick Süskind is perhaps the most intriguing, since one of his novels, *Das Parfum: Die Geschichte eines Mörders* [Perfume: The story of a murderer], published in 1985 and adapted into a film in 2005 directed by Tom Tykwer and starring Ben Whishaw, has clear thematic parallels with the legend of the murderous bookman.

44 By skimming over the surface of his books, Fra Vicents performs an act of appropriation that Sartre describes through the image of skiers sliding over snow. Although skiers traverse only the surface-level of snow, they posit its breadth and depth as a unified field and use it as an instrument for reaching a goal. What is more, because they are in continuous movement, they feel as if their freedom were unbounded:

> En glissant, je demeure, dit-on, superficiel. Cela n'est pas exact; certes, j'effleure seulement la surface. ... Mais ... le glissement est action *à distance*, il assure ma maîtrise sur la matière sans que j'aie besoin de m'enfoncer dans cette matière et de m'engluer en elle pour la dompter. Glisser, c'est le contraire de s'enraciner. (*L'Être* 644)
>
> [We think of sliding as remaining on the surface. This is inexact; to be sure, I only skim the surface. ... Nevertheless ... the sliding is action *at a distance*; it assures my mastery over the material without my needing to plunge into that material and engulf myself in it in order to overcome it. To slide is the opposite of taking root. (*Being* 745)]

Skiers, as well as "readers" like Fra Vicents, remain on the surface of the objects of which they are conscious. Yet according to Sartre, their actions are not necessarily "superficial," for through them they experience the extraordinary power of freedom and, by extension, a veritable ontological joy.

45 In the poetry of Mallarmé, Sartre writes, "il faut que le moment de la plénitude poétique corresponde à celui de l'annulation. Ainsi la vérité *devenue* de ces poèmes, c'est le Néant" (*Mallarmé: La lucidité* 164) ["the moment of Poetry's fulfillment must correspond to the moment of its annihilation. Thus, the truth these poems have come to embody is Nothingness" (*Mallarmé, or the Poet* 142)].

**Part 2: Bibliophiles, Bibliographers, and Bookstore Browsers**

1 Sainz y Rodríguez discusses Menéndez Pelayo's perception of Gallardo in his introduction to the *Obras escogidas* of Gallardo (1: viii). The words of Fernández Espino appear in a letter he wrote to Adolfo de Castro, dated 29 August 1851, and cited by Rodríguez-Moñino (*Historia* 99). Most of Gallardo's letters are contained in the early twentieth-century work of Sainz y Rodríguez and in the mid-twentieth-century works of Rodríguez-Moñino.

2 For the sake of clarity, I have modernized some of Gallardo's spelling.

3 In *Vida y trabajos de un libro viejo (contados por él mismo)* [The life and labours of an old book (narrated by itself)], Jorge Campos humorously depicts the adventures of a book, beginning with its printing in early

sixteenth-century Spain and ending with its placement in the Biblioteca Nacional de España in the nineteenth century. In part 6, the book recounts how Gallardo acquired it in Lisbon, transported it to London, and eventually lost it in Spain. It remarks that while Gallardo was in England, he was able to dedicate himself to his passion of giving refuge to wayward books. It further describes him as the quintessential bibliophile of the period:

> Conque así le tenemos, con su rostro patilludo, metido en la bata, pantalón ajustado, ya hasta el suelo, y no como otros dueños anteriores míos, que lucían media, y con una seda siempre arrebozada al cuello, con estampa de lo que más tarde habían de llamar romántico, y leyendo o escribiendo o hablando de lo que leía y escribía. (55)
>
> [So, here we have him, his face with big sideburns, tucked in his robe and his tight trousers, already to the floor and unlike those of my other previous masters, who wore them half-length, and always covering his neck with a silk scarf, with the look of what later was to be called Romantic, and reading or writing or talking about what he was reading and writing.]

4 Heber was initially interested in English literature, but by the time of his death he had accumulated well over 100,000 books from throughout Europe, which were housed in his private libraries in England, Holland, Belgium, and Germany. He was a Member of Parliament from 1821–6, but he was forced to give up his seat and flee England when the newspaper *John Bull* implied that he and Charles Henry Hartshorne, a young man twenty-nine years his junior, were lovers. Heber met Hartshorne at the Roxburghe Club, one of the oldest bibliophile societies in the world, which he had helped establish in 1812. Heber was also a friend of the noted British bibliophile, Frances Mary Richardson Currer.

5 Gallardo refers to these bookmen as the Hermanos Orea [Brothers Orea]. They were probably the publishers Francisco López de Orea and José Orea, whom Dowling speculates were related (108). In a letter to Böhl de Faber's wife, Francisca Larrea de Böhl, dated 27 November 1836, Gallardo expresses his anger at the situation by referring to "los manejos puercos del librero Orea" (Sainz y Rodríguez 32) [the filthy manipulations of the bookman Orea].

6 This comment is dated 15 July 1832. It appears in the essay, "*La tía fingida* ¿es novela de Cervantes?" [*The Pretended Aunt*, is it a novel of Cervantes?], which was published in the first volume of *El Criticón*.

7 Pérez Vidal recognizes the tensions between Gallardo and his nephew that these letters reveal. He nevertheless argues that in general the relationship between the two was positive (49–51).

8 Castro was the author of a text titled *El Buscapié*, which he claimed had been written by Cervantes. According to Pérez Vidal, Gallardo repeatedly

challenged the authenticity of *El Buscapié*, arguing that it was a literary hoax, even though Castro himself spoke highly of Gallardo in his prologue to the volume. In response, Castro penned a series of articles critical of Gallardo, which he eventually developed into *Aventuras*. Gallardo then published a text titled *Zapatazo a Zapatilla, y a su falso* Buscapié *un puntillazo* [A hard kick to little Zapata, and to his false *Buscapié* a mortal blow]. In this piece, Gallardo referred to Castro as Lupianejo Zapatilla, a diminutive of the name of Lupián Zapata, a falsifier of historical chronicles with whom Castro sought to identify (Pérez Vidal 52–3).

9 According to Castro, Gallardo was envious of the literary success of some of his exiled compatriots in London including Antoni Puig i Blanch, whose treatise *La Inquisición sin máscara* [The Inquisition unmasked] was published abroad in translation, whereas Gallardo's *Diccionario crítico-burlesco* was not. When a friend of Puig i Blanch launched a Spanish-language newspaper in London, Gallardo supposedly became jealous and tried to start a newspaper of his own. But the undertaking failed. Castro's narrative is replete with such anecdotes. Yet it offers no balanced assessment of Gallardo, and is thus intentionally polemical.

10 This scene is clearly reminiscent of the scene in *Don Quixote*, just prior to the burning of the books, when Don Quixote rose in the night "y proseguía en sus voces y en sus desatinos, dando cuchilladas y reveses a todas partes" (Cervantes Saavedra, *Don Quijote* 76) ["and continued his raving and ranting, laying about him with his sword all over the room with slashes and backstrokes" (Cervantes Saavedra, *Don Quixote* 93)].

11 Gallardo's dreams about books are not all nightmares. In a letter to José de la Peña Aguayo, dated 11 April 1830, he writes of a dream in which he finds himself in a field in springtime, surrounded by friends. As he gazes at the scene, he sees meadows, fountains, and nymphs, as well as a "tesorejo de oro viejo enpapelado qe [él] and[a] buscando por el mundo" (Rodríguez-Moñino, *Don Bartolomé* 293) [a little treasure of old gold wrapped in paper that he has searched for throughout the world]. This image can be read as a distillation of the ideal book of his bibliophile fantasies.

12 Although Menéndez Pelayo recognized that Gallardo was tireless in his bibliographical work, he criticized him because Gallardo was a liberal and a mason (Senabre 7). As Pérez Vidal remarks, Menéndez Pelayo's assessment of Gallardo was in fact biased by his own traditionalism (4). In *Historia de los heterodoxos españoles* [History of heterodox Spaniards], Menéndez Pelayo writes that Gallardo "expolió todo género de bibliotecas públicas y particulares, [y] fue admirado y temido por cuantos poseían libros" (709n22) [plundered all sorts of public and private libraries, and was admired and feared by all those who possessed books].

13 The most noted examples are Sainz y Rodríguez (1921), Buchanan (1923), Rodríguez-Moñino (1955 and 1965), Senabre (1975), Fernández Sánchez (1994), Pérez Vidal (2001), and Gallego Lorenzo (2008).
14 Lucian of Samosata wrote one of the first known diatribes against a bibliophile in his "Remarks Addressed to an Illiterate Book-Fancier."
15 Two of these letters, dated 22 and 23 February 1850, were published that year by Jannet in the *Journal de l'amateur de livres* [Journal of the book lover] and were subsequently translated into Spanish and republished by del Val, in 1951, in *Bibliografía romántica española (1850)* [Spanish Romantic bibliography (1850)]. As del Val suggests, they may have constituted one letter (Sobolevsky xxv).
16 Del Val notes that according to the Spanish novelist Juan Valera, a friend of Sobolevsky, the conversations between Sobolevsky and Gallardo took place over a period of three days (Sobolevsky xli).
17 Numerous contemporaries of Gallardo, including Castro, describe him as irascible. Reig Salvá, a descendent of Vicente Salvá, indicates that her illustrious ancestor "no tenía precisamente carácter suave" (102) [did not exactly have a gentle character]. When preparing her biography of Vicente, she had access to his correspondences. Her study is thus a key source of information on his life and his relationship with his son, Pedro. See also Mourelle Lema and Rueda for biographical details of the Salvá family.
18 Reig Salvá notes that there remains no documentation indicating where Salvá obtained the financial backing for the shop (95).
19 With regard to the library of Thomas Phillipps, the largest private manuscript collection of the nineteenth century, John Michell notes with obvious irony that "[d]isposing of [it] was far beyond the powers of his heirs for several generations" (121).
20 Strictly speaking, a book that is "unopened" (*sin abrir*) is one whose leaves have never been cut open, whereas a book that is "uncut" (*intonso*) is one whose leaves have been cut open but have not been trimmed on the edges and made uniform. Uncut books allow bibliophiles to appreciate many of their original characteristics. But as John Carter and Nicolas Barker point out, traditional books were in fact "intended to be cut smooth, even if they were not thereafter gilded, marbled, sprinkled, gauffred or stained with colour. Any copy of such a book, therefore, which has survived with its edges entirely uncut is an accident, a specimen of the embryo stage in book production: rare no doubt, bibliographically interesting, but not representative of the book as intended for the reader's shelf" (224).
21 Hidalgo published "Mi biografía" in his *Diccionario general de bibliografía española*, vol. 1, 1862, xi–xvii. The text was reprinted in 1945 under the title "Autobiografía del librero-impresor don Dionisio Hidalgo"

[Autobiography of the bookseller-printer don Dionisio Hidalgo] in *Catálogos de libreros españoles (1661–1840): Intento bibliográfico*, edited by Antonio R. Rodríguez Moñino, Langa, 1945, 194–204. I cite from the original version in the *Diccionario*.

22 Hidalgo remarks that during the Napoleonic period his father allied himself with the supporters of the French (xii).

23 Juan Delgado Casado indicates that Hidalgo entered the Seminario Conciliar of Burgos in 1825 and began his study of law in Valladolid in 1827 (512).

24 During this period, Hidalgo volunteered to join the liberal forces in the first Carlist War, serving with Mariano Miguel de Reinoso (1799–1863) in the theatre of Valladolid (*Diccionario* xiii).

25 In making this choice, Hidalgo imagines that he is actualizing the potential essence with which he was born. Yet according to Sartre's theory of bad faith, this essence is not given but rather constructed through the process of self-realization. Hidalgo wants to believe he is answering his call, but he also chooses (and throughout the rest of his life re-chooses) his calling. In so doing, he takes on the seemingly contradictory task of becoming what he already is. For Sartre, this contradiction – that determinism can and should be freely assumed – undergirds the bourgeois notion of freedom and is reiterated through Hidalgo's own writing.

26 Luis María de Salazar y Salazar (1758–1838) was a naval officer and government minister. In 1830, Fernando VII conferred upon him the title of Conde de Salazar. For further information, see O'Donnell.

27 Botrel identifies these figures as "José" Bonnat and "Andrés" (or André) Jaymebon (546).

28 For further information on the editorial career of Carlos Bailly-Baillière, see Botrel 565–70.

29 According to Fernández Sánchez, the *Diccionario* is Hidalgo's most important work (197). The first volume was published in 1862, and the following six volumes were published under the direction of Hidalgo's son, Manuel Fernández Hidalgo. The final one appeared in 1881. The entire seven-tome corpus was reprinted in facsimile form by the German publisher, Georg Olms Verlag, in 1973.

30 Menéndez Pelayo cites Antoni Puig i Blanch as the author of the line, "acarreadores y faquines de la república de las letras."

31 In 1859, Hidalgo entered his *Diccionario bibliográfico español del siglo XIX* in the annual bibliography contest of the Biblioteca Nacional de España. Delgado Casado speculates that this particular *Diccionario*, which was never published, was a compilation of already published material and for this reason was considered less worthy by the contest committee. But he and Fernández Sánchez also comment on how it did not meet the

prevailing expectations for bibliographies of the day (see Delgado Casado 512–17 and Fernández Sánchez 200).

32 In issue 18, volume 7, of the *Boletín*, Manuel Fernández Hidalgo announced his father's death, as well as his own intention to continue editing the journal with Arturo Piera as publisher (Hidalgo, *Boletín* 7: 197).

33 According to Checa Cremades, some scholars, including E. Inman Fox, Roberta Johnson, and Magdalena Rigual Bonastre, have broached the subject of Azorín's bibliophilia, but in his view the topic is far from exhausted ("Azorín" 331). He in fact recognizes the need for a thorough investigation of the bibliophilia of several early twentieth-century Hispanophone writers, including Pío Baroja, Rubén Darío, and Miguel de Unamuno (330).

34 Most of the essays reprinted by Fuster García were first published in *La Prensa* (Buenos Aires) and *ABC* (Madrid), as well as *Blanco y Negro*, *Destino*, *Luz*, and *La Vanguardia*. Some were also reprinted in the earlier collection, *Azorín y los libros: Exposición* (Azorín 1993). Unless otherwise indicated, I cite Azorín from the edition of Fuster García. For a discussion of Azorín's long collaboration with *La Prensa* of Buenos Aires, see Sotelo Vázquez.

35 This image of mist is reminiscent of the passage in Unamuno's novel, *Niebla*, in which the protagonist, Augusto Pérez, declares that through love "la niebla de la existencia" (141) [the mist of existence] becomes concrete.

36 See Francisco Fuster García, "Azorín y los libros," for an overview of Azorín's discussion of reading and in particular his insistence that young people be allowed to read freely the books of their choosing, even if these seem beyond their level of comprehension.

37 For a discussion of how reading affects Azorín's perception of the world, constituting his "peculiar sensibilidad libresca" (6) [peculiar bookish sensibility], as well as the way Azorín rewrites the Spanish classics, see Fox "Lectura."

38 For a discussion of the relationship between Azorín and Baroja, see Fuster García, "Azorín y Baroja."

39 Azorín notes that the word "librería" [bookshop] initially referred to a private library, and in his childhood home the family library, which contained books from a monastery library confiscated by the Spanish government in the nineteenth century, was called the "librería" [*Libros* 72–3].

40 Azorín's bibliophilia clearly differs from that of traditional bibliophiles. According to Checa Cremades, traditional bibliophiles typically seek specific kinds of books and organize their libraries around unifying themes (*El libro* 2012, 144). For González Manzanares, their penchant for specialization is in fact what sets them apart from mere "aficionado[s] a los libros" (39), or book enthusiasts.

41 Azorín uses the word "catálogo" to indicate both a simple listing of books as well as an annotated bibliography.

42 For "Azorín: Primores de lo vulgar," see Ortega y Gasset, *Obras completas* 2. I use Jurkevich's perceptive translation of the title (*In Pursuit* 220n21).

43 In this novel the protagonist, Doña Inés, relives the love affair of an ancestor from the Middle Ages.

44 Azorín cites the full title of Bejarano's book as *Sentimientos patrióticos o conversaciones cristianas que un cura de aldea, verdadero amigo del país, inspira a sus feligreses* [Patriotic feelings and Christian conversations that a village priest, a true friend of the country, inspires in his parishioners]. César Pérez Gracia wonders if Bejarano was a fictional creation of Azorín. Bejarano's identity, however, has now been corroborated, and in her doctoral dissertation Quintanilla López-Tafall identifies copies of his book in various libraries in Spain and other countries (95–8).

45 Dodeman stereotypes the various nationalities of bibliophiles he observes browsing the bookstalls of the Seine. With regard to the Spanish he writes: "L'Espagnol est, en effet, grandiloquent. 'La France, Monsieur, est une grande nation!' Ou bien, il est triste comme don Quichotte et il a le sens de l'évaluation exorbité" (88) [The Spaniard is, in fact, grandiloquent. "France is a great nation, Monsieur!" Or instead, he is sad, like Don Quixote, and he has a huge sense of self-worth].

46 See the studies of Joiner for a discussion of the affinities between Azorín and Proust.

47 Miguel Enguídanos describes this passage of *Doña Inés* as symphonic, as if the hands were musical notes resonating in perfect accord and *in crescendo* (28). As he insightfully suggests, Azorín's prose is characterized not only by a visual dimension, as numerous critics have noted, but by a musical quality as well.

48 The contemporary Spanish writer Antonio Gala is also intrigued by the thought of all the hands that have touched and held old books.

> Y me alegra suponer que unas manos que ya no existen (¿que no existen?) abrieron esta cubierta, volvieron estas hojas; que una mirada que no existe (¿que no existe?) resbaló sobre estas líneas, descifró esta frase, se sumergió en este laberinto. Me rejuvenece la vida imaginar que alguien, como yo ahora – antes, siglos antes que yo – interrumpió un momento la lectura y reflexionó con un dedo entre estas mismas páginas, mirando hacia el vacío, entre paredes quizá ya destruidas, ante un paisaje quizá irreconocible. (61)
>
> [And it delights me to imagine that hands that no longer exist (that no longer exist?) opened this cover and turned these pages; that a look that no longer exists (that no longer exists?) glided over these lines, deciphered this sentence, and sank into this labyrinth. It rejuvenates me to imagine that

someone, like myself now – but before, centuries before me – interrupted his reading for a moment and reflected with a finger between these same pages, gazing into the emptiness, between walls perhaps now destroyed, at a landscape perhaps now unrecognizable.]

This passage in fact echoes the tone of Azorín's own musings on books and the past.

49 Azorín prefers to refer to used bookshops by the traditional Spanish term, "librerías de lance," rather than the Gallic "librerías de ocasión" (166).

50 The term "intrahistoria" [intra-history] is associated primarily with Unamuno. In *En torno al casticismo*, Unamuno speaks metaphorically of the history of great people and events as waves on the ocean, in contrast to the "intrahistoria," or unchanging essence of the people, which he compares to the waters beneath the surface. See Dobón for a discussion of the relation of Unamuno's concept of "intrahistoria" to Azorín's notion of "historia interna" [internal history] in *El alma castellana* (1900) [The Castilian soul] and its development in *La ruta de Don Quijote* (1905) [The route of Don Quixote].

51 The expression "little philosopher" derives from the title of the third novel of Azorín's quasi-autobiographical trilogy, *Las confesiones de un pequeño filósofo* (1904) [The confessions of a little philosopher].

## Part 3: Lost Books and Textual Restitution

Some material in Part 3 previously appeared in the following article: "Reading the Spanish Past: Library Fantasies in Carlos Ruiz Zafón's *La sombra del viento*." *Bulletin of Spanish Studies*, vol. 83, no. 6, 2006, pp. 839–54.

1 "Wove paper," developed by James Whatman in the eighteenth century, became one of the most common forms of paper in the modern period. It is made through a process in which paper pulp is applied to a finely woven metal mesh (see Basdenes, *On Paper* 61 and 296). Despite its name, it has a smoother surface than traditional "laid paper," which dries on more widely spaced vertical and horizontal chains and retains their imprint. The mesh used to make wove paper is itself woven, but laid paper, when held up to light, can actually look woven.

2 Proteomics, which involves the study of proteins in living organisms, has been applied to various kinds of artworks in order to identify the traces of those in the past who had physical contact with them. For a non-technical discussion of this subject, see Knight.

3 This is particularly apparent in Azorín's own books. As Roberta Johnson explains, Azorín marked up his books, often with an index on the front and/or back cover indicating topics and pages of interest (18).

4 The most extreme albeit light-hearted representation of the rebellious bookman is the protagonist of Arturo Pérez-Reverte's *El club Dumas, La novena puerta* [The club Dumas, the ninth gate], who is actually compared to the Devil. For an analysis of this blockbuster detective novel about stolen books and murder, see Ellis "Detectives."

5 *La sombra del viento* is the first of a four-volume cycle of novels, including *El juego del ángel* (2008) [The angel's game], *El prisionero del cielo* (2011) [The prisoner of heaven], and *El laberinto de los espíritus* (2016) [The labyrinth of spirits].

6 See Obiols, 40.

7 Foucault contrasts Flaubert's conscious incorporation of other texts with that of Cervantes in *Don Quixote* and Sade in *La nouvelle Justine*, arguing that these texts maintain an ironic distance from the tales of knight-errantry and the virtuous novels of the eighteenth century. *La Tentation de saint Antoine* is thus for Foucault a first in the history of the book. But as a matter of fact, its originality owes precisely to its explicit derivativeness.

8 El Cementerio de los Libros Olvidados, in keeping with the library imagined by Borges in "La biblioteca de Babel," is seemingly infinite. Like the library in Eco's *Il nome della rosa*, it also appears otherworldly: "la biblioteca era al tempo stesso la Gerusalemme celeste e un mondo sotterraneo al confine fra la terra incognita e gli inferi" (217) ["the library was at once the celestial Jerusalem and an underground world on the border between terra incognita and Hades" (*The Name* 184)].

9 As in Michael Ende's *Die unendliche Geschichte* [The neverending story], the title of the book that the character reads is the same as the title of the book in which he appears. In a sense, both child-readers – Daniel Sempere and Ende's Bastian Balthazar Bux – will save a seemingly fantastic textual world from oblivion.

10 This is reminiscent of a passage in Carmen Martín Gaite's *El cuarto de atrás* [*The Back Room*], in which the narrator, after recognizing the fluidity of all historical and literary narratives, remarks: "Mi imagen se desmenuza y se refracta en infinitos reflejos" (167) ["My image shatters and is refracted in infinite reflections" (166–7)].

11 Book burning has haunted the western imaginary since the destruction of the Library of Alexandria, although as Battles points out, most books succumb to slower, less dramatic processes of decay. Julián stands in a long line of book burners, including the murderous bookman of Barcelona, that culminates most recently with the pyro-bibliomaniacs of Elias Canetti's *Auto-da-Fé*, Ray Bradbury's *Fahrenheit 451*, and Eco's *Il nome della rosa*.

12 Labanyi, following Jacques Derrida's argument in *Spectres de Marx* [Specters of Marx], explains such ghost-like figures as "the traces of those

who have not been allowed to leave a trace ... the victims of history who return to demand reparation; that is, that their name, instead of being erased, be honoured" (66).

13 The Ruiz Zafón text validates lowbrow culture through its sympathetic (and at times tongue-in-cheek) references to Julián's hackneyed writing and indeed through its own melodramatic style. But in interviews, Ruiz Zafón lashes out against what he regards as the banality of contemporary writing. According to Neuman, "[l]a misión de Daniel Sempere es, entre muchos significados, el rescate de una cultura en vías de inmolarse en la banalidad" [the mission of Daniel Sempere is, among other things, the recovery of a culture in the process of burning itself out in banality]. Yet as Ruiz Zafón's own writing confirms, the boundaries separating highbrow from lowbrow are porous at best, if not illusory.

14 The "pila de cuartillas que crece y crece" evokes the magical "montón de folios" (206) ["pile of sheets of paper" (205)] depicted in *El cuarto de atrás*. In contrast, the "enfermedad de los libros y las palabras" seems to prefigure a similar condition – albeit in the father rather than the son – that Enrique Vila-Matas describes in *El mal de Montano* [Montano's malady].

15 The parallel with *El cuarto de atrás* is intriguing. In this text, the narrator's interlocutor implies that her writing may be a kind of love letter she has written to herself, and that the other is simply a vehicle for her own self-expression: "Usted no necesita que exista, usted si no existe, lo inventa, y si existe, lo transforma" (196) ["You have no need for him to exist. If he doesn't exist, you invent him, and if he does exist, you transform him" (196)].

16 Gómez-Montero describes the burned books as "portadores de la memoria reprimida de la ciudad ... que van reapareciendo una y otra vez como manifestación del subconsciente colectivo de la ciudad bajo la fórmula del regreso de algo reprimido socialmente que se trata de despertar del subconsciente urbano" (414–15) [bearers of the repressed memory of the city that continue to reappear again and again as a manifestation of the collective subconscious of the city and that signify the return of something socially repressed that attempts to awaken from the urban subconscious].

17 Following Nora, Romero argues that "*lieux de mémoire* normally refer to 'official' places of memory, those that are systematic, institutionalized and self-referential, such as cemeteries, museums, archives and monuments, whose function is usually to impose a 'learned memory' that is uniform, deliberate and external, and that buries a 'lived memory'" (Romero 299; Nora 12). As a site of memory, *Os libros arden mal* strives to reconstitute memories that official versions of the past (that is, Francoist, anti-democratic, and anti-Galician versions) sought to erase.

18 Diego reveals that during the Argentine dictatorship of the 1970s he buried two boxes of books, including several volumes of Karl Marx, on

the outskirts of the city of La Plata. He imagines that at some future date someone will dig them up and gain insight into the history of subversive books, as occurred in Barcarrota, Spain in 1992, when a sixteenth-century library of books excoriated by the Inquisition was discovered behind the wall of a house undergoing renovation (314).

19 In the *Poesía completa* of García Lorca, these verses appear as follows: "Cabelos que van ô mar / onde as nubens teñen seu nidio pombal" (564).

20 Borrow is amused to find that the liberal group thinks he is actually the pretender Carlos, whom the Carlists fought to place on the throne of Spain.

21 In fact, Borrow does not mention the inscription in the passage of *The Bible in Spain* in which he describes this episode.

22 *The Bible in Spain* is replete with anti-Catholic diatribes, which Borrow directs at Spain and above all the Vatican. In the preface he writes: "It is true that, for nearly two centuries, she [Spain] was the she-butcher, *La Verduga*, of malignant Rome; the chosen instrument for carrying into effect the atrocious projects of that power" (3). He is surprised to find that the inhabitants of the Iberian Peninsula often have no knowledge of the existence of the Bible. At the beginning of his sojourn he remarks: "I have questioned the lower class of the children of Portugal about the Scripture, the Bible, the Old and New Testament, and in no one instance have they known what I was alluding to, or could return me a rational answer, though on all other matters their replies were sensible enough" (17). Ironically, some of the more educated, secular Spaniards he encounters likewise have little knowledge of the Bible, which they relegate to an obscurantist past. The mayor who ultimately frees Borrow when he is mistakenly identified as a Carlist finds his interest in the New Testament strange given that he hails from a country that has produced such giants of enlightened thinking as Jeremy Bentham: "I have heard that the English highly prize this eccentric book. How very singular that the countrymen of the grand Baintham [*sic*] should set any value upon that old monkish book" (290).

In another passage Borrow recounts a conversation with a young Portuguese woman. When he criticizes a book in her possession that he deems inimical to religion, her spontaneous reaction is to burn it. Ironically, it is the Protestant Borrow who elicits this fanatical and, from his perspective, decidedly Catholic gesture.

> They [her books] consisted principally of popular stories, with lives and miracles of saints, but amongst them was a translation of Volney's *Ruins of Empires*. I expressed a wish to know how she became possessed of this book. She said that a young man, a great Constitutionalist, had given it to her some months previous, and had pressed her much to read it, for that it was one of

> the best books in the world. I replied, that the author of it was an emissary of Satan, and an enemy of Jesus Christ and the souls of mankind; that it was written with the sole aim of bringing all religion into contempt, and that he inculcated the doctrine that there was no future state, nor reward for the righteous nor punishment for the wicked. She made no reply, but going into another room, returned with her apron full of dry sticks and brushwood, all which she piled upon the fire, and produced a bright blaze. She then took the book from my hand and placed it upon the flaming pile; then sitting down, took her rosary out of her pocket, and told her beads till the volume was consumed. This was an auto da fé in the best sense of the word. (35)

23 Joseba Gabilondo identifies Ríos as the owner of the typing school where Gabriel learns to write. In analyzing the dynamic of father-son relationships in *Os libros arden mal*, he argues that Casares Quiroga and Ríos function for Gabriel as symbolic father figures from opposite ends of the political spectrum (95).

24 Books like flagstones form a pathway, and books like arks carry us through darkened waters to safe shores. The image of the ark not only alludes to the biblical vessel but is also suggestive of the Russian film director Alexander Sokurov's vision of the Hermitage Museum in the film *The Russian Ark*, which he depicts as a bearer and preserver of the Russian cultural tradition during centuries of autocracy and dictatorship.

25 In this passage Ren hails Gabriel as the *katechon*. Yet his use of the word seems misguided if, as the text has suggested, the *katechon* is in fact the "lawless one," or Antichrist. As the namesake of the Angel of the Annunciation, Gabriel is instead the harbinger of a new discursive tradition (or Word) made possible through a reconnection with the multiple discursive traditions of the past that have been repressed in official historical narratives.

26 In analyzing this passage, Gabilondo writes: "It is interesting to analyze the shift in the conversation from the Bible to the *Ulysses*, which is not justified by the narrative but signifies the universality of that Galician progressive modern bourgeoisie who could read – and in fact translated fragments into Galician of – the most foundational novel of the 20th century before it appeared anywhere else in Spain" (95).

27 This implicit parallel between the architectural styles of Bosnia and Iberia is but one of the many passages in the text in which the Muslim cultures of the two regions are compared.

28 Goytisolo's account of the destruction of the National and University Library of Bosnia and Herzegovina parallels Joshua Hammer's account of the attack by Al-Qaeda-sponsored jihadis on the collection of ancient Islamic manuscripts housed in the Ahmed Baba Institute of Higher Learning and Islamic Research in Timbuktu, Mali. At the time of the attack,

most of the 377,000 manuscripts held in the Institute and other libraries of Timbuktu had already been removed to safe-sites outside the city. But on the morning of 25 January 2013, a group of jihadis occupying the Institute took some 4,200 manuscripts and burned them. As Hammer writes, "[i]n minutes, the work of some of Timbuktu's greatest savants and scientists, preserved for centuries, hidden from the nineteenth-century jihadis and the French conquerors, survivors of floods and the pernicious effects of dust, bacteria, water, and insects, were consumed by the inferno" (209–10).

29 For a thorough discussion of the historical background of the destruction of books during the Balkan wars of the 1990s, see Knuth 105–34.

30 Although Genaro J. Pérez warns us not to confuse the extra-textual author, Goytisolo, with the authorial voices or figures in the text (398), Manuel Hierro detects "transferencias textuales y reverberaciones temáticas" [textual transferences and thematic reverberations] from several narratives including *Paisajes después de la batalla* [*Landscapes after the Battle*] and *Coto vedado* [*Forbidden Territory*], the first volume of Goytisolo's autobiography (144). For further analysis of the intersections of fiction, autobiography, and history in *El sitio de los sitios*, see the studies of Davis ("Life" and "Narrative") and Puebla Pedrosa.

31 In *Coto vedado* Goytisolo describes a real person named Eusebio Borrell, who is fictionalized in both *El sitio de los sitios* and Goytisolo's subsequent novel, *Las semanas del jardín* [*The Garden of Secrets*] (see Conte 125n7). In *El sitio de los sitios* the narrator first hears the name of his Uncle Eusebio, a homosexual who disappears during the Spanish Civil War, "en aquella habitación con las paredes tapizadas de libros" (151) ["in that room whose walls were lined with books" (126)]. In *Las virtudes del pájaro solitario* a character with a similar story appears. Again, what draws the attention of the narrator are his uncle's books.

> [É]stás en el despacho del tío y examinas los libros encuadernados de rojo y oro alineados en los estantes de la librería, manuales de historia, recopilaciones de obras jurídicas, tratados de divulgación médica y científica, obras piadosas, estampa en color de un santo varón cobardemente asesinado por los del otro bando ... (119)
>
> [(Y)ou are in your uncle's study and you examine the books bound in red and gold lined up on the shelves of the bookcase, history textbooks, collections of works on jurisprudence, popular treatises on medicine and science, manuals of piety, a color print of a pious man, victim of a cowardly assassination by those on the other side ... (111)]

Eventually, the narrator observes "las pavesas y cenizas de la biblioteca [de este] ya fusilado señor mayor" (140) ["the embers and ashes of the library of (this) older gentleman now executed by a firing squad" (130)].

32 As Kunz argues in his analysis of *El sitio de los sitios* and *Las semanas del jardín*: "The central figure is not composed like a mosaic which, bit by bit, acquires its definitive and complete form, but rather like a kaleidoscope which, with each twist that it is given, offers us a new vision, sometimes similar to the previous one, sometimes completely different but always based on constant elements" (99).

33 In what follows I use the word "narrator" simply to refer to the narrative voice as it appears at any given moment in the text. Although this voice has no single or stable identity, it is usually depicted as male. When speaking of the narrative voice I therefore employ the pronouns "he" and "him" and the possessive adjective "his."

34 The Latin word "situs" can in fact refer not only to a site as a geographical space but also to a structure, such as a library building.

35 In *Cuaderno de Sarajevo*, Goytisolo blames the "memoricide" not only on the perpetrators of the attack on the library but also on the Serbian writers who promoted the assertion of the Serbian state.

> En verdad – y tal era el propósito de la gavilla de mediocres novelistas, poetas e historiadores con vocación de pirómanos, cuyo *Informe* a la Academia de Belgrado fue el germen de la ascensión de Milosevic al poder y del subsiguiente desmembramiento de Yugoslavia – dicho crimen [la destrucción de la biblioteca] no puede ser definido cabalmente sino como *memoricidio*. (56)
>
> [In truth – and this was the aim of that gang of mediocre novelists, poets, and historians whose real calling was pyromania and whose *Report* to the Belgrade Academy was the seed of Milosevic's ascent to power and the subsequent dismembering of Yugoslavia – this crime (the destruction of the library) cannot be properly defined except as a *memoricide*.]

36 The multifaceted collection of the library could also be interpreted as a symbol of the cosmopolitanism of Sarajevo before the war. In *Cuaderno de Sarajevo*, Goytisolo describes the city as "[un] espacio de encuentros y convergencias, punto en donde las diferencias, en vez de ser causa de exclusión, se entremezclan y fecundan por ósmosis y permeabilidad" (58) [(a) space of encounters and convergences, a point where differences, instead of being the cause of exclusion, intermingle and inseminate by osmosis and permeability]. Reading books in a library similarly leads to encounters, convergences, interminglings, and inseminations of discourses that are by nature osmotic and permeable.

37 For a depiction of a book maker who participated in the burning of his own condemned books, see Javier Azpeitia's *El impresor de Venecia* [The printer of Venice]. When seeing his books burn, he wonders to what we owe our "anhelo ilusorio de atrapar en palabras el murmullo de nuestra especie, si al final ese discurso inmenso de la vida, que todo lo devora,

se reproduce en el crepitar de una hoguera de libros mucho mejor que en ninguna historia narrada o por narrar" (303) [illusory desire to trap in words the murmur of our species, if in the end that immense discourse of life, which devours everything, is better represented in the crackling of a bonfire of books than in any story ever told or to be told].

38 The *Haggadah* is a Jewish text read at the Passover Seder. The Sarajevo *Haggadah* was composed in Barcelona in the fourteenth century and taken from Spain by exiled Sephardic Jews. During the seventeenth century it appeared in Venice, where it avoided the fate of many Jewish books burned by the Inquisition. As Riedlmayer explains, it entered the library of the National Museum of Bosnia and Herzegovina in Sarajevo in the late nineteenth century. During the Second World War it was saved from the Nazis by a Muslim librarian, and in 1992 it was saved again, when the contents of the museum library were removed for safekeeping (7). While in Sarajevo, Goytisolo interviewed a man descended from Sephardic Jews, who spoke a form of Spanish fully intelligible to him and who identified in part as a Spaniard (*Cuaderno* 59–62). This anecdote functions to connect once again the victims of the siege of Sarajevo with the Jewish and Muslim victims of the Christian reconquest of Spain.

39 The English translation suggests a breaking of meaning rather than an uprooting of meaning, as indicated by the word "descuajo."

40 Not only the recovery of the lost books but also the story of the biblioclasm itself (as either reported or imagined in books like Goytisolo's) provides solace for those experiencing similar tragedies. In the narrative *Les Passeurs de livres de Daraya: Une bibliothèque secrète en Syrie* [The book smugglers of Daraya: A secret library in Syria], the French journalist Delphine Minoui recounts a series of Skype conversations that she had with a group of young revolutionaries in Daraya, a suburb of Damascus, who opposed both Daech and the regime of Bashar al-Assad during the Syrian Civil War. While under constant assault by the forces of al-Assad, they managed to recover thousands of books from the rubble of the bombardments and create an underground library for the use of the inhabitants of Daraya. In their conversations with Minoui they speak of the experience of finding among the books several accounts of the siege of Sarajevo and the destruction of the National and University Library of Bosnia and Herzegovina, which they regard as a mirror of their own plight. One of them remarks:

> Lire sur Sarajevo, c'est se sentir moins seul. Se dire que d'autres, avant nous, ont traversé la même épreuve. Dans un autre pays. Un autre contexte. Mais, grâce à leur récit, je me sens moins vulnérable. Je retrouve une force intérieure qui me fait avancer. (109)

[To read about Sarajevo is to feel less alone. To think that others, before us, have undergone the same ordeal. In another country. Another context. But, thanks to their story, I feel less vulnerable. I discover an inner force that makes me go forward.]

41 The term "Sotadic Zone" was coined by Sir Richard Francis Burton to describe areas of the world, from southern Europe to the South Seas, where he considered homosexual practice endemic. See Conte 136n8.

42 Hierro comments on the etymology of the word "ficha" [index card], which is related to the Spanish word "filiación" [affiliation or parentage], and which derives from the Latin word "filius" [son]. According to Hierro, the trope of the "ficha" in *El sitio de los sitios* "engloba el programa de la memoria" (153n12) [encompasses the project of memory]. He relates it to the attempt of Goytisolo to sustain the memory of his mother, who, like the woman killed by a sniper's bullet on the streets of Sarajevo, perished on the streets of Barcelona during the early days of the Spanish Civil War. As living "fichas," the narrative voices in *El sitio de los sitios* become the progeny of the books incinerated in the siege of the library and thereby renew their discourses. Interestingly, in *Cuaderno de Sarajevo* Goytisolo notes that while visiting the ruins of the library, he picked up a piece of scorched paper and discovered "una ficha clasificadora del Archivo" (57) [an index card from the Archive]. He kept it to remind himself of the barbarism, and perhaps also to serve as a sort of link between the books destroyed in the fire and his own act of writing *El sitio de los sitios*.

43 See Conte for a magisterial elucidation of Goytisolo's desire to "evitar con dignidad la erosión" (83) ["avoid erosion with dignity" (155)] (the final verse of the appendix of poems) and his "poética de las ruinas" (Conte 129) [poetics of ruins].

44 The Spanish original suggests not only that he is reading his own work but also that he is reading himself ["leyendo a mí mismo"], as if he were literally the inscribed text of the poems. If this is the case, then what is recovered is both a lost discourse and a life that exists only insofar as it is expressed discursively.

45 The image of discourse as a trap is evocative of a passage in *Las virtudes del pájaro solitario* in which the narrator describes the exegesis of a text as an attempt to "capturar la sutileza del viento con una red" (59) ["capture the subtlety of wind in a net" (55)].

46 In *Les Passeurs de livres de Daraya*, Minoui notes that after the forces of Bashar al-Assad occupied Daraya, the books in the underground library were not burned, and many were simply sold off in the flea markets of Damascus: "La culture au rabais. Quatre ans de sauvetage du patrimoine de Daraya troqués contre quelques pièces de monnaie" (143) [Culture at

a discount. Four years of rescuing the patrimony of Daraya swapped for several coins].

**Part 4: Nuria Amat and the Persistence of Books**

Some material in this section previously appeared in the following article: "The Nostalgia for Lost Books: Nuria Amat as Librarian and Writer." *Romance Notes*, vol. 45, no. 3, Spring 2005, pp. 347–55.

1 Although Amat has written most of her works in Castilian, in 2011 she penned a Catalan-language novel, titled *Amor i guerra* [Love and war].
2 Since the publication of "Escritores que lloran," Amat has in fact produced a number of successful narratives, including the award-winning *Reina de América* [*Queen Cocaine*] (2001).
3 Walter Mehring recalls the similar words of his own father: "'All the books will be yours when I am dead,' my father used to say whenever I came to borrow a volume from him" (14–15). Whereas the library of Amat's father was dispersed after he gave it to her brother, the books of Mehring's Viennese father were destroyed by the Nazis, despite Mehring's own efforts to save them.To a certain extent, Amat's discussion of her relationship with her father parallels Simone de Beauvoir's analysis in *Le deuxième sexe* [The second sex] of father-daughter relationships, as well as the analysis of her own relationship with her father in *Mémoires d'une jeune fille rangée* [Memoirs of a dutiful daughter].
4 This displacement of the self is emphasized in "Escritores que lloran" through the use of the third person. Here, Amat not only formulates the notion of "el efecto biblioteca" but even demonstrates it through a conscious parody of the formal essay. She also explicitly distances herself from her textual subject, whom she refers to not as "yo" [I], but as "la niña" [the girl], "la bibliotecaria" [the librarian], "la escritora" [the writer], etc.
5 I am thinking here of the Aristotelian notion of form, which, with entities such as humans, is not imposed on matter (as a carpenter might impose the form of a table on wood), but rather reveals itself as the inherent logic or structure of a being.
6 The terms "electronic library" and "digital library" refer to collections stored digitally rather than through paper, microfilm, and other non-digital materials.
7 Conducting an online library search might seem less like an expression of bibliophilia than would reading a paper-based book in a traditional library space. Yet as the literature of bibliophilia reveals, many bibliophiles are in fact more interested in searching for books than in actually reading them.

The so-called bibliomaniac thus shares psychological motivations not only with compulsive bibliographers but also with compulsive searchers of digital information and digital texts.

8 The individual who made this declaration ("The library is dead. Long live the librarian!") was Frederick Wilfrid Lancaster. See Lancaster 171.

9 Amat also discusses the effects of emerging digital technology on late twentieth-century writers in *El libro mudo: Las aventuras del escritor entre la pluma y el ordenador* (1994) [The mute book: The adventures of the writer between the pen and the computer].

10 In *Mal d'archive: Une impression freudienne* (1995) [*Archive Fever: A Freudian Impression* (1996)], Jacques Derrida undertakes a psychoanalytic study of the phenomenon of archive creation as it is affected by the structures of both human memory and political power. Davis invokes Derrida's theorization of archives in his study of literary canons, in a chapter of his book *Writing Heritage in Contemporary Spain*, titled "Never-Ending Story: Canon Fever" (48–73). The metaphorical fever that provokes Alejandra to seek respite through self-fashioning in texts and books is evocative of the titles of Derrida and Davis, although it is expressed in a more limited context.

11 Alejandra clearly shares commonalities with the autobiographical and fictional characters of Unamuno, who believe that they achieve a degree of immortality when their stories are written, even if it is these stories, rather than they themselves, that will survive after they die.

12 Stark's virulent diatribes against digital technology in fact far exceed the apprehension that Amat expresses over the perceived obsolescence of personal libraries. As he categorically declares: "Il n'y a pas de culture des ordinateurs. Il n'y a pas de civilisation numérique" (207) [There is no computer culture. There is no digital civilization].

13 See, for example, the study of Legros.

14 In describing his library, Montaigne writes: "Là je feuillette à cette heure un livre, à cette heure un autre, sans ordre et sans dessein, à pièces décousues" (1294; qtd. in Compagnon 58) [There, at one moment, I leaf through one book and at another moment through another book, without order or plan, in a disjointed fashion]. Compagnon cites the widely held assumption that in the digital age the practice of linear and prolonged reading will disappear. But as he sees it, Montaigne defended a versatile style of reading, whimsical and spontaneous, that anticipates the reading practices of many contemporary internet users (59). Although confined to his library, the figure of Montaigne is thus also similar to Azorín's wandering bibliophile.

15 Various writers speak of their identification with books, including Sartre in his autobiography *Les Mots* [*The Words*]. Eakin in fact describes the young Sartre as "[t]he boy who wanted to be a book" (126).

**Part 5: Miquel Plana and the Book as a Work of Art**

1 Antoni Monturiol and Magda Pujolàs describe Plana's edition of Jacint Verdaguer i Santaló's epic poem *L'Atlàntida* [Atlantis], which he completed in 1992, as the "cim de la bibliofília catalana i hispànica" (22) [summit of Catalan and Hispanic bibliophilia]. As Pilar Vélez sees it, Plana's work represents a bibliophilia situated between the end of the world of Gutenberg and the consolidation of the world of digital technology ("Miquel Plana: Un fenómeno" 49).
2 For critics like Carrión Gútiez, binding is what makes a book a book: "un libro sin encuadernar no es un libro" ("El libro" 139) [an unbound book is not a book]. This is in fact the view of most traditional bibliophiles. According to the renowned Spanish bookbinder Antolín Palomino Olalla, bookbinding is the highest of the book arts, and the most beautiful aspect of bound books is the *papel pintado*, or marbled paper, that decorates the inside and outside of traditional book covers (*Autobiografía* 63–4). For examples of Palomino Olalla's exquisite *papeles pintados*, see Palomino Olalla, *Mis papeles*.
3 Two Spanish-language authors associated with Oulipo are the Spaniard, Pablo Martín Sánchez, and the Argentine, Eduardo Beti.
4 Rimbaud begins the poem with the famous verse "A noir, E blanc, I rouge, U vert, O bleu" (126) [A black, E white, I red, U green, O blue].
5 From the José Escada retrospective, *Eu não evoluo, viajo* [I do not evolve, I travel] at the Museu Calouste Gulbenkian, 9 July 2016–31 October 2016.
6 When examining Plana's works in the Biblioteca Nacional de España, I was struck by the fact that several, including *Barcelona 1888–1992*, were too large for the librarian to carry and had to be wheeled to me in a cart.

# Works Cited


Ainaud de Lasarte, Josep M. "Bibliòfils per força." *Bibliofília a Catalunya: Des del s. XIX*, Fundació Jaume 1, 2001, pp. 66–7.

Albero, Miguel. *Enfermos del libro: Breviario personal de bibliopatías propias y ajenas*. U de Sevilla, Secretariado de Publicaciones, 2009.

Alexander, Charles. "Between Poetics, the Poetics of Between, Pressing Between." *Threads Talk Series*, edited by Steve Clay and Kyle Schlesinger, Granary Books/Cuneiform Press, 2016, pp. 18–37.

Almela y Vives, Francisco. *Ramillete de bibliófilos valencianos*. Castalia, 1950.

Amat, Nuria. *La biblioteca electrónica*. Fundación Germán Sánchez Ruipérez/ Ediciones Pirámide, 1990.

– *La biblioteca fantasma: El laboratorio de lo imaginario*. Montena, 1989.

– *Escribir y callar*. Siruela, 2010.

– *El ladrón de libros y otras bibliomanías*. Muchnik, 1988.

– *Letra herida*. Alfaguara, 1998.

– *Todos somos Kafka*. Prologue by Carlos Fuentes, Reverso, 2004.

Arnella, Jaume. "El llibreter monjo." *Les Cançons del Pont de Les Formigues*, Tram, 1999, www.cancioneros.com/lyrics/song/69490/el-llibreter-monjo-jaume-arnella.

Augustine. *The City of God: Books XVII–XXII*. Translated by Gerald G. Walsh and Daniel J. Honan, Catholic U of America P, 1981.

Ayén, Xavi. "Radiografía de un éxito literario." *La Vanguardia*, 26 Nov. 2002, www.xtec.es/~jducros/Carlos%20Ruiz%20Zafon.html.

Azorín. *Azorín y los libros: Exposición*. Ministerio de Cultura, Dirección General del Libro y Bibliotecas, Centro de las Letras Españolas, 1993.

– *Doña Inés*. *Obras completas*, vol. 4, edited by Ángel Cruz Rueda, Aguilar, 1948, pp. 735–847. 9 vols.

– *Libros, buquinistas y bibliotecas: Crónicas de un transeúnte: Madrid-París*. Edited by Francisco Fuster (García) and preface by Andrés Trapiello, Ediciones Fórcola, 2014.

– *Un pueblecito: Riofrío de Ávila. Obras completas*, vol. 3, edited by Ángel Cruz Rueda, Aguilar, 1947, pp. 527–95. 9 vols.

Azpeitia, Javier. *El impresor de Venecia*. Tusquets, 2016.

Baker, Edward. *La biblioteca de don Quijote*. Marcial Pons, 1997.

Balaguer, Víctor. *Las ruinas de Poblet*. Tello, 1885.

Balcells, Albert. *Catalan Nationalism: Past and Present*. Edited by Geoffrey J. Walker and translated by Jacqueline Hall, St. Martin's Press, 1996.

Barrière, Didier. "'Un Petit Francisque Michel,' Médiéviste, Bibliomane Romantique, Mauvais élève de Charles Nodier." *Fragmentos*, vol. 31, 2006, pp. 113–40.

Basdenes, Nicholas A. *A Gentle Madness: Bibliophiles, Bibliomanes, and the Eternal Passion for Books*. Henry Holt, 1999.

– *On Paper: The Everything of Its Two-Thousand-Year History*. Vintage Books, 2013.

Battles, Matthew. "Burning Isn't the Only Way to Lose a Book." Review of *The Library of Alexandria: Centre of Learning in the Ancient World*, edited by Roy MacLeod. *London Review of Books*, 13 Apr. 2000, pp. 20–1.

Batur, Enis. *D'une bibliothèque l'autre*. Translated by François Skvor, Bleu autour, 2008.

Benjamin, Walter. "Little History of Photography." *Selected Writings* 2.2 (1931–1934), translated by Rodney Livingstone et al. and edited by Michael W. Jennings et al., Belknap Press of Harvard UP, 2005, pp. 507–30.

Bersani, Leo. *Homos*. Harvard UP, 1995.

Bonet Correa, Antonio. "Pregón de la XVIIIa Feria Nacional del Libro de Ocasión Antiguo y Moderno, Madrid, 1994." *Pregones y carteles: Homenaje a Antolín Palomino Olalla*, Ayuntamiento de Madrid, 1997, pp. 137–8.

Borges, Jorge Luis. "La biblioteca de Babel." *Obras completas, 1923–1972*. Emecé, 1974, pp. 465–71.

Borrow, George [Henry]. *The Bible in Spain*. J.M. Dent and Sons/E.P. Dutton, 1947.

Borsuk, Amaranth. *The Book*. MIT P, 2018.

Botrel, Jean-François. *Libros, prensa y lectura en la España del siglo XIX*. Translated by David Torra Ferrer, Fundación Germán Sánchez Ruipérez, 1993.

Buchanan, Milton A. *Notes on the Life and Works of Bartolomé José Gallardo*. New York and Paris, 1923.

Burke, Edmund. *A Philosophical Enquiry into the Origin of Our Ideas of the Sublime and Beautiful*. Edited by J.T. Boulton, Columbia UP, 1958.

Burns, Gerald L. "Mallarmé: The Transcendence of Language and the Aesthetics of the Book." *The Journal of Typographic Research*, vol. 3, no. 3, July 1969, pp. 219–34.

Caballé, Anna, and Francesc X. Puig Rovira, editors. *Bibliofilia y amistad: Juan José Gómez-Fontecha y Jaume Pla: Correspondencia (1975–2002)*. Milenio/Associació de Bibliòfils de Barcelona, 2014.

Cadena, Josep M. "Joan Vila i la catalanitat d'un il·lustrador." *D'Ivori: La màgia de la il·lustració*, edited by Josep M. Cadena et al., Ajuntament de Barcelona, 1996, pp. 11–36.
– "Miquel i Planas, bibliófilo y exlibrista." *Diario de Barcelona*, 29 Aug. 1971, p. 13.
Calderón, Emilio. *La memoria de un hombre está en sus besos*. Stella Maris, 2016.
Calvino, Italo. *If on a Winter's Night a Traveler*. Harcourt, 1981.
– *Se una notte d'inverno un viaggiatori*. Einaudi, 1979.
Campos, Jorge. *Vida y trabajos de un libro viejo (contados por él mismo)*. Castalia, 1949.
Carrière, Jean-Claude, and Umberto Eco. *N'espérez pas vous débarrasser des livres: Entretiens menés par Jean-Philippe de Tonnac*. Grasset and Fasquelle, 2009.
– *This Is Not the End of the Book: A Conversation Curated by Jean-Philippe de Tonnac*. Translated by Polly McLean, Vintage Books, 2012.
Carrión, Jorge. *Librerías*. Anagrama, 2013.
Carrión, Ulises. *El arte nuevo de hacer libros: Archivo Carrión 1*. Edited by Juan J. Agius and translated by Heriberto Yépez, Colección Anómalos, 2012.
Carrión Gútiez, Manuel. "Encuadernación y destino del libro (loa y guía de pequeños y grandes coleccionistas)." *Bibliofilias: Exposición con motivo del 38° Congreso Internacional y la 21a Feria Internacional de ILAB*, Fundación Lázaro Galdiano, 2008, pp. 57–65.
– "El libro encuadernado como consumación." *El libro como objeto de arte: Actas del II Congreso nacional sobre bibliofilia, encuadernación artística, restauración y patrimonio bibliográfico. Cádiz, abril de 2004*, Ayuntamiento de Cádiz, 2008, pp. 139–47.
Carter, John, and Nicolas Barker. *ABC for Book Collectors*. 8th ed., Oak Knoll Press, 2006.
Cartopiés Cartonera. www.cartopies.blogspot.com/. Accessed 30 May 2020.
Castellanos, Jordi. "Mercat del llibre i cultura nacional (1882–1925)." *Els Marges*, vol. 56, 1996, pp. 5–38.
Castillo, Montserrat. "Joan Vila, 'D'Ivori,' il·lustrador." *D'Ivori: La màgia de la il·lustració*, edited by Josep M. Cadena et al., Ajuntament de Barcelona, 1996, pp. 37–142.
Castoldi, Alberto. *Il libro che uccide*. Bergamo UP, 2002.
Castro, Adolfo de. *Aventuras literarias del iracundo bibliopirata estremeño don Bartolomico Gallardete, escritas por el buen don Antonio de Lupián Zapata (La horma de su zapato)*. Francisco Pantoja, 1851.
Cervantes Saavedra, Miguel de. *Don Quijote de La Mancha*. Edited by Martín de Riquer, Editorial Juventud, 1968.
– *Don Quixote of La Mancha*. Translated by Walter Starkie, Signet Classic, 1979.
Checa Cremades, José Luis. "Azorín, bibliofilia y encuadernación." *Encuadernación: Doce ensayos sobre bibliofilia y artes del libro (siglos XX-XXI)*, Turpin Editores, 2012, pp. 329–48.

– *El libro antiguo: Materia bibliográfica y objeto de deseo*. 2nd ed., Praha, 2011.
– *El libro antiguo: Materia bibliográfica y objeto de deseo*. 3rd ed., Praha, 2012.
– "La vanguardia poética del 27 y la bibliofilia española: En la biblioteca de José Alburquerque Dueñas." *Encuadernación: Doce ensayos sobre bibliofilia y artes del libro (siglos XX–XXI)*, Turpin Editores, 2012, pp. 351–82.
Collins, Jim. *Bring on the Books for Everybody: How Literary Culture Became Popular Culture*. Duke UP, 2010.
– "Reading, in a Digital Archive of One's Own." *PMLA*, vol. 128, no. 1, Jan. 2013, pp. 207–12.
Comadira, Narcís. *Triomf de la vida*, Miquel Plana, 1993.
Compagnon, Antoine. *Un été avec Montaigne*. Éditions des Équateurs, 2013.
Conte, David. "La retracción frente al asedio: El fundamento poemático de *El sitio de los sitios*." *Pesquisas en la obra tardía de Juan Goytisolo*, edited by Brigitte Adriaensen and Marco Kunz, Rodopi, 2009, pp. 117–39.
Corberto, Albert. "Notícia històrica sobre el colofó." *Colofons de Domènec Moli en els llibres de Miquel Plana*, by Domènec Moli, 2012, pp. 107–15.
Cvetkovich, Ann. *An Archive of Feelings: Trauma, Sexuality, and Lesbian Public Cultures*. Duke UP, 2003.
Dahan, Jacques-Rémi. *Visages de Charles Nodier*. PUPS, 2008.
Dante Alighieri. *La divina commedia*. 5th ed., Rizzoli, 2013.
– *The Divine Comedy*. Translated by Melville Best Anderson, The Heritage Press, 1944.
Davis, Stuart. "Life, Death and the Name: The Case of Juan Goytisolo." *Forum of Modern Language Studies*, vol. 41, no. 4, Sept. 2005, pp. 365–74.
– "Narrative Battles: War and Memory in the Novels of Juan Goytisolo." *Bulletin of Hispanic Studies*, vol. 86, no. 4, July 2009, pp. 521–36.
– *Writing and Heritage in Contemporary Spain: The Imaginary Museum of Literature*. Tamesis, 2012.
De Bury, Richard. *The Love of Books: The Philobiblon of Richard de Bury*. Translated by E.C. Thomas, Luce, 1907.
Delgado Casado, Juan. *Un siglo de bibliografía en España: Los concursos bibliográficos de la Biblioteca nacional (1857–1953)*, vol. 2. Ollero y Ramos Editores, 2001. 2 vols.
Dibdin, Thomas Frognall. *Bibliomania, or Book Madness: A Bibliographic Romance, in Six Parts, Illustrated with Cuts*. J. McCreery, 1811.
*Diccionario de la lengua española*. 23rd ed., Real Academia Española, 2014, https://dle.rae.es/.
Diego, José Luis de. *La otra cara de Jano: Una mirada crítica sobre el libro y la edición*. Ampersand, 2017.
Dobón, María Dolores. "*La ruta de Don Quijote*, 'intrahistoria,' e 'historia interna.'" *Azorín, 1904–1924: IIIè colloque international*, U de Pau et des Pays de l'Adour/U de Murcia, 1996, pp. 87–91.

Dodeman, Charles. *Le Journal d'un bouquiniste*. Tancrède, 1922.
Domènech i Montaner, Lluís. *Historia y arquitectura del Monasterio de Poblet*. Montaner y Simón, 1927.
Domínguez, Carlos María. *La casa de papel*. Alfaguara, 2004.
– *The House of Paper*. Translated by Nick Caistor, Harcourt, 2005.
Dorfman, Ariel. "My Lost Library: Books, Exile, and Identity." *Chronicle of Higher Education*, 18 Sept. 2011, pp. B6–11.
Dowling, John. "Las *Noches lúgubres* de Cadalso y la juventud romántica del Ochocientos." Biblioteca Virtual Miguel de Cervantes, 2002, www.cervantesvirtual.com/obra/las-noches-lugubres-de-cadalso-y-la-juventud-romantica-del-ochocientos--0/.
Drucker, Johanna. *The Century of Artists' Books*. Granary Books, 1995.
Eakin, Paul John. *Fictions in Autobiography: Studies in the Art of Self-Invention*. Princeton UP, 1985.
Eco, Umberto. *The Name of the Rose*. Translated by William Weaver, Harcourt, 1983.
– *Il nome della rosa*. Bompiani, 2016.
Eisenberg, Daniel. "La biblioteca de Cervantes." *Studia in honorem Prof. M. de Riquer*, Quaderns Crema, 1987, pp. 271–328.
– "Did Cervantes Have a Library?" *Hispanic Studies in Honor of Alan D. Deyermond: A North American Tribute*, edited by John S. Miletich, Hispanic Seminary of Medieval Studies, 1986, pp. 93–106.
Ellis, Robert Richmond. "'Les adieux irréversibles': Simone de Beauvoir and Oreste F. Pucciani." *Simone de Beauvoir Studies*, vol. 17, 2000–1, pp. 156–61.
– "Detectives, Mad Bookmen, and the Devil's Disciples: A Reading of *El club Dumas, La novena puerta* of Arturo Pérez-Reverte." *Anales de la Literatura Española Contemporánea*, vol. 31, no.1, Winter 2006, pp. 29–45.
– "The Legend of Fra Vicents in European and Catalan Culture." *Symposium: A Quarterly Journal in Modern Literatures*, vol. 56, no. 3, 2002, pp. 123–33.
– "The Nostalgia for Lost Books: Nuria Amat as Librarian and Writer." *Romance Notes*, vol. 45, no. 3, Spring 2005, pp. 347–55.
– "Reading the Spanish Past: Library Fantasies in Carlos Ruiz Zafón's *La sombra del viento*." *Bulletin of Spanish Studies*, vol. 83, no. 6, 2006, pp. 839–54.
Ender, Evelyne, and Deidre Shauna Lynch. "Introduction: Reading Spaces." *PMLA*, vol. 134, no. 1, Jan. 2019, pp. 9–17.
Enguídanos, Miguel. "Azorín en busca del tiempo divinal." *Papeles de Son Armadans*, vol. 15, no. 43, 1959, pp. 13–32.
Epps, Brad. "*Modernisme* in Catalonia." *Modernism*, edited by Astradur Eysteinsson and Vivian Liska, John Benjamins, 2007, pp. 781–800.
Estruga, Jordi, et al. *Tres arquitectes del llibre: Lluís Jou, Jaume Pla, Miquel Plana*. Ziggurat, 2004.
Fabra, Pompeu. *La llengua catalana i la seva normalització*. Edited by Francesc Vallverdú, Edicions 62, 1980.

Fernández Sánchez, José. *Historia de la bibliografía en España*. Compañía Literaria, 1994.
Flaubert, Gustave. "Bibliomanie: Conte." *Appendice aux oeuvres complètes de Gustave Flaubert, Vol. 1: Oeuvres de jeunesse inédites: 1830–1838*, Conard, 1910, pp. 132–47. 3 vols.
Fonalleras, Josep M. "Lletres premsades: Miquel Plana i la literatura." *Miquel Plana: Arquitecte del llibre, 1943–2012*, Museu de la Garrotxa d'Olot, Institut de Cultura de la Ciutat d'Olot, 2015, pp. 69–71.
Fontbona, Francesc. "La bibliofília vuitcentista." *Bibliofília a Catalunya: Des del s. XIX*, Fundació Jaume 1, 2001, pp. 12–19.
– "Miquel Plana, artista singular." *Miquel Plana: Arquitecte del llibre, 1943–2012*, Museu de la Garrotxa d'Olot, Institut de Cultura de la Ciutat d'Olot, 2015, pp. 39–41.
Foucault, Michel. *The Archaeology of Knowledge*. Translated by A.M. Sheridan Smith, Pantheon, 1972.
– *L'Archéologie du savoir*. Gallimard, 1969.
– *La Bibliothèque fantastique: À propos de "La Tentation de saint Antoine" de Gustave Flaubert*. La Lettre volée, 1995.
– "Fantasia of the Library." *Language, Counter-Memory, Practice: Selected Essays and Interviews*, edited by Donald F. Bouchard and translated by Donald F. Bouchard and Sherry Simon, Cornell UP, 1977, pp. 87–109.
Fox, E. Inman. "Azorín y la nueva manera de mirar las cosas." *Anales Azorinianos*, vol. 7, 1999, pp. 11–22.
– "Lectura y literatura (En torno a la inspiración libresca de Azorín)." *Cuadernos Hispanoamericanos*, vol. 205, 1967, pp. 5–26.
Fuster García, Francisco. "Azorín y Baroja: Una extraña pareja." *Cuadernos Hispanoamericanos*, vol. 779, no. 5, 2015, pp. 92–103.
– "Azorín y los libros: Autorretrato de un lector." *Cuadernos Hispanoamericanos*, vol. 762, no. 12, 2013, pp. 71–84.
Gabilondo, Joseba. "Masculine Masochism as Dominant Fiction in Minority Literatures in Spain: An Analysis of Manuel Rivas's Narrative." *Galicia*, vol. 21, C, 2011, pp. 78–103.
Gala, Antonio. "Pregón de la VIIa Feria Nacional del Libro de Ocasión Antiguo y Moderno, Madrid, 1983." *Pregones y carteles: Homenaje a Antolín Palomino Olalla*, Ayuntamiento de Madrid, 1997, pp. 59–61.
Gallardo, Bartolomé José. *El Criticón: Papel volante de literatura y bellas-artes*. 2 vols. Ayuntamiento de Campanario, 1999.
– *Obras escogidas*. 2 vols. Edited by Pedro Sainz y Rodríguez, Compañía Iberoamericana de Publicaciones, 1928.
Gallego Lorenzo, Josefa. "Breves pinceladas sobre el bibliógrafo Bartolomé José Gallardo." *El libro como objeto de arte: Actas del II Congreso nacional sobre bibliofilia, encuadernación artística, restauración y patrimonio*

*bibliográfico. Cádiz, abril de 2004*, Ayuntamiento de Cádiz, 2008, pp. 211–21.

García Lorca, Federico. *Poesía completa*. 2nd ed., Galaxia Gutenberg, 2012.

García Márquez, Gabriel. *Cien años de soledad*. Edited by Joaquín Marco, Espasa-Calpe, 1982.

– *One Hundred Years of Solitude*. Translated by Gregory Rabassa, Harper and Row, 1970.

Gikandi, Simon. "The Fantasy of the Library." *PMLA*, vol. 128, no. 1, Jan. 2013, pp. 9–20.

Glendinning, Nigel. "Spanish Books in England: 1800–1850." *Transactions of the Cambridge Bibliographical Society*, vol. 3, no. 1, 1959, pp. 70–92.

Gómez Escámez, Vicente. *La huella de los libros*. Alhulia, 2011.

Gómez-Montero, Javier. "El conjuro anamnésico de *Os libros arden mal* de Manuel Rivas." *Romanistisches Jahrbuch*, vol. 62, no. 1, 2011, pp. 405–24.

González Manzanares, Joaquín. *La pasión libresca extremeña: Retazos de bibliografía, bibliofilia y bibliotecas*. Alborayque Libros, 2009.

Goytisolo, Juan. *Cuaderno de Sarajevo: Anotaciones de un viaje a la barbarie*. El País / Aguilar, 1993.

– *El sitio de los sitios*. Seix Barral, 2002.

– *State of Siege*. Translated by Helen Lane, City Lights Books, 2002.

– *Las virtudes del pájaro solitario*. Seix Barral, 1990.

– *The Virtues of the Solitary Bird*. Translated by Helen Lane, Serpent's Tail, 1991.

Graeber, Eric, editor. *Magic and Madness in the Library*. Birch Brook Press, 1999.

Guillén Ramón, José Manuel, and Dolores Pascual Buyé. "Libros alternativos: Los otros libros." *El libro como objeto de arte: Actas del II Congreso nacional sobre bibliofilia, encuadernación artística, restauración y patrimonio bibliográfico. Cádiz, abril de 2004*, Ayuntamiento de Cádiz, 2008, pp. 255–9.

Guitert y Fontseré, Joaquín. *Historia del Real Monasterio de Poblet, Vol. 6: Continuación de la historia del Padre Finestres*. 1955.

– *Poblet: Curiosidades, leyendas y tradiciones*. Pompeyo Vidal Molné, 1937.

Hammer, Joshua. *The Bad-Ass Librarians of Timbuktu: And Their Race to Save the World's Most Precious Manuscripts*. Simon and Schuster, 2016.

Hart, Thomas R. "Two *Noucentistes*: Eugeni d'Ors and Pompeu Fabra." *Hispanic Research Journal*, vol. 2, no. 3, Oct. 2001, pp. 211–19.

Hayles, N. Katherine. "Combining Close and Distant Reading: Jonathan Safran Foer's *Tree of Codes* and the Aesthetic of Bookishness." *PMLA*, vol. 128, no. 1, Jan. 2013, pp. 226–31.

Hesse, Hermann. *Une Bibliothèque idéale*. Translated by Nicolas Waquet, Éditions Payot and Rivages, 2012.

Hidalgo, Dionisio. *Boletín Bibliográfico Español*, vol. 1. Imprenta de las Escuelas Pías, 1860. 9 vols.

– *Boletín Bibliográfico Español*, vol. 7. Imprenta de Julián Peña, 1866. 9 vols.

– *Diccionario general de bibliografía española*, vol. 1. Imprenta de las Escuelas Pías, 1862. 7 vols.
Hierro, Manuel. "La memoria sitiada de Juan Goytisolo en *El sitio de los sitios.*" *Antípodas*, vol. 8–9, 1997, pp. 144–54.
Hoffmann, E.T.A. *Das Fräulein von Scuderi. Gesammelte Werke, Vol. 4: Erzählungen*, Atlantis Verlag, 1982, pp. 269–344. 5 vols.
Huizing, Klaas. *Der Buchtrinker: Zwei Romane un neun Teppiche*. Knaus, 1994.
Huysmans, J.K. *À Rebours: Avec une préface de l'auteur écrite vingt ans après le roman*. Fasquelle, 1970.
Iwasaki, Fernando. *Somos libros, seámoslo siempre*. U de Sevilla, 2014.
Jackson, Holbrook. *The Story of Don Vincente*. Corvinus, 1939.
Johannot, Yvonne. *Tourner la page: Livre, rites et symboles*. Éditions Jérôme Millon, 1988.
Johnson, Roberta. *Bibliotecas de Azorín*. Caja de Ahorros del Mediterráneo, 1996.
Joiner, Lawrence D. "The Portrayal of the Artist in Proust and Azorín." *Revista de Estudios Hispánicos*, vol. 10, no. 2, May 1976, pp. 181–92.
– "Proust, Azorín, and the Past." *Hispanófila*, vol. 60, May 1977, pp. 45–51.
Jou, Lluís, et al. *Jou, Pla i Plana: Arquitectes del llibre: Museu d'Història de Catalunya, Barcelona, 18 gener–20 març 2005*. Associació de Bibliòfils de Barcelona, 2005.
Jurkevich, Gayana. "Azorín's Magic Circle: The Subversion of Time and Space in *Doña Inés*." *Bulletin of Hispanic Studies*, vol. 73, no. 1, 1996, pp. 29–44.
– *In Pursuit of the Natural Sign: Azorín and the Poetics of Ekphrasis*. Bucknell UP, 1999.
– "A Poetics of Time and Space: Ekphrasis and the Modern Vision in Azorín and Velázquez." *MLN*, vol. 110, no. 2, Mar. 1995, pp. 284–301.
Kies, Albert. "La Bibliothèque de Charles Nodier." *Charles Nodier: Colloque du deuxième centenaire, Besançon – Mai 1980*, Les Belles-Lettres, 1981, pp. 223–8.
Knight, Sam. "Hidden Traces: How Historical Manuscripts Are Giving up Their Secrets." *The New Yorker*, 26 Nov. 2018, pp. 38–45.
Knuth, Rebecca. *Libricide: The Regime-Sponsored Destruction of Books and Libraries in the Twentieth Century*. Praeger, 2003.
Kornetis, Kostis. "'Let's get laid because it's the end of the world!': Sexuality, Gender and the Spanish Left in Late Francoism and the *Transición*." *European Review of History/Revue européenne d'histoire*, vol. 22, no. 1, Jan. 2015, 176–98, doi.org/10.1080/13507486.2014.983433.
Kunz, Marco. "Egocentrism and Polycentric Writing: The Inscription of the Author in *Las semanas del jardín*." Translated by Stanley Black. *Juan Goytisolo: Territories of Life and Writing*, edited by Stanley Black, Peter Lang, 2006, pp. 95–124.
Labanyi, Jo. "History and Hauntology; or, What Does One Do with the Ghosts of the Past? Reflections on Spanish Film and Fiction of the Post-

Franco Period." *Disremembering the Dictatorship: The Politics of Memory in the Spanish Transition to Democracy*, edited by Joan Ramon Resina, Rodopi, 2000, pp. 65–82.
Lacan, Jacques. *Écrits*. Éditions du Seuil, 1966.
– *Écrits: The First Complete Edition in English*. Translated by Bruce Fink, Norton, 2006.
– *Le Séminaire de Jacques Lacan. Livre 1: Les écrits techniques de Freud, 1953–1954*. Éditions du Seuil, 1975.
– *The Seminar of Jacques Lacan. Book 1: Freud's Papers on Technique, 1953–1954*. Translated by John Forrester, Norton, 1991.
Lancaster, Frederick Wilfrid. *Libraries and the Future: Essays on the Library in the Twenty-First Century*. Haworth Press, 1993.
Lang, Andrew. *The Library: With a Chapter on Modern English Illustrated Books by Austin Dobson*. Macmillan, 1881.
Lázaro Carreter, Fernando. "Pregón de la XIIIa Feria Nacional del Libro de Ocasión Antiguo y Moderno, Madrid, 1989." *Pregones y carteles: Homenaje a Antolín Palomino Olalla*, Ayuntamiento de Madrid, 1997, pp. 107–9.
Lazzarin, Stefano. "Biblio-détectives, mystifications romanesques, plagiaires heureux: Nodier et le 'roman' des livres." *Dérision et supercheries dans l'œuvre de Charles Nodier. Actes du colloque de Dole, 18 octobre 2008*, Les Éditions de La Passerelle, 2008, pp. 51–66.
Lee, Christopher A. "E.T.A. Hoffmann's 'Mademoiselle de Scudéry' as a Forerunner of the Detective Story." *Clues: A Journal of Detection*, vol. 15, no. 2, 1994, pp. 63–74.
Legros, Alain. *Essais sur poutres: Peintures et inscriptions chez Montaigne*. Klincksieck, 2000.
Lista y Aragón, Alberto. "De la sublimidad." *Ensayos literarios y críticos*, vol. 1, Calvo-Rubio, 1844, pp. 20–2. 2 vols.
Liu, Alan. "The End of the End of the Book: Dead Books, Lively Margins, and Social Computing." *Michigan Quarterly Review*, vol. 48, no. 4, Fall 2009, pp. 499–520.
Llamas, Manuel. *L'edició a Catalunya: El segle XX (fins a 1939)*. Gremi d'Editors de Catalunya, 2005.
Llorens, Vicente. *Liberales y románticos: Una emigración española en Inglaterra (1823–1834)*. Castalia, 2006.
Löwy, Michael. "The Romantic and Marxist Critique of Modern Civilization." *Theory and Society*, vol. 16, no. 6, Nov. 1987, pp. 891–904.
Lucian. "Remarks Addressed to an Illiterate Book-Fancier." *The Works of Lucian of Samosata*, vol. 3. Translated by H.W. Fowler and F.G. Fowler, Clarendon Press, 1905. 4 vols.
Macias i Arau, Pere, et al. *Miquel Plana: Trajectòria gràfica*, Comissió Premis Ciutat d'Olot, 1992.

Mainer, José-Carlos. "1898–1910: La constitución de un mercado literario." *Cánovas y Lázaro: Dos bibliófilos de fin de siglo*, edited by Juan Antonio Yeves Andrés, Fundación Lázaro Galdiano, 1998, pp. 83–99.

Mandrell, James. "The Literary Sublime in Spain: Meléndez Valdés and Espronceda." *MLN*, vol. 106, no. 2, Mar. 1991, pp. 294–313.

Manguel, Alberto. *The Library at Night*. Yale UP, 2008.

Marchamalo, Jesús. *Las bibliotecas perdidas*. Renacimiento, 2008.

Martín Abad, Julián. "Incunables y post-incunables: Bibliografía y bibliofilia." *El libro como objeto de arte: Actas del II Congreso nacional sobre bibliofilia, encuadernación artística, restauración y patrimonio bibliográfico. Cádiz, abril de 2004*, Ayuntamiento de Cádiz, 2008, pp. 57–95.

Martín Gaite, Carmen. *The Back Room*. Translated by Helen R. Lane, Columbia UP, 1983.

– *El cuarto de atrás*. Destino, 1978.

Martín Rodrigo, Inés. "Las librerías están cerradas, pero puedes seguir comprando libros." *ABC*, 23 Mar. 2020, www.abc.es/cultura/libros/abci-coronavirus-librerias-estan-cerradas-pero-puedes-seguir-comprando-libros-202003191609_noticia.html.

Martín Rodrigo, Inés, et al. "La crisis del libro según los editores." *ABC*, 5 May 2012, www.abc.es/cultura/libros/abci-cinco-editores-hablan-cambiar-201205110000_noticia.html.

Mateos Pérez, Prudencio. "Miquel i Planas, arquetipo del bibliófilo." *Anticuaria*, vol. 51, 1988, pp. 62–4.

Max, Gerry. "Gustave Flaubert: The Book as Artifact and Idea: *Bibliomanie* and Bibliology." *Dalhousie French Studies*, vol. 22, 1992, pp. 9–22.

Mehring, Walter. *The Lost Library: The Autobiography of a Culture*. Translated by Richard and Clara Winston, Bobbs-Merrill, 1951.

Mendoza Díaz-Maroto, Francisco. *Introducción a la bibliofilia*. Vicent García, 2004.

– *La pasión por los libros: Un acercamiento a la bibliofilia*. Espasa-Calpe, 2002.

Menéndez Pelayo, Marcelino. "De re bibliographica." *Revista Europea*, vol. 8, no. 125, 16 July 1876, pp. 65–73.

– *Historia de los heterodoxos españoles II (último): Protestantismo y sectas místicas, Regalismo y Enciclopedia, Heterodoxia en el siglo XIX*. 3rd ed., Biblioteca de Autores Cristianos, 1978.

Mengual Català, Josep. *A dos tintas: Josep Janés, poeta y editor*. Random House Mondadori, 2013.

Mennessier-Nodier, Marie. *Charles Nodier: Épisodes et souvenirs de sa vie*. Didier, 1867.

Michell, John. "Bibliomaniacs." *A Passion for Books: A Book Lover's Treasury of Stories, Essays, Humor, Lore, and Lists on Collecting, Reading, Borrowing, Lending, Caring for, and Appreciating Books*, edited by Harold Rabinowitz and Rob Kaplan, Random House, 1999, pp. 111–21.

Mingote, Antonio. "Pregón de la XIIa Feria Nacional del Libro de Ocasión Antiguo y Moderno, Madrid, 1988." *Pregones y carteles: Homenaje a Antolín Palomino Olalla*, Ayuntamiento de Madrid, 1997, pp. 101–2.

Minoui, Delphine. *Les Passeurs de livres de Daraya: Une bibliothèque secrète en Syrie*. Éditions du Seuil, 2017.

Miquel i [y] Planas, Ramon [Ramón] [R.]. *El arte en la encuadernación*. Edición de la Cámara Oficial del Libro de Barcelona, 1933.

– *El arte hispano-árabe en la encuadernación*. Miquel-Rius, 1913.

– *Els cent aforismes del bibliòfil*. Miquel-Rius, 1925.

– *Contes de bibliòfil: Originals de C. Nodier, G. Flaubert, A. Bonnardot, C. Asselineau, A. Daudet, O. Uzanne, G. Doucet, P. Louys, P. Mille, J. Pons y Massaveu, R. Casellas y M. S. Oliver*. Institut Català de les Arts del Llibre, 1924.

– "Contra la Reforma Lingüística: Conferencia d'en Ramon Miquel y Planas al Atenèu Barcelonès els dies 21 y 25 d'aquest mes." *Catalana: Revista Setmanal*, vol. 1, no. 13, 1918, pp. 297–356.

– *De tonterías o sea de cosas y dichos de bibliómanos: Lectura de sobremesa en la comida de la noche del 20 de diciembre de 1948 de la Asociación de Bibliófilos de Barcelona*. Miquel-Rius, 1949.

– *Ensayos de bibliofilia: Reunidos y publicados con motivo de los XXV años de vida editorial del autor*. Miquel-Rius, 1923.

– *Los ex libris y su actual florecimiento en España: Con LXXIV ilustraciones reproduciendo ejemplares antiguos españoles y extranjeros, y modernos de Triadó, Riquer, Diéguez, Cornet, Renart y otros*. Tipolitografía Salvat y C., S en C., 1905.

– *La fiesta del libro y de las artes gráficas: Discurso de R. Miquel y Planas en la inauguración del curso de 1926–1927 de la Escuela Práctica de las Artes del Libro, el día 7 de octubre de 1926*. Instituto de las Artes del Libro de Barcelona, 1926.

– *La formación del libro*. Prologue by Fernando Bruner Prieto, Mejías y Susillo, 1926.

– *La llegenda del llibreter assassí de Barcelona*. Miquel-Rius, 1928.

– *La llegenda del llibreter assassí de Barcelona*. Adapted by Federico Pablo Verrié, Aguilar, 1951.

– *Memoria del editor de la "Biblioteca Catalana" al Ilustríssim Consell de la Mancomunitat de Catalunya*. Elzeviriana, 1918.

– *La novel·la d'un bibliòfil: (diàlegs de llibres)*. L'Avenç, 1918.

– *El purgatori del bibliòfil*. Renaixença, 1920.

Molas, Joaquim. "Miquel Plana y la literatura." *Miquel Plana: Artista y bibliófilo en la Biblioteca Nacional*, edited by Elena Luxán Rodríguez et al., Biblioteca Nacional, 2003, pp. 140–2.

Moli, Domènec. *Colofons de Domènec Moli en els llibres de Miquel Plana*. GraDeFajol, D.L., 2012.

– "Miquel Plana, un treballador inesgotable." *Miquel Plana (1943–2013): Poètica d'un ofici*, edited by Antoni Monturiol and Magda Pujolàs, Museu d'Art de Girona, 2012, pp. 11–15.

– "2015: En Miquel és aquí, com tantes vegades. Miquel – el faulista – veu en off." *Miquel Plana: Arquitecte del llibre, 1943–2012*, edited by Antoni Monturiol and Madga Pujolàs, Museu de la Garrotxa d'Olot, Institut de Cultura de la Ciutat d'Olot, 2015, pp. 17–37.

Montaigne, Michel de. *Les Essais*. Edited by Jean Céard, Livre de Poche, 2001.

Montobbio Jover, José Ignacio. "Elogi de la bibliofília." *Bibliofília a Catalunya: Des del s. XIX*, Fundació Jaume 1, 2001, pp. 4–9.

Monturiol, Antoni, and Magda Pujolàs, editors. *Miquel Plana (1943–2013): Poètica d'un ofici*, Museu d'Art de Girona, 2012, pp. 6–10.

Moreno-Caballud, Luis. "La imaginación sostenible: Culturas y crisis económica en la España actual." *Hispanic Review*, vol. 80, no. 4, Fall 2012, pp. 535–55, www.jstor.org/stable/23275308.

Morgades, Bernardo. *Historia de Poblet*. Prologue by Felipe Bertrán Güell, 1948.

Mourelle Lema, Manuel. *Datos inéditos para una biografía de Vicente Salvá*. Imprenta Aguirre, 1965.

Muller, Renaud. *Une Anthropologie de la bibliophilie: Le désir de livre*. L'Harmattan, 1997.

Neuman, Lilian. "La Barcelona es un gran fabulador." *La Vanguardia*, 19 June 2001, www.xtec.es/~jducros/Carlos%20Ruiz%20Zafon.html.

*The New Oxford Annotated Bible with the Apocrypha: Revised Standard Version*. Edited by Herbert G. May and Bruce M. Metzger, Oxford UP, 1973.

Nieva, Francisco. "Pregón de la XVIIa Feria Nacional del Libro de Ocasión Antiguo y Moderno, Madrid, 1993: Sacramento de la identidad, el libro viejo." *Pregones y carteles: Homenaje a Antolín Palomino Olalla*, Ayuntamiento de Madrid, 1997, pp. 131–3.

Nodier, Charles. *Le Bibliomane*. Conquet, 1893.

Nora, Pierre. "Between Memory and History: *Les Lieux de Mémoire*." *Representations*, vol. 26, Apr. 1989, pp. 7–24.

Obiols, Isabel. "Carlos Ruiz Zafón, escritor: 'La narrativa clásica siempre vuelve, es el centro de todo.'" *El País*, 18 Nov. 2002, www.elpais.com/diario/2002/11/18/cultura/1037574007_850215.html.

O'Donnell, Hugo. "Luis María de Salazar, capitán de navío y ministro de marina." *Cuadernos monográficos del Instituto de Historia y Cultura Naval*, vol. 54, 2007, pp. 115–28.

Ollé Pinell, Antonio. "Ramón Miquel y Planas: Artista creador de libros." *Homenaje a la memoria del ilustrísimo Señor D. Ramón Miquel y Planas: Organizado por la Asociación de Bibliófilos de Barcelona, la Real Academia Catalana de Bellas Artes de San Jorge, y el Gremio Sindical de Maestros Impresores de Barcelona*, Altés, 1951–2, pp. 67–84.

Ortega y Gasset, José. "Azorín: Primores de lo vulgar." *Obras completas*, vol. 2, Revista de Occidente, 1954, pp. 157–91. 6 vols.

Pageaux, Daniel-Henri. "L'Espagne de Charles Nodier." *Charles Nodier: Colloque du deuxième centenaire, Besançon – Mai 1980*, Les Belles-Lettres, 1981, pp. 183–95.

Palau y [i] Dulcet, Antoni. *Corona d'Aragó y sos antichs dominis: Catalunya, Valencia, Balears, Sardenya, Nápols y Sicilia. Catálech de llibres en venda en la llibrería antiquaria d'Antoni Palau, Carrer de S. Pau, 41, Barcelona.* Fills de Jaume Jepús, 1916.

– *Memorias de un librero catalán, 1867–1935*. Librería Catalonia, 1935.

Palomino Olalla, Antolín. *Autobiografía: Conocimientos y recuerdos sobre el arte de la encuadernación*. Ayuntamiento de Madrid, 1986.

– *Mis papeles pintados*. Centro Cultural del Conde Duque, 1990.

Patxot y Ferrer, Fernando. *Las ruinas de mi convento*. Apostolado de la Prensa, 1920.

Pérez, Genaro J. "*La cuarentena* y *El sitio de los sitios* de Juan Goytisolo: Intertextualidad, creación y recreación autorial." *Letras Peninsulares*, Winter 2001–2, pp. 391–403.

Pérez Bowie, José Antonio. "*Las esquinas del aire* o las permeables fronteras de la ficción." *Juan Manuel de Prada: De héroes y tempestades*, edited by José Manuel López de Abiada and Augusta López Bernasocchi, Verbum, 2003, pp. 358–83.

Pérez Gracia, César. "La novela dieciochesca en Azorín." *Cuenta y razón del pensamiento actual*, vol. 134, 2004, https://nanopdf.com/download/num134-007_pdf.

Pérez-Reverte, Arturo. *The Club Dumas*. Translated by Sonia Soto, Vintage Books, 1998.

– *El club Dumas, La novena puerta*. Alfaguara, 2000.

Pérez-Rioja, José Antonio. *La edición de libros en el Madrid isabelino (1833–1868)*. Artes Gráficas Municipales, 1993.

– "Los exlibris y el exlibrismo." *Historia ilustrada del libro español: La edición moderna. Siglo XIX y XX*, edited by Hipólito Escolar, Germán Sánchez Ruipérez, 1996, pp. 541–53.

Pérez Vidal, Alejandro. *Bartolomé José Gallardo: Perfil literario y biográfico*. Editora Regional de Extremadura, 2001.

Pla, Jaume. *Técnicas del grabado calcográfico y su estampación, con unas notas de bibliofilia*. Omega, 1986.

Plana, Miquel. *Barcelona 1888–1992: Vista per vuit escriptors, i il·lustrada amb aiguaforts per vint artistas*. Miquel Plana, 1991.

– *En defensa de la lletra: Vint-i-sis apologies per vint-i-sis literats*. Introduction by Modest Prats and illustrations by Miquel Plana, Casa Neufville, 1990.

Porter, José. "La bibliofilia catalana y Miquel y Planas." *Homenaje a la memoria del ilustrísimo Señor D. Ramón Miquel y Planas: Organizado por la Asociación de Bibliófilos de Barcelona, la Real Academia Catalana de Bellas Artes de San Jorge, y el Gremio Sindical de Maestros Impresores de Barcelona*, Altés, 1951–2, pp. 43–62.

– *Los libros*. 1973.

Prada, Juan Manuel de. *Las esquinas del aire: En busca de Ana María Martínez Sagi*. Planeta, 2000.

Pressman, Jessica. "The Aesthetic of Bookishness in Twenty-First-Century Literature." *Michigan Quarterly Review*, vol. 48, no. 4, Fall 2009, pp. 465–82.

Price, Leah. *What We Talk About When We Talk About Books: The History and Future of Reading*. Basic Books, 2019.

Proust, Marcel. *Le Temps retrouvé. À la recherche du temps perdu*, vol. 4, Gallimard, 1989. 7 vols.

– *Time Regained. In Search of Lost Time*, vol 6. Translated by Andreas Mayor and Terence Kilmartin, Modern Library, 2003. 7 vols.

Puebla Pedrosa, Ceferino. "Claves autobiográficas y metafóricas de *El sitio de los sitios*." *Hispánica*, vol. 41, 1997, pp. 89–103.

Puig i Borràs, Núria. "La tipografia en la simfonia compositiva de Miquel Plana." *Miquel Plana: Arquitecte del llibre, 1943–2012*, Museu de la Garrotxa d'Olot, Institut de Cultura de la Ciutat d'Olot, 2015, pp. 93–7.

Puig Rovira, Francesc X. "L'interès pel llibre: Gabinets de lectura, bibliofília i exlibrisme." *L'exaltació del llibre al vuitcents: Art, indústria i consum a Barcelona*, edited by Pilar Vélez, Biblioteca de Catalunya, 2008, pp. 169–200.

– "Miquel Plana: Aproximación a un concepto actual de la bibliofilia." *Miquel Plana: Artista y bibliófilo en la Biblioteca Nacional*, edited by Elena Luxán Rodríguez et al., Biblioteca Nacional, 2003, pp. 133–8.

– "El paper del paper, segons Miquel Plana." *Miquel Plana: Arquitecte del llibre, 1943–2012*, Museu de la Garrotxa d'Olot, Institut de Cultura de la Ciutat d'Olot, 2015, pp. 87–91.

Pujol, Josep M. "Miquel Plana, artista del libro." *Miquel Plana: Artista y bibliófilo en la Biblioteca Nacional*, edited by Elena Luxán Rodríguez et al., Biblioteca Nacional, 2003, pp. 154–7.

– *Tècniques: Reverberacions gràfiques*. Departament de Cultura i Mitjans de Comunicació, U de Barcelona, 2008.

Quílez i Corella, Francesc. "Graphic Arts: Posters, Prints and Book-plates." *Modernisme in the MNAC Collections*, edited by Mercè Doñate et al. and translated by Andrew Langdon-Davies, Museu Nacional d'Art de Catalunya and Lunwerg, 2009, pp. 189–219.

Quiney, Aitor. "Les *encuadernacions* de Miquel Plana." *Miquel Plana: Arquitecte del llibre, 1943–2012*, Museu de la Garrotxa d'Olot, Institut de Cultura de la Ciutat d'Olot, 2015, pp. 77–9.

Quintanilla López-Tafall, Rocío. "Jacinto Bejarano y sus *Sentimientos patrióticos*. Edición crítica." 2015. Universidad Complutense de Madrid, PhD dissertation.

Rabinowitz, Harold, and Rob Kaplan, editors. *A Passion for Books: A Book Lover's Treasury of Stories, Essays, Humor, Lore, and Lists on Collecting, Reading, Borrowing, Lending, Caring for, and Appreciating Books*. Times Books, 1999.

Raven, James. *What Is the History of the Book?* Polity Press, 2018.

Reig Salvá, Carola. *Vicente Salvá: Un valenciano de prestigio internacional*. Instituto de Literatura y Estudios Filológicos, Institución Alfonso el Magnánimo, 1972.

Resina, Joan Ramon. "The Catalan *Renaixença*." *The Cambridge History of Spanish Literature*, edited by David T. Gies, Cambridge UP, 2004, pp. 470–8.

– "Modernism in Catalonia." *The Cambridge History of Spanish Literature*, edited by David T. Gies, Cambridge UP, 2004, pp. 513–19.

– "*Noucentisme*." *The Cambridge History of Spanish Literature*, edited by David T. Gies, Cambridge UP, 2004, pp. 532–7.

Ribeiro de Menezes, Alison. "Juan Goytisolo's *Cuaderno de Sarajevo*: The Dilemmas of a Committed War Journalist." *Journal of Iberian and Latin American Studies*, vol. 12, no. 2–3, Aug. 2006, pp. 219–31.

Riedlmayer, András. "Erasing the Past: The Destruction of Libraries and Archives in Bosnia-Herzegovina." *Middle East Studies Association Bulletin*, vol. 29, no. 1, July 1995, pp. 7–11.

Rimbaud, Arthur. *Poésies: Derniers vers; Une saison en enfer; Illuminations*. Edited by Daniel Leuwers, Le Livre de Poche, 1972.

Rivas, Manuel. *Books Burn Badly*. Translated by Jonathan Dunne, Vintage Books, 2011.

– *Os libros arden mal*. 2nd ed., Xerais, 2007.

Robert, Maurice. *Code de la bibliophilie moderne*. Union Latine d'Éditions, 1936.

Rodergas Calmell, Josep. *Semblança y bibliografia de R. Miquel y Planas*. Elzeviriana, 1951.

Rodríguez-Moñino, Antonio. *Don Bartolomé José Gallardo (1776–1852): Estudio bibliográfico*. Sancha, 1955.

– *Historia de una infamia bibliográfica: La de San Antonio de 1823. Realidad y leyenda de lo sucedido con los libros y papeles de don Bartolomé José Gallardo*. Castalia, 1965.

Roig, Montserrat. "El profesor y el librero asesino." *Cuentos barceloneses*, Icaria, 1989, pp. 203–13.

Romero, Eugenia R. "Popular Literary *lieux de mémoire* and Galician Identity in Manuel Rivas's *En salvaxe compaña*." *Bulletin of Hispanic Studies*, vol. 86, no. 2, Mar. 2009, pp. 293–308.

Rouveyre, Édouard. *Connaissances nécessaires à un bibliophile: Accompagnées de notes critiques et de documents bibliographiques*, vol. 1. 5th ed., Édouard Rouveyre, 1899. 10 vols.
Rueda, Ana, editor. *Irene y Clara, o La madre imperiosa*, by Vicente Salvá y Pérez. U de Salamanca, 2003.
Ruiz García, Elisa. "El libro tardo antiguo: Un íntimo objeto de deseo." *Bibliofilias: Exposición con motivo del 38° Congreso Internacional y la 21a Feria Internacional de ILAB*, Fundación Lázaro Galdiano, 2008, pp. 19–25.
Ruiz Zafón, Carlos. *The Shadow of the Wind*. Translated by Lucia Graves, Penguin Press, 2004.
– *La sombra del viento*. Planeta, 2002.
Sainz y Rodríguez, Pedro. *Estudio sobre la historia de la crítica literaria en España: Don Bartolomé José Gallardo y la crítica literaria de su tiempo*. New York and Paris, 1921.
Salter, James. "L'amour des livres." Translated by Christophe Jaquet. *Des Bibliothèques pleines de fantômes*, by Jacques Bonnet, Arléa, 2014, pp. 9–16.
Salvá y Mallén, Pedro. "Prólogo." *Catálogo de la biblioteca de Salvá*, vol. 1, Ferrer de Orga, 1872, pp. v–xxiv. 2 vols.
Salvá y Pérez, Vicente. *La bruja, o cuadro de la corte de Roma. Novela. Hallada entre los manuscritos de un respetable teólogo, grande amigote de la curia romana*. Librería Hispano-Americana, 1830.
Sánchez Mariana, Manuel. "La bibliofilia y sus especialidades." *Bibliofilias: Exposición con motivo del 38° Congreso Internacional y la 21a Feria Internacional de ILAB*, Fundación Lázaro Galdiano, 2008, pp. 67–73.
– *Bibliófilos españoles: Desde sus orígenes hasta los albores del siglo XX*. Biblioteca Nacional, Ministerio de Cultura/Ollero and Ramos, 1993.
Sartre, Jean-Paul. *Being and Nothingness: A Phenomenological Essay on Being*. Translated by Hazel E. Barnes, Pocket Books, 1978.
– *L'Être et le néant: Essai d'ontologie phénoménologique*. Gallimard, 1980.
– *The Family Idiot: Gustave Flaubert 1821–1857*, vol. 1. Translated by Carol Cosman, U of Chicago P, 1981. 3 vols.
– *L'Idiot de la famille: Gustave Flaubert de 1821–1857*, vol. 1. Gallimard, 1983. 3 vols.
– *Mallarmé: La lucidité et sa face d'ombre*. Edited by Arlette Elkaïm-Sartre, Gallimard, 1986.
– *Mallarmé, or the Poet of Nothingness*. Translated by Ernest Sturm, Pennsylvania State UP, 1988.
– *Les Mots*. Gallimard, 1964.
– *Qu'est-ce que la littérature*. Gallimard, 1976.
– *What Is Literature?* Translated by Bernard Frechtman, Philosophical Library, 1949.
– *The Words*. Translated by Bernard Frechtman, Random House, 1981.

Satz, Mario. *Meditaciones kabalísticas: Fuego negro, fuego blanco*. Kairós, 2015.

Schwartz, Marcy. *Public Pages: Reading along the Latin American Streetscape*. U of Texas P, 2018.

Sedgwick, Eve Kosofsky. *Between Men: English Literature and Male Homosocial Desire*. Columbia UP, 1985.

Serret, José María. "Bibliofilia y bibliófilos." *El libro como objeto de arte: Actas del I Congreso nacional sobre bibliofilia, encuadernación artística, restauración y patrimonio bibliográfico, Cádiz, 21–24 de abril de 1999*, Ayuntamiento de Cádiz, 1999, pp. 253–60.

Senabre, Ricardo. *Notas sobre el estilo de Bartolomé José Gallardo*. Diputación Provincial de Badajoz, 1975.

Setbon, Raymond. "Un détracteur 'progressiste' de la Révolution: Charles Nodier." *Les Lettres Romanes*, vol. 32, no. 1, 1978, pp. 52–77.

Silverman, Gillian. *Bodies and Books: Reading and the Fantasy of Communion in Nineteenth-Century America*. U of Pennsylvania P, 2012.

Silverman, Willa Z. *The New Bibliopolis: French Book Collectors and the Culture of Print, 1880–1914*. U of Toronto P, 2008.

Silvestre, María Soledad. "Una guerra todas las guerras: El viaje a la barbarie de Juan Goytisolo." *I° Congreso Internacional de Literatura y Cultura Españolas Contemporáneas, 1 al 3 de octubre de 2008, La Plata, Argentina. Los siglos XX y XXI*, Centro de Estudios de Teoría y Crítica Literaria, 2008, www.aacademica.org/000-095/99.pdf.

Snyder, Jonathan. *Poetics of Opposition in Contemporary Spain: Politics and the Work of Urban Culture*. Palgrave Macmillan, 2015.

Sobolevsky, Sergio. *Bibliografía romántica española (1850)*. Introduction and translation by Joaquín del Val and notes by Antonio Rodríguez-Moñino, Castalia, 1951.

Sopena, Mireia. "Miquel Plana, arquitecte de complicitats." *Colofons de Domènec Moli en els llibres de Miquel Plana*, by Domènec Moli, 2012, pp. i–v.

Sotelo Vázquez, Adolfo. "Azorín en 'La Prensa' de Buenos Aires." *Cuadernos Hispanoamericanos*, vol. 756, no. 6, 2013, pp. 43–50.

Stark, Virgile. *Crépuscule des bibliothèques*. Les Belles Lettres, 2015.

Stauffer, Andrew M. "An Image in Lava: Annotation Sentiment, and the Traces of Nineteenth-Century Reading." *PMLA*, vol. 134, no. 1, 2019, pp. 81–98.

Steegmuller, Francis, editor. *The Letters of Gustave Flaubert*, vol. 2. Harvard UP, 1982. 2 vols.

Steinmetz, Jean-Luc. "Au bonheur des livres." *"L'Amateur de livres" précédé du "Bibliomane," de "Bibliographie des fous," et "De la monomanie réflective,"* by Charles Nodier. Edited by Jean-Luc Steinmetz, Le Castor Astral, 1993, pp. 7–23.

Still, Judith, and Michael Worton, editors. *Textuality and Sexuality: Reading Theories and Practices*. Manchester UP, 1993.

Süskind, Patrick. *Das Parfum: Die Geschichte eines Mörders*. Diogenes, 1985.

Taylor, Barry. "Ramón Miquel y Planas and His *Biblioteca Catalana*: Medievalism, Publishing and Bibliophilia in Early Twentieth-Century Barcelona." *The British Library Journal*, vol. 19, no. 1, Spring 1993, pp. 58–82.

Trenc, Eliseu. "Del llibre il·lustrat al llibre decorat: D'Apel·les Mestres al Modernisme." *L'exaltació del llibre al vuitcents: Art, indústria i consum a Barcelona*, edited by Pilar Vélez, Biblioteca de Catalunya, 2008, pp. 101–22.

Unamuno, Miguel de. *Niebla*. 19th ed. Edited by Mario J. Valdés, Cátedra, 2004.

Urbani García, Fabiola. "El libro de artista, capricho, juego, objeto ..." *El libro como objeto de arte: Actas del I Congreso nacional sobre bibliofilia, encuadernación artística, restauración y patrimonio bibliográfico, Cádiz, 21–24 de abril de 1999*, Ayuntamiento de Cádiz, 1999, pp. 261–8.

Uzanne, Octave. *La nouvelle bibliopolis: Voyage d'un novateur au pays des néo-icono-bibliomanes*. Henri Floury, 1897.

Valentí Fiol, Eduard. *El primer modernismo literario catalán y sus fundamentos ideológicos*. Ediciones Ariel, 1973.

Van-Halen, Juan. "Pregón de la XXa Feria Nacional del Libro de Ocasión Antiguo y Moderno, Madrid, 1996: Viejos pájaros de papel." *Pregones y carteles: Homenaje a Antolín Palomino Olalla*, Ayuntamiento de Madrid, 1997, pp. 149–51.

Vélez (i Vicente), Pilar. "D'Ivori: Bibliofília i exlibrisme." *D'Ivori: La màgia de la il·lustració*, edited by Josep M. Cadena et al., Ajuntament de Barcelona, 1996, pp. 143–90.

– "El libro como objeto." *Historia de la edición y de la lectura en España, 1472–1914*, edited by Víctor Infantes et al., Germán Sánchez Ruipérez, 2003, pp. 552–6.

– *El llibre com a obra d'art a la Catalunya vuitcentista (1850–1910)*. Biblioteca de Cataluyna, 1989.

– "Miquel Plana (1943–2012): Editor de bibliofília, singular i inconfusible." *Miquel Plana: Arquitecte del llibre, 1943–2012*, Museu de la Garrotxa d'Olot, Institut de Cultura de la Ciutat d'Olot, 2015, pp. 43–9.

– "Miquel Plana: Un fenómeno singular dentro de la bibliofilia catalana del siglo XX." *Miquel Plana: Artista y bibliófilo en la Biblioteca Nacional*, edited by Elena Luxán Rodríguez et al., Biblioteca Nacional, 2003, pp. 17–20.

Vila-Matas, Enrique. *Dublinesca*. Seix Barral, 2010.

– *Dublinesque*. Translated by Rosalind Harvey and Anne McLean, Harvill Secker, 2012.

Vilarrubias, Felio A. *Poblet: Monjes, arte, historia*. Casulleras, 1965.

Villamandos, Alberto. "Against Nostalgia: Esther Tusquets and the Remembering of the Gauche Divine." Women's and Gender Studies, University of Missouri-Kansas City, 13 Mar. 2012, info.umkc.edu/

wgs/2012/03/13/against-nostalgia-esther-tusquets-and-the-remembering-of-the-gauche-divine/#.
Villena, Luis Antonio de. "Pregón de la XIXa Feria Nacional del Libro de Ocasión Antiguo y Moderno, Madrid, 1995: Elogio y fascinación del libro antiguo." *Pregones y carteles: Homenaje a Antolín Palomino Olalla*, Ayuntamiento de Madrid, 1997, pp. 143–5.
*Webster's Third New International Dictionary of the English Language Unabridged*. Edited by Philip Babcock Gove, Merriam-Webster, 1986.
Weiner, Norman D. "On Bibliomania." *The Psychoanalytic Quarterly*, vol. 35, no. 2, 1966, pp. 217–32.
Winter, Michael F. "Umberto Eco on Libraries: A Discussion of 'De Bibliotheca.'" *The Library Quarterly*, vol. 64, no. 2, Apr. 1994, pp. 117–29.
Yeves Andrés, Juan Antonio. "Bibliofilias: José Lázaro Galdiano y su biblioteca." *Bibliofilias: Exposición con motivo del 38° Congreso Internacional y la 21a Feria Internacional de ILAB*, Fundación Lázaro Galdiano, 2008, pp. 9–17.

# Index

# Toronto Iberic



1 Anthony J. Cascardi, *Cervantes, Literature, and the Discourse of Politics*
2 Jessica A. Boon, *The Mystical Science of the Soul: Medieval Cognition in Bernardino de Laredo's Recollection Method*
3 Susan Byrne, *Law and History in Cervantes'*Don Quixote
4 Mary E. Barnard and Frederick A. de Armas (eds), *Objects of Culture in the Literature of Imperial Spain*
5 Nil Santiáñez, *Topographies of Fascism: Habitus, Space, and Writing in Twentieth-Century Spain*
6 Nelson Orringer, *Lorca in Tune with Falla: Literary and Musical Interludes*
7 Ana M. Gómez-Bravo, *Textual Agency: Writing Culture and Social Networks in Fifteenth-Century Spain*
8 Javier Irigoyen-García, *The Spanish Arcadia: Sheep Herding, Pastoral Discourse, and Ethnicity in Early Modern Spain*
9 Stephanie Sieburth, *Survival Songs: Conchita Piquer's*Coplas*and Franco's Regime of Terror*
10 Christine Arkinstall, *Spanish Female Writers and the Freethinking Press, 1879–1926*
11 Margaret Boyle, *Unruly Women: Performance, Penitence, and Punishment in Early Modern Spain*

12 Evelina Gužauskytė, *Christopher Columbus's Naming in the* diarios *of the Four Voyages (1492–1504): A Discourse of Negotiation*
13 Mary E. Barnard, *Garcilaso de la Vega and the Material Culture of Renaissance Europe*
14 William Viestenz, *By the Grace of God: Francoist Spain and the Sacred Roots of Political Imagination*
15 Michael Scham, Lector Ludens*: The Representation of Games and Play in Cervantes*
16 Stephen Rupp, *Heroic Forms: Cervantes and the Literature of War*
17 Enrique Fernandez, *Anxieties of Interiority and Dissection in Early Modern Spain*
18 Susan Byrne, *Ficino in Spain*
19 Patricia M. Keller, *Ghostly Landscapes: Film, Photography, and the Aesthetics of Haunting in Contemporary Spanish Culture*
20 Carolyn A. Nadeau, *Food Matters: Alonso Quijano's Diet and the Discourse of Food in Early Modern Spain*
21 Cristian Berco, *From Body to Community: Venereal Disease and Society in Baroque Spain*
22 Elizabeth R. Wright, *The Epic of Juan Latino: Dilemmas of Race and Religion in Renaissance Spain*
23 Ryan D. Giles, *Inscribed Power: Amulets and Magic in Early Spanish Literature*
24 Jorge Pérez, *Confessional Cinema: Religion, Film, and Modernity in Spain's Development Years, 1960–1975*
25 Joan Ramon Resina, *Josep Pla: Seeing the World in the Form of Articles*
26 Javier Irigoyen-García, *"Moors Dressed as Moors": Clothing, Social Distinction, and Ethnicity in Early Modern Iberia*
27 Jean Dangler, *Edging toward Iberia*
28 Ryan D. Giles and Steven Wagschal (eds), *Beyond Sight: Engaging the Senses in Iberian Literatures and Cultures, 1200–1750*
29 Silvia Bermúdez, *Rocking the Boat: Migration and Race in Contemporary Spanish Music*
30 Hilaire Kallendorf, *Ambiguous Antidotes: Virtue as Vaccine for Vice in Early Modern Spain*
31 Leslie Harkema, *Spanish Modernism and the Poetics of Youth: From Miguel de Unamuno to* La Joven Literatura
32 Benjamin Fraser, *Cognitive Disability Aesthetics: Visual Culture, Disability Representations, and the (In)Visibility of Cognitive Difference*
33 Robert Patrick Newcomb, *Iberianism and Crisis: Spain and Portugal at the Turn of the Twentieth Century*
34 Sara J. Brenneis, *Spaniards in Mauthausen: Representations of a Nazi Concentration Camp, 1940–2015*

35 Silvia Bermúdez and Roberta Johnson (eds), *A New History of Iberian Feminisms*
36 Steven Wagschal, *Minding Animals In the Old and New Worlds: A Cognitive Historical Analysis*
37 Heather Bamford, *Cultures of the Fragment: Uses of the Iberian Manuscript, 1100–1600*
38 Enrique García Santo-Tomás (ed), *Science on Stage in Early Modern Spain*
39 Marina Brownlee (ed), *Cervantes'*Persiles*and the Travails of Romance*
40 Sarah Thomas, *Inhabiting the In-Between: Childhood and Cinema in Spain's Long Transition*
41 David A. Wacks, *Medieval Iberian Crusade Fiction and the Mediterranean World*
42 Rosilie Hernández, *Immaculate Conceptions: The Power of the Religious Imagination in Early Modern Spain*
43 Mary Coffey and Margot Versteeg (eds), *Imagined Truths: Realism in Modern Spanish Literature and Culture*
44 Diana Aramburu, *Resisting Invisibility: Detecting the Female Body in Spanish Crime Fiction*
45 Samuel Amago and Matthew J. Marr (eds), *Consequential Art: Comics Culture in Contemporary Spain*
46 Richard P. Kinkade, *Dawn of a Dynasty: The Life and Times of Infante Manuel of Castile*
47 Jill Robbins, *Poetry and Crisis: Cultural Politics and Citizenship in the Wake of the Madrid Bombings*
48 Ana María Laguna and John Beusterien (eds), *Goodbye Eros: Recasting Forms and Norms of Love in the Age of Cervantes*
49 Sara J. Brenneis and Gina Herrmann (eds), *Spain, World War II, and the Holocaust: History and Representation*
50 Francisco Fernández de Alba, *Sex, Drugs, and Fashion in 1970s Madrid*
51 Daniel Aguirre-Oteiza, *This Ghostly Poetry: Reading Spanish Republican Exiles between Literary History and Poetic Memory*
52 Lara Anderson, *Control and Resistance: Food Discourse in Franco Spain*
53 Faith Harden, *Arms and Letters: Military Life Writing in Early Modern Spain*
54 Erin Alice Cowling, Tania de Miguel Magro, Mina García Jordán, and Glenda Y. Nieto-Cuebas (eds), *Social Justice in Spanish Golden Age Theatre*
55 Paul Michael Johnson, *Affective Geographies: Cervantes, Emotion, and the Literary Mediterranean*

56 Justin Crumbaugh and Nil Santiáñez (eds), *Spanish Fascist Writing: An Anthology*
57 Margaret E. Boyle and Sarah E. Owens (eds), *Health and Healing in the Early Modern Iberian World: A Gendered Perspective*
58 Leticia Álvarez-Recio (ed), *Iberian Chivalric Romance: Translations and Cultural Transmission in Early Modern England*
59 Henry Berlin, *Alone Together: Poetics of the Passions in Late Medieval Iberia*
60 Adrian Shubert, *The Sword of Luchana: Baldomero Espartero and the Making of Modern Spain, 1793–1879*
61 Jorge Pérez, *Fashioning Spanish Cinema: Costume, Identity, and Stardom*
62 Enriqueta Zafra, *Lazarillo de Tormes: A Graphic Novel*
63 Erin Alice Cowling, *Chocolate: How a New World Commodity Conquered Spanish Literature*
64 Mary E. Barnard, *A Poetry of Things: The Material Lyric in Habsburg Spain*
65 Frederick A. de Armas and James Mandrell (eds), *The Gastronomical Arts in Spain: Food and Etiquette*
66 Catherine Infante, *The Arts of Encounter: Christians, Muslims, and the Power of Images in Early Modern Spain*
67 Robert Richmond Ellis, *Bibliophiles, Murderous Bookmen, and Mad Librarians: The Story of Books in Modern Spain*